D1408955

MARK JUERGENSMEYER is Professor of Sociology and Director of Global and International Studies at the University of California, Santa Barbara. He is the winner of the Grawemeyer Award for his book, *Terror in the Mind of God* (UC Press). He is the editor of *Global Religions: An Introduction* and is also the author of *The New Cold War? Religious Nationalism Confronts the Secular State* and *Gandhi's Way: A Handbook of Conflict Resolution*, both from UC Press.

Global Rebellion

COMPARATIVE STUDIES IN RELIGION AND SOCIETY

Mark Juergensmeyer, editor

Global Rebellion

Religious Challenges to the
Secular State, from Christian
Militias to al Qaeda

Mark Juergensmeyer

UNIVERSITY OF CALIFORNIA PRESS
Berkeley · Los Angeles · London

University of California Press, one of the most
distinguished university presses in the United States,
enriches lives around the world by advancing
scholarship in the humanities, social sciences, and
natural sciences. Its activities are supported by the UC
Press Foundation and by philanthropic contributions
from individuals and institutions. For more
information, visit www.ucpress.edu.

University of California Press
Berkeley and Los Angeles, California

University of California Press, Ltd.
London, England

This is a revised, updated, and expanded version of a
work originally published as *The New Cold War?
Religious Nationalism Confronts the Secular State*
(Berkeley and Los Angeles: University of California
Press, 1993).

Library of Congress Cataloging-in-Publication Data

Juergensmeyer, Mark.
   Global rebellion : religious challenges to the secular
state, from Christian militias to al Qaeda / Mark
Juergensmeyer.—Rev. ed.
      p.   cm.   —   (Comparative studies in religion
and society, 16)
   Includes bibliographical references and index.
   ISBN: 978–0–520-25554-8 (cloth : alk. paper)
   1. Religions.   2. Radicalism—Religious aspects.
   I. Title.

BL80.3.G56   2008
322'.1—dc22   2007023293

Manufactured in the United States of America

17   16   15   14   13   12   11   10   09   08
10   9   8   7   6   5   4   3   2   1

This book is printed on New Leaf EcoBook 50, a
100% recycled fiber of which 50% is de-inked post-
consumer waste, processed chlorine-free. EcoBook 50
is acid-free and meets the minimum requirements of
ANSI/ASTM D5634–01 (*Permanence of Paper*).

for Sucheng

Contents

Preface and Acknowledgments

The turn of the twenty-first century has been marked by both globalization and religious politics—and the two may well be related. Global social change has weakened the nation-state and eroded confidence in the European and American idea of secular nationalism, provoking some to take a strident religious path.

This book provides a road map to this global pattern of religious activism and offers an attempt to make sense of it. Virtually every religious tradition has been touched by religious forms of political protest—from American Christianity and Israeli Judaism to Indian Hinduism and Japanese Buddhism; it is not purely a product of the Islamic activism of the Middle East. This book surveys these forms of religious activism in all of their diversity and attempts to answer some basic questions: why are they religious? and why are they happening now?

To seek the answers to these questions I have done what scholars usually do—I have read what I could, and thought about it all. I have also talked with people, especially those people directly involved with movements of religious activism in recent years in various parts of the world. For this reason, I am grateful to those whom I interviewed and to experts and colleagues around the world who are familiar with the case studies on which my observations are based, and who provided me with insights and advice.

In Iraq, Mary Kaldor, director of the Center for Global Governance at the London School of Economics, helped to provide access to a variety of political and religious leaders, facilitated by her colleague Yahia Said. Hanna Edwards, director of the Iraqi al-Amal Human Rights Association of Baghdad, provided hospitality and arrangements. Shirouk al-Abayaji provided insights and help in translation, and Will Thomas assisted with video- and audiotaping and transcribed the interviews.

In Egypt, I valued the cooperation of Saad Ibrahim, Kent Weeks, and Leila el-Hamamsy of the American University in Cairo; Muhammad Khalifa and Ibrahim Dasuqi Shitta of Cairo University; Mohamed Elmisilhi Salem of Al-Azhar University, Cairo; and Gehad Auda and other scholars and journalists connected with the *Al-Ahram* newspaper and institute. William Brinner and Alan Godlas helped in arranging contacts in Cairo, for which I am very grateful. On a later trip to Cairo, Va'Shajn Parr provided hospitality and insights, and Juan Campo made helpful comments on the revision.

In Israel and Palestine, my mentors were Ifrah Zilberman in Jerusalem, Ehud Sprinzak, Emmanuel Sivan, and Gideon Aran at Hebrew University, and Ariel Merari at Tel Aviv University. I appreciated the support of the Yitzhak Rabin Center for Israel Studies and the Tantur Ecumenical Institute. I valued the insights of Zaid Abu-Amr of Bir Zeit University, and independent researchers Anne Marie Oliver and Paul Steinberg, now research scholars at the Orfalea Center of Global and International Studies at the University of California, Santa Barbara. I thank Robin Wright of the *Washington Post* as well as other journalists in Jerusalem, the West Bank, and Gaza for their help in securing interviews. In Lebanon I benefited from the hospitality of Joseph Jabbra, president of the Lebanese American University, the assistance of Paul Orfalea and his family, and the insights of Eddie Saade.

In India I was assisted by Harish Puri and Surjit Singh Narang at Guru Nanak Dev University, Amritsar; and I greatly benefited from the comments of Manoranjan Mohanty, T. N. Madan, J. P. S. Oberoi, and members of the department of political science at Delhi University, where an initial version of one section of this book was presented. I have also learned from the comments of Gurinder Singh Mann, my colleague at Santa Barbara, and Mohinder Singh at the National Institute for Punjab Studies in New Delhi on the case study of the Sikhs. In Jummu and Kashmir, I appreciated the arrangements provided by Pramod Kumar and the Institute for Development and Communications in Jummu. And I always turn to Ainslie Embree for advice on things related to India and Pakistan.

In Sri Lanka my research was facilitated by S. W. R. deA. Samarasinghe and Radhika Coomaraswamy of the Kandy and Colombo branches, respectively, of the International Centre for Ethnic Studies; Sarath Amunugama of Worldview International Foundation; Mangala Moonesinghe of the Marga Institute, Colombo; and Padmasiri deSilva of the philosophy department, Peradeniya University, Kandy. I also appreciate the comments of Stanley Tambiah of Harvard University on the Sri Lankan case and on the theoretical perspective of the project as a whole. Useful advice on initial contacts in Sri Lanka came from Don Swearer, Ashis Nandy, and Diana Eck. In the original research for this section, Antony Mattessich provided both help and insight.

In Japan, I appreciated the help and advice of Susumu Shimazono, Koichi Mori, and Ian Reader. In Mongolia I appreciated the support of the faculty and administrators of Mongolian State University. In Ireland I relied on Jim Gibney and the Sinn Fein press office, and I learned much from Tom Buckley, Brian Murphy, and Martin O'Toole. For an introduction to the Algerian community in Paris I thank François Godement and Michelle Zimney. My access to some Christian activists in the United States was facilitated by Julie Ingersoll. Prison interviews in Lompoc, California, were facilitated by Warden David Rardin, Terry Roof, and Representative Walter Capps.

In addition to these helpful scholars and advisors, I also wish to thank the many participant-observers who shared their insights with me. Their names appear in the list of interviews at the end of this book.

Shortly after the end of the old Cold War I produced an earlier version of this book under the title "The New Cold War," with a question mark after the phrase. Though the events that have transpired since that time have removed all doubt, this is in many ways a new book. Most of the case studies are new or are vastly altered. Yet to a surprising degree the original ideas that animated this book remain salient. The revival of religious politics at the dawn of the twenty-first century is due in large part to the loss of faith in secular nationalism in an increasingly globalized world. Thus, though virtually every sentence in this book is either new or newly revised, many of the observations in the original version of this book remain intact.

The initial research for this book was begun while I was a fellow at the Woodrow Wilson International Center for Scholars at the Smithsonian Institution, Washington, D.C., in 1986. Additional grants for research in 1987–88 came from the Harry Frank Guggenheim Foundation, from 1989 to 1991 from the United States Institute of Peace in Washington, D.C., and in 1996–97 from the American Council of Learned Societies. Research from 2003 to 2007 was facilitated by funds from the

Grawemeyer Award in Religion. Earlier versions of some of the material included in this book have been published as "The Logic of Religious Violence" in the *Journal of Strategic Studies* and *Contributions to Indian Sociology;* "What the Bhikkhu Said: Reflections on the Rise of Militant Religious Nationalism" in *Religion;* "Sacrifice and Cosmic War" in *The Journal of Terrorism and Political Violence;* and the essays on India and Sri Lanka in Stuart Mews, ed., *Religion in Politics: A World Guide.* The sections on the Aum Shinrikyo, Christian militia, and other cases are based on material that was gathered for a previous book, *Terror in the Mind of God: The Global Rise of Religious Violence.* Portions of the last chapter were published in my essay in the proceedings of an international conference on counterterrorism sponsored by the Club de Madrid.

In the years that I have worked on this topic my colleagues in Berkeley, Washington, Honolulu, and Santa Barbara have enriched my thinking about these matters enormously, as have other colleagues around the world and a host of competent research assistants. Some, such as Darrin McMahon, have gone on to become significant scholars on their own. At Santa Barbara, Barzin Pakandam provided helpful suggestions for revisions of the section on the Islamic Revolution in Iran; Robert Schaerges offered insights and accurate information on the sections about Iraq, Afghanistan, and the global jihadi movement; Brent Linas helped to make the footnotes make sense, and Mike Hoff clarified the bibliography. Other cheerful assistants at Santa Barbara included Paul Lynch, John Ucciferri, Ryan Bushek and Jeff McMillan.

The original version of this book, and parts of the revisions, were groomed by my friend and spouse, Sucheng Chan, to whom this book is dedicated. She has helped immensely in bringing organization and clarity to both versions of the manuscript, and her consistent support for this project over the years has helped to keep it alive. In one way or another, she and all others named above have helped to improve this book's accuracy and flow of thought, and have demonstrated, once again, the benefits of having such patient and intelligent friends.

The Rise of Religious Rebellion

"Islam is under attack," a mullah in Baghdad told me in 2004, the year after the American military forces invaded and occupied his country. He was responding to a question about why the resistance to the American military occupation of Iraq had become so stridently religious. In his reckoning, the United States had imposed its presence in the region not only to liberate Iraq from a dictator but also to establish an American-style secular political regime, and the Iraqis were responding in kind.[1]

"You Americans will not succeed," he went on to tell me, "for Islam will prevail." What was striking about his comment was the idea that the United States was opposed not just to Saddam Hussein but also to Islam. In his view the presence of the U.S. military forces was directed at his nation's religion, and he thought that Iraq would not be truly free until it had established Muslim rule.

Earlier a Muslim professor in Egypt had given me a similar explanation for the rise of religious activism in his country. He told me that there was "a desperate need for religion in public life."[2] He viewed Islam as "a culturally liberating force," which Egypt needed in order to free itself from the vestiges of its colonial past. "Western colonialism has gone," he explained, "but we still have not completed our independence. We will not be free until Egypt becomes a Muslim state."

I heard similar comments from Jewish militants in Israel, Hindu and Sikh partisans in India, Buddhist fighters in Sri Lanka, and members of Christian militias in the United States. A rabbi in Jerusalem said that Israel needed to adhere to the principles of the Torah, and a Lutheran minister in Maryland told me that America desperately needed a Christian form of government in order to "cleanse its soul."[3] The pastor said that he would not be satisfied until the legal status of the U.S. Constitution was replaced by the moral codes of the Bible.

In interviews I have conducted over two decades throughout the world, I found that these points of view are far from unusual. In fact, what appeared to be an anomaly when the Islamic revolution in Iran challenged the supremacy of Western culture and its secular politics in 1979 became a major theme in international politics by the beginning of the twenty-first century. The new world order that replaced the bipolar powers of the old Cold War was characterized not only by the rise of new economic forces, a crumbling of old empires, and the discrediting of communism, but also by the resurgence of parochial identities based on ethnic and religious allegiances. Although many observers in the West maintained that the ending of the old Cold War had led to an "end of history" and a worldwide ideological consensus in favor of secular liberal democracy, the rise of new religious and ethnic politics belied that assertion.[4] Moreover, the extent of the dichotomy between these ways of conceiving civil order and the presence of such strong passions on either side suggest that the global confrontation has all the hallmarks of a new Cold War.

In many ways the current conflict is more a global rebellion than a war, since few of the movements of religious resistance to the secular state have an alternative government in mind. They know what they are against but not exactly what they are for.

Yet there are many similarities between these movements and the ideological challenges of the earlier conflict. Like the old Cold War, the contest between these new forms of culture-based politics and the secular state has been global in its scope, binary in its opposition, occasionally violent, and essentially a difference of ideologies. Like the old Cold War, each side tends to stereotype the other. According to an Islamic political strategist in Sudan, the post–Cold War West needed a new "empire of evil to mobilize against."[5] Similarly, he and other religious politicians needed a stereotype of their own: a satanic secular foe that would help them mobilize their own forces. Today, the West (now aligned with the secular leaders of the former Soviet Union) confronts an opposition that, unlike that of the old Cold War, is neither politically united nor, at present, militarily strong. Yet the violence persists.

Some blame religion for the problem. In a comment on the rise of Sikh militancy in India, an editor of the *Atlantic Monthly* described the manner in which religion had inflamed the Third World as "one of the grimmer and more ironic developments of the late twentieth century." He claimed that religion is "on the whole a benign force in Western societies"; but in the non-Western world of Asia, Africa, and the Middle East it "often combines combustibly with nationalism to fuel political murder."[6] The underlying assumption was that something is seriously wrong with religion in the non-Western world.

In this book, I have adopted a different approach. I have tried to see the points of view of the activists whom the *Atlantic* editor disparaged. From the perspectives of the mullah in Iraq, the rabbi in Jerusalem, and the Lutheran pastor in Maryland, it is secular nationalism, and not religion, that has gone wrong. They see the Western models of nationhood— both democratic and socialist—as having failed, and they view religion as a hopeful alternative, a base for criticism and change.

Why has secular nationalism failed to inspire them? Why has religion been raised as an alternative? Why has the rejection of secular nationalism on religious grounds been so violent? And what ideology and political organization will replace it? In searching for answers to these questions, I have sought the opinions of politically active religious leaders in various parts of the world. Some I interviewed in person; others I encountered through their published interviews, transcripts of their speeches, and their writings. I have tried to make sense of their positions, determine what they have in common with their counterparts in other parts of the globe, place them in a wider context of political and cultural change, and understand why they are so optimistic about their role in what one Algerian Islamic nationalist described as "the march of history."[7]

My interest in this topic began with the Sikhs. Having lived in northern India from time to time and written on religion and politics in the Punjab, and having known the Sikhs generally to be delightful and sensible people, I was profoundly disturbed to witness the deadly spiral of violence involving militant Sikhs and the Indian government that began in the early 1980s and ended a little over a decade later. In trying to make sense of this situation, I turned to the recorded sermons and transcripts of one of the leaders of the militant movement, Sant Jarnail Singh Bhindranwale.[8] His message seemed to be one of despair about the present state of society: he saw it characterized by an absence of a sense of moral community and led by politicians incapable of being anything but corrupt. The despair, however, was tempered by a radical hope: that a religious crusade could bring about a political revolution, one that would usher in a new politics and a new moral order.

The rhetoric of Bhindranwale—at once critical and hopeful, oriented both to modern needs and to traditional values of the past—was not unique, I found, as I began to compare it with other cases. Turning first to the language of Buddhist monks in the militant Sinhalese movement in nearby Sri Lanka and to the rhetoric of India's Hindu nationalists, I soon expanded my interests from the discourse of politically active religious leaders in those two countries to the ideological language of their counterparts in Egypt, Iran, Israel, Israeli-occupied Palestine, Central Asia, and eventually to Japan, Iraq, Afghanistan, Indonesia, North Africa, Europe, the United States, and other parts of the world.[9] The differences among the religious and political movements in these regions are considerable. There is a great deal of variation among their religious values and goals and their political and historical settings, but many of their concerns are surprisingly similar. They are united by a common enemy— secular nationalism—and by a common hope for the revival of religion in the public sphere.

While urging that these movements be taken seriously, however, I do not want to exaggerate their importance. Although some religious activists have already achieved a great deal of political influence in their regions of the world, others have not and never will. Many will forever remain members of a strident minority. I include them in this study, however, because they fit into a larger, virtually global pattern. I have tried to include most, if not all, forms of contemporary religious activism around the world, focusing on religious groups that actively criticize the secular political order and attempt to replace it with one founded on religious principles.

In many parts of the world religious and ethnic identities are intertwined. The nationalist aspirations of Muslims in China and Central Asia have been rightly described by the anthropologist Dru Gladney as "ethnoreligious."[10] But even in these locales, the crucial symbols and beliefs of the regions' cultural heritages are most often those associated with religion. Perhaps for that reason religious activists there, as elsewhere in the world, have become secular leaders' most formidable foes.

It would be easy to characterize these religious activists *as fundamentalists,* but I hesitate to do so for several reasons. First, the term is pejorative. It refers, as one Muslim scholar observed, to those who hold "an intolerant, self-righteous, and narrowly dogmatic religious literalism."[11] The term is less descriptive than it is accusatory: it reflects our attitude toward other people more than it describes them. By implication such persons should not be taken seriously as thoughtful political actors, and that characterization does not fit most of the people whom I encountered in this study, either directly or through their writings.

Second, *fundamentalism* is an imprecise category for making comparisons across cultures. The term stems from the attempt of a group of conservative Protestants early in the twentieth century to define what they held to be the "fundamentals" of Christianity, including the inerrancy of scripture, and it is unclear how they can be compared with those who adhere to other forms of revitalized Christianity, much less to religious activists of other faiths in other parts of the world.[12] The only thing that most religious activists around the world have in common, aside from their fervor, is their rejection of modern secularism. For that reason, a better comparative category would be *antimodernism,* the term that Bruce Lawrence uses to define fundamentalism as a global concept, for it suggests a religious revolt against the secular ideology that often accompanies modern society.[13] One of the advantages of this term is that it allows one to make a distinction between those who are *antimodern* and those who are *antimodernists*—that is, between those who disdain the features of modern society and those who go further and reject the secular ideologies that dominate modern cultures.[14]

This distinction is important because in most cases religious activists, while opposing the values of modernism, are themselves very modern persons. The dean of Islamic theology in Cairo, to whom I referred in one of the opening paragraphs of this introduction, lived in London for a number of years and appreciated its modern efficiency. Rabbi Meir Kahane, a right-wing Jewish nationalist in Israel, ran his movement like a political campaign and loved to discuss American baseball. Khalid Sheik Mohammed, the colleague of Osama bin Laden who was the architect of the September 11, 2001, attacks, studied mechanical engineering in the United States. The Islamic resistance in Iraq uses cell phones and website technology and relies on international television to rally its support. Such religious activists are modern in the sense that they are organization-minded and empirical in their outlook.[15] Yet their modernity is such that it also allows them to embrace traditional religious values and reject secular ones.

My third objection to the use of the term *fundamentalism* in this study is the most salient: it does not carry any political meaning. To call someone a fundamentalist suggests that he or she is motivated solely by religious beliefs rather than by broad concerns about the nature of society and the world. The religious activists I met and studied are politically astute and deeply concerned about the society in which they live. No doubt many of them have friends who may be fixated exclusively on religious matters, and they may rightly be called conservatives, fundamentalists, or simply antimodernists. But when such people fuse their religious perspective with a broad prescription for the world's political and social destiny of the world, one must find an inclusive term. For that reason, I call them religious activists.

By characterizing the subjects of this study as religious activists, I mean to suggest that they are individuals with both religious and political interests. To understand their perspective is an exercise in both comparative religion and comparative politics, for they appear—at least from our point of view—to be responding in a religious way to a political situation. Many of them, however, agree with the observation of the founder of the Palestinian Hamas movement, Sheik Ahmed Yassin, who told me that there is "no clear distinction between religion and politics" and that the distinction itself is a mark of Western ways of thinking.[16] Rather, religious critics of secular nationalism see a deficiency in society that is both spiritual and political in character, one that requires a response that is religious as well as worldly.

Although they reject secular ideas, religious activists do not necessarily reject many aspects of secular politics, including the political apparatus of the modern nation-state. To show how this can be possible, I must explain how I use certain terms. By the *state,* I mean the locus of authority and decisionmaking within a geographical region. By the *nation,* I mean a community of people associated with a particular political culture and territory that possesses autonomous political authority.[17] A *nation-state* is a modern form of nationhood in which a state's authority systematically pervades and regulates an entire nation, whether through democratic or totalitarian means. The modern nation-state is morally and politically justified by a concept of *nationalism,* by which I mean not only the xenophobic extremes of patriotism but also the more subdued expressions of identity based on shared assumptions regarding why a community constitutes a nation and why the state that rules it is legitimate.[18]

Many of the new religious rebels described in this book are able to accept the idea of the nation-state even though they reject the idea of secular nationalism. This means that they are less concerned about the political structure of the nation-state than they are about the political ideology that underlies it. They focus on the rationale for having a state, the moral basis for politics, and the reasons why a state should elicit loyalty. They often reject the European and American notion that nationalism can be defined solely as a matter of secular contract.[19] At the same time, however, many of them see no contradiction in affirming certain forms of political organization that have developed in the West, such as the democratic procedures of the nation-state, as long as they are legitimized not by the secular idea of a social contract but by traditional principles of religion. Other religious activist reject the idea of the modern nation altogether and advocate a kind of religious transnationalism. But there is no inherent bias against the nation-state by religious activists in general.

A *bhikkhu* (a male Buddhist monk) in Sri Lanka told me that what he despised was "not democracy, but your idea of nationalism."[20] He and others like him reject the notion that what draws people together as a nation and what legitimizes their political order is a rational compact that unites everyone in a geographical region through common laws and political processes. Such secular nationalism underlies both the parliamentary democracies of Europe and the Americas and the socialist bureaucracies that once characterized Eastern European countries and the formerly Soviet republics of the Commonwealth of Independent States. This way of thinking about nationalism comes naturally to most Americans and Europeans, but it contains assumptions about the universal and secular nature of a moral social order that many religious people in the rest of the world simply do not take for granted.

I find it striking that religious activists so strongly dismiss secular nationalism as fundamentally bereft of moral or spiritual values. How shocking this rejection would have been to the Western social scientists who in the 1950s proclaimed that the advent of secular nationalism in the Third World was not only a triumph of Western political influence but also one of the West's finest legacies to public life throughout the world.

I begin, in the first chapter of this book, with this sense of promise that so buoyed the spirits of proponents of Western nationalism in a post-Enlightenment era. I examine how the promise faded and how the value of secular nationalism began to be questioned in many parts of the world. I also explore the underlying issue: the competition between religion, in its various forms, and the European and American model of secular nationalism. The next four chapters of this book provide case studies from the Middle East, South Asia, Europe, United States, and elsewhere, including the transnational movement of global jihad. These chapters provide a comprehensive overview of thirty years of religious militancy throughout the world and the various religious traditions associated with it. Virtually every religion is associated with some form of religious rebellion. The sixth chapter looks at several concerns that have been raised about religious activists: their proclivity toward violence and their apparent disregard for democracy and human rights, and how we can learn to live with at least some aspects of the religious political agenda. The concluding chapter of the book is devoted to the question of where we go from here: how this rebellion has developed in stages and where it may be heading, what religion has to do with it, and how it can move beyond the rhetoric and violence and come to a graceful accommodation with civil order and public life.

CHAPTER I

The Religious Challenge to the Secular State

One of the more puzzling features of the *fatweh* in which Osama bin Laden proclaimed war on the American and European West in 1996 was his comparison of Western presence in the Middle East with the Crusades and colonialism. This may have surprised many Westerners who were not used to hearing issues of international relations expressed in cultural terms—especially not in images derived from the Middle Ages and the colonial era. Most Americans and Europeans thought that this kind of cultural oppression was buried in the unhappy past.

To many in the non-Western world, however, these images aptly characterized the present. When the Ayatollah Khomeini railed against American and European influence in Iran, what he had in mind was a new kind of colonialism. Though Iran had never been colonized by European powers, the domination of Western cultural and economic control seemed like colonialism all the same.

The ayatollah and many other leaders of what used to be known as the "third world" of Africa, Asia, Latin America, and the Middle East regarded Western influence as an intrusion that did not end with European political and military retreat in the mid-twentieth century. They regarded it as having continued for the next forty years of the Cold War era under the guise of political ideology and economic control and into the twenty-first century in the form of American-orchestrated globalization. The new secular nationalism that was Europe's legacy in the developing world began to be perceived by many in those regions as morally vacuous and politically corrupt—the worse features of the colonial past.

THE LOSS OF FAITH IN SECULAR NATIONALISM

In the celebrations following the first stages of elections that threatened to bring Islamic nationalists to power in Algeria in the 1990s, a jubilant supporter of the Islamic Front spied a foreigner on the streets of Algiers and grabbed her by the arm. "Please give my condolences to President Mitterrand," the Algerian said.[1] Behind this amusing bit of sarcasm is an impression shared by many Muslims in Algeria: that the nation's ruling party, the National Front, which came to power during the war of independence with France and which controlled the country afterward, was, in a cultural sense, an extension of French colonial rule. Independent Algeria was seen as not entirely independent, but rather a vestige of a past that was itself in need of liberation. An Islamic Algeria would finally mark the country's true freedom from colonialization.

In the middle of the twentieth century, when Algeria and many other former colonies in the developing world gained political independence, Europeans and Americans often wrote with an almost religious fervor about what they regarded as these new nations' freedom—by which they meant the spread of nationalism throughout the world. Invariably, they meant a secular nationalism: new nations that elicited loyalties forged entirely from a sense of territorial citizenship. These secular-nationalist loyalties were based on the idea that the legitimacy of the state was rooted in the will of the people in a particular geographic region and divorced from any religious sanction.

The secular nationalism of the day was defined by what it was—and what it was not. It distanced itself especially from the old ethnic and religious identities that had made nations parochial and quarrelsome in the past. The major exception was the creation of the state of Israel in 1948 as a safe haven for Jews, but even in this case the nation's constitution was firmly secular, and Israeli citizenship was open to people of all religious backgrounds—not only Jews but also Christians and Muslims. In general, mid-twentieth-century scholars viewed the spread of secular nationalism in a hopeful, almost eschatological, light: it was ushering in a new future. It meant, in essence, the emergence of mini-Americas all over the world.

Hans Kohn, his generation's best-known historian of nationalism, observed in 1955 that the twentieth century was unique: "It is the first period in history in which the whole of mankind has accepted one and the same political attitude, that of nationalism."[2] In his telling, the concept had its origins in antiquity. It was presaged by ancient Hebrews and fully enunciated by ancient Greeks. Inexplicably, however, the concept stagnated for almost two thousand years, according to Kohn's account, until suddenly it took off in earnest in England, "the first modern nation," during the seventeenth century.[3] By the time of his writing, in the mid-twentieth century, he cheerfully observed that the whole world had responded to "the awakening of nationalism and liberty."[4]

Not only Western academics but also a good number of new leaders—especially those in the emerging nations created out of former colonial empires—were swept up by the vision of a world of free and equal secular nations. The concept of secular nationalism gave them an ideological justification for being, and the electorate that subscribed to it provided them power bases from which they could vault into positions of leadership ahead of traditional ethnic and religious figures. But secularism was more than just a political issue; it was also a matter of personal identity. A new kind of person had come into existence—the "Indian nationalist" or "Ceylonese nationalist" who had an abiding faith in a secular nationalism identified with his or her homeland. Perhaps none exemplified this new spirit more than Gamal Abdel Nasser of Egypt and Jawaharlal Nehru of India. According to Nehru, "there is no going back" to a past full of religious identities, for the modern, secular "spirit of the age" will inevitably triumph throughout the world.[5]

There was a cheerful optimism among the followers of Nehru after India's independence, writes the political scientist Donald Smith: "The Indian nationalist felt compelled to assert that India was a nation," even though some "embarrassing facts"—such as divisive regional and religious loyalties—had to be glossed over.[6] The reason for this compulsion, according to Smith, was that such people could not think of themselves as modern persons without a national identity. "In the modern world," writes Smith, "nationality and nationalism were the basic premises of political life, and it seemed absolutely *improper* for India to be without a nationality."[7] A similar attitude predominated in many other new nations, at least at the beginning.

Leaders of minority religious communities—such as Hindu Tamils in Ceylon and Coptic Christians in Egypt—seemed especially eager to embrace secular nationalism because a secular nation-state would ensure that the public life of the country would not be dominated completely by the majority religious community. In India, where the Congress Party became the standard-bearer of Nehru's vision, the party's most reliable supporters were those at the margins of Hindu society—untouchables and Muslims—who had the most to fear from an intolerant religious majority.

The main carriers of the banner of secular nationalism in these newly independent countries, however, were not members of any religious community at all, at least in a traditional sense. Rather, they were members of the urban educated elite. For many of them, embracing a secular form of nationalism was a way of promoting its major premise—freedom from the parochial identities of the past—and thereby avoiding the obstacles that religious loyalties create for a country's political goals. By implication, political power based on religious values and traditional communities held no authority.

The problem, however, was that in asserting that the nationalism of their country was secular, the new nationalists had to have faith in a secular culture that was at least as compelling as a sacred one. That meant, on a social level, believing that secular nationalism could triumph over religion. It could also mean making secular nationalism a suprareligion of its own, which a society could aspire to beyond any single religious allegiance. In India, for example, political identity based on religious affiliation was termed *communalism*. In the view of Nehru and other secular nationalists, religion was the chief competitor of an even higher object of loyalty: secular India. Nehru implored his countrymen to get rid of what he called "that narrowing religious outlook" and to adopt a modern, nationalist viewpoint.[8]

The secular nationalists' attempts to give their ideologies an antireligious or a suprareligious force were encouraged, perhaps unwittingly, by their Western mentors. The words used to define *nationalism* by Western political leaders and such scholars as Kohn always implied not only that it was secular but that it was competitive with religion and ultimately superior to it. "Nationalism [by which he meant secular nationalism] is a state of mind," Kohn wrote, "in which the *supreme loyalty* of the individual is felt to be due the nation-state."[9] And he boldly asserted that secular nationalism had replaced religion in its influence: "An understanding of nationalism and its implications for modern history and for our time appears as fundamental today as an understanding of religion would have been for thirteenth century Christendom."[10]

Rupert Emerson's influential *From Empire to Nation,* written several years later, shared the same exciting vision of a secular nationalism that "sweeps out [from Europe] to embrace the whole wide world."[11] Emerson acknowledged, however, that although in the European experience "the rise of nationalism [again, secular nationalism] coincided with a decline in the hold of religion," in other parts of the world, such as Asia, as secular nationalism "moved on" and enveloped these regions, "the religious issue pressed more clearly to the fore again."[12] Nonetheless, he anticipated that the "religious issue" would never again impede the progress of secular nationalism, which he saw as the West's gift to the world. The feeling that in some instances this gift had been forced on the new nations without their asking was noted by Emerson, who acknowledged that "the rise of nationalism among non-European peoples" was a consequence of "the imperial spread of Western European civilization over the face of the earth." The outcome, in his view, was nonetheless laudable: "With revolutionary dynamism . . . civilization has thrust elements of essential identity on peoples everywhere. . . . The global impact of the West has . . . run common threads through the variegated social fabrics of mankind, . . . [and it] has scored an extraordinary triumph."[13]

When Kohn and Emerson used the term *nationalism* they had in mind not just a secular political ideology and a religiously neutral national identity but a particular form of political organization: the modern European and American nation-state. In such an organization, individuals are linked to a centralized, all-embracing democratic political system that is unaffected by any other affiliations, be they ethnic, cultural, or religious. That linkage is sealed by an emotional sense of identification with a geographical area and a loyalty to a particular people, an identity that is part of the feeling of nationalism. This affective dimension of nationalism is important to keep in mind, especially in comparing secular nationalism with religion. In the 1980s, the social theorist Anthony Giddens described nationalism in just this way—as conveying not only the ideas and "beliefs" about political order but also the "psychological" and "symbolic" element in political and economic relationships.[14] Scholars such as Kohn and Emerson recognized this affective dimension of nationalism early on; they felt it appropriate that the secular nation adopt what we might call the spirit of secular nationalism.

Secular nationalism as we know it today—as the ideological ally of the nation-state—began to appear in England and America in the eighteenth century. Only by then had the idea of a nation-state taken root deeply enough to nurture a loyalty of its own, unassisted by religion or tradition, and only by then had the political and military apparatus of the nation-state expanded sufficiently to encompass a large geographic region. Prior to that time, as Giddens explains, "the administrative reach" of the political center was so limited that rulers did not govern in "the modern sense."[15] Although there were embryonic forms of secular nationalism before then, the power of the state had been limited.[16] Until the advent of the nation-state, the authority of a political center did not systematically and equally cover an entire population, so that what appeared to be a single homogeneous polity was in fact an aggregation of fiefdoms. The further one got from the center of power, the weaker the grip of centralized political influence, until at the periphery entire sections of a country might exist as a political no-man's-land. For that reason, one should speak of countries prior to the modern nation-state as having frontiers rather than boundaries.[17]

The changes of the late eighteenth and nineteenth centuries included boundaries; the development of the technical capacity to knit a country together through roads, rivers, and other means of transportation and communication; the construction of the economic capacity to do so, through an increasingly integrated market structure; the emergence of a world economic system based on the building blocks of nation-states;[18] the formation of mass education, which socialized each generation of youth into a homogeneous society; and the rise of parliamentary democracy as a system of representation and an expression of the will of the people. The glue that held all these changes together was a new form of nationalism: the notion that individuals naturally associate with the people and place of their ancestral birth (or an adopted homeland such as the United States) in an economic and political system identified with a secular nation-state. Secular nationalism was thought to be not only natural but also universally applicable and morally right.

Although it was regarded almost as a natural law, secular nationalism was ultimately viewed as an expression of neither God nor nature but of the will of citizens.[19] It was the political manifestation of the Enlightenment view of humanity. John Locke's ideas of the origins of a civil community[20] and Jean-Jacques Rousseau's social-contract theories required little commitment to religious belief.[21] Although Locke and Rousseau had religious sensibilities and allowed for a divine order that made the rights of humans possible, these ideas did not directly buttress the power of the church and its priestly administrators. Their secular concepts of nation and state had the effect of taking religion—at least church religion—out of public life.

The medieval church once possessed "many aspects of a state," as one historian put it, and it commanded more political power "than most of its secular rivals."[22] By the mid-nineteenth century, however, Christian churches had ceased to have much influence on European or American politics. The church—the great medieval monument of Christendom with all its social and political diversity—had been replaced by *churches*: various denominations of Protestantism and a largely depoliticized version of Roman Catholicism. These churches functioned like religious clubs, voluntary associations for the spiritual edification of individuals in their leisure time, rarely cognizant of the social and political world around them.[23]

At the same time that religion in the West was becoming less political, its secular nationalism was becoming more religious. It became clothed in romantic and xenophobic images that would have startled its Enlightenment forebears. The French Revolution, the model for much of the nationalist fervor that developed in the nineteenth century, infused a religious zeal into revolutionary democracy; the revolution took on the trappings of church religion in the priestly power meted out to its demagogic leaders and in the slavish devotion to what it called the temple of reason. According to Alexis de Tocqueville, the French Revolution "assumed many of the aspects of a religious revolution."[24] The American Revolution also had a religious side: many of its leaders had been influenced by eighteenth-century deism, a religion of science and natural law that was "devoted to exposing [church] religion to the light of knowledge."[25] As in France, American nationalism developed its own religious characteristics, blending the ideals of secular nationalism and the symbols of Christianity into what has been called "civil religion."[26]

The nineteenth century saw the fulfillment of Tocqueville's prophecy that the "strange religion" of secular nationalism would, "like Islam, overrun the whole world with its apostles, militants, and martyrs."[27] It spread throughout the world with an almost missionary zeal and was shipped to the newly colonized areas of Asia, Africa, and Latin America as part of the ideological freight of colonialism. It became the ideological partner of what came to be known as nation building. As the colonizing governments provided their colonies with the political and economic infrastructures to turn territories into nation-states, the ideology of secular nationalism emerged as a byproduct. As it had in the West during previous centuries, secular nationalism in the colonized countries during the nineteenth and twentieth centuries came to represent one side of a great encounter between two vastly different ways of perceiving the sociopolitical order and the relationship of the individual to the state: one informed by religion, the other by a notion of a secular compact.

In the West this encounter, and the ideological, economic, and political transitions that accompanied it, took place over many years, uncomplicated by the intrusion of foreign control of a colonial or neocolonial sort. The new nations of the twentieth and twenty-first centuries, however, have had to confront the same challenges in a short period of time and simultaneously contend with new forms of politics forced on them as byproducts of colonial rule. As in the West, however, the challenge they have faced is fundamental: it involves the encounter between an old religious worldview and a new one shaped by secular nationalism.

When Europeans colonized the rest of the world, they were often sustained by a desire to make the rest of the world like themselves.[28] Even when empires became economically burdensome, the cultural mission seemed to justify the effort. The commitment of colonial administrators to a secular-nationalist vision explains why they were often so hostile to the Christian missionaries who tagged along behind them: the missionaries were the liberal colonizers' competitors. The church's old religious ideology was a threat to the new secular ideology that most colonial rulers wished to present as characteristic of the West.[29]

In the mid-twentieth century, when the colonial powers retreated, they left behind the geographical boundaries they had drawn and the political institutions they had fashioned. Created as administrative units of the Ottoman, Hapsburg, French, and British empires, the borders of most Third World nations continued to survive after independence, even if they failed to follow the natural divisions between ethnic and linguistic communities. By the middle of the twentieth century, it seemed as if the cultural goals of the colonial era had been reached: although the political ties were severed, the new nations retained all the accoutrements of Westernized countries.

The only substantial empire that remained virtually intact until 1990 was the Soviet Union. It was based on a different vision of political order, of course, one in which international socialism was supposed to replace a network of capitalist nations. Yet the perception of many members of the Soviet states was that their nations were not so much integral units in a new internationalism as colonies in a secular Russian version of imperialism. This reality became dramatically clear after the breakup of the Soviet Union and its sphere of influence in the early 1990s, when old ethnic and national loyalties sprang to the fore.

Even in the twenty-first century, the nation-state continued to be critical to world politics, not only for ideological reasons but also for economic ones: despite the growing power of transnational corporations, nation-states remained the essential units of the global economic system. In the past, religion had little role to play in this scheme, and when it did become involved, it often threatened it.[30] Contemporary religious politics, then, is the result of an almost Hegelian dialectic between two competing frameworks of social order: secular nationalism (allied with the nation-state) and religion (allied with large ethnic communities, some of them transnational). The clashes between the two have often been destructive, but, as we shall see, they have also offered possibilities for accommodation. In some cases these encounters have given birth to a synthesis in which religion has become the ally of a new kind of nation-state. At the same time, other liaisons with contemporary political trends have led to a different vision: religious versions of a transnationalism that would supplant the nation-state world.

THE COMPETITION BETWEEN TWO IDEOLOGIES

The encounter between religion and secularism is linked to the very terms used to describe these two ways of looking at the world. Prior to the European Enlightenment the words "religion" and "secularism" scarcely existed. As the scholar of comparative religion Wilfred Cantwell Smith has pointed out, the word "religion" began to be widely used in modern Europe and America only in the nineteenth century. Though it appears in ancient Roman writings, the term did not reappear until the Renaissance, and then only occasionally, coming into prominence only in the last two centuries.[31] Before that time and in most parts of the world even today, words that translate as "tradition," "community," and "faith" have been used for what we think of as religious customs, groups, and devotion. It was unthinkable that "religion" in this sense might be separate from other parts of life.

The Enlightenment ushered in a new way of thinking about religion—a narrower definition of the term that encompassed institutions and beliefs that were regarded as problematic, and conceptually separated them from the rest of social life, which was identified by a new term, "secular." What many people in Europe were afraid of at the time was the economic and political power of the clergy, and the fanaticism associated with the terrible wars of religion of the sixteenth and seventeenth centuries. These would be controlled in a society in which "religion" had its limitations within "secular" society.

It is interesting to note that the terms "religious" and "secular" came from the church. In the Middle Ages the Roman Catholic Church had made a distinction between those clergy associated with religious orders that were separated from the world, and were "religious," and those clergy who officiated in local parishes in society and were "secular." After the Enlightenment, the whole church and all of its customs, practices, and beliefs were conceptually encompassed by the term "religion." Everything else—including the moral basis for public order, social values, and the idea of moral communities—was secular. Before the Enlightenment, and in most parts of the world down to the present time, all of these moral elements of social and political life have been conceived as being part of the tradition, customs, and practices of religion.

Perhaps it is useful, then, to think of religion in two senses, in post- and pre-Enlightenment ways of thinking. One is the narrow idea of religious institutions and beliefs that are set apart from secular social values in the modern West. The other is the broad idea of moral values, traditional customs, and spiritual sensibility that includes much of what the secular West regards as public virtue and purposeful life—values shared by most thoughtful and concerned citizens within a society.

Hence the elusive term "religion," in the broad sense, can point to a moral sensibility toward the social order that in many ways is remarkably similar to the civic values of those who feel most ardently about secularism. This is especially so in the non-Western world. In traditional India, for instance, the English term "religion" might be translated as the word for moral order—*dharma*—as well as for belief *(mazhab)*, fellowship *(panth)*, or community *(qaum)*. As *dharma*, Hindu thought is like political or social theory, the basis of a just society. The Enlightenment thinkers who were most insistent on secularism did not see religion in this way; what they saw was an arrogant religious hierarchy keeping the masses enslaved to superstition in order to avoid justice and reason. They thought of religion as competitive with Enlightenment values, yet religion as *dharma* looks very much like that moral ground on which the Enlightenment thinkers were able to build the edifice of a just society. In ways that might surprise them, religion—at least in its broad sense, as a conveyer of public values—and secularism as a social ideology might well be two ways of talking about the same thing.

If so, how should we describe this similarity between religion and secularism that put them in competition in the West several centuries ago and more recently elsewhere in the world? Our terms are important because they color how we think about Western history and how we think about contemporary world affairs. Because the functions of traditional religious and secular social values are so similar, it might be useful to designate a general category that includes both terms: a "genus" of which religion and secularism are the two competing "species." Wilfred Cantwell Smith recommended enlarging the idea of "traditions" to include secular humanism; Benedict Anderson suggested "imagined communities" for all national societies; and Ninian Smart offered "worldviews" as the common term for nationalism, socialism, and religion.[32] Their choices have the benefit of including a wide range of concepts, from attitudes toward sexuality and natural science to views about the cosmos, and they explicitly include both what we call *religion* (in both narrow and broad senses) and what we call *secularism*. Because our discussion is focused on conceptual frameworks that legitimize authority, however, we might consider a phrase with more political connotations, such as *ideologies of order*.

I use the word *ideology* with a certain amount of trepidation, knowing that it comes freighted with meanings attached to it by Karl Marx and Karl Mannheim and that a great deal of controversy still lingers over its interpretation today.[33] The term is useful for our purposes, however, because it originated in the late eighteenth century in the context of the rise of secular nationalism.[34] A group of French *idéologues,* as they called themselves, sought to build a science of ideas based on the theories of Francis Bacon, Thomas Hobbes, John Locke, and René Descartes that would be sufficiently comprehensive to replace religion, in the broad sense, and provide a moral weight to counter the violent excesses of the French Revolution. According to one of the *idéologues,* Destutt de Tracy, whose book *Elements of Ideology* introduced the term to the world, "logic" was to be the sole basis of "the moral and political sciences."[35]

The French originators of the term "ideology" would be surprised at the way it has come to be redefined, especially in contemporary conversations, where it is often treated as an explanatory system that is specifically "nonscientific."[36] But in proposing their own "science of ideas" as a replacement for religion, the *idéologues* were in fact putting what they called *ideology* and what we call *religion* (in the broad sense) on an equal plane. Perhaps Clifford Geertz, among modern users of the term, has come closest to its original meaning by speaking of ideology as a "cultural system."[37] Geertz includes both religious and political cultural systems within this framework, as well as the many cultural systems that do not distinguish between religion and politics. Religion and secular nationalism could both be considered cultural systems in Geertz's sense of the word, and, hence, as he uses it, they are ideologies.

I would prefer, then, to call both religion and secularism ideologies and have done with it. But to make clear that I am referring to the original meaning of the term and not to political ideology in a narrow sense, or to a Marxian or Mannheimian notion of ideology, I will refer to what I have in mind as *ideologies of order*. Both religious and secular frameworks of thought conceive of the world in coherent, manageable ways; they both suggest that there are levels of meaning beneath the day-to-day world that give coherence to things unseen; and they both provide the authority that gives the social and political order its reason for being. In doing so, they define for the individual the right way of being in the world and relate persons to the social whole.

Secular nationalism is the social form of secularism that locates an individual within the universe. The idea of a secular nation ties him or her to a particular place and a particular history. A number of social scientists have argued that the phenomenon of secular nationalism is linked to the innate need of individuals for a sense of community. Karl Deutsch has pointed out the importance of systems of communication in fostering a sense of nationalism.[38] Ernest Gellner argues that the political and economic network of a nation-state can function only in a spirit of nationalism based on a homogeneous culture, a unified pattern of communication, and a common system of education.[39] Other social scientists have stressed the psychological aspect of national identity: the sense of historical location that is engendered when individuals feel they have a larger, national history.[40]

But behind these notions of community is a more stern image: that of order. Nationalism involves loyalty to an authority who, as Max Weber observed, holds a monopoly over the "legitimate use of physical force" in a given society.[41] Giddens describes nationalism as the "cultural sensibility of sovereignty," implying that, in part, the awareness of being subject to an authority—an authority invested with the power of life and death—gives nationalism its potency.[42] Secular nationalism, therefore, involves not only an attachment to a spirit of social order but also an act of submission to an ordering agent.

Scholarly attempts to define religion also stress the importance of order, though in a post-Enlightenment context where religion is thought of in the narrower sense, the orderliness is primarily metaphysical rather than political or social.[43] In providing its adherents with a sense of conceptual order, religion often deals with the existential problem of disorder. The disorderliness of ordinary life is contrasted with a substantial, unchanging divine order.[44] Geertz sees religion as the effort to integrate messy everyday reality into a pattern of coherence at a deeper level.[45] Robert Bellah also thinks of religion as an attempt to reach beyond ordinary phenomena in a "risk of faith" that allows people to act "in the face of uncertainty and unpredictability" on the basis of a higher order of reality.[46] This attitude of faith, according to Peter Berger, is an affirmation of the sacred, which acts as a doorway to a truth more certain than that of this world.[47] Louis Dupré prefers to avoid the term *sacred* but integrates elements of both Berger's and Bellah's definitions in his description of religion as "a commitment to the transcendent as to *another reality*."[48] In all these cases there is a tension between this imperfect, disorderly world and a perfected, orderly one to be found in a higher, transcendent state or in a cumulative moment in time. As Émile Durkheim, whose ideas are fundamental to each of these thinkers, was adamant in observing, religion has a more encompassing force than can be suggested by any dichotomization of the sacred and the profane. To Durkheim, the religious point of view includes both the notion that there is such a dichotomy and the belief that the sacred side will always, ultimately, reign supreme.[49]

Even on the metaphysical level, religion, like secular nationalism, can provide the moral and spiritual glue that holds together broad communities. Members of these communities—secular or religious—share a tradition, a particular worldview, in which the essential conflict between appearance and deeper reality is described in specific and characteristically cultural terms. This deeper reality has a degree of permanence and order quite unobtainable by ordinary means. The conflict between the two levels of reality is what both religion and secular nationalism are about: the language of both contains images of chaos as well as tranquil order, holding out the hope that, despite appearances to the contrary, order will eventually triumph and disorder will be contained.

Because religion (in both broad and narrow senses) and secular nationalism are ideologies of order, they are potential rivals.[50] Either can claim to be the guarantor of orderliness within a society; either can claim to be the ultimate authority for social order. Such claims carry with them an extraordinary degree of power, for contained within them is the right to give moral sanction for life-and-death decisions, including the right to kill. When either secular nationalism or religion assumes that role by itself, it reduces the other to a peripheral social role.

Earlier in history it was often religion that denied moral authority to secular politicians, but in recent centuries it has been the other way around. Secular political authorities now monopolize the authority to

sanction violence. Political leaders attempted to do so long before the advent of the nation-state but usually in collusion with religious authority,
not in defiance of it. Seldom in history has the state denied so vehemently
the right of religious authorities to be ultimate moral arbiters as in the
modern period, and seldom before has it so emphatically taken on that
role itself. The secular state, and the state alone, is given the power to kill
legitimately, albeit for limited purposes: military defense, police protection, and capital punishment. Yet all the rest of the state's power to per-
suade and to shape the social order is derived from this fundamental
power. In Weber's view, the monopoly over legitimate violence in a society is the very definition of a state.[51] In challenging the state's authority, today's religious activists, wherever they assert themselves around the
world, reclaim the traditional right of religious authorities to say when
violence is moral and when it is not.

Religious conflict is one indication of the power of religion to sanction killing. The parties in such an encounter may command a greater degree of loyalty than do contestants in a purely political war. Their interests can subsume national interests. In some cases such a religious battle
may preface the attempt to establish a new religious state. It is interesting to note, in this regard, that the best-known incidents of religious violence throughout the contemporary world have occurred in places
where it is difficult to define or accept the idea of a nation-state. At the
end of the twentieth century, these places included Palestine, the Punjab,
and Sri Lanka; in the twenty-first century they include Iraq, Somalia, and
Lebanon, areas where uncertainties abound about what the state should
be and which elements of society should lead it. In these instances, religion has often provided the basis for a new national consensus and a new
kind of leadership.

Islam, Judaism, and Christianity have provided religious alternatives
to secular ideology as the basis of nationalism. So also has Hinduism,
Sikhism, and perhaps most surprisingly, Buddhism. In Thailand, for example, the king must be a monk before assuming political power—he
must be a "world renouncer" before he can become a "world conqueror," as Stanley Tambiah has put it.[52] Burmese leaders established a
Buddhist socialism, guided by a curious syncretic mix of Marxist and
Buddhist ideas, and even the protests against that order in Burma—
renamed Myanmar—had a religious character: many of the demonstrations in the streets were led by Buddhist monks.[53] Thus in most traditional
religious societies, including Buddhist ones, "religion," as Donald Smith
puts it, "answers the question of political legitimacy."[54] In the modern

West that legitimacy is provided by nationalism, a secular nationalism. But even there, religion continues to wait in the wings, a potential challenge to the nationalism based on secular assumptions. Perhaps nothing indicates this potential more than the persistence of religious politics in American society, including the rise of the Christian militia and the American religious right.[55] Religion, like secular nationalism, has provided a faith in the unitary nature of a society that authenticates both political rebellion and political rule.

When the mullahs in Iraq told me that America was the enemy of Islam, they were equating a secular state with religion. It is a comparison that would have startled many of the twentieth-century proponents of secular nationalism. Scholars such as Kohn and Emerson and nationalist leaders such as Nasser and Nehru regarded secular nationalism as superior to religion in large measure because they thought it was categorically different. Yet it seems clear in hindsight that to believe in the notion of secular nationalism required a great deal of faith, even though the idea was not couched in the rhetoric of religion. The terms in which it was presented were the grandly visionary ones associated with spiritual values. Secular nationalism, like religion, embraces what one scholar calls "a doctrine of destiny."[56] One can take this way of looking at secular nationalism a step further and state flatly, as did one author writing in 1960, that secular nationalism is "a religion."[57]

Talal Asad has made this point in a different way by showing how secularism has become a natural successor to religion in the evolution from premodern to modern societies. In Asad's view, secularism is a sort of advanced form of religion that relocates the sphere of the sacred in communal values, such as human rights. Hence religion and secularism are closely intertwined.[58] A scholar of comparative religion, Ninian Smart, has gone further to specify the characteristics that make secular nationalism akin to a certain kind of religion—"a tribal religion."[59] Employing six criteria to define the term, he concluded that secular nationalism measured up on all counts: on doctrine, myth, ethics, ritual, experience, and social organization.

This structural similarity between secular nationalism and religion is complemented by what I regard as an even more basic, functional similarity: they both serve the ethical function of providing an overarching framework of moral order, a framework that commands ultimate loyalty from those who subscribe to it. A further point, one that will be explored later in this book, bears mentioning here: nowhere is this common form of loyalty more evident than in the ability of nationalism and religion,

alone among all forms of allegiance, to give moral sanction to martyrdom and violence.

Though it may be true that other entities, such as the Mafia and the
Ku Klux Klan, also sanction violence, they are able to do so convincingly
only because they are regarded by their followers as (respectively) quasi-
governmental or quasi-religious organizations. For that reason, I believe
the line between secular nationalism and religion has always been quite
thin. Both are expressions of faith, both involve an identity with and a
loyalty to a large community, and both insist on the ultimate moral legitimacy of the authority invested in the leadership of that community.
The rise of secular nationalism in world history, as Benedict Anderson
observes, has been an extension of "the large cultural systems that preceded it, out of which—as well as against which—it came into being."[60]
Anderson, in observing the ease with which secular nationalism is able
to justify mass killings, finds a strong affinity between "nationalist imagining" and "religious imagining." This affinity leads to a blurring of the
lines between them. Secular nationalism often evokes an almost religious
response and it frequently appears as a kind of "cultural nationalism" in
the way that Howard Wriggins once described Sinhalese national sentiments.[61] It not only encompasses the shared cultural values of people
within existing, or potentially existing, national boundaries but also
evokes a cultural response of its own.

The implication of this position—that secular nationalism has a cultural dimension—is that there is no such thing as a concept of nationalism that stands above culture. The Western notion of secular nationalism is precisely that: a Western construct. Perhaps in time, as Kohn and
Emerson prophesied, the concept will spread throughout the globe, not
because it is inherently universal but because it has been deliberately
adapted to particular situations and clearly accepted within certain regions as a legitimate expression of indigenous sentiments. In contrast, in
many regions during the 1950s there was superficial acceptance of a concept that was promoted by leaders of new nations who may have genuinely believed in the idea of secular nationalism but who also found it
useful in buttressing their own legitimacy at home and enlisting economic support and fostering political liaisons abroad.

The proposition that the Western notion of secular nationalism is a
European construct has been bandied about from time to time in Western intellectual circles. At least one scholar, a Christian theologian, suggested that the idea of a secular basis for politics is not only culturally
European but specifically Christian. In an arresting book, *Christianity in*

World History, Arend Theodor van Leeuwen argued that the idea of sep-
arating out the things of God from the things of people in such a way as
to deny the divine nature of kingship was first formulated in ancient Israel and then became a major motif of Christianity.[62] As Christianity
spread across Europe, it brought the message of secularization with it:
"Christianization and secularization are involved together in a dialecti-
cal relation," van Leeuwen claimed.[63] By secularization, van Leeuwen
did not mean secularism—the worship of worldly things—but rather the
separation of religious and temporal spheres.[64] The great liaison between
the medieval church and state was something of a mistake, from this
point of view, and the Enlightenment brought Christianity's secularizing
mission back on track. In general, van Leeuwen proclaimed, "the revolutionary history of the West up to the present time is rightly held to have
been a continuous, ongoing process of secularization"; and, he added, it
is a process that "nothing has been able to halt, let alone reverse."[65]

Van Leeuwen noted that the encounter between Western (implicitly
Christian) secular culture and the traditional religious cultures of the
Middle East and Asia "begins a new chapter in the history of secularization."[66] Secular culture was, in his mind, Christianity's gift to the
world, and he fully expected that as a result of the encounter Hindus
would shed their "myth of *sanatana dharma*" (traditional duties) and
Muslims their "myth of the all-embracing authority of the *shari'a*" (religious law), just as Christians had fled from pagan gods and the ancient
Israelites had abandoned the Tower of Babel.[67] This result was inevitable, van Leeuwen thought, for "once the ontocratic pattern of the
pagan religions has been disrupted fundamentally, there can be no returning to a pre-Christian situation."[68] Still, in the short run, van
Leeuwen anticipated trouble: "Never in the past," he wrote, "has there
been such an encounter" as the present one between Christianity "in
such a thoroughly secularized phase" and "the great pre-Christian societies and the post-Christian Muslim world." Van Leeuwen concluded,
somewhat darkly, "We do not know what may happen."[69]

As it turned out, the encounter between Islamic and other traditional
religious societies and the secular West was as unpleasant as van
Leeuwen feared. Van Leeuwen's thesis about the Christian origins of
modern Western secularism is increasingly regarded as true, especially in
developing countries, by people who have never heard of van Leeuwen
and who once were uncritically accepting of Western nationalism as the
wave of the future. The finer points of van Leeuwen's argument are still
problematic, however. The long history of secularism is doubtful. The

idea that secularism was uniquely Christian can be challenged by the observation that most other religious traditions have as complicated a pattern of church/state relations as Christianity has. In ancient India and in many Buddhist countries, for instance, a distinction similar to that made by the ancient Hebrews and early Christians was drawn between priestly and secular authority. Moreover, the instances of religious complicity with the state are at least as frequent in Christian history as they are in the history of other traditions. Yet van Leeuwen is correct in saying that the particular form of secular society that has evolved in the modern West is a direct extension of its past, including its religious past, and is not some supracultural entity that came into being only after a radical juncture in history.

Van Leeuwen thus stated some years ago what today is taken to be a fact in many parts of the world: the secular nationalism of the West is a mask for a certain form of European Christian culture. This point of view is adopted increasingly by many who have never read van Leeuwen but who agree with his premise: that the rise of specific political ideologies is part of a much larger unfolding of ideas in world history, ideas that in most cases are colored in particular religious hues. Although Christian religious activists in the United States also object to the secularization of their country's politics, this position is most frequently heard among the religious and political leaders of previously colonized countries.

THE MUTUAL REJECTION OF RELIGION AND SECULARISM

In places like the United States and Europe, where secular nationalism, rather than religion, has become the dominant paradigm in society, religion has been shunted to the periphery. This transposition is most dramatically illustrated by the clublike church religion that is common in the United States. Yet, even there, attempts have been made to assimilate some aspects of religion into the national consensus. The reasons for doing so are varied: coopting elements of religion into nationalism keeps religion from building its own antinational power base; it provides religious legitimacy for the state; and it helps give nationalism a religious aura. To accomplish these goals, national leaders have borrowed various elements of a society's religious culture. The secular nationalism of the United States is to some extent colored by a religiosity such as this, as Bellah has pointed out in his analysis of the "civil religion" sprinkled throughout the inaugural addresses of American presidents and the rhetoric of other public speakers.[70]

Despite these attempts to coopt it, and despite its relegation to the pe-riphery of society, church religion occasionally intrudes into the politi-cal sphere. In what Jaroslav Krejci calls "the American pattern" of society—the attempt to blend "ethnopolitical relationships" into a ho-mogeneous whole—some religious groups resist the blending.[71] This re-sistance was seen dramatically during the civil-rights movement of the 1960s, when the African American church and its clergy became central political actors, and religious movements such as the Black Muslims arose as vehicles of protest. In a different way the ascendance of an Evan-gelical Protestant political activism some thirty years later was a new as-sault on the presumptions of secular nationalism in the United States. Secular nationalism in Europe is also not completely immune from reli-gion. In what Krejci calls "the European pattern," where strong ethnic and religious communities are supposedly insulated from political life, the insulation sometimes wears thin.[72] The events in Eastern Europe in the early 1990s and the xenophobic Christian responses to Muslim im-migrants in the twenty-first century are cases in point.

So the West has found that religion does not always stay tightly leashed. But if accommodating religion has been difficult for the West, efforts to bridle religion in the new nations in Africa, Asia, and the Mid-dle East have been a thousand times more problematic. There, the need to deal with religion is much more obvious. Given religious histories that are part of national heritages, religious institutions that are sometimes the nations' most effective systems of communication, and religious lead-ers who are often more socially devoted, efficient, and intelligent than government officials, religion cannot be ignored. The attempts to ac-commodate it, however, have not always been successful, as the follow-ing examples indicate.

In Egypt, following the revolution of 1952, Gamal Abdel Nasser was caught in a double bind. Because his support came from both the Muslim Brotherhood and the modern elite, he was expected to create a Muslim state and a modern secular state at the same time. His ap-proach was to paint a picture of an Egypt that was culturally Muslim and politically secular, and he cheerfully went about "Egyptizing along with modernizing," as a professor in Cairo put it.[73] The compromise did not work, and especially after Nasser attempted to institute "sci-entific socialism," which the Muslim Brotherhood regarded as anti-Islamic, the Brotherhood became Nasser's foe. It attempted to over-throw his government, and Nasser jailed its members and executed its leader, Sayyid Qutb.

Nasser's successor, Anwar al-Sadat, repeated the pattern, which turned out to be a tragic and fatal mistake. Like Nasser, Sadat raised Muslim expectations by currying favor with the Muslim Brotherhood. In 1971, he released many of them from jail, but by 1974 he and the Brotherhood were at loggerheads, and again the organization was outlawed. Sadat attempted to assume the mantle of Islam by calling himself "Upholder of the Faith," announcing that his first name was really Muhammad rather than Anwar, and promoting religious schools. None of these attempts worked. His wife was thought to be an improper role model for Muslim women, and Sadat himself was accused of being a Muslim turncoat. With this image in mind, members of the al-Jihad, a radical fringe group of the Muslim Brotherhood, assassinated Sadat in 1981. His successor, Hosni Mubarak, tried to steer more of a middle course, making no promises to the Muslim activists but making no new secular or socialist departures either.[74]

In India, three generations of prime ministers in the Nehru dynasty—Jawaharlal, his daughter Indira Gandhi, and her son Rajiv—all tried to accommodate religion as little as possible. Yet at times they were forced to make concessions to religious groups almost against their wills. Nehru seemed virtually allergic to religion, putting secularism alongside socialism as his great political goal. Nonetheless the Indian constitution and subsequent parliamentary actions have given a great deal of public support to religious entities.[75] Special seats have been reserved in the legislature for Muslims and members of other minority communities; religious schools have been affiliated with the state; and temples and mosques have received direct public support. In general the Indian government has not been indifferent to religion but has attempted to treat—and foster—each religion in the country equally. As Ainslie Embree puts it, "Advocates of secularism in India always insisted . . . that far from being hostile to religion, they valued it."[76]

Even so, these concessions have not been sufficient to stem the tide of religious politics in India. The 1980s was a decade of tragedy in that regard. Hindu nationalists wanted more and more access to power, prompting defensiveness on the part of Muslim and Christian minorities and a bloody rebellion on the part of the Sikhs. The assassinations of Prime Minister Gandhi and her son Rajiv did not put an end to their sense of dissatisfaction, and the Hindu nationalist Bharatiya Janata Party displaced the Congress Party in providing national leadership from 1998 to 2004, when it was defeated by a revived Congress Party led by

Rajiv Gandhi's widow, Sonia, who stepped aside to allow an economist, Manmohan Singh, to become prime minister.

These attempts to accommodate religion in secular nationalism lead to a double frustration: those who make these compromises are sometimes considered traitors from both a spiritual and a secular point of view. Moreover, these compromises imply that spiritual and political matters are separate—an idea that most religious activists reject and see as a capitulation to secularism. They sense that behind the compromises is a basic allegiance not to religion but to the secular state.

This suspicion about secularism's competition with religion has led to the conclusion that secular nationalism is "a kind of religion," as one of the leaders of the Iranian revolution put it. The Iranian leader, Abolhassan Bani-Sadr, wrote this in a matter-of-fact manner that indicated that what he said was taken as an obvious truth by most of his readers.[77] Bani-Sadr went on to explain that it was not only a religion but one peculiar to the West, a point echoed by one of the leaders of the Muslim Brotherhood in Egypt.[78] Behind his statement was the assumption that secular nationalism responds to the same needs for collective identity, ultimate loyalty, and moral authority that religion has traditionally responded to and that this similar response makes secular nationalism de facto a religion. One of his colleagues went further and stated that the Western form of secular nationalism is Christian. He claimed that the West is "not as secular as it pretends," for it has "Christian governments."[79] For evidence, he offered the fact that the word *Christian* is used in the title of socialist parties in Europe.[80]

Others have given a more sophisticated version of this argument, saying that although secular nationalism in the West may not be overtly Christian, it occupies the same place in human experience as does Islam in Muslim societies, Buddhism in Theravada Buddhist societies, and Hinduism and Sikhism in Indian society. Thus it is a religion in the same sense as Islam, Theravada Buddhism, Hinduism, and Sikhism. One might as well call it Christian nationalism or European cultural nationalism, they declare, and make clear what seems to many Muslims, Buddhists, Hindus, and Sikhs to be perfectly obvious: that it competes in every way with religion as they know it.

Behind this charge is a certain vision of social reality, one that involves a series of concentric circles. The smallest circles are families and clans; then come ethnic groups and nations; the largest, and implicitly most important, are global civilizations. Among the global civilizations are Islam, Buddhism, and what some who hold this view call "Christendom" or simply "Western civilization."[81] Particular nations such as Germany, France, and the United States, in this conceptualization, stand as subsets of Christendom/Western civilization; similarly, Egypt, Iran, Pakistan, and other nations are subsets of Islamic civilization.

From this vantage point, it is a serious error to suggest that Egypt or Iran should be thrust into a Western frame of reference. In this view of the world they are intrinsically part of Islamic, not Western, civilization, and it is an act of imperialism to think of them in any other way. Even before the idea of a "clash of civilizations" gained popularity, religious activists around the world asserted that their views about religious politics reflected basic differences in worldviews. They were anticipating the controversial thesis that the Harvard political scientist Samuel Huntington propounded in the mid-1990s.[82]

One notable pre-Huntington adherent of the "clash of civilization" thesis was the Ayatollah Khomeini, who lamented what in prerevolutionary Iran he and others referred to as "West-toxification" or "Westomania."[83] According to Khomeini, Islamic peoples have been stricken with Westomania since the eighth century, and partly for that reason they readily accepted the cultural and political postures of the shah. More recent attempts to capitalize on Westomania, he maintained, have come from the insidious efforts of Western imperialists.[84] The goal of the Islamic revolution in Iran, then, was not only to free Iranians politically from the shah but also to liberate them conceptually from Western ways of thinking.

When the leaders of some formerly colonized countries continue to espouse Western ideas—including, especially, the idea of secular nationalism—they are accused by other indigenous leaders of perpetuating colonialism. "We have yet to be truly free," a Buddhist leader in Sri Lanka remarked in reference to the Western-style government in his country.[85] In some Middle Eastern Islamic countries, the injury of the colonial experience was compounded with the insult of having lost their connection with a great Islamic power, the Ottoman Empire. At the end of the First World War, the old empire came under the jurisdiction of Britain and other European powers, which carved the region into secular nation-states. Countries such as Iraq and Jordan were lines drawn in the sand. Hence secular nationalism was for them literally the legacy of colonial rule.

Islamic revolutionaries in Iran have also regarded the secular government under the shah as a form of Western colonialism, even though Iran was never a colony in the same sense that many Middle Eastern and

South Asian countries were. The heavy-handed role of the U.S. Central Intelligence Agency in Iranian politics and the force-feeding of Western ideas by the shah were regarded as forms of colonialism all the same. According to one Iranian leader, Abolhassan Bani-Sadr, the religious character of Western nationalism made it a competitor with Islam. He claimed that Western nationalism suffers from a pretension of universality so grand it has religious proportions, and this claim to universality makes its cultural and economic colonialism possible by allowing a "national entity" from the West to assume that it has "prior rights to the rest of the world."[86]

These leaders regard as especially pernicious the fact that the cultural colonialism of Western ideas erodes confidence in traditional values. For that matter, they maintain, it also undermines traditional religious constructs of society and the state. Concerns over both these matters and over the erosion of religion's influence in public life unite religious activists from Egypt to Sri Lanka, even those who bitterly oppose one another. A leader of the religious right in Israel and a spokesperson for the Islamic movement in Palestine, for instance, used exactly the same words to describe their sentiments: "Secular government is the enemy."[87]

Though secular nationalism has been criticized by proponents of every religious tradition, some commentators have focused on Islam as if it were unique. According to the historian Bernard Lewis, "the very notion of a secular jurisdiction and authority . . . is seen as an impiety, indeed as the ultimate betrayal of Islam."[88] He goes on to say that "the righting of this wrong is the principal aim of Islamic revolutionaries."[89] Ignoring other political, economic, and cultural goals of Islamic activists, Lewis asserts that their main purpose around the world is to rid their societies of what they regard as the corrosive influence of Western secular institutions.

Indeed, some religious revolutionaries—although certainly not all of them—adopt this point of view and deny the possibility that secular institutions can exist in a religious society, but these criticisms of secular politics come from every religious tradition. A supporter of the Christian militia in the United States, for instance, said that the American legal system should be based on the Bible. A leader of the Jewish religious right in Israel asserted that "secular government is illegitimate."[90] A similar sentiment was echoed by one of his rivals, a Muslim leader in Palestine, who declared that "a secular state is anti-Islamic" and that "no such thing exists in Islam."[91] Some would go so far as to denounce the very idea of secular society. When secular ideas are described in articles published by the Palestinian Hamas movement, they are dubbed *al-muniya,* which means "knowledge that does not come from Islam."[92] By implication, it is no knowledge at all.

One of the reasons secular ideas and institutions are so firmly rejected by some religious leaders is that they hold these ideas and institutions accountable for the moral decline within their own countries. The moral impact of Western secularism in Sri Lanka was devastating, according to the calculations of some leaders of Buddhist monastic organizations. One of them, in discussing this matter, carefully identified the evils of the society around him and then laid them fully at the feet of the secular government. "We live in an immoral world," the bhikkhu (monk) stated, giving as his examples of immorality gambling, slaughtering animals for meat, and drinking *arrack* (a locally produced alcohol that is popular in the countryside).[93] In each case the government was implicated: the state lottery promoted gambling, the state encouraged animal husbandry, and it licensed liquor shops. The institutions of government were all suspect, the bhikkhu implied: "People in public office are not to be trusted."[94]

Interestingly, one of the concepts that most disturbed the bhikkhu was an activity that most Westerners regard as a cardinal strength of the secular political system: the ability to respond impartially to the demands of a variety of groups. The political expediency of giving in to the demands of particular interests, such as those of the Tamils, was cited by the bhikkhu as evidence of the government's immorality. He felt that such politicians were incapable of standing up for truth in the face of competing, selfish interests, and their impartiality indicated that they ultimately cared only about themselves. He scoffed at secular politicians who cloaked themselves in Buddhist rhetoric. "They are the enemy of Buddhism," he said.[95]

Secular nationalists within developing countries are thought to be enemies in part because they are in league with a more global enemy, the secular West. To some religious nationalists' way of thinking, there is a global conspiracy against religion, orchestrated by the United States. For this reason virtually anything the United States does that involves non-Western societies, even when its stated intentions are positive, is viewed as part of a plot to destroy or control them. During the 1991 Gulf War, Islamic political groups in Egypt initially condemned Iraq's secular leader, Saddam Hussein, for invading Kuwait. But when the United States sent troops to defend the Kuwaitis, militant Egyptian Muslims began to defend him. They claimed that American military and economic control was the major obstacle to "the liberation of the Third World" and prohibited the establishment of a pan-Islamic consciousness that would unify Arab Muslim people.[96]

At the extreme of this critique of secular power is the notion that the United States is not just power-hungry but evil. The Palestinian Islamic movement Hamas issued a communiqué stating that the United States "commands all the forces hostile to Islam and the Muslims." It singled out George H. W. Bush, who, it claimed, was not only "the leader of the forces of evil" but also "the chief of the false gods."[97] As the communiqué indicates, this line of reasoning often leads down a slippery slope, for once secular institutions and authorities begin to loom larger than life and are seen as forces of evil, the conclusion rushes on, inevitably and irretrievably, that secular enemies are more than mortal foes: they are mythic entities and satanic forces.

An early example of this process of satanization occurred during the Iranian revolution when both the shah and President Jimmy Carter were referred to as *Yazid* (in this context, an agent of Satan). "All the problems of Iran," Khomeini elaborated, are "the work of America."[98] He meant not only political and economic problems but also cultural and intellectual ones, fostered by "the preachers they planted in the religious teaching institutions, the agents they employed in the universities, government educational institutions, and publishing houses, and the Orientalists who work in the service of the imperialist states."[99] The vastness and power of such a conspiratorial network could be explained only by its supernatural force.

The process of satanization indicates that secular nationalism is seen as a religious entity, albeit a sinister one, and this view can be explained, in part, by the "fallen-angel" syndrome: the higher the expectations, the more severe the recriminations when expectations are not met.[100] Many members of formerly colonized countries had maintained such high expectations of secular nationalism, and put such great faith in it, that their disappointment in its failure was also extreme. Where anticipation of secularism's performance had assumed messianic proportions, the anger at the lack of performance reached satanic depths.

Hence the loss of faith in secular nationalism is part of a profound disappointment: the perception that secular institutions have failed to perform. In many parts of the world the secular state has not lived up to its own promises of political freedom, economic prosperity, and social justice. Some of the most poignant cases of disenchantment with secularism have been found among educated members of the middle class who were raised with the high expectations propagated by secular-nationalist political leaders. Some of them were propelled toward religious nationalism after trying to live as secular nationalists and feeling betrayed, or at least unfulfilled. Many of them also felt that Western societies betrayed themselves: the government scandals, persistent social inequities, and devastating economic difficulties of the United States and the former Soviet Union made both democracy and socialism less appealing as political models than they had been during the more innocent 1940s and 1950s. The global mass media, in their exaggerated way, brought to religious leaders in non-Western nations the message that there was a deep malaise in the United States caused by the social failures of unwed mothers, divorce, racism, and drug addiction, the political failures of various political scandals, and the economic failures associated with trade imbalances and the mounting deficit.

But mass media or no, religious leaders in the new nations did not need to look any further than their own national backyards for evidence that the high expectations raised by secular nationalists in their own countries were not being met. "It is an economic, social, and moral failure," a Muslim leader in Egypt said, speaking of the policies of his nation's secular state.[101] Other new religious revolutionaries were disturbed not so much by the failure of the experiment in secular nationalism as by the failure to fully implement religious nationalism, except in Iran and Afghanistan.

Among some followers the hopes for religious politics have been utopian. Christian revolutionaries in Latin America have spoken of instituting the "kingdom of God" promised in the New Testament. The "*dhammic* society" that the bhikkhu in Sri Lanka desired as the alternative to secular nationalism resembled a paradise: "The government would be supported by the people and trusted by them; it would uphold *dhamma* [moral teachings of the Buddha], and it would consult monks regarding proper policies."[102] In a Halakhic society, Jewish leaders in Jerusalem promised, Israel would become more harmonious, all its aspects integrated under religious law. "Man can't live by bread alone," one of the leaders reminded his supporters; "religion is more than just belief and ritual; it is all of life."[103] Another contrasted secular rule with the rule of God: "Secularism lacks God and idealism," he said, pointing out that the state "only has laws, and that's not enough. There is a need to be in touch with the God behind the justice and the truth that secular society espouses."[104] The vision of religious activists has been appealing in part because it promises a future that cannot easily fail: its moral and spiritual goals are transcendent and not as easy to gauge as are the more materialistic promises of secular nationalists.

In many parts of the world, the profound disappointment in secular nationalism has led to disillusionment. Many have lost faith in its relevance and its vision for the future. In their own way, these critics of secular nationalism have experienced what Jürgen Habermas has dubbed a modern "crisis of legitimation," in which the public's respect for political and social institutions has been deflated.[105] Perhaps many religious leaders never really believed in the moral validity of secular nationalism, and over time they were able to convince the masses of people within their societies of its invalidity, not for moral reasons but because great numbers of them no longer saw secular nationalism as an expression of their own identities or related to their social and economic situations. More important, they failed to see how the Western versions of nationalism could provide a vision of what they would like themselves and their communities to become. Secular nationalism came to be seen as alien, the expression of only a small, educated, and privileged few within non-Western societies. As both capitalist and formerly socialist governments wrestled with their own constituencies over the moral purpose of their nations and the directions they might take, their old, tired forms of nationalism seemed less appealing elsewhere.

Yet even though secular nationalism does not easily accommodate religion and religion does not accept the ideology of secular nationalism, religion can sometimes be hospitable to the institution of the nation-state—albeit on religion's terms. Religious activists are well aware that if a nation is based from the start on the premise of secular nationalism, religion is often made marginal to the political order. This outcome is especially unfortunate from many radical religious perspectives—including Jihadi militants, messianic Jewish Zionists, and Christian militias—because they regard the two ideologies as unequal: the religious one is far superior. Rather than starting with secular nationalism, they prefer to begin with religion.

According to one Sinhalese writer, whose tract *The Revolt in the Temple* was published shortly after Sri Lankan independence and was influential in spurring on the Buddhist national cause, "it is clear that the unifying, healing, progressive principle" that held together the entity known as Ceylon throughout the years has always been "the Buddhist faith."[106] The writer goes on to say that religion in Sri Lanka continues to provide the basis for a "liberating nationalism" and that Sinhalese Buddhism is "the only patriotism worthy of the name," worth fighting for or dying for.[107] In India, Hindu nationalists have been equally emphatic that Hindutva, as they call Hindu national culture, is the defining characteristic of Indian nationalism. Similar sentiments are echoed in movements of religious nationalism elsewhere in the world.

The implication of this way of speaking is not that religion is antithetical to nationalism, but that religious rather than secular nationalism is the appropriate premise on which to build a nation—even a modern nation-state. In fact, most references to nationhood used by religious activists assume that the modern nation-state is the only way in which a nation can be construed. (The major exception is the global jihad movement, which envisages a transnational Islamic state.) The term *religious nationalism* refers to the contemporary attempt to link religion and the nation-state. This is a new development in the history of nationalism, and it immediately raises the question of whether such a linkage is possible: whether what we in the West think of as a modern secular nation— a unified, democratically controlled system of economic and political administration—can in fact be accommodated within religion.

It is an interesting question and one to which many Western observers would automatically answer no. Even as acute an interpreter of modern society as Giddens regards most religious cultures as, at best, a syncretism of "tribal cultures, on the one hand, and modern societies, on the other."[108] Yet by Giddens's own definition of a modern nation-state, postrevolutionary Iran would qualify. The Islamic revolution in Iran solidified not just central power but also systemic control, a dominance over the population that in some ways was more conducive to nationhood than the monarchical political order of the shah. The Iranian case will be explored later in this book, but suffice it to say here that at least in this instance a new national entity came into being that was quite different from previous kinds of Muslim rule. It was also different from the secular regime that the shah ineptly attempted to build. The shah dreamed of creating Kemal Ataturk's Turkey in Iran and bringing to his country the instant modernity that he perceived as Ataturk's gift to Turkey. Ironically, it was Khomeini—with his integrative religious ideology and his grass-roots network of mullahs—who brought Iran closer to the goal of a unified nation.

Does religion lose some essential aspects in accommodating modern politics? Some religious leaders think that it does. In favoring the nation-state over a particular religious congregation as its major community of reference, religion loses the exclusivity held by smaller, subnational religious communities, and the leaders of those communities lose some of their autonomy. For that reason, many religious leaders are suspicious of religious nationalism. Among them are the transnational activists associated with the global jihad movement, religious utopians who would rather build their own isolated political societies than deal with the problems of an entire nation, religious liberals who are satisfied with the secular nation-state the way it is, and religious conservatives who would rather ignore politics altogether. Some Muslims accused Khomeini of transforming Islam into a political ideology and reducing it to a modern political force.[109] Moreover, most Islamic rebellions are aimed in the opposite direction: to rid Islam of what many activists regard as the alien idea of the nation-state.[110] Yet, even if that is their aim, one of the curious consequences of their way of thinking is the appropriation of many of the most salient elements of modern nationhood into an Islamic frame of reference. Rather than ridding Islam of the nation-state, they too are creating a new synthesis.

Perhaps the most brazen of the new religious activists are those who move beyond the nation-state to think in transnational terms. The Aum Shinrikyo movement in Japan, for example, imagined a global apocalypse in which their movement's leaders would survive to become the rulers of a unified postwar world. As I have mentioned, the global jihad movement associated with Osama bin Laden, Khalid Sheik Mohammed, and others also has had a transnational agenda. Though the movement targeted what it regarded as corrupt governments—including Saudi Arabia, Egypt, Iraq, the United States, and many European countries—the diverse network of activists associated with the jihadi cause have come from a variety of national backgrounds. Its organizations have defied national boundaries. Moreover, for all of its carefully orchestrated violence against what it regarded as evil powers—including the destruction of the World Trade Center on September 11, 2001, the subsequent attacks on the transportation systems of London and Madrid, and the many bombings in Iraq—no clear plans for alternative governments or politics have emerged. Rather, the rhetoric of bin Laden and his associates, including Ayman al-Zawahiri and Abu Musab al-Zarqawi, have referred only obliquely to a future transnational Islamic polity. They have been clear, however, about what they do not want: a secular nation-state. From this point of view, even religiously defined nation-states are insufficient, and religious regimes such as Afghanistan's Taliban are welcomed only because they are stepping-stones toward some inchoate vision of a broader Islamic political entity. What made the Taliban so useful, from their perspective, was the safe haven that it provided for leaders in the transnational Islamic struggle.

Modern movements of religious activism, therefore, are subjects of controversy within both religious and secular circles. The marriage between those old competing ideologies of order—religion and secular nationalism—has produced the mutant offspring of contemporary religious politics. This is an interesting turn in modern history, and one fraught with dangers, for the radical accommodation of religion to the ideologies of nationalism and transnationalism may not be good either for religion or for political order. The rebellious religious movements that emerged in many parts of the world in the late twentieth and early twenty-first centuries have exhibited both the dangers and the possibilities inherent in religious activists' appropriation of the instruments of political power, including global networks and the enduring notion of the nation-state.

The Front Line of Religious Rebellion: The Middle East

Religious rebellion has been around for a long time. Although the religious rebellions of the last two decades of the twentieth century and the beginning of the twenty-first have been shaped by modern politics, they inherit a long tradition of religious protest and social change. Religious and political ideas have been intertwined throughout history and around the globe, and a number of rebellions against authority, from the Maccabean revolt in ancient Israel to the Taiping Rebellion in China, the Wahhabiya movement in Arabia, and Puritanism in England, have been religious in character. Some of these, like the movements to be discussed here, were rebellions against political authorities. The Puritans—who launched a theocratic revolt against the seventeenth-century English political system—may be regarded as precursors of modern religious radicals.[1]

The new movements are different from their historical predecessors in that they are reactions to the modern nation-state and in some cases are attempts to forge a synthesis with it. Since the nation-state is a specific political form that originated in the modern West, responses to it evoke specific ethnic loyalties and religious commitments. Many of these movements are also identified with particular geographic and linguistic regions. To understand the phenomenon, then, these movements must be considered in the context of the cultures that produced them. In this chapter and those to follow, I have attempted to survey the major movements of religious rebellion around the world that have arisen in the late twentieth century and the first decade of the twenty-first.

These movements are rebellious in that they challenge the legitimacy of the old order and call for changes that have far-reaching consequences. I hesitate to label them revolutionary, since this would imply that they envision a specific alternative political order. The accounts that follow document a great variety of political goals. They may be vaguely democratic, socialist, theocratic, or autocratic; in many instances the leaders simply have not thought that far ahead.

Some social scientists have seen violent political change as eruptions along fault lines in a social system in which pressure has been building for years.[2] This model can be applied to some of the current cases as well. Gary Sick has done so in describing the Iranian revolution as almost a "textbook case" of Crane Brinton's theory that revolutions occur when rising expectations are thwarted.[3]

Iran is indeed one of the few places where a religious rebellion has become a revolution and replaced a secular regime. In other locations where religious rule has been established—such as Afghanistan, Sudan, and Somalia—the revolutionary regimes have been shaky, and the duration of their political control has been brief. Some have been toppled, and others have been transformed. In other cases, such as electoral success of the Hindu nationalist Bharatiya Janata Party in India and the Islamic Hamas movement in the Palestinian legislative elections, a more moderate element of religious politics came to power.

Whether or not they have presented viable political alternatives to established regimes, these movements of religious activism have posed a serious threat to public order. Public security in the latter part of the twentieth century became defined as protection against the possibility of terrorism and political violence, and the source of this unrest was invariably associated with movements of political rebellion associated with religion. And the threat has been real. Five heads of state have been assassinated by religious radicals—Anwar al-Sadat in Egypt, Yitzhak Rabin in Israel, S. W. R. D. Bandaranaike in Sri Lanka, Indira Gandhi in India, and Muhammad Boudiaf in Algeria—and thousands, on both sides of the struggles, have lost their lives.

The goals of these movements are both national and transnational. Like the ideological rhetoric of the old Cold War, the political ambitions of many of the movements are directed toward both local needs and a supranational ideal, particularly so among the movements in the Middle East covered in this chapter. The longing for a global state of religious harmony is an old Islamic dream, and for years the great Islamic empires appeared to be on the verge of making that dream a reality. For that reason, many Muslim activists I interviewed hesitated to speak solely of national interests and instead expressed pan-Islamic ideals.

When I visited Sheik Ahmed Yassin, the founder and spiritual leader of the Palestinian Hamas movement, I found that one of the pictures on the walls of his home portrayed the global reach of Islam. Superimposed on a map of the world was the Qur'an drawn as if it had hands extending from Morocco to Indonesia.[4] Some Muslim writers harken back to the ideas of mid-twentieth-century Muslim political thinkers such as Maulana Maududi, Hassan al-Banna, and Sayyid Qutb in considering the very idea of nationalism anti-Islamic. Kalim Siddiqui described nationalism as "the greatest evil that stalks the modern world," and although he acknowledged that many Muslim movements are indeed nationalist, he saw their nationalism as a short-term goal and looked forward to Islamic unity "beyond the Muslim nation-states."[5] The ideologies of Osama bin Laden and some of the strident Sunni jihadi activists in Iraq are unapologetically transnational in their goals.

Even though the yearning for a single Islamic nation runs deep in Muslim consciousness, most Muslim activists have been content to settle for an Islamic nationalism limited to the particular countries in which they reside. In the modern period, as Ira Lapidus explains, "the capacity of Islam to symbolize social identity has been merged into national feeling."[6] The most obvious example is Iran, where the Shi'ite form of Islam (elsewhere largely a minority) that predominates provides a convenient cultural base for Iranian nationalism. But even in Sunni areas, such as Egypt and Palestine—as the case studies in this chapter show—religious sentiments are fused with national concerns. The religious rebels there fight for an Egyptian or a Palestinian identity as well as for a Muslim one. Even the proponents of a worldwide Islamic nation concede the necessity for "a succession of Islamic Revolutions in all Muslim areas of the world."[7] They expect that these will eventually be united through " 'open' or 'soft' frontiers" to replace the boundaries between Islamic states.[8] My guess, however, is that the borders will stay immutable and solid, for the pan-Islamic sentiments of Arabs and other Muslims have always been vexed by intra-Islamic rivalries, and the enduring idea of the nation-state.[9]

EGYPT'S ORIGINS OF MUSLIM REBELLION

In 1981, Egypt's president, Anwar al-Sadat, was assassinated by members of an extremist movement, al-Jihad. A *fatweh* authorizing the assassination had been proclaimed by Sheik Omar Abdul-Rahman, a former professor of Islamic law. Though Abdul-Rahman was not convicted, he left Egypt soon after the trial, eventually ending up in Afghanistan and then in the United States, where he became the leader of the storefront mosque in New Jersey with which many of the accused conspirators in the 1993 World Trade Center bombing were affiliated. His vision eventually widened to global jihad. The same is true of one of his colleagues at the time, Ayman al-Zawahiri, who was a leader of the Egyptian al-Jihad movement and who eventually became Osama bin Laden's associate and personal physician in Afghanistan. But in the early 1980s, Abdul-Rahman and his followers in the al-Gamaa al-Islamiya ("the Muslim group") and al-Zawahiri and his al-Jihad movement were committed to a vision of Islamic rule in Egypt that would rival Khomeini's Iran. In 1990, the speaker of the Egyptian Assembly, Rifaat al-Mahgoub, second in power to President Hosni Mubarak, was brutally assassinated. Members of the al-Gamaa al-Islamiya were charged with the crime but were acquitted in 1993 for lack of evidence. At the time, Mahgoub's death was attributed to Egypt's support of the United States in the Gulf War, but another factor may have been his efforts to block the use of Islamic law in Egypt's courts.[10] In Egypt, as in many other Arab countries, trifling with Islam is serious business.

The al-Jihad movement was at the extreme edge of Egypt's Muslim Brotherhood, which was founded in 1928 by Hassan al-Banna. Another radical Muslim movement, the Young Egypt Society (which advocated a kind of Islamic socialism), was founded soon after, in 1933.[11] The leaders of these early Islamic political movements were reacting against the transnational modernism that was the legacy of the British Empire (and before it, the Ottoman Empire). Western culture, political influence, and economic control were the elements of a modernity that some of the early nationalists sought to reject. For that reason, Egyptian nationalism grew in both religious and secular directions from the outset. The Muslim Brotherhood represented the Islamic form of Egyptian nationalism, and the Wafd Party represented its secular side. When King Farouk and the tradition of Egyptian monarchy were overthrown in 1952, it was largely the Wafd vision of a secular Egypt that emerged triumphant.

Yet even after Farouk, Islamic nationalism continued to be a potent force in Egyptian politics. The leader of the revolution, Gamal Abdel Nasser, had at one time been allied with the Muslim Brotherhood, as had his successor, Anwar al-Sadat. Despite their willingness to defend the Islamic aspects of Egyptian nationalism, neither Nasser nor Sadat was sufficiently strident in his ideology nor sufficiently accommodating in his response to the Muslim leadership to remain in the good graces of Islamic activists. By the 1960s, the leaders of the Muslim Brotherhood and Nasser were locked in bitter opposition; when leaders of the Brotherhood attempted to overthrow his government, Nasser promptly threw them in prison.

Egypt's love-hate relationship between Muslim leaders and secular politicians continued in the 1970s during Sadat's presidency. On the one hand, Sadat released the leaders of the Muslim Brotherhood from prison, lifted a ban on the writings of Muslim radicals, and was instrumental in the drafting of the 1971 version of the Egyptian Constitution, which proclaimed, in Article 2, that the goal of the judicial system was to make *shari'a* (Islamic law) the law of the land. On the other hand, Sadat did little to carry out this goal or the other Islamic reforms he had earlier touted. His concessions to Coptic Christians were widely denounced by Muslim activists, and his wife was portrayed as promiscuous. (Pictures of her dancing with U.S. president Gerald Ford at a formal occasion at the White House were circulated as evidence of her infidelity.) The accords with Israel arranged by President Carter were considered further signs of Sadat's moral decay, and he eventually succeeded in "having everyone turn against him," as one Egyptian scholar explained, in part because "he tried too hard to please everyone."[12]

The movement with which Sadat's assassins were associated made a deep political impact, largely because its ideology is more radical than that of Egypt's moderate Muslim leadership. One of the most strident positions was taken by Abd Al-Salam Faraj, who was the author of a remarkably cogent argument for waging war against the political enemies of Islam. His pamphlet, *Al-Faridah al-Gha'ibah* ("The Neglected Duty"), states more clearly than any other contemporary writing the religious justifications for violence. It was published and first circulated in Cairo in the early 1980s.[13] This document grounds the activities of Islamic terrorists firmly in Islamic tradition, specifically in the sacred text of the Qur'an and the acts and sayings of the Prophet Muhammad recorded in the *hadith*.

Faraj argues that the Qur'an and the *hadith* are fundamentally about warfare. Their concept of jihad—holy war—is meant to be taken literally, not allegorically. According to Faraj, the "duty" that has been profoundly "neglected" is jihad, and jihad calls for "fighting, which means confrontation and blood."[14] Moreover, Faraj regards those who deviate from the moral and social requirements of Islamic law—apostates within the Muslim community as well as the more expected enemies from without—as fit targets for jihad.[15]

Perhaps the most chilling aspect of Faraj's political philosophy is his conclusion that peaceful and legal means for fighting apostasy are inadequate. The true soldier for Islam is authorized to use virtually any means available to achieve a just goal.[16] Deceit, trickery, and violence are specifically mentioned as available options.[17] Faraj sets some moral limits on the tactics that may be used—innocent bystanders and women are to be avoided, whenever possible, in assassination attempts—but he emphasizes that the duty to engage in such actions when necessary is incumbent on all true Muslims. The reward for doing so is nothing less than an honored place in paradise. Such a place was presumably earned by Faraj himself in 1982 after he was tried and executed for his part in Sadat's assassination.

This way of thinking, although extreme, is not unique to Faraj. He is part of a tradition of radical Islamic political writers that reaches back to the beginning of the twentieth century and earlier. Among Sunni Muslims worldwide, the most important radical thinker has been Maulana Abu al-Alaa al-Maududi, the founder of and ideological spokesman for Pakistan's Jamaat-i-Islami (Islamic Association), who was born in 1903 and rose to prominence in the 1940s.[18] His ideas were echoed by his contemporary and Egypt's most influential writer in the radical Muslim political tradition, Sayyid Qutb. Qutb, born in 1906 and, like Faraj, executed for his political activities, did not define the techniques of terror that were acceptable for the Islamic warrior as explicitly as did Faraj.[19] Rather, he laid the groundwork for Faraj's understanding of jihad as an appropriate response to those who advocated a modernity hostile to Islam.

Qutb specifically faulted those who encouraged the cultural, political, and economic domination of the Egyptian government by the West. He had spent several years in the United States studying educational administration, but Qutb's experience only confirmed his impression that American society was essentially racist and that American policy in the Middle East was dictated by Israel and what he regarded as the Jewish lobby in Washington.[20] Alarmed at the degree to which the new government in Egypt was modeled after Western political institutions and informed by Western values, Qutb, in the early 1950s, advocated a radical return to Islamic principles and Muslim law. In *This Religion of Islam*, he maintained that humanity is fundamentally defined by religion rather than by race or nationality and that religious war is the only morally acceptable form of killing.[21] For Qutb, the ultimate war is between truth and falsehood, and satanic agents of falsehood, he argued, were entrenched in the Egyptian government. Needless to say, Egypt's government officials found such ideas dangerous. Qutb was put in prison for most of the rest of the 1950s and was executed for treason in 1966.

Maududi, Qutb, and Faraj's radicalism has circulated widely in Egypt through two significant networks: universities and the Muslim clergy. The two networks intersect in the Muslim educational system, especially in schools and colleges directly supervised by the clergy. Among these, the most important is Cairo's Al-Azhar University. The Muslim schools enroll only a small percentage of Egyptian students—5 percent or so—at all levels of the educational system.[22] It is a significant number, nonetheless, because of the impact of education in relating the traditional truths of Islam to modern ideas. As the dean of the faculty of education at Al-Azhar University explained to me, the school's mission is to show how modern academic subjects and fields of professional training—including business, medicine, law, and education—can be taught from an Islamic perspective.[23] Though most subjects are similar to those in secular universities, they often have an Islamic twist. Al-Azhar is often viewed as a fountainhead of radical Islamic ideas, and a great number of militant Muslim activists were educated there.

Despite its aspirations, the radical Muslim movement has yet to be sufficiently united to threaten President Hosni Mubarak with revolution. Even though it showed its destructive power in the 1990 assassination of the speaker of the People's Assembly, the movement remains small and splintered. The main organization within the movement, the Muslim Brotherhood, has progressively moderated its politics. Though not accepted as a legal party, it is well represented in the legislature. Members of the Brotherhood, running as independent candidates in the 1987 elections, won 38 seats out of the 448 in the People's Assembly. In the 2005 elections they again ran as independents, garnering 88 seats, some 20 percent of the total, which made them the largest opposition bloc in the Egyptian Assembly. The Brotherhood's political platform was clearly articulated by its leader, Abu al-Nasr, in an open letter to President Mubarak. According to Nasr, the movement had four main positions: pride in its Egyptian identity and tradition, the conviction that Egypt's problems are largely spiritual and moral in nature, the expectation that Islamic values will be made the basis for all aspects of Egyptian society, and the desire for Islamic organizations to have the freedom to operate as they wish.[24]

These relatively reasonable positions have made the Muslim Brotherhood look quite respectable—especially compared with the strident
rhetoric of the extremists. In 1991, during the Gulf War, divisions between moderate and radical factions in the Islamic movement widened.[25]
In the mid-1990s the terrorist acts of al-Gamaa al-Islamiya further alienated it from the Muslim mainstream. In addition to the World Trade
Center bombing in New York, tourists were attacked near Luxor and in
a café in Cairo, a luxury ship was fired on as it cruised down the Nile,
and a bomb was placed in one of the Pyramids. A succession of attacks
that began in 2004 on tourist sites in Egyptian resorts along the Red Sea
was said to be motivated by radical Islamic opposition to what was regarded as the loose morals of visiting tourists, including Israelis. Three
bombs ignited almost simultaneously on a single day in Sharm el-Sheik
in 2005, killing eighty-eight people. In contrast to these acts of terrorism, the Muslim Brotherhood presented a more viable, if gradual, Islamic revolution. What worries its secular opponents is the possibility
that shifts of ideology and power in a gradual revolution could be as un-
settling as the more extreme measures—and far more enduring in their
impact.

IRAN'S PARADIGMATIC REVOLUTION

Muslim activists in Iran have achieved what for many of their colleagues
in other parts of the world is still an elusive goal: a successful revolution
and the establishment of a religious state. Even so, Shi'a Muslim politics
are different from Sunni politics, and Egyptian activists have been influenced far more by Arab and Pakistani ideas than by Iranian ones.[26] Despite their common goals there is little connection between radical religious leaders in Sunni and Shi'a areas. "They have their political
problems," a member of the Muslim Brotherhood in Cairo told me, "and
we have ours."[27] There is, however, sometimes a tremor of admiration
in their voices when they speak of the power of the Iranian revolution.[28]
And the example of Iran shows that an Islamic revolution is not just
empty rhetoric but a realistic possibility.[29]

Some of the early movements of Muslim activism in Iran were influenced by Egyptian ideas—the thinking of al-Banna and Qutb, for
example—and by Egypt's radical religious organizations. In the late
1940s and early 1950s, the Fedayeen-i-Islam was created in Iran in imi-
tation of the guerrilla Muslim Brotherhood (Jam'iyat al-Ikhwan al-
Muslimin), which at the time was spreading terror throughout Egypt. By

the time the Iranian Islamic movement gathered steam in the 1970s, however, the motives and the organization were distinctly Iranian.

"An entire population has risen up against the Shah," the Ayatollah Khomeini announced to a professor from the University of California who visited him in France during the declining days of the Pahlavi regime.[30] This "revolutionary movement," as Khomeini described it, was an "explosion" that occurred as a direct result of American intervention and the repression of Islam over the preceding fifty years. At the time of the interview, 1978, Khomeini remarked that the situation had "intensified to an extraordinary degree."[31] A few days later, he was bound for Iran and his headquarters in Qom, where he presided over the new regime until his death on June 4, 1989.

Although the revolution was marked by the unique personality of the ayatollah, the particular circumstances of Iranian politics, and the distinctive character of Shi'ite Islam, this regime and the remarkable transfer of power that inaugurated it can be seen as the paradigm of religious revolution. The demon of the revolution was the secular nationalism patterned on the West that was ineptly promoted by the shah. The critique of the shah's Westernized regime was couched in religious terms, the rebellion was led by religious figures, and the new order was fashioned as a utopian religious state. It was not simply a revival of an earlier form of Muslim rule, but a new form of Islamic politics. In a curious way, it provided a unified political system for the country and made the shah's vision of an Iranian nationalism come true.

The new politics of the Iranian revolution were fundamentally Muslim—and particularly Shi'ite. Politics of various kinds have always been part and parcel of Islam. The Prophet Muhammad himself was a military as well as a spiritual leader, and there have been strong Muslim rulers virtually from the tradition's inception. In classical Islam, as in most traditional religious societies, there was no distinction between church and state, and the concept of secularism was alien to Islam—as it was to most religious traditions—until quite recently.[32] All aspects of social and personal behavior were subject to divine guidance, and all political authority ultimately derived from sacred authority. This continues to be a general principle in Islamic societies. What is novel about the new Islamic movements is their struggle to infuse—in a distinctively modern way—this religious authority into the institution of the nation-state.

Perhaps nowhere in Islam is struggle more a part of its tradition than in Shi'ite societies. The world of Islam is largely Sunni, and only a small minority—probably less than 20 percent—is Shi'a. They are concentrated in the Arabian Peninsula, southern Lebanon, Iraq, Pakistan, India, Azerbaijan, and especially in Iran, where 90 percent are Shi'a of a particular form. This dominant, Ithna Ashari (Twelver) brand of Shi'ism is based on the belief that there will be twelve great leaders, or imams, in world history. Shi'ite Islam began with a political struggle, and over time the tradition developed its own separate theological emphases. In his interpretation of the tradition, Khomeini capitalized on traditional Shi'ite themes, sharpening them to fit the situation of revolutionary Iran. The most important of these themes are the Shi'a tradition of struggle against oppression, the vesting of political power in the clergy, and a pattern of messianic and utopian expectations.

The Shi'a Tradition of Struggle.   Shi'ism was born in conflict, in the struggle for power immediately after the death of the Prophet Muhammad. The term *shi'a* means "partisans," followers of a particular religious and political position. The dispute was between those who felt that the spiritual and temporal authority of Islam resided in the caliphs who came after him and those who believed that it dwelled in the members of the Prophet's own family—specifically in the descendants of Ali—the Prophet's cousin and son-in-law. The critical moment in this conflict came in 680 C.E., with the assassination of Ali's son, Hussain, who led the Shi'ite community in Karbala (in present-day Iraq). The assassin, Yazid, was a caliph of the Sunni's Umayyad dynasty. To this day, that event is recognized as the tragic turning point in Shi'ite history—rather as the Crucifixion is regarded in Christian history.

The assassination of Hussain is commemorated annually in massive parades throughout Shi'ite communities. Men stripped to the waist march down city streets, flagellating themselves with whips and barbed wire until their backs become raw and bloody. On these occasions—the Ashura celebrations held every year during the first ten days of the Islamic month of Muharram—the faithful remember the suffering of Hussain and grieve for his death and their own vicarious guilt for not having stood by him in his time of trial.

In Iran, from the early 1960s on, the Ashura took a political turn. The Ayatollah Khomeini and his colleagues began to alter the emphasis from personal mourning to collective outrage against oppression. They had in mind especially the shah's oppression of Islam, and they likened him to Yazid, Hussain's assassin. In his messages the ayatollah urged his followers to avenge the martyrdom of Hussain by attacking the Yazids of the present age. "With the approach of Muharram," he told his flock, "we are about to begin the month of epic heroism and self-sacrifice—the month in which blood triumphed over the sword, . . . the month in which the leader of the Muslims taught us how to struggle against all the tyrants of history."[33] In case the listener had missed the point, Khomeini would soon mention the shah by name—the particular tyrant he had in mind.

The Political Power of the Clergy.   Islam is primarily a layperson's religion, and although political leaders are expected to adhere to its precepts and to use the state's apparatus to administer Muslim law, the clergy in most parts of the Muslim world has little political influence. In such predominantly Sunni societies as Egypt and Syria, for instance, the clergy has been relatively uninvolved in radical Islamic politics.[34] The Shi'a tradition is different, in part for theological reasons. The idea of an imam, a great leader who shapes world history, has conditioned Shi'ites to expect strong leadership in what we would regard as both secular and religious spheres. During a period of history when an imam is not physically present—such as the contemporary period, when the imam is supposedly "hidden"—his power resides in the mullahs, the Shi'a clergy. Another source for the power of certain religious leaders is their ancestral ties to the family of Ali and hence to the Prophet himself. The Ayatollah Khomeini could claim such ties, and even the modern Iraqi leader, Saddam Hussein, let it be known that he had such connections. The shah's family, however, lacked such spiritual links, and from the point of view of the Shi'a clergy, that made them unfit for leadership. The shah's family name—Pahlavi—identified them with ancient Persians. But, as it turned out, religion was a more powerful source of identity in Iran than ethnicity.

Rebellions of one sort or another have been led by Shi'a clergy in Iran for at least a century. In 1892 a revolt against the use of tobacco was fomented by mullahs, and their influence on the Constitutional Revolution of 1905–9 ensured that laws would not be passed that the mullahs deemed injurious to Islam. During the 1950s, after the campaign of the shah to blunt the mullahs' influence, some of them conspired against secular Iranian leaders, several of whom were assassinated. The groups they organized were modeled on Egypt's Muslim Brotherhood, including the Fedayeen-i-Islam (Supporters of Islam) and the Mujahadin-i-Islam (Fighters for Islam), led by Mullah Nawab Safavi and the Ayatollah Abul Qasim Kashani, respectively. By 1963, the radical opposition to the shah had crystallized around the leadership of the Ayatollah Khomeini, and the Iranian revolution began in earnest.

Messianic and Utopian Expectations. In the Shi'a view of history, the hidden imam will return again at the end of history in the form of the Mahdi, the Messiah who will overthrow the evil forces and institute a realm of justice and freedom. It would have been heresy to suggest that the Ayatollah Khomeini was the Mahdi and that the Iranian revolution was that realm, and no Shi'ite dared do so. (Most of Khomeini's followers in Iran called him *imam* (rather than *ayatollah*, the label by which he is best known in the West), but the title is often applied to Shi'ite religious leaders with no implication that they are in the pantheon of the twelve great imams.)[35] Even so, some of Khomeini's followers claimed that he was actually a "mystical emanation issuing directly from the Mahdi," serving as a harbinger of the Mahdi's return.[36] While the belief was not widespread, the very notion of a Mahdi created hospitable cultural conditions for salvific leadership.

These three aspects of Shi'ite Islam—its history of struggle against oppression, the political power it has traditionally vested in the clergy, and its tradition of messianic and utopian expectations—made Islam in Iran ripe for revolutionary political exploitation. That the revolution happened so easily was due in part to the vulnerability of its adversaries. Few characters in the Shi'ite drama of the forces of good struggling against the forces of evil have been so effectively thrust into the role of evil as the members of the Pahlavi dynasty—Riza Shah, who established a military dictatorship in 1921, and his son Muhammad Riza Shah, who succeeded him in 1941. The Pahlavi reign was interrupted from 1951 to 1953 by a democratically elected prime minister, Mohammed Mossadegh (Musaddiq), who attempted to nationalize the oil industry and, with the help of the U.S. Central Intelligence Agency, was promptly overthrown.

When the shah returned, he attempted to mollify the mullahs by giving them free rein in developing their organizations and helping them to finance Islamic schools. To some extent this policy was successful, and even Khomeini's predecessor, Ayatollah Hosain Burujirdi, supported the shah in the 1950s; at this time the clergy was accused of being a "pillar of the Pahlavi state."[37] This accommodation of the mullahs changed in the 1960s, however, when the shah sought to institute land reforms that threatened religious institutions and extended the right to vote to women—acts that many of the mullahs regarded as threatening. Impressed by Kemal Ataturk's experiment at secularization in Turkey, the shah introduced similar sweeping reforms, replacing most of Islamic law with secular rules adapted from the French Napoleonic code. Although they tried publicly to appear to be good Muslims, the Pahlavis were faulted for destroying traditional Muslim schools and seminaries, Westernizing the universities, and creating a modern secular bureaucracy to administer the state. Women were forbidden to wear the veil (although the shah later relaxed that rule). In Teheran and other cities Western culture began to thrive, bringing in its wake not only Coca-Cola and Western movies but also discos, girlie magazines, and gay bars. It was not the Islamic utopia the mullahs had in mind. The mullahs described it, in fact, as "a satanic rule."[38]

The government's control of the media and the presence of the sinister SAVAK, the secret police, made opposition difficult. According to one observer, it was "impossible to breathe freely in Iran."[39] The group that was most difficult to contain and had the largest capacity to organize was the clergy, which found a natural leader in Ruhullah al-Musavi al-Khomeini, who began his career as the protégé of one of Iran's leading theologians, Sheik 'Abd al-Karim Ha'iri of the pilgrimage city of Qom. Following the death of Ha'iri in 1937, the leadership fell to the Ayatollah Burujirdi; when he died in 1961, there was no immediate consensus over who the new leader at Qom should be. It is probably not a coincidence that Khomeini's increasingly outspoken public pronouncements against the shah at that time were concomitant with his rising popularity and the solidification of his power within the Shi'ite community. In any event, the protest, and Khomeini's leadership of it, surfaced in a massive demonstration in Qom in the spring of 1963. The demonstration led to Khomeini's imprisonment, followed by his release in 1964, and reimprisonment again in that year, and then his expulsion from the country. Khomeini continued to live in exile—first in Turkey, then in Iraq, and finally in France—until after the revolution was completed in 1979. Although he was out of the country during those critical years, he was certainly not silent, and perhaps he was able more effectively to articulate the grievances and lead the revolution from the French village of Neauphle-le-Chateau than from Qom.

To the surprise of everyone, the end came quite suddenly. Perhaps most caught off guard were the Americans, who had great difficulty even conceiving the possibility that a band of bearded, black-robed rural mullahs might pose a serious threat to the poised and urbane shah, with all his worldly connections and military power.[40] Even more inconceivable was that the power of the shah should crumble so effortlessly. Only a few months before, U.S. president Jimmy Carter had praised the shah for creating an "island of stability" in the region.

Although the new revolutionary regime did not live up to its utopian promises, it introduced radical changes in Iran's government and culture. After the revolution, Islamic law became the law of the land, and most marks of "Westoxification" were systematically erased. These reforms have not always been introduced with subtlety—some seven thousand people were executed for purported "crimes" as varied as homosexuality and believing in the Baha'i faith—and the revolutionary spirit has not been easily contained. For a time bands of young people in the Hizbollah (Party of God) roamed the streets, attacking anyone or anything that appeared anti-Islamic, and a group of rowdy youths, without government authorization (at least at the beginning), precipitated a foreign-policy crisis by taking hostages at the American Embassy in Teheran.[41]

Following the revolution and the establishment of an Islamic Republic of Iran in 1979, the regime has gone through several stages. It began as a moderate, secular rule led first by Mehdi Bazargan and then by Abolhassan Bani-Sadr, until Khomeini used the hostage crisis as a means of forcing out the moderates.[42] After Bani-Sadr fled the country in 1981, a period of repression set in, during which thousands were killed, moderate and leftist political forces were destroyed, and the power of the clergy was consolidated.[43] In 1985, the revolutionary regime began something of a Thermidorean return, for a time, to a more pragmatic and moderate rule. From 1980 to 1988, the resources of the country were drained by a war with Iraq. The Iraqi military forces of Saddam Hussein were supported by the United States, which at the time considered Iran the greater evil.

After the death of the Ayatollah Khomeini on June 4, 1989, his son, Ahmad Khomeini, remained virtually the only radical member of the clergy in the government's inner circles; the new president of Iran, Ali-Akbar Heshemi-Rafsanjani, continued to steer a pragmatic course. During the Gulf War, Rafsanjani refused to side with Iraq and his criticism of the United States was relatively restrained, to the disappointment of the conservative clergy.[44] At the end of 1991, Iranian leaders negotiated the release of American hostages held for years in Lebanon. In the first months of 1992, apparently to impress upon the conservative clergy that he had not capitulated to the Americans, Rafsanjani denounced the American-sponsored Arab-Israeli peace talks and described the United States as "an arrogant power."[45] Although the April 1992 election was a triumph for the moderates, its reforms were largely economic. The nation's radical political posture persisted, and in 1993 Iran greatly increased its financial aid to Islamic political movements in Algeria, Bosnia, Lebanon, Pakistan, Tajikistan, and elsewhere.[46]

The elections of 1997 swept a reform politician, Seyyed Mohammad Khatami, into power. Khatami was supported by intellectuals and urban youth, and his presidency was accompanied by expectations of social reform that would mitigate the harsher aspects of Islamic rule. Internationally, Khatami called for a "dialogue of civilizations" to replace the clash of civilizations, a sentiment that was supported by the United Nations General Assembly, which designated the year 2001 as the year of the Dialogue of Civilizations. In skirmishes with the Guardian Council appointed by the Supreme Leader, Ali Khamenei, Khatami was regularly defeated and his authority undermined. By the 2005 elections, even his own followers had become disillusioned.

This struggle between reformists and the hard-line Muslim clergy was a central issue in the 2005 Iranian presidential elections. Though the moderate former president, Ali-Akbar Hashemi-Rafsanjani, was favored, an upset victory resulted in the ascension to power of Tehran's former mayor, Mahmoud Ahmadinejad, who was supported by Khamenei and was popular among disaffected villagers and the urban poor. He also benefited from his anti-Americanism, a position that was popular in part because of the inclusion of Iran in the "axis of evil" by U.S. president George W. Bush in his State of Union address in 2002. After the election, Ahmadinejad, who is said to be an adherent of an unusually conservative and apocalyptic Shi'a sect, the Hojjatieh, consolidated his political control, indirectly challenged Khamenei's authority, and presented himself as the spokesman for the conservative political wing of the Muslim world. He took a hard line against Israel, wrote an open letter to U.S. president George W. Bush criticizing America's foreign policy, and antagonized the United States and much of the world through his defense of Iran's nuclear program. Domestically, he stepped up the enforcement of Islamic customs and purged the universities in an attempt to Islamicize the curriculum. He also attempted to rid the country's language of Western words, favoring the Farsi word for "flexible loaves," for instance, rather than "pizza." Though he did not institute the economic reforms that many of his supporters expected, he did provide food and social services to the poor.

During the 2006 Israeli incursion into Lebanon, Ahmedinejad supported the Hizbollah leader Sheik Hassan Nasrallah, whom the U.S. government had dubbed an Iranian puppet. There is some evidence to support the contention that for many years prior to the 2006 clashes between Israel and Lebanon's Hizbollah, Iran had been building up the Lebanese militant Shi'ite movement and arming its militia. Iran also supported the regime of Hafez al-Assad and his son Bashar in Syria, members of the small but powerful Shi'a religious movement known as Alawites.

On the eastern side of the country, Iran has long supported the Shi'a Hazara tribal group in Afghanistan; and it has had ties to Tajiks, the Persian ethnic communities in Afghanistan and Central Asia that are largely Sunni. Iran supported the Tajik Afghan leader Ahmed Shah Massoud and his Northern Alliance militia in their resistance to the Pashtun's Taliban movement. After Massoud was killed by operatives close to Osama bin Laden shortly before the September 11, 2001, attacks on the World Trade Center and the Pentagon, Iran favored the destruction of the Taliban. Iran also has had ties to other Tajik communities in Tajikistan, Uzbekistan, Pakistan, and the Xinjiang province of China. Many of these have been involved in militant religious movements of their own.

Perhaps the most enduring legacy of the Islamic revolution in Iran are the constitutional privileges granted to religion in Iran's public life and the creation of an Iranian nationalism that the shah tried but failed to achieve.[47] Iranian nationalist goals have become fused with Shi'ite political ideology, the Muslim clergy has substantial political authority, and religion plays a leading role in the country's administration. The extent of the religious leadership's political authority is particularly interesting, for the architects of the revolution have taken the concept of the just ruler (al-sultan al-'adil) in Shi'ite Islam and transformed it into a political position—an elder statesman who guides and advises the president and other governmental officials.[48] During Khomeini's lifetime, he himself played that role, and after his death he was succeeded by the Ayatollah Ali Khamenei. The extent of the Supreme Leader's authority is ambiguous, for, as Khomeini explained, "the religious leaders do not wish to be the government, but neither are they separate from the government."[49] Separate or not, Khomeini warned that the clergy would be prepared to "intervene" if the secular leaders of the government make "a false step."[50] Religious revolutionaries in other parts of the world would give almost anything to acquire this remarkable political leverage.

ISRAEL'S MILITANT ZIONISM

Though Israel's religious rebels are Jewish rather than Muslim, their situation is not unlike that of many Muslim activists. But they are more like the Muslim rebels in Egypt than Iran. Rather than confronting entirely secular rulers like the shah, they oppose moderate leaders who are more than nominally committed to their nation's dominant religion—in this case, Judaism. While extreme Jewish activists view the state of Israel as a largely secular entity, for many (including its Arab opponents), Israel is an example of religious nationalism achieved. Muslim nationalism in the Middle East has been fueled in part by a kind of religious competition, since many Muslim political observers feel that they deserve what the Jews have—their own state. Some Egyptian activists claim that the Jewish nation's religious zeal—in contrast to the secular indifference of their own country—contributed to Israel's victory in the 1967 war.[51]

However, within Israel itself a large contingent of politically active Jews regard their homeland as the expression of an incomplete form of religious nationalism, at best. Although Israel is hospitable to Jewish refugees, it is essentially a secular state, informed by the rules and mores of European and American society, and that leaves many Jewish religious nationalists deeply dissatisfied.

One of the most vocal of these Jewish nationalists was Rabbi Meir Kahane, the spokesman for the radical Kach ("Thus!") Party. Not surprisingly, perhaps, he had a certain admiration for the Ayatollah Khomeini.[52] He told me that he felt closer to Khomeini and other militant Muslims than he did to such framers of secular political thought as John Locke or even to secular Jews.[53] The reason, he explained, was that Khomeini believed in the relevance of religion to everyday life and especially in the importance of religion in shaping a nation's morality and communal identity. From Kahane's point of view, that belief was far more important than any politically expedient secular arrangement even if it privileged one religious group over another.

Kahane's views on Jewish nationalism are not entirely unprecedented. Tensions between the religious and secular dimensions of the state have been a persistent theme in the recent struggle for Israeli nationhood. When the first meeting of the World Zionist Organization (WZO) was held in 1897, the organization's goal was defined as the formation of a modern national community based on the common cultural and historical heritage of the Jewish people—not to re-create the biblical Israel. The founder of the WZO, Theodor Herzl, had dreamed of Jewish assimilation into European society and hoped to achieve that dream by providing the Jews with "a new, modern symbol system—a state, a social order of their own." And Herzl added, it needed "above all a flag."[54]

Herzl designed such a flag. It was intended to celebrate the laboring-class character of the new Israeli society and featured symbols for the

seven hours he thought were sufficient for a working day. For other
Jews, however, a flag—especially the secular flag that Herzl designed—
was not enough. They formed another nationalist group, the Merkaz
Ruhani, or Mizrahi, which called for the formation of a religious state,
one that would follow the precepts of the Torah. At the same time, another group of orthodox Jews, Agudat Israel, adopted a somewhat different attitude: its members were in favor of Jews settling in Palestine but
were largely indifferent to whether the nation should be a Jewish state.
From the Agudat Israel's point of view, until the Temple was rebuilt and
a new David installed as king, there could be no true Israel.

These and other groups continued their assaults on secular Israel after
the establishment of an independent state in 1948, even though significant compromises had been made to accommodate their positions. Jewish religious courts created during the British Mandate from 1943 to
1947 became integrated into the new legal system, and a "status quo
agreement" between the religious parties and the prestate administration, the Jewish Agency, called for religious concessions that included the
government's observance of dietary laws and maintenance of religious
schools.

Yet many nationalist Jews in Israel regarded these concessions as insufficient. The most influential advocate of further religious reforms, the
Mafdal Party, was a direct descendant of the old Mizrahi Party and its
various offshoots. The Mafdal has consistently held a dozen or so seats
in the Knesset and has been a coalition partner in virtually every government formed since Israel's independence. The Agudat Israel Party, despite its ambivalence toward a Jewish state, maintained representation
in the Knesset as well. The ties of these two parties to the Likud Party
during its long rule led to the enactment of strong laws against public ob-
scenity, working on the sabbath, and the sale of pork.

More recently, a movement has formed in Israel based on the idea that
the present secular Jewish state is the precursor of an ideal religious Israel.[55] It is the revival of an old idea, one advocated by Rabbi Avraham
Yitzhak ha-Kohen Kuk, the chief rabbi of pre-Israeli Palestine. According
to Kuk (and his son and successor, Z. Y. Kuk), the secular state of Israel
prepares the way for a nation based explicitly on faith; it contains a "hidden spark" of the sacred.[56] The implications of this position are that the
coming of the Messiah is likely to happen soon, and the religious purification of the state of Israel could help make that arrival occur more quickly.

Kuk's ideas ignited the religious imaginations of many Israelis after
the Six-Day War in 1967. The war had two results that affected the

growth of Jewish nationalist movements. The success of the military engagement led to widespread national euphoria, a feeling that Israel was
suddenly moving in an expansive and triumphant direction. At the same
time, Israel's military success raised the questions of what to do with the
conquered territory and the Palestinian Arab residents of the West Bank
and the Gaza Strip.

Jewish nationalists who were impressed with the theology of Rabbi
Kuk felt strongly that history was leading to the moment of divine redemption and the re-creation of the biblical state of Israel. This meant
that the Palestinians living in the West Bank were in the way: at best
they were an annoyance to be controlled, at worst an enemy to be destroyed. The *intifada,* or "rebellion," that erupted in the Arab areas of
Gaza, Jerusalem, and the West Bank in December 1987 only inflamed
the sentiments of the Kukists. The influx of Soviet and Ethiopian Jews
increased the pressure on living space and visibly supported the claim
that Jews throughout the world are looking toward Israel as a redemp-
tive nation.

One of the most vocal of the Jewish nationalists in the Kuk lineage
was Meir Kahane. Kahane, an American who had a long history of Jewish political activism in Brooklyn, formed the Jewish Defense League
(JDL) in the 1960s to counter acts of anti-Semitism.[57] In 1971 he came
to Israel and turned to a more messianic vision of Jewish politics; in 1974
he created the Kach party, whose main platform was that Israel should
be ruled according to a strict construction of Jewish law; non-Jews—for
that matter, even secular Jews—had no place in this sacred order. Unlike
Kuk, Kahane saw nothing positive in the establishment of a secular Jewish state: the true religious creation of Israel was yet to come. Unlike
other Jewish conservatives with this point of view, however, he felt that
it was going to happen fairly soon and that he and his partisans could
help bring about that messianic event. Kahane was elected to the Knesset in 1984, but after he served a term, his party was banned in 1988 because of its "racist" and "undemocratic positions."[58]

Kahane's aggressive stance toward Judaism's detractors had worked
well in the liberal political atmosphere of the United States. There, Jews
were in the minority, and Kahane's JDL was portrayed in the mass media
as a Jewish version of the Black Panthers, which claimed to defend the
rights of the oppressed. In Israel, however, where the Jews were the status quo, Kahane's belligerence struck many secular nationalists as
bigotry—some called it Jewish Nazism. His statements about Arabs were
parsed and found to be surprisingly similar to Hitler's remarks on the

Jews.[59] A biography of the rabbi published in the mid-1980s was sardonically titled *Heil Kahane*.[60]

Kahane's main inspiration was not Hitler, however, but the messianic strain in Judaism. In Kahane's view, the coming of the Messiah was imminent, and the Arabs were simply in the wrong place at the wrong time. He told me that he did not hate the Arabs; he "respected them" and felt that they "should not live in disgrace in an occupied land."[61] For that reason, they should leave. The problem, for Kahane, was not that they were Arabs but that they were non-Jews living in a place designated by God for Jewish people since biblical times.[62] From a biblical point of view, Kahane argued, the true Israel is the West Bank of the Jordan River and the hills around Jerusalem—not the plains where Israel's largest city, Tel Aviv, is located.[63] The desire to reclaim the West Bank was therefore not simply irredentism: it was a part of a sacred plan of redemption. Kahane felt that modern Jews could hasten the coming of the Messiah by beginning to reclaim the sacred land. "Miracles don't just happen," Kahane said, referring to the messianic return, "they are made." And, he added, his own efforts and those of his followers would help "change the course of history."[64]

Although most Jewish settlers do not agree with what Ehud Sprinzak describes as Kahane's "catastrophic messianism" and subscribe instead to Kuk's incremental theory of messianic history, they view their occupation of the West Bank not only as a social experiment but as a religious act.[65] Rabbi Moshe Levinger, a leader of the Gush Emunim—an organization that encourages the new settlements and claims Rabbi Kuk as its founder—told me that the settlers' "return to the land is the first aspect of the return of the Messiah."[66] The religious settlers are by no means the majority of those who have established residential colonies on the West Bank—they are only a small percentage—but their presence colors the entire movement. Many of them regard the Palestinian Arabs around them with contempt. Hostility from the Arabs—and, for that matter, from many secular Jews—has hardened many of the members of the Gush Emunim and turned what began as a romantic venture into a militant cult.[67]

Much the same can be said about those who long for the rebuilding of the Temple in Jerusalem. According to Kuk's theology, the event that will trigger the return of the Messiah and the start of the messianic age is the reconstruction of the Temple on Temple Mount.[68] Again, like the Jewish conquest of biblical lands, it is an act of God that invites human participation: Jewish activists can join this act of redemption by helping to rebuild the Temple. The main practical constraint against doing so is the fact that Judaism's holiest place is simultaneously one of Islam's most sacred sites. The Dome of the Rock (Qubbat as-Sakhra) occupies precisely the Temple site, which is known by Arabs as Haram al-Sharif, the location from which the Prophet Muhammad is said to have ascended into heaven. No other location is acceptable for rebuilding the Temple, however, and for that reason many messianic Jews are convinced that sooner or later the Dome has to go.

This conviction has led to several attempts to destroy the existing Muslim shrine, some of them involving elaborate tunnels bored from a site near the Western Wall, the only portion of the original Temple still standing. According to Yoel Lerner, a former colleague of Kahane who was imprisoned for his involvement in a plot to blow up the Dome of the Rock, the three conditions necessary for messianic redemption are the restoration of the biblical lands, the revival of traditional Jewish law, and the rebuilding of the Temple.[69] He told me that Israel is well on its way to fulfilling the first two conditions; the absence of the Temple is the sole remaining obstacle to the realization of this messianic vision.

Another Jewish nationalist who laments the absence of the temple is Gershon Salomon. He heads a small group known as the Faithful of Temple Mount—one of several groups committed to rebuilding the Temple. Salomon explained to me that the construction of the Temple will precipitate an "awakening" of the Jewish people and the advent of the messianic age.[70] For years, on the seventh day of the festival of Sukkot, Salomon and his small band of followers marched on Temple Mount and attempted to pray, and, according to some, also lay the cornerstone for rebuilding the Temple.[71] Each year, the *waqf* organization of Muslim clergy, which at the time policed the area, turned Salomon away.

During the celebration of Sukkot in October 1990, the charged atmosphere of the *intifada* and the presence of American troops in nearby Saudi Arabia made the situation more tense than usual. As Salomon and his group slowly moved toward Temple Mount, the Waqf leaders were joined by a large number of young people associated with the Islamic Palestinian resistance movement Hamas and by a contingent of Israeli police who were, as it turned out, insufficient in number to control what became an ugly incident. Salomon and his group were barred from the Temple Mount area, but the damage had been done: in the confusion rocks were thrown, bullets were fired, and seventeen Palestinians were killed by the Israeli police in the melee.[72] The Security Council of the

United Nations censured Israel for its heavy-handedness and called for an outside investigation, which Israel refused to allow.

Less than a month after the Temple Mount incident, the messianic wing of Jewish nationalism received another shock with the assassination of Meier Kahane in New York City, where he had come to give a speech. The suspected assassin, El Sayyid Nosair, was a recent immigrant from Egypt associated with the al-Salam Mosque in Jersey City. Other members of the mosque had been arrested for attempting to send ammunition to the Palestine Liberation Organization (PLO), and several of Nosair's colleagues were later convicted of conspiracy in their participation in the 1993 bombing of the World Trade Center. Leaders of the mosque invoked the theology of Muslim nationalists such as Qutb and Faraj. They explained that the killing of Kahane did not violate the Qur'an because Kahane was an enemy of Islam.[73] Within a day of Kahane's death, two elderly Palestinian farmers were shot dead along the roadside near the West Bank city of Nablus, apparently in retaliation for Kahane's killing. Thus the spiral of violence that Kahane encouraged continued even after his death. An editorial writer for the *New York Times,* who described Kahane's life as "a passionate tangle of anger and unreason," referred to his death as the product of a "legacy of hate."[74]

In September 1993, when many Israelis were celebrating the mutual recognition of Israel and the PLO, leaders of Kahane's Kach party denounced the historic accord, calling it a fraud. They joined members of opposition parties, the Gush Emunim, and West Bank settlers in launching a campaign of civil disobedience against the accord, and vowed to fight by "any means." The passion of their protest—reminiscent of the style of Rabbi Kahane, whom they considered a martyr—came from the conviction that an Israeli retreat from the biblical lands of the West Bank was not only bad politics but bad religion. In their view, a religious state ruled by Jewish law and located on the site of biblical Israel was essential for the redemption of the entire cosmos. For this reason, not long after the accord was signed, a follower of Kahane slaughtered a group of Arabs as they worshiped in the mosque at Hebron's Tomb of the Prophets.

On February 24, 1994, the night before the celebration of Purim—a holiday marking the deliverance of Jews from extinction at the hands of their oppressors—a medical doctor from Brooklyn, Baruch Goldstein, who had adopted Kahane's Jewish messianic beliefs, went to the shrine at the Tomb of the Patriarchs in the town of Hebron, also known by its Arabic name, al-Khalil. The shrine is located above the Cave of Machpelah, the site where Abraham, Sarah, Isaac, and other biblical figures venerated by the three Abrahamic faiths—Judaism, Christianity, and Islam—were said to have been entombed more than three thousand years ago. The shrine, a large fortresslike stone building, contained halls of worship for both Jews and Muslims; the Mosque of Ibrahim (Abraham, in Arabic) had been standing on this site since the seventh century. Goldstein went to the Jewish side, where worshippers had gathered to listen to a reading of the Scroll of Esther, as is traditionally done on Purim eve. But his meditation was interrupted by boisterous voices outside, and the terrible words were shouted—"*itbah al-yahud*" (Death to Jews)—this time by a gang of Arab youths. Goldstein turned and saw that the armed guards that the Israeli government had stationed at the site were ignoring the commotion. Dr. Goldstein was outraged and felt that both Judaism and the Jewish people had been deeply humiliated.

Before dawn the next morning, on the day of Purim, Goldstein returned to the shrine. This time he entered the mosque on the Muslim side of the building, where early-rising worshippers were beginning their morning prayers. Goldstein pulled out a Galil assault rifle he had hidden in his coat and began firing indiscriminately into the crowd of men and boys who were kneeling in prayer on the carpeted floor. After firing 111 shots and killing more than thirty worshippers and injuring scores more, Goldstein was overwhelmed by the crowd and beaten to death.

Some months after the awful incident at the elaborate gravesite that had been constructed near Goldstein's home in Kiryat Arba, the volunteer guard Yochay Ron told me that the doctor was a hero. "Dr. Goldstein did the right thing," said the thin young man, who was wearing blue jeans, a white t-shirt, and an embroidered skullcap, and carrying an automatic rifle.[75] At the time of Goldstein's funeral, more than a thousand of the settlement's six thousand residents came to honor him during a driving rainstorm. Soon thereafter the grave had become a shrine, and the raised granite slab was surrounded by a concrete plaza and ringed by pillared lamps. Most Israelis, however, regarded Goldstein as a menace at best, a terrorist at worst—someone whose acts have tragically escalated the violence in the region.

An even greater demon in the eyes of most Israelis is the Jewish activist Yigal Amir, who thought he was helping save Israel's honor when he assassinated the country's prime minister, Yitzhak Rabin. On the evening of November 4, 1995, on their way to a large peace rally held in the plaza of the city hall in Tel Aviv, Rabin and his wife, Leah, discussed the possibility of violence and the precautions that they should take against it. What they feared were reprisals from militant members of Hamas against the peace overtures that Rabin had made. They were aware of militant Jewish opposition to the peace process as well, but "never in our wildest imaginations," Leah Rabin told me, "did we ever think he would be attacked by a Jew. We simply did not think it possible that one Jew could even think of killing another."[76]

Later that evening Rabin addressed a cheering crowd of 100,000, telling them Israelis believed in peace and were "ready to take a risk for it."[77] Observers said that it was one of Rabin's finest hours, a high point in his political career, and a moment of great personal satisfaction. Minutes later, just after he had descended the staircase and was walking to his car beside the government building, Amir, a student from Tel Aviv's conservative Bar-Ilan University, aimed his pistol and shot the prime minister at point-blank range. As Rabin lay dying on the sidewalk next to the car, Amir was apprehended by the police. He was quoted as saying that he had no regrets for what he had done, adding that he had "acted alone and on orders from God."[78]

Amir, a former combat soldier who had studied Jewish law, said that his decision to assassinate the prime minister was not a casual one and that he had attempted to carry out the act on two previous occasions. At those times, however, the conditions had not been right. His decision to kill the prime minister was influenced by the opinions of militant rabbis that such an assassination would be justified by the "pursuer's decree" of Jewish legal precedent.[79] The principle morally obligates a Jew to halt someone who presents "a mortal danger" to Jews. Such a danger, Amir reasoned, was created by Rabin in allowing the Palestinian Authority to expand on the West Bank.

The assassination of Rabin did not deter succeeding Israeli governments from selectively withdrawing from some areas of Palestinian control, including Gaza and parts of the West Bank. In August 2005, over 9,500 settlers and the troops that supported them were required to leave the area. By September, Israel had withdrawn support from all Jewish settlements in Gaza, despite the fierce opposition of extreme religious opponents who felt that any withdrawal of Jewish control over what they regarded as the biblical lands of Israel was an act of treason and a violation of the faith. Some protestors threw eggs, bottles, and paint at the soldiers who were sent to evacuate the area; others barricaded themselves in synagogues. Many of the protestors were young people from religious settlements in the West Bank who claimed that God had given the land to the Jews and considered allowing any piece of it to be given away a violation of divine will.

Jewish settlers on the West Bank were even more resistant to relinquishing territory in areas that they claimed had been occupied by Jews in biblical times. But in fact only a few isolated Jewish settlements in the West Bank were dismantled by the Israeli government. Many of the settlements around the city of Jerusalem were simply absorbed into redefined boundaries of the city limits. Settlements in other parts of the West Bank were incorporated into Israeli territory by the construction of a network of controlled highways that was begun in 2004. Many of the settlements were protected by a controversial barrier, described by the Israeli government as a security fence and by most Palestinians as a wall. Construction of the 420-mile barrier began in 2002 and continued for some years. In many sections it was indeed a metal fence; in other areas, including the city of Jerusalem, it was a thirty-foot-tall concrete wall. Opposition to the barrier included concerns not only about the divisive nature of the barrier but also about its location. The barrier created a de facto demarcation of boundaries that absorbed an estimated 40 percent of formerly Palestinian-controlled areas. Though Jewish extremists were still unhappy with what they thought were unnecessary compromises with the Palestinians, the protected settlements, the network of highways, and the extensive barrier created a significant expansion of direct Israeli control over what had been regarded as Palestinian territory. The dream of incorporating into the Jewish state of Israel the biblical land on the West Bank had largely been fulfilled.

HAMAS: THE ISLAMIC *INTIFADA*

The day that Israel's Yitzhak Rabin and the PLO's leader, Yasser Arafat, boarded airplanes to fly to Washington D.C. to witness the historic signing of an Israeli-PLO accord in September 1993, protests erupted not only in Israel but also in the West Bank, Gaza, and much of the adjacent Arab world. Eight were killed in Gaza alone. The demonstrations were waged not only by Jewish nationalists but also by their Muslim counterparts. The Jewish extremists thought that their government had given away too much; the Muslim extremists thought Israel's concession insufficient. Israeli Jewish and Palestinian Muslim activists were each fighting on two fronts: against each other and against their own secular leaders. The antisecular attacks were often more vicious. Many observers thought that the secular leaders, Rabin and Arafat, were propelled into the September 1993 alliance in part because they feared the rising strength of the religious nationalists in their camps. In Israel, the most ardent opponents of the secular government were Kahane's Kach party and the Gush Emunim. In Palestine, it was Hamas.

At first Hamas was an underground movement—actually a coalition of several movements with no single leader. Prominent among those identified with the movement were several religious figures: Sheik 'Abd al-Aziz 'Odeh (Uda); Sheik As'ad Bayud al-Tamimi, a resident of Hebron who was a preacher at the al-Aqsa Mosque in Jerusalem; and especially Sheik Ahmed Yassin from Gaza.[80] Sheik Yassin, who was described as "a charismatic and influential leader," commanded the Islamic Assembly, which had ties to virtually all the mosques in Gaza, and within a few years Hamas was able to gain 65 to 75 percent of the votes of both students and faculty in the local councils of Gaza's Islamic University.[81] Sheik Yassin claimed that he and his Muslim colleagues initiated the *intifada,* the popular uprising against the Israeli occupation of Gaza and the West Bank.[82]

Although Sheik Yassin was almost completely incapacitated by a degenerative nerve condition and had to be carried from place to place, he drew an extraordinary following. When I visited him in 1989, his small house at the outskirts of Gaza City was crowded with admirers and associates who came for advice and the benefit of his spiritual presence. They sat on the carpeted floor of a plain meeting room adjacent to his bedroom and listened patiently to the sheik's rambling discourse. His monologue on the evils of Israeli occupation and the virtues of Muslim society was interrupted only by an occasional question and by daily prayers. These Sheik Yassin managed with great difficulty, tottering back and forth as he uttered the sacred words. His mind was sharp, however, and his opinions on current political matters were clearly expressed.

Sheik Yassin described his Islamic resistance movement as the heart of the Palestinian opposition. He told me that the idea of a secular liberation movement for Palestine is profoundly misguided because there "is no such thing as a secular state in Islam."[83] At that time, prior to the September 1993 accords, he nominally supported the PLO. He referred to Arafat as "President Arafat" and claimed that after the liberation of Palestine, "the people will decide" whether there should be an Islamic state.[84] Clearly, Sheik Yassin was confident that the people would decide in favor of Islam.

Leaders of the PLO, however, were not as certain as Sheik Yassin about the outcome of the vote.[85] They were clearly nervous about the Hamas challenge to their legitimacy, and before I was allowed to interview Sheik Yassin, representatives of the PLO in Gaza stopped my taxi and insisted that the driver take me to a pro-PLO refugee camp where I could hear the secular Palestinian point of view. On another occasion, Yasser Arafat's brother, Fathi Arafat, assured me that only "a small percentage of Palestinians are in favor of an Islamic state."[86] Arafat told me that religion should be a personal matter. He would not want his daughter to wear the Islamic veil, he said, but he would respect the right of others to do so if they wished. Yet he affirmed that his movement was democratic: should the Palestinian people vote in favor of an Islamic state, he would support it.[87]

From the 1990s onward, Palestinians have been caught between these two competing visions of an independent Palestine. Long before the 2006 elections that brought Hamas to power, many observers felt that the competition was about equal. In Gaza, supporters of Hamas were in the majority; there was also considerable support for Islamic nationalism on the West Bank.[88] Yet Palestinians told me that they supported both secular and religious movements for Palestinian independence. "The distinction between the PLO and Hamas is artificial," said a Palestinian student leader who was studying Islamic theology in Cairo. "We should now be united against a common enemy; tomorrow, when we are free, we can discuss our differences."[89]

Still, the differences are considerable. In the late 1990s, the competition was between Yasser Arafat, who envisioned Palestine as a modern nation-state, patterned largely on the Western secular model, and Sheik Yassin, who told me that "shari'a should be the sole basis for Islamic politics."[90] Although Sheik Yassin admired Khomeini's revolution in Iran and valued certain aspects of conservative Islamic rule in Saudi Arabia, he was critical of both the Iranians and the Saudis. Sheik Yassin was most strongly influenced by Islamic nationalist leaders in nearby Egypt; he is said to have been familiar with the writings of both Qutb and Faraj.

The roots of militant Islamic Palestinian resistance to the Israeli occupation of their homeland stretches back to the 1970s, when an Islamic alternative to the PLO was proposed.[91] One of the constituent groups of the short-lived movement was a Palestinian version of Egypt's Muslim Brotherhood. This group, in which Sheik Yassin was active, did not expand until the 1980s, when many Palestinian Islamic activists associated with the Muslim Brotherhood became impatient with what they viewed as its passivity and split off to form several new associations. Sheik Yassin became president of the al-Mujamma' al-Islami (the Muslim Gathering). It had ties to another confederation of groups known as the Islamic Jihad, over which Sheik 'Odeh presided.[92] In 1983 the Islamic

Jihad was implicated in the killing of a young Israeli settler in the occupied territories. In October 1984 Sheik Yassin and his colleagues were arrested and jailed for stockpiling weapons to be used for "the destruction of Israel and the creation of an Islamic state."[93] In 1986, after Sheik Yassin and other prisoners were freed through a prisoner exchange, the Islamic Jihad launched a cluster of new military actions targeting Israeli military officers; in Gaza; several Israeli soldiers were killed, as were members of the Jihad. Sheik 'Odeh was arrested and expelled from the country.[94] At the same time, the Islamic resistance began to organize Palestinians outside the Israeli-occupied areas. Communiqués were circulated in Paris and London, and a magazine, *al-Islam wa Filastin (Islam and Palestine),* began publication in Cyprus, with circulation throughout Europe and the United States. The magazine listed a mailing address in Tampa, Florida, in addition to the main Cyprus office.[95]

The last month of 1987 saw the beginning of the *intifada*—a popular uprising that relied not on sophisticated weapons used by a few well-trained cadres, but on rocks, barricades, and any other materials that ordinary Palestinians could marshal in their resistance to Israeli occupation. It was a dramatic turn in the movement's strategy, not only because the simplicity of the weaponry drew in virtually any Palestinian, but also because its populist style gave the cause an image of a moral crusade rather than a terrorist plot. For a time it also changed the nature of the Islamic resistance. As a popular crusade, the *intifada* was identified with the religion—and the religious leaders—of the people. The Islamic resistance movement Hamas emerged at roughly the same time as the *intifada*, and although there is no question of a connection between the two, there is some debate over Sheik Yassin's boast that he and other Muslim activists created the *intifada*. It is equally possible that the *intifada*, in a sense, created Hamas. Without the *intifada,* a broad-based Muslim activist movement outside the PLO would have been unrealizable.

The word *hamas* means zeal or enthusiasm, but it is also an acronym for the formal name of the movement: Harakat al-Muqawama al-Islamiyya (Islamic Resistance Movement). The name first appeared publicly in a communiqué circulated in mid-February 1988. The communiqué was one in a series that began about the time that the *intifada* began in December 1987, but it was not clear whether the Muslim Brotherhood, the Jihad organizations, or some other group was behind these early communiqués. Jean-François Legrain suggests that Yassin and the Muslim Brotherhood were not involved in the early communiqués or with the *intifada* but joined the *intifada* bandwagon only in February

1988.[96] The February communiqué that mentions the name *Hamas* describes the movement as "the powerful arm of the Association of Muslim Brothers."[97] It is possible, therefore, that Hamas marked a new phase in the Islamic resistance movement, one in which militant Palestinian Muslim activists were united under an old Muslim Brotherhood leadership based in Gaza for the purpose of capturing the leadership of the *intifada*.

Hamas placed the ideology of Islam and the organization of the mosque at the service *of intifada*. The struggle between the Palestinians and the Israelis was described in eschatological terms as "the combat between Good and Evil."[98] Committees were set up in mosques to provide alternative education when schools were closed because of the *intifada*, and other mosque committees collected *zakat* (donations) to give to victims of the uprising. Most of the leaders of Hamas had religious titles. The movement's communiqués justified its positions on the basis of Islamic beliefs and tradition, and they cast even the most specific issues of policy in a theological light. The communiqués criticized the Arab states' compromises with Israeli and U.S. positions and called for general strikes to protest the sponsorship of peace envoys by the Americans. In August 1988 Hamas published a forty-page covenant, which presented its vision of an Islamic Palestine and implied that the only moral course for Palestinians was to reject the secular ideology and compromising strategy of the PLO and wage direct jihad against Israel.[99]

The PLO did not take kindly to the Hamas's declaration of independence, and for a month or so the two organizations seemed to be competing for public support. They announced general strikes at different times, and although the Hamas strikes were usually smaller, the movement was especially successful in garnering support in Gaza and increasingly in such West Bank cities as Nablus, Ramallah, Bethlehem, and Hebron. By late September 1988 Hamas and the PLO had at least temporarily patched up their differences; for some months after that, most of the general strikes were called by both groups at the same time.

The mutual suspicion that marred relations between Hamas and the PLO may have been goaded, in part, by the Israeli government. In the last months of 1988, while members of the PLO were being imprisoned, Sheik Yassin was interviewed on Israeli television. There were rumors that he and Hamas were tolerated by the Israeli government because they were obstructing the path of the PLO.[100] By the middle of 1989, however, the leaders of Hamas were regarded as too troublesome to be ignored. The Israeli government rounded up many of them, including Sheik Yassin, who was put under house arrest.

Despite the suppression of its leaders, Hamas did not disappear. Its message was spread through underground circulars and journals, such as *Al-Sabil (The Way)*, which was printed in Oslo, Norway, and smuggled into Israel. For several reasons, the Islamic resistance movement in Palestine continued to grow. The longer the *intifada* continued, the more restless the Palestinian populace became with the official PLO leadership. Moreover, the educated PLO elite was often at some remove from the masses—and, in the case of those who were in exile, physically distant—whereas the Islamic leaders were a part of the local communities and close at hand. In addition, the masses of American troops assigned to Saudi Arabia in 1990 following Saddam Hussein's invasion of Kuwait were seen by many Palestinians as a direct threat. The *intifada* was rejuvenated and, with it, the growing sentiment that the conciliatory attitude of the PLO was not working and that further direct action was necessary.

This sentiment was heightened by a second event in 1990, the October confrontation on Temple Mount. Temple Mount had become an increasingly important symbol in the Hamas resistance struggle. Unlike the PLO, which had only an imagined Palestinian capital to defend, Hamas's moral assets were real and tangible: the Dome of the Rock and the al-Aqsa Mosque. Defending the sacred shrine and cleansing it of "foreign" (Israeli) influence became a major theme in Hamas publications. The sacred hill also became an important site for recruiting young Palestinian men from Jerusalem—many of them former members of street gangs—to the cause. Many were initiated into the Hamas movement in a dramatic nighttime ritual at the Dome of the Rock.[101] When the Israeli activist Gershon Salomon and his followers in the Faithful of Temple Mount let it be known that they were going to march on the site and lay the cornerstone for a new temple, Hamas leaders spread the word among their youthful followers that the time had come to defend the faith against the Israeli intruders. What happened then, as I recounted earlier in this chapter, was one of the bloodiest incidents of the *intifada*.

Hamas made the most of the incident. The Temple Mount confrontation had the immediate effect of consolidating Hamas's power in Arab Jerusalem and the West Bank. It also expanded the terms of the Palestinian cause: at issue were not only land and political rights but also religion. "The massacre at al-Aksa," leaders explained in one of their communiqués, "showed that our fight with Zionism is a fight between Islam and Judaism."[102] One might add that the al-Aqsa incident demonstrated that members of the Islamic resistance would lay down their lives in defense of the faith at a time when their more secular compatriots were quiescent.

Several violent incidents involving Hamas in November and December 1990 indicated either that the movement was becoming bolder and more aggressive or that bolder and more aggressive individuals were joining the movement and championing its cause as their own. In either event the events signaled a significant change in Hamas's position. During those two months, at least eight Israelis were killed by individuals associated with Hamas. After the knife slaying of three Israeli workers in Jaffa in mid-December, nearly a thousand Palestinians associated with Hamas (including six hundred in Gaza and another two hundred on the West Bank) were said to have been arrested.[103] Among them was Abdul Aziz Rantisi, a colleague of Sheik Yassin, who has been described as "the co-founder of Hamas."[104]

By 1991 the Islamic resistance movement had become a significant contender for Palestinian leadership, in large part because of the weakening of Yasser Arafat's power after the defeat of the PLO's ally, Iraq, in the Gulf War. Unlike Arafat, whose disastrous support of Saddam Hussein during the Gulf War had decimated the PLO's coffers and undermined its political support, the leaders of Hamas did not take a clear stand—perhaps stimulated by the fact that the government of Kuwait had been by far a greater financial supporter of Hamas than of the PLO.[105] After the Gulf War, Hamas began to demand greater representation on Palestinian councils, and for the first time Arafat's authority began to be challenged by local leaders. By the middle of 1991 feuds between religious and secular Palestinian leaders had turned violent.[106] Supporters of Hamas were beginning to win elections on the West Bank as well as in Gaza.[107] In October 1991, Sheik Yassin was again imprisoned by Israel.

In 1992, the peace talks between Israeli and Palestinian leaders commanded the attention of most Palestinians, and the *intifada* degenerated from a popular uprising involving makeshift weapons into a well-armed struggle conducted by small groups of youthful cadres. Among these were groups associated with the Fateh and Marxist branches of the PLO as well as groups associated with Hamas.[108] Many of the older leaders of Hamas adopted a wait-and-see attitude toward the peace talks, while the younger members fought, at times violently, against the members of the PLO who supported the talks.[109] Supporters of Hamas questioned the degree to which Islamic law and leadership would be factors in the settlement eventually negotiated with the Israelis.

As it turned out, Islamic principles were not even mentioned in the September 1993 accord sponsored by Rabin and Arafat. From Hamas's point of view, the circumstances surrounding the accord could not have been worse: It was a thoroughly secular document, negotiated in secret with Israeli leaders and signed in Washington with the blessings of what is often seen as Islam's global enemy, the government of the United States.

The day the document was signed, Hamas supporters in Gaza City used wooden clubs to disperse a rally sponsored by a new pro-agreement political party. Arafat supporters opened fire with submachine guns over the heads of those attending a rally organized by Hamas in the Gaza town of Rafah. And in Damascus, a coalition of ten anti-PLO groups— including Hamas and another radical Islamic group, the Islamic Jihad— pledged to scuttle the accord, calling Arafat a traitor. The continuing tensions and attempts on his life proved the seriousness of these accusations. Many outside the Middle East wondered why Palestinians were so adamantly opposed to what seemed a major Israeli concession and a giant step toward their own independence.

On one level, the disagreement over the 1993 accord was a matter of who would lead the movement: the Hamas leadership came from the poorest areas of the villages and towns. On another level, Hamas put into question the character of both the Palestinian movement and the hoped-for Palestinian state. Sheik 'Odeh saw the increased Islamicization of the *intifada* as "a sign from God to the people that they need Islam as a center,"[110] challenging the secular PLO's monopoly on power. For although Sheik Yassin admitted that a secular Palestinian government could go far in helping to protect Islamic values in Palestine, it could never go far enough. It ultimately would be an illegitimate form of government because, according to Sheik Yassin and many of his followers in Hamas, "the only true Palestinian state is an Islamic state," and that would mean strict adherence to *shari'a* and its moral rules.[111]

The establishment of the Palestinian National Authority in 1994 was a milestone toward Palestinian independence and a triumph for Arafat. It also transformed the Palestinian Islamic movement. Rather than being a dissident branch of the Palestinian resistance, Hamas, as the enemy of the secular Palestinian state, became the vanguard of a new revolutionary posture. With the establishment of the Palestinian Authority, the frequency of Hamas-perpetrated suicide bombings in Tel Aviv, Jerusalem, and elsewhere in Israel increased. They were widely seen not only as attacks on Israel but also as attempts to discredit the conciliatory policies of Arafat's Palestinian Authority.

In the beginning, as I was told by Abdul Aziz Rantisi, the political leader of Hamas, the movement's military operation targeted only soldiers. The movement took "every measure" to stop massacres and to discourage suicide bombings.[112] But according to Rantisi, two events changed things. One was the attack by Israeli police on Palestinians demonstrating in front of the al-Aqsa mosque near the Dome of the Rock in 1990, and the other was the massacre in Hebron by Baruch Goldstein in 1994 during the month of Ramadan. Rantisi pointed out that both of these incidents were directed at mosques, and he maintained that the timing of Goldstein's attack, during Ramadan, was not coincidental. He concluded that these were attacks on Islam as a religion as well as on Palestinians as a people. He was also convinced that Israel's military had played a role in the incidents, despite the government's denial that it supported the extremist Jews who had precipitated the al-Aqsa incident or provoked the Hebron massacre. Rantisi pointed out that in Goldstein's attack, Israeli soldiers were standing nearby. Goldstein had befriended them, and he was able to change his rifle magazine clip four times during the incident without being stopped by soldiers.

Rantisi explained that the young Hamas supporters' suicide bombings were authorized only in response to these and other specific acts of violence from the Israeli side, acts that frequently affected innocent civilians. In that sense they were defensive: "If we did not respond this way," Rantisi explained, "Israelis would keep doing the same thing."[113] Moreover, he said, the bombings were a moral lesson. "We want to do the same to Israel as they have done to us," he explained, indicating that just as innocent Muslims had been killed in the Hebron incident and in many other skirmishes during the Israeli-Palestinian conflict, it was necessary for the Israeli people to experience the violence before they could understand what the Palestinians had gone through.[114] Rantisi said virtually the same thing on international television following the Israeli air strike in Gaza in July 2002 that killed several women and children in addition to the intended target, the head of the military wing of Hamas.

"It is important for you to understand," Rantisi told me, "that we are the victims in this struggle, not the cause of it."[115] He repeated this point at the end of my interview when I asked Rantisi in what way he thought Hamas was misunderstood and what misrepresentations he would like to correct. "You think we are the aggressors," Rantisi said.

"That is the number one misunderstanding. We are not: we are the victims."[116]

Many Palestinians regarded Rantisi and his mentor, Sheik Yassin, as victims indeed when both were killed in 2004 by Israeli missile strikes. Rantisi had served as leader of the movement for two months following Sheik Yassin's assassination. The enormous outpouring of Palestinian support for the cause of the departed leaders during funeral processions throughout Gaza and the West Bank were portents of a strengthened Hamas. If Israeli military officials thought they had destroyed Hamas by executing its most visible leaders, they were soon to receive a rude awakening.

On January 25, 2006, elections were held for the Palestinian Legislative Council, the legislative body for the Palestinian National Authority. These were the first elections since the death of Yasser Arafat in 2004, and his Fateh party, led by Palestinian president Mahmoud Abbas, was widely expected to win. Among their electoral opponents were politicians representing Hamas, which had decided to present candidates after their favorable showing in municipal elections in 2005. To widespread surprise, Hamas won. The radical Muslim party secured 44 percent of the popular vote with 56 percent of the seats, while the secular Fateh party won 42 percent of the popular vote but only 34 percent of the seats. Soon after, Hamas leader Ismail Haniya formed a new government in a testy relationship with Abbas, who continued to serve as president under Palestinian constitutional rules.

Several months later, militant factions loyal to Hamas and Fateh were warring with each other, and the Palestinian community was on the brink of civil war. In the summer of 2006 its internal difficulties were deflected by an international political crisis that began when Hamas supporters captured an Israeli soldier to secure an exchange of political prisoners and Israel responded with a military incursion into Gaza. The crisis escalated when Hizbollah forces in southern Lebanon attempted to use a similar tactic to force a swap of prisoners. Hizbollah's capture of two Israeli soldiers precipitated a major Israeli military intervention into Lebanon in July 2006. The war in Lebanon ended in August with a U.N.-brokered ceasefire. In February 2007 a fragile agreement for a unity government between Hamas and Fateh was signed in Mecca, but the peace between the secular and religious camps of Palestinians soon broke down, collapsing into a bitter civil war. By summer 2007, Hamas controlled all of Gaza, while Fateh held tenuous reins on the West Bank and what remained of the Palestinian Authority.

INSURGENTS IN IRAQ

The Israeli attack in 2004 that killed the Palestinian Hamas leader Sheik Ahmed Yassin had repercussions in a different part of the Arab world: the al-Anbar province of post-Saddam Iraq. At the time that Sheik Yassin was killed, Sunni activists in Iraq were beginning to mobilize protests against the U.S. occupation of their country that began with the American-led military coalition that toppled Saddam Hussein's government in April 2003.

"We hated Saddam," a Sunni Muslim cleric told me, indicating that he and his colleagues in the Sunni triangle of al-Anbar and adjacent provinces had no use for the secular dictator.[117] Nonetheless, he and his allies regarded the American coalition authority that replaced Saddam's government as an even worse choice. They saw the U.S. occupation as a repressive force, imposing a Western-style government on Muslim territory, much as America's ally, Israel, imposed itself on the Middle East. For this reason they saw parallels to their own experience in Iraq with Hamas and the Muslim struggle in Palestine.

The killing of Sheik Yassin had an impact especially on the insurgency in Fallujah during the critical month of March 2004. The Iraqis in Fallujah had identified themselves with the Palestinians, and Sheik Yassin had been widely revered in Iraq's Sunni stronghold. Televised scenes of the site of the crippled leader's death outraged Muslims in Fallujah, who poured out into the streets in a spontaneous demonstration. The U.S. military used a show of force to control the demonstration, but the American presence reinforced the idea that the politics of the United States and Israel were essentially identical. It was a common belief among Iraqis that the United States supported what was regarded as Israel's oppression of Palestinian freedom. Thus the anger against Israel's control over Palestine became merged with the hatred of the U.S. occupation of Iraq. In the eyes of many in Fallujah, the Palestinian and Iraqi cause was the same. One of the city's main streets, which ended in a square metal bridge over the Euphrates River—was renamed in honor of the fallen Sheik Yassin.

For over a week tension mounted. On March 31, several American-made sport-utility vehicles came hurtling through Fallujah on the newly named Sheik Yassin Street. The passengers in the vehicles were security staff employed by a North Carolina firm, Blackwater Security Consulting, but from the Iraqi point of view these armed Americans were either soldiers or spies. The vehicles were ambushed.[118] Soon the stalled vehicles burst into flames with the occupants caught inside.[119]

The gruesome scene of four men burned alive soon became even more horrific. A crowd of some forty to fifty men and boys gathered, dancing and shouting anti-American slogans. Videotapes of the scene show men beating the lifeless charred corpses with a metal pipe. A young boy stomped his heel onto a burned head and called to a reporter to tell President Bush to "come and look at this!"[120] The remains of two of the burned bodies were dragged down Sheik Yassin Street to the bridge. "This is what these spies deserve," said one 28-year-old Iraqi who observed the incident.[121]

According to some accounts, the car that dragged one of the bodies through the streets of Fallujah had a picture of Sheik Yassin in the window. The Associated Press reported that members of the crowd held pictures of the assassinated sheik as the bodies were mutilated. Later a statement was issued from a previously unknown group, the Brigade of Martyr Ahmed Yassin. The statement claimed responsibility for the attack and described it as "a gift from the people of Fallujah to the people of Palestine and the family of Sheik Ahmed Yassin who was assassinated by the criminal Zionists."[122]

This was a critical moment in the increasing intensity of the insurgency and in the militancy of the U.S. occupation authority's response. Against the advice of the American generals on the scene, orders came from the Pentagon to quell the insurgency by directly attacking Fallujah. A major military assault ensued in the following month, and after a difficult ceasefire during the summer, the city was virtually emptied by a U.S. military campaign in November 2004 that was determined to rid the city of insurgents. The intensity of the American assault, however, hardened the opposition and created a more dedicated resistance. A Marine general who participated in the April assault on Fallujah later regretted it and said "it had increased the level of animosity."[123]

The fall of Fallujah marked a turning point in jihadi influence on the insurgency. Though the U.S. attack was meant to weaken the insurgency, at the same time it strengthened the hand of foreign jihadi activists operating in Iraq, some of whom were associated with the transnational al Qaeda movement. Prior to November 2004 Islamic activists in Fallujah were largely under the influence of local clergy.[124] The destruction of Fallujah's social network by the U.S. military weakened those ties, however, and scattered the insurgents. Increasingly they came under the influence of the more radical activists. Before the fall of Fallujah, the jihad outsiders had been mistrusted; the destruction of Fallujah provided evidence in the eyes of many that the jihadi rhetoric of cosmic war was real.

When I was in Baghdad in 2004, my interviews with clerics associated with the Sunni resistance convinced me that at that time their main concern had been the religious consequences of the U.S. occupation of Iraq, not global jihad. One of them told me that he was certain that the purpose of the U.S. invasion and occupation of his country was to coopt an Islamic revolution against the secular government; he regarded the U.S.-supported regime in Baghdad as simply a continuation of the anti-Islamic secular policies of Saddam Hussein.[125] From the cleric's point of view, the purpose of the insurgency was not only to end the American occupation of Iraq but also to usher in a new Islamic regime. In this sense the mission of the Iraq insurgency was much like that of Hamas. The respect paid to Sheik Yassin reflected a style of Islamic politics, in many cases outright religious nationalism, that focused on local control.

The jihadi elements that came into Iraq in the months following the U.S. military invasion were different from these local insurgents—they were more strident, more expansive in their vision of global religious struggle. They were transnationalists. The jihadi warriors from Jordan, Syria, and elsewhere in the Middle East saw Iraq as a new battleground in the global confrontation between Islam and what they regarded as the anti-Islamic forces of the secular West. One of the leaders of these new jihadi soldiers who helped to transform the Iraqi resistance was the Jordanian militant Abu Musab al-Zarqawi.

Al-Zarqawi's lasting impact on Iraq's civil strife was his effort to create religious conflict between Arab Sunnis and Shi'ites. In March 2004, his group launched an attack on Shi'a shrines in Karbala and Baghdad. In December 2004 the group attacked the leading Shi'a shrine in Najaf and again bombed the Karbala mosque. Perhaps the most destructive attack was the February 2006 bombing of the al-Asqari mosque in Samarra—one of Shi'a Islam's holiest sites—destroying its striking golden dome and killing 165 people. Al-Zarqawi had publicly proclaimed his intention to foment Sunni-Shi'a animosity, and the destruction of the shrine was clearly meant to accomplish that goal.

Al-Zarqawi's goal of sectarian strife indeed came to fruition, and these hostilities outlived al-Zarqawi himself. On June 7, 2006, U.S. military intelligence received information regarding Al-Zarqawi's location near the city of Baquba, and attacked the location with a missile strike that killed him, along with one of his wives and one of his children. There was considerable speculation about who might have divulged al-Zarqawi's whereabouts; some thought that he might have been betrayed by members of his own movement. He was succeeded by an Egyptian jihadi, Abu Ayyub al-Masri.

In the meantime, the momentum of sectarian strife had taken on a life of its own. Soon after the February 2006 bombing of the Samarra mosque, over a hundred Sunni mosques were attacked and ten Sunni imams were killed. Fifteen more were kidnapped. A tit-for-tat litany of reprisal killings between Shi'a and Sunni neighborhoods intensified during the following year.

Much of the fervor of Shi'a retaliation against Sunnis was urged on by the radical Shi'a cleric Muqtada al-Sadr. Though relatively young and undistinguished among Shi'a clergy in Iraq, Muqtada had imposing family ties. He was the son of one of Iraq's most famous clerics, the late Grand Ayatollah Mohammad Sadeq al-Sadr, and son-in-law of another distinguished cleric, the Grand Ayatollah Mohammad Baqir as-Sadr. Perhaps more important, he had set up something of a theocratic rule in one of Baghdad's most crowded districts, Sadr City, which consisted almost entirely of poor Shi'a immigrants. Moreover, Muqtada served as the commander of a large paramilitary force, the Mahdi Army, that drew its manpower from former units of the disbanded Iraqi army and was said to have received covert support from Iran.

Muqtada had no use for the American-led coalition government, which sought his arrest in 2004. At the same time he despised al-Zarqawi's forces, whose terrorists attacks were directed at Shi'a targets. After the destruction of the Samarra mosque, rogue elements related to the Muqtada camp undertook unusually savage acts of terrorism, aimed at the Sunni population in retaliation for car bomb assaults in Shi'a neighborhoods, many of them in Sadr City. The Shi'a reprisals were equally brutal. Groups of ordinary Sunni citizens were rounded up, tortured, and murdered, their bodies mutilated by electric drills and dumped in the Tigris River or in fields outside of the city of Baghdad.

Though the sectarian violence in Iraq was often described as Sunni-Shi'a civil war, there was little support for the violence from moderates and mainstream religious leaders on either side. On the Sunni side, the Sunni Association of Muslim Clerics resisted the attempts of the al-Tawhid jihadis to coopt it, and the association often played a positive role in helping to moderate the violence. I spoke with one Sunni cleric who told me that he had sought to mediate between extremist insurgents and the Iraqi government for the sake of Iraqi unity.[126] The jihadi extremists became increasingly impatient with what they regarded as compromises by the nationalistic-minded Sunni leaders.

By 2007 the tensions between moderate Iraqi Sunni leaders and the jihadi outsiders had erupted into dissention and violence between their factions. Sunni militia in al-Anbar Province—who had worked with the foreign jihadis in attacks on the U.S. and Iraqi military—were now colluding with U.S. forces in apprehending their former allies and in some instances torturing and killing them. On the Shi'a side, the Shi'a-dominated Iraq government pledged to control Muqtada's gangs, and leading clerics such as Grand Ayatollah Sayyid Ali Husaini al-Sistani distanced themselves from Shi'a extremists. Sistani carried considerable political weight, not only because of his religious authority but also because of his relationship with the leading Shi'a political party, the Supreme Council for the Islamic Revolution in Iraq, led by Abdul Aziz al-Hakim.

I was assured that Iraqi Shi'ites and Sunnis had an innate sense of hospitality toward one another by Nuri Kamal al-Maliki, who later became prime minister of Iraq (at the time of my interview with him in 2004, he was deputy director of the Shi'a Dawa Party).[127] Al-Maliki told me that his own party was 15 percent Sunni and that Shi'a-Sunni intermarriage was common. He also told me that the threat of Muqtada al-Sadr—who was one of his primary supporters—was greatly exaggerated. Yet in the years following, the threat proved quite real. In 2007 al-Maliki pledged to bridle Muqtada's forces in order to support a troop surge strategy promoted by U.S. president George W. Bush. For a time Muqtada went into hiding, and the violence temporarily subsided. Nonetheless, rogue elements from the Shi'a side soon continued their acts of terror and reprisal, imitating those of Sunni extremists. As in other parts of the world, the most extreme elements of society used violence to attempt to impose their agendas on the populace.

OTHER MOVEMENTS IN THE MIDDLE EAST AND AFRICA

Iraq was vulnerable to the rise of religious rebellion following the overthrow of the secular regime of Saddam Hussein in 2003 in part because of the political influence of the adjacent neighborhood. Even if the country had not been invaded by a host of jihadi activists from neighboring Syria, Jordan, and Saudi Arabia, the Muslim activists within Iraq would have been affected by models of religious activism in the Middle East and North Africa. Though some of the activist movements were Christian (in Lebanon) and Jewish (in Israel), most were associated with the dominant religion of the regions: Islam in both its Shi'a and Sunni forms. Models of activist Shi'a politics were provided not only by the revolutionary Islamic regime of Iraq but also by the Hizbollah para-military movement in Lebanon. Radical Sunni political activists are found throughout the Middle East, North Africa, and in pockets of sub-Saharan Africa as well.

Lebanon, Syria, and Jordan

In Lebanon, Shi'ite and Christian allegiances have defined the nation's major political factions, each claiming to represent a true Lebanese nationalism. The Hizbollah party was founded in 1982 as a resistance movement against Israeli incursions into the southern parts of the country. It was responsible for a series of acts of terrorism, including suicide attacks on Israel and the bombing of the U.S. Marine barracks in Beirut in 1983. After the end of Lebanon's civil war in 1990, the movement continued to maintain its radical opposition to the state of Israel at the same time that it enlisted broad public support from the Shi'a minority in Lebanon. It created a network of social services and a parliamentary political wing. In 2006, its leader, Sheik Hassan Nasrallah, instigated the kidnapping of two Israeli soldiers along the Lebanon-Israeli border, to which Israel responded with a major military offensive. The United States, charging that Hizbollah was supported by Iran and Syria, backed Israel in the hope of diminishing the influence of these two rivals to American power in the region. After the withdrawal of Israeli troops in August 2006, the movement declared victory and resurfaced with even greater public support than before. Hizbollah protests since then appear to be aimed at tearing apart Lebanon's fragile ethnic alliances and creating a new government dominated by Hizbollah and its Syrian allies.

In Syria, the government has been under fire from Sunni Islamic activists opposed to the Ba'ath Party's socialist ideology and its attempts to accommodate Christians and other minority groups, including the Shi'ite Alawite community that produced the country's ruling family.[128] They challenged the secular politics of the Alawite president Hafez al-Assad and al-Assad's successor, his son Bashar, whom they have accused of "gross corruption, brutal repression of dissent, collusion with Zionism and imperialism, and sectarianism."[129]

In Jordan, where the Heshemite royal family has presided over a modern Muslim regime ever since the country was created out of the remnants of the Ottoman Empire in 1921, radical religious movements have arisen from time to time to punctuate the political calm. After Israel and the independent nation of Jordan were created out of the British Mandate of Palestine, hundreds of thousands of Palestinian refugees flooded into Jordanian territory. Even more arrived after the 1967 Arab-Israeli war, and in 1970 the struggle between Palestinian activists and the Jordanian government—known as Black September—resulted in thousands killed, primarily on the Palestinian side. The religious transformation of one wing of the Palestinian movement in Gaza and the West Bank affected the Palestinian refugee activism in Jordan as well. The reaction against U.S. policy in the region, beginning with the Gulf War, also fueled Muslim activism in the country. In 1991, members of the Muslim Brotherhood secured the largest single bloc in the Jordan parliament in elections. Since then, even more extreme Muslim groups have threatened to destabilize the Jordanian government.[130] Some have been associated with the Jamaat al-Tawhid wa'l-Jihad (Unity and Jihad Group) founded by the Jordanian jihadi leader Abu Musab al-Zarqawi that was a major source of violence in post-Saddam Iraq. Iraqi activists loyal to al-Zarqawi perpetrated terrorist attacks on hotels in the heart of Jordan's capital, Amman, including a suicide bombing in November 2005 that killed fifty-four and injured hundreds.

Gulf States

Even in Saudi Arabia, Kuwait, and the other Gulf Emirates, where a kind of state Islamic culture prevails and Islamic law is observed, Muslim activists continue to threaten the status quo. In Saudi Arabia, even though the state protects the dominant conservative Wahhabi form of Islam, Muslim activists have lambasted the royal family and its alliance with the United States, and cassette tapes and CDs recording the radicals' fiery speeches have been distributed (illegally) by the thousands.[131] In 1996 a Saudi Hizbollah group destroyed a U.S. military housing complex in Khobar, and in 2003 activists said to be acting on instructions from Osama bin Laden's al Qaeda movement bombed a suburb of Riyadh, the Saudi capital, largely inhabited by Westerners. Several other attacks were carried out in Riyadh and Jeddah in the following year.

One of bin Laden's first acts of terrorism was a bombing in Yemen in 1992, directed at U.S. soldiers who fortunately had just checked out of the hotel that was targeted for attack. An al Qaeda attack on the USS *Cole* docked in the Yemeni harbor of Aden on October 12, 2000, killed seventeen U.S. sailors and injured more than thirty.

North Africa

In Sudan, across the Red Sea from Saudi Arabia, Islamic activism has been part of the political culture for decades. After 1989, when Lieutenant General Omar Hassan Ahmed Bashir established an Islamic regime in Sudan, thousands of young Muslim revolutionaries came to study in Sudanese universities and to train in its military camps.[132] Hassan Abdullah Turabi, the Islamic leader described as the "behind-the-scenes power" in Khartoum, was also mentioned as "one of the key architects" of Islamic movements in Algeria, Tunisia, Egypt, Ethiopia, Nigeria, Chad, and Afghanistan.[133] Even before Turabi's fall from power in 1999, however, the Sudanese government had begun to take a less stridently Muslim stance. It even cooperated with the United States in expelling Osama bin Laden from the country in 1996. Religious rhetoric continued to inform policies of the Sudanese state, however, especially with regard to the government's treatment of non-Arab ethnic minorities. These policies have been extremely repressive—genocidal, in fact—in southern Sudan and the region of Darfur.

Even during the most active years of Sudan's Islamic regime it is doubtful that its influence had a decisive political effect on other Islamic countries. The impetus toward Islamic politics is distinctively tied to each country's history and culture. In Algiers, for instance, when the Islamic Salvation Front in 1991 resoundingly defeated the party that had ruled Algeria since its independence from France in 1962, the Islamic leaders emulated the earlier independence movement and promised to fulfill it by giving Algeria "a firm beginning for building an Islamic state."[134] It was a short-lived promise, however, for in January 1992 the army annulled the elections and established a secular military junta, accomplishing, as the leader of a local mosque put it, "a *coup d'état* against the [Algerian] Islamic state before it was created."[135] Leaders of the Islamic Salvation Front were jailed, and a ban was imposed on meetings at mosques, which had become venues of protest and organization for the Islamic opposition. On March 5 the party was officially outlawed. Later that year, the standoff between the army and Muslim activists erupted into violence, and the Casbah in Algiers's Old City became an arena of guerrilla warfare reminiscent of Algeria's war of independence.[136] Hundreds of supporters of the Islamic Salvation Front were killed, and on June 29, 1992, Muhammad Boudiaf, the civilian head of the military-supported Council of State, was assassinated, allegedly by militant supporters of the Islamic Salvation Front.[137] Elections resumed in 1995, and by 2002 much of the Islamic resistance had been defeated or defused by an amnesty program aimed at reconciling dissident elements.

Islamic political movements have also been directed toward local and national concerns in other parts of North Africa. In neighboring Tunisia, the outlawed Islamic Renaissance Party and the Nahda movement mounted a serious challenge to the government.

In Somalia, an Islamic-based government established theocratic rule over most of the country for six months in 2006. The country had been in a state of political collapse since 1991, when a coalition of local warlords brought down the regime of President Siad Barre. The political turmoil of the country was exacerbated by a prolonged famine. When U.S. forces tried to protect United Nations relief operations in the country in 1993, they suffered significant casualties and the public specter of the bodies of American soldiers dragged through jeering crowds. The U.S. forces soon withdrew. Years later, Osama bin Laden would claim that his network had supported the Somalia anti-American insurgents. In 2004 a transitional federal government was established in Somalia—largely a coalition of warlords—supported by the United States. It was in this context that Islamic forces under leadership of the Islamic Courts Union (known also as the Somalia Islamic Courts Council [SICC]), said to be supported by al Qaeda, gained control of the capital, Mogadishu, in June 2006 and conquered much of the rest of the country shortly thereafter. Sharif Sheik Ahmed, the head of the council, became the leader of the country and imposed a religious dictatorship, although he claimed to be open to international relations with other countries. At the end of December 2006, Ethiopian forces—said to have been supported by the U.S. military—ousted the Islamic regime and reestablished the previously ensconced transitional federal government.

Morocco has been the site of a host of terrorist attacks, including a series of suicide bombings in 2007. In May 2003, a hotel, a restaurant and the Belgian consulate were badly damaged in Casablanca. Morocco's Prince Moulay Hicham told me that the organizers of these attacks were outsiders connected with the wider global jihad movement associated with al Qaeda (I discuss these attacks in that context in chapter 5).[138] In an effort to diffuse Muslim political organization in the country, the previous king of Morocco, Hassan II, had proclaimed himself "commander of believers" *(Amir al-Mouminin)*. Yet the group implicated in the recent acts, the Salafia Jihadia group, consists entirely of Moroccans. In addition to the fourteen militants who were killed in the

2003 attacks, another fifteen were convicted later that year, all from the southern Moroccan city of Agadir.

Morocco's Salafia Jihadia was founded in the early 1990s by fighters returning from Afghanistan. Their grievances are aimed not only at the American and European influence in the region but also at the Moroccan state. Most of the followers are recruited from poor neighborhoods of Morocco's urban areas.[139] Another group, al-Adl wal-Ihsan (Justice and Welfare Group), the largest Muslim political organization in Morocco, claims more than thirty thousand members. The founder, Sheik Abdessalam Yassine, is especially critical of the royal family, and the movement's spokesperson, Nadia Yassine, proclaims herself a feminist as well as an Islamist. The movement has been banned, though many of its members also support the moderate Muslim group, the Party of Justice and Development (PJD). The PJD received the largest number of votes in the September 2007 parliamentary elections.

Sub-Saharan Africa

In sub-Saharan Africa, religion and politics have been intertwined for most of Africa's history, even though there have been no significant attempts to overthrow the secular states of the continent and establish religious regimes.[140] Kings and chiefs in traditional African society claimed divine right to legitimize their rule. In Uganda, for instance, the Baganda people have traced their political origins to a divinely inspired king. The Yoruba people of Nigeria claim that their political ancestry is linked to a god, Oduduwa. The charismatic authority of many of the leaders of new religious movements in Africa has raised the possibility that they could become politically influential.

Though most Africans below the Sahara Desert are either Christian, observers of traditional African religious customs, or practitioners of a synthesis between the two, conversions to Islam are on the rise. The relations between the Muslim, Christian and traditional African communities are often tense. In Nigeria, for instance, where the northern part of the country is Muslim, efforts to impose *shari'a* law in the area have led to protests and confrontations by organized groups of Christian activists.

Some African Muslims have joined the global jihadi cause—including those Tanzanians and Kenyans involved in the 1998 United States embassy bombings in the capital cities of Dar es Salaam, Tanzania, and Nairobi, Kenya. Osama bin Laden's al Qaeda network was implicated in the planning of the attack. In 2002, a group of suicide bombers attacked a tourist hotel in Mombassa, Kenya, frequented by Israeli tourists, and surface-to-air missiles were fired at an airplane filled with Israeli tourists as it took off from the Mombassa airport. In this case the alleged perpetrators were from Somalia. Like the U.S. embassy bombings, the target was the presence of foreigners and not the secular state of Kenya or Tanzania.

During the late twentieth century, and extending into the beginning of twenty-first, Muslim political activism has been on the rise throughout the world, but the movements associated with it are not orchestrated by a central command, nor are their goals necessarily antithetical to national interests. Many Muslim activists are indeed nationalists: some support subnational, local, and ethnic entities, and a few favor a pan-Islamic federation of states. Most, however, are united in opposing the prospect of Western-style secular nationalism in the Middle East while espousing an Islamic nationalism of their own. Like religious activists elsewhere, they have criticized secular rule from a religious perspective: they employ religious language, leadership, and organization in their attempts to change it, and they hold up as their ideal the promise of a new religious order.

Each of the religious movements surveyed in this chapter opposed not only secular nationalism but also the compromise efforts of secular leaders. Each offered its own model of religious protest: the Shi'ite movement in Iran achieved a total revolution; the Sunni Muslim movement in Egypt combined violent extremism with nonviolent measures; the Israeli religious right attempted to move its nominally religious nation further in the direction of religious commitment; and Hamas and the jihadi wing of the Iraqi insurgency attempted to Islamicize what had been largely secular movements of resistance. Although the particular course that each movement has taken is distinctly its own, the diverse pattern of religious activism that they illustrate has been replicated in movements of religious activism throughout the world.

CHAPTER 3

Political Targets of Rebellion: South, Central, and Southeast Asia

The specter of Buddhist monks breaking up a peace rally in the capital of Sri Lanka and angry Hindu sadhus destroying a mosque in the northern Indian town of Ayodhya indicates the passion of religious activism in the region. But Asia is also a region in which Islamic political parties and Hindu nationalist movements have peacefully come to power. Perhaps more so than in the Middle East, religious activists in South, Central, and Southeast Asian have employed a great variety of strategies for change. Their targets have been at times traditional political parties, at other times the political process itself, and sometimes the political culture undergirding the process. This diversity characterizes the religious ferment in the region, especially the activities that are the focus of this chapter—Hindu and Sikh movements in India, Buddhist activists in Sri Lanka and Mongolia, and Islamic militants in Afghanistan, Central Asia, and Southeast Asia.

What is striking about these movements is that the union of religion and politics not only enhances the power of local political forces but also buttresses a new religious leadership; often its leaders are activists at odds with the traditional religious elite. Hence, the secular political targets of these movements help to consolidate religious identity and influence. The forms that these new religious politics have taken in Asia have been diverse: political parties have been formed in the name of religion, terrorist squads have attacked political and cultural targets, and constitutions have been amended or reformulated to accommodate religious rules. In India and Sri Lanka, the magnitude of the movements' following is staggering. India's Bharatiya Janata Party (BJP) is probably the largest religious nationalist movement in the world. Although its leaders do not usually advocate violence, members of other movements in the region do, and the level of religious violence in society at large is often intense: the number of political assassinations in the name of religion in South Asia rivals or exceeds that in the Middle East.

The cases that follow in this chapter are useful for understanding the variety of traditions that engender religious activism. In Asia, the new religious militants are Hindu, Christian, and Buddhist as well as Muslim. These cases also demonstrate the diverse ways in which their adherents have been politically involved: from militant guerrilla movements fomenting revolution to organized involvement in electoral politics. What these various kinds of religious politics have in common is a challenge to the legitimacy of the secular state.

RESURGENT ISLAM IN SOUTH AND CENTRAL ASIA

Afghanistan

The five-year reign of the Taliban in Afghanistan from 1996 to 2001 is a worst-case scenario of what can happen when religious politics prevail. The regime imposed draconian limitations on women's public roles, brutal forms of judicial punishment, and austere restrictions on popular culture. Women were not allowed to attend schools, limbs were chopped off for what many might regard as minor offences, and music and videos were banned.

Yet the Taliban is only the extreme of a spectrum of Islamic politics in Afghanistan that is more varied than the regime's hard-line policies would indicate. As in other parts of South and Central Asia, where Islamic political movements have flourished in the post–Cold War era, the movements have often clashed with one another as well as with their secular opponents.

The Taliban was one of several contending Islamic parties in the aftermath of the fall of the Soviet-backed regime that had ruled the country since the Saur Revolution brought a Socialist government to power in Afghanistan in 1978. After a long and debilitating struggle against the Islamic resistance forces—the *mujahadin* ("fighters")—the Soviet Union withdrew its support for the regime of Mohammad Najibullah in 1989. His government was soon toppled. Individuals who had come to join the mujahadin from throughout the Muslim world returned to their own countries and to expatriate communities in Europe and the United States, having been trained in guerrilla warfare and fired with rebellious zeal. Some became terrorists of the new jihadi struggle against the secular governments backed by Europe and the United States and changed the course of international relations.

The mujahadin forces transformed Afghanistan's politics. Shortly after April 25, 1992, when Kabul, the capital of Afghanistan, fell to Islamic guerrilla fighters associated with the Jamiat-i-Islami (Islamic Society), the Hezb-i-Islami (Islamic Party), and other rebel cadres allied to or sympathetic with the *mujahadin,* the country was proclaimed an Islamic republic, and the crowds in the streets roared their approval with the cry *Allahu akbar:* "God is great."[1] The Muslim rebels had been supported by the United States, which considered them freedom fighters opposed to communist rule. From the rebels' point of view, they were trying to oust a secular regime that had been propped up by foreign forces. Ultimately they succeeded. In their mind, Islam had won.

Burhanuddin Rabbani, an ethnic Tajik, was installed as the president of the Islamic Council of Afghanistan while rival Muslim groups continued to struggle for power from 1992 to 1996. The new government began a process of Islamicizing the Afghan legal code: it promulgated a laws enforcing Muslim customs, including a ban on alcohol, a requirement that women wear veils in public, and the use of flogging, amputations, and other violent forms of punishment prescribed by Islamic law.[2]

Militia supporting rival warlords represented the different ethnic factions within the country. Gulbuddin Hekmatyar, who served as prime minister for a time, was a member of the largest ethnic group, the Pashtuns (also known as Pathans), and General Abdul Rashid Dustom was an Uzbek. The other major Tajik leader was Ahmed Shah Massoud, who together with Rabbini led what came to be known as the Northern Alliance. Though the groups battled intensely with one another, all were conservative Muslims and maintained strict standards of traditional behavior.

In the midst of this civil strife, an even more conservative religious group became militarized and seized the reigns of power. The name of this group, the Taliban, means "student," alluding to the origins of the movement among young men who had attended madrassas, or Muslim schools, in the Pashtun-dominated areas of southern and eastern Afghanistan and of the Baluchistan, Waziristan, and North-West Frontier provinces of Pakistan. The leader of the movement, Mullah Mohammed

Omar, came from a village near Kandahar, attended a madrassa, and served as a mullah. He had lost an eye in the resistance against the Soviet occupation of Afghanistan. He is said to have never flown on a plane and was uneasy around foreigners.

Though the Taliban was best known outside of Afghanistan for its religious conservatism, the main differences between it and the other religiously conservative groups in the country, such as the Northern Alliance headed by Massoud, were ethnic. Massoud and most of his followers were Tajik, and Mullah Omar and his Taliban cadres were Pashtun. Mullah Omar was also distinguished by his military manpower, rumored to have been supplemented by Pakistan intelligence operatives. By 1995 Taliban forces had captured Kabul, and in 1996 most of the country was under their control. In 1997 Omar renamed the country the Islamic Emirate of Afghanistan. By August 1998 almost all of the remaining outposts of opposition in northern Afghanistan had come under his power, though the Tajik forces of the Northern Alliance led by Massoud fought on.[3] Massoud's armies were at the forefront of the U.S.-based military conquest of the Taliban in 2001, though Massoud himself had been killed, most likely by Osama bin Laden's cadres, shortly before the September 11, 2001, attacks on the World Trade Center and the Pentagon.

When the Taliban first came to power in Kabul they did not adapt easily to modern urban life. The young leaders displayed the trappings and organization of their brigand past. They wore the traditional clothing of their rural homelands and treated the modern city of Kabul as if it were a village. Their leader, Mullah Omar, refused to live in the capital, preferring his village home near Kandehar. Adopting an even stricter interpretation of Islamic law than most of the Kabul clergy, the Taliban leaders barred women from attending school or working, even as nurses and doctors in mixed-gender hospitals or as teachers in all-female schools. Cinema, videos, and popular music were banned. Crimes such as petty theft were punished by the amputation of a hand, and rape and murder by public execution. The punishments were carried out as public spectacles in the former soccer stadium.

Not surprisingly, the Taliban never won the hearts of most Afghanis, not even the traditional Muslim clergy, who were largely marginalized by the regime. After the September 11, 2001, attacks, when the United States government accused the Taliban of harboring al Qaeda terrorists, a convention of the country's religious leaders seemed ambivalent about the Taliban's support for al Qaeda, and asked Osama bin Laden and his Saudi retinue to leave the country. When the U.S. military attacked

Afghanistan several days later, and the combined efforts of American military air strikes and the revived forces of the Northern Alliance caused the Taliban regime to crumble at the end of 2001, it was clear that very few Afghanis had risen to defend the Taliban government. Even members of the Taliban's own ethnic community, the Pashtuns, celebrated.

The new government that came to power through democratic elections, headed by Hamid Karzai, was considerably less strict than the Taliban. In the cities women were able to return to school and employment, and films and music were again broadcast and sold in stores. Many elements of conservative religious influence remained, however, and in time the Taliban regained some of its strength in the southern and western regions of the country. Many Afghanis began to regard Karzai and the American forces that supported him as new incarnations of the secular Soviet-supported puppet regime that they had ousted before. Hence, the specter of militant Islamic resistance has continued to haunt Afghanistan.

Pakistan

Pakistan had been one of only three countries to recognize the Taliban government (the others were Saudi Arabia and the United Arab Emirates). Pakistan had provided the regime with financial support, and some say that agents of Pakistan's intelligence forces had been in collusion with Taliban leaders.[4] But after the attacks of September 11, 2001, when the United States accused the Taliban of harboring Osama bin Laden and housing the headquarters of his al Qaeda organization, Pakistan's president, Pervez Musharraf, consented to the American military invasion and occupation of Afghanistan. Some observers thought that Musharraf was motivated by a desire not only to destroy the Taliban, which had become an erratic and dangerous neighbor, but also to undercut its support for the extreme wing of Islamic political parties in Pakistan, which was potentially a threat to Musharraf's power and the country's stability.[5]

In Pakistan, Islamic parties such as the Jamaat-i-Islami, Jami'at al' Ulama-i-Islam (Party of the Community of Islam) and Jami'at al' Ulama-i-Pakistan (Party of the Community of Pakistan) were challenged by even more extreme Islamic political groups, including a virulent coalition in Pakistan's Punjab region: the Islami Jamhoori Ittehad (Islamic Democratic Front), which opposed Benazir Bhutto's brief rule and was a critical factor in her electoral defeat in 1990. Since then, Islamization has become a major aspect of politics in Pakistan. The Islamic legal code, the *shari'a*, has been proclaimed the law of the land; secular civil laws have been repealed.

Nonetheless Pakistan is not yet the Islamic country envisioned by its most influential Islamic political theorist, Sayyid Abdul A'la Maududi, usually referred to as Maulana Maududi. The leading Islamic party in Pakistan, the Jamaat-i-Islami, was created by Maududi in 1941, years before the country was established as part of the legacy of the British extrication from colonial rule of the Indian subcontinent. When the region was partitioned into India and Pakistan (Pakistan's eastern wing later seceded and became the country of Bangladesh), Maududi opposed the creation of Pakistan as a secular state, arguing that the very concept was foreign to the Islamic political tradition. Yet when the nation came into being, Maududi and his Jamaat-i-Islami party focused on the internal politics of the nation and what he regarded as the necessity for an Islamic state.

Though the Jamaat-i-Islami remains the most influential Islamic party in Pakistan, it is only one of several.[6] Power struggles within the Jamaat-i-Islamiya, compounded with ideological differences, resulted in the rise of many new parties, including the Muttahida Qaumi Movement (MQM), founded by radical Muslim students at the University of Karachi in 1978. It drew its support from the *mohajir*, immigrants from India. Rumors floated that the movement was supported initially by Pakistan's secretive Directorate for Inter-Services Intelligence (ISI) to undercut the political support for Prime Minister Benazir Bhutto in the state of Sindh. Since its founding, the MQM has been accused of carrying out terrorist incidents, including political assassinations in Sindh in 1992. Hundreds of death were blamed on the government's heavy-handed crackdown on the MQM in 1996. The revived MQM has moderated its tactics, and in 2005 it won a majority of seats in the Karachi municipal elections. After the 2001 invasion of Afghanistan, it generally supported Musharraf's position on the war on terrorism. In 2007, however, members of the MQM movement were accused of fomenting riots in Karachi against rival political and religious groups.

After September 11, 2001, and President Musharraf's declaration of support for U.S. policy on terrorism, the Jamaat-i-Islami took a strong stand against the U.S.-led invasion of Afghanistan and enjoyed a revival in its popularity. The movement was at the center of a coalition of Islamic parties opposing Musharraf. In the legislative elections of Pakistan on October 20, 2002, Jamaat-i-Islami received 11.3 percent of the popular vote and seated 53 of 272 elected members of the national assembly. Opposition to Musharraf and what was perceived to be his pro-U.S. stance deepened in 2007 after a bloody confrontation between government security forces and radical Muslim clerics and students at Islamabad's Red Mosque. The leading cleric at the mosque, Abdul Rashid Ghazi, had openly announced his support of the Taliban and Osama bin Laden, and many of the students in the schools and seminaries located in the mosque compound came from Taliban-influenced Pashtun tribal areas of Waziristan along the Afghanistan border. Invoking the fear of terrorism and the specter of religious rebellion, Musharraf established emergency rule in November 2007, precipitating a constitutional crisis that anticipated the end of his regime. The wave of opposition surged after the assassination of his political rival, Benazir Bhutto, at the end of the year. Radical religious organizations capitalized on the political insecurity of the country. As in other instances around the world, the harsh measures used to combat terrorism paradoxically created fertile grounds for the violence that the extra-legal measures were meant to quell.

Kashmir

The Jamaat-i-Islami and other militant Islamic groups in Pakistan have been accused of trying to export their ideologies to Islamic revolutionaries in Kashmir and nearby Central Asian states. The princely state of Kashmir has been a thorn in the side of Indian and Pakistani relations ever since the two independent states were created from the remnants of the British Empire in 1948.[7] At that time the British had let each state decide whether it would be affiliated with the Muslim-majority Pakistan or the Hindu-majority India. Kashmir was a difficult case, in part because the state's ruler was a Hindu maharaja and the population divided among Muslims and Hindus. Control of Kashmir was sought by both Pakistan and India—not only because of its beauty and its historical significance, but also because of its strategic location at the intersection of India, Pakistan, China, Afghanistan, and the Central Asian states associated with the Soviet Union. Almost immediately after Pakistan and India's independence, fighting broke out between Indian and Pakistani forces. A tenuous line of ceasefire was established, dividing Kashmir; it has been patrolled by United Nations peacekeeping forces ever since.

Despite the ceasefire, discontent has simmered on the Indian side of Kashmir for many years, especially among members of the Muslim majority population, who feel marginalized by New Delhi's increasingly

Hindu political posture. Over the years, a movement for independence has developed on the Indian side of Kashmir—or rather, several movements, which often quarrel with one another. Some seek a united Kashmir, independent of both Pakistan and India. Others—allegedly promoted by Pakistani forces—seek a united Kashmir associated with Pakistan. Still others, said to be encouraged by al Qaeda, see themselves as part of a global jihadi movement.

The insurgency broke out in the open in 1989. Some claimed that it had a distinctly religious cast from the beginning, influenced by the large number of mujahadin from Afghanistan who took up the Kashmiri cause after the end of the Soviet-Afghan war. The government of India claimed that Pakistan harbored the militants and supported them, though Pakistan denied any direct support, accusing the Indian army of human rights abuses in its heavy-handed measures to counter the insurgency. Tensions between secularists and Muslim militants have surfaced within the Kashmiri independence movement.

In 1993, a report by a committee of the U.S. House of Representatives claimed that members of one of Kashmir's most militant Islamic movements, the Hizbul Mujahadin, were supported by Pakistan's Jama'at-i Islamiya party, "from which they receive funding, weapons and training assistance" in addition to that allegedly provided by the Pakistan government's secret intelligence agency, the Directorate for Inter-Services Intelligence (ISI).[8] According to other reports, the ISI encouraged the creation of the Hizbul Mujahideen as the Kashmiri wing of the Jama'at-i Islamiya in order to counter the influence of the leading militant separatist movement, the Jammu and Kashmir Liberation Front, which longed for the Indian side of Kashmir to be a separate country, rather than to unite with Pakistan, as the Hizbul Mujahadin preferred.

The presence of al Qaeda operatives in neighboring Afghanistan was said to have encouraged the movement to take a more militant, pro-Islamic direction. After the attacks of September 11 and the U.S. invasion of Afghanistan, Pakistan's government pledged to help rein in the Muslim militants in Kashmir. This pledge was renewed after a terrorist attack on the Indian Parliament on December 13, 2001, allegedly perpetrated by militant Muslim supporters of the movements for Kashmiri separatism. Peace negotiations between India and Pakistan resulted in a ceasefire on November 26, 2003, followed by increased communication between the two countries and renewed cooperation in economic areas. India and Pakistan cooperated even more closely after the 2005

Kashmir earthquake, which killed over 80,000. Both countries opened roads previously barred to aid in the disaster relief.

The militant Muslim supporters of the Kashmiri cause watched the mounting rapprochement between Pakistan and India with suspicion. They launched new terrorist acts in India, and were blamed for bombings in Delhi on October 29, 2005, and a catastrophic attack on the Mumbai train system on July 11, 2006. Seven bomb blasts took place over a period of eleven minutes on the suburban railway in India's financial capital, resulting in 207 dead and over seven hundred injured. Muslim extremists from the Islamic separatist movement, Lashkar-e-Toiba, and the banned Students Islamic Movement of India initially were implicated, but evidence also showed the involvement of international jihadi operations linked to al Qaeda. A telephone call to the government from someone claiming to be associated with the transnational movement gave India's treatment of Muslim minorities, including the Kashmiri separatists, as the reason for the attack.[9] Thus the Kashmir political issue was framed increasingly within the context of global jihad and the contest between the Islamic and non-Islamic world.

Bangladesh

Muslim groups and parties have been a significant feature of Bangladesh's political dynamics for more than a quarter century. Bangladesh was a part of the new nation of Pakistan, which was created in 1947 out of the Indian subcontinent, and like the western wing of Pakistan, its political parties were initially largely secular. After the eastern wing of Pakistan seceded from the union in a bloody civil war in 1971 and changed its name to Bangladesh, it faced many of the internal political tensions as the western wing, which after 1971 became known simply as Pakistan. Mounting pressure from Islamic political parties forced the government to emulate Pakistan and publicly endorse the identity of Bangladesh as an Islamic state.[10]

The largest of the several Islamic political parties in Bangladesh is the Jamaat-e Islami Bangladesh, which is a partner of the similarly named parties in India and Pakistan, all of which trace their origins to the formative Islamic political thinker Maulana Maududi, who was born in India and emigrated to Pakistan after the partition of the subcontinent into India and Pakistan in 1947. In the 2001 elections, the Jamaat-e Islami Bangladesh won 7.5 percent of the votes, which gave them seventeen seats in the three-hundred-member national assembly.

More important than their representation in the national assembly, however, has been the ability of the Jamaat-e Islami Bangladesh and other Islamic parties, such as the Islami Oikya Jot, to play a pivotal role in forming coalition governments in the absence of a majority among either of the two major national parties—the Bangladesh Nationalist Party (BNP) and the Bangladesh Awami League. In general the Islamic parties have favored the BNP.

The Jamaat-e Islami Bangladesh played a critical role in bringing to power the BNP coalition government in 1991 led by Begum Khaleda Zia, the widow of General Ziaur Rahman (popularly known as Zia), who instituted a military coup in 1975 that was legitimized through general elections in 1978, and who ruled until his assassination in 1991. He was succeeded by his widow, Khaleda Zia, until the 1996 elections, when the opposition Awami League and its coalition (led by another woman, Sheik Hasina) came to power. In the 2001 elections, the BNP coalition, led by Khaleda Zia and supported by the Jamaat-e Islami Bangladesh, returned to power.

The Jamaat-e Islami Bangladesh has attempted to use its political muscle to encourage the government to adopt conservative religious standards for society and to proclaim Islamic *shari'a* as the basis of the nation's law. In the years immediately following the 1971 independence struggle with Pakistan, their influence was muted due to the fact that many of the organization's top leadership supported Pakistan in resisting the secession efforts. Gradually their reputation and influence have improved, especially in the post-2001 climate of Islamic activism throughout the Muslim world, when their Islamic political ideology appeared to be part of a global trend. Members of the Jamaat-e Islami Bangladesh have been accused of fomenting demonstrations and acts of terrorism against symbols of American power in the country. Many alleged terrorists have been members of the student wing of the party, the Islami Chhatra Shibir.[11]

Even more radical Islamist parties, the Jagrata Muslim Janata Bangladesh and Jama'atul Mujahideen Bangladesh, have been blamed for a proliferation of other attacks. The parties were banned in February 2005, and hundreds of suspected members were detained. The first recorded case of a suicide bomb attack in Bangladesh took place in November 2005, when a series of bombs aimed at judges, courts, and journalists killed ten. Members of the Jama'atul Party were implicated. In

2006 the heads of both of the extremist Muslim parties were placed under arrest.

Central Asia

The models of radical politics offered by the Taliban and the religious extremists of Pakistan and Bangladesh were also considered a threat in the capitals of the Central Asian republics—Uzbekistan, Turkmenistan, Kazakhstan, Tajikistan, and Kyrgyzstan—and in areas of Islamic influence west of the Caspian Sea, including Azerbaijan and three of Russia's federal territories: Dagestan, Tatarstan, and Chechnya. Rebels in Chechnya have been waging a separatist struggle against the Russian army since 1991, and although it has largely been a movement of ethnic nationalism, the Islamic character of Chechan society has made it susceptible to militant Muslim influences.[12] The only government to have recognized the Chechen Republic as a separate nation was Afghanistan's Taliban in 2000, shortly before it was toppled by the U.S.-supported military invasion. Allegations have been made of connections between Islamic radicals and the Chechen mafia, one of the most powerful criminal gangs operating in the region.

A rise of Islamic rhetoric in association with the Chechnya separatist movement began in 2002. Attempts have been made both within and outside the region to link the Chechnya struggle to a wider confrontation: the global contest between Islamic politics and Western-style nationalism. Even the pro-Moscow leadership in Chechnya felt it necessary to proclaim its adherence to Islamic values, and during the Danish cartoon incident in 2005 it decried the Danish government's support of the cartoonists. Many militant Muslims, including Osama bin Laden, have proclaimed the Chechan independence movement as an Islamic cause.

The major force of Islamic power in the post-Soviet region has been elsewhere, however: in Central Asia, in the "-stans" that constituted the Soviet Central Asian region. Everything that the Muslim rebels in Afghanistan said about the secular and communist takeover of Afghanistan could be said about these Central Asian countries.[13] Like the Afghan government, the Central Asian governments had been backed by a Soviet military and economic power that was imperial in its attitudes and designs. As in Afghanistan, groups of Muslim nationalists in each of the Central Asian republics and Russian Muslim regions were eager to take the secular leaders' place and create Islamic states.[14] The new Central

Asian secular leaders—many of them former communists—were concerned about the rise of new movements aimed at reviving Central Asia's Islamic political power.[15]

The fears of the secular leaders were warranted. Less than two weeks after the fall of the socialist government in Kabul in 1992, a coalition of democratic politicians and Muslim activists formed a revolutionary council in Tajikistan and seized power in Dushanbe, the capital. On May 7, 1992, the old Communist leader, Rakhman Nabiyev, barricaded himself inside the KGB headquarters, and the new leaders proclaimed Tajikistan a democratic Muslim state. Again, as in Kabul, the crowds roared in response the slogan *Allahu akbar,* "God is great."[16]

The vast region of Central Asia southeast of Moscow is home to some fifty million Muslims. These Muslims were all but ignored by the outside world during the heyday of the Soviet Union, even though their numbers made the Soviet Union the fifth-largest Muslim nation in the world (following Indonesia, Pakistan, Bangladesh, and India). Although each of the countries has its own identity—and its own cultural nationalism— the region as a whole is a part of an area known as Turkestan, which briefly in the pre-Soviet era was a nation of its own (not to be confused with Turkmenistan, which is only one of the present-day Central Asian nations). Some Islamic nationalists in the region see the revival of the nation of Turkestan as the wave of the future. The cultural area known as Turkestan reached beyond the boundaries of the five countries currently in Central Asia—the Xinjiang region of China, for instance, is known as East Turkestan—so the attempt to revive the nation would have international implications.

"In my lifetime," the founder of Uzbekistan's Islamic political movement, Birlik (Unity), claimed, "there will be a Turkestan that extends beyond Central Asia."[17] Other Muslim leaders in Kazakhstan and Uzbekistan are said to dream of a Central Asian empire united by an Islamic radicalism. In the Uzbekistan capital of Tashkent, the senior Muslim cleric of Central Asia proposed dismantling the borders of the separate states and reviving Turkestan once again.[18] Although Turkestan was only briefly a political entity, the idea of it remains a powerful image of Central Asian unity.

Religious nationalism in Central Asia is thus really two issues. One is whether Muslim nationalists within each of the five Central Asian nations have sufficient force to challenge the secular order—the order that is often led by old communists who have adopted a new, secular democratic posture. The other is whether the various religious nationalists in the region will be able to come together under a common banner, even if it is a loose federation of states.

Both these forms of religious nationalism and regionalism are fueled by a strong anticommunism. The deep disdain for communism in the region is in part a result of its repression of Islam, in part the result (despite Lenin's policy of divide and rule), of communism's painting over traditional ethnic identities with the same gray Soviet brush and in part the perception of Marxist ideology as a cover for Russian imperialism. Thus the region's antisecularism is to a large degree a protest against the years of what is regarded as Russian colonial rule.

In a newly opened *madrassa* in the old Muslim capital of Bukhara in Uzbekistan, several students made explicit the link between communism and Russian colonialism. In Soviet days, they explained, the dead could not be buried in a shroud. "Why is it communist to be buried in a coffin," one of them asked, "but not in a shroud?"[19] The same pattern of prejudice was to be seen in the restrictions on married women covering their heads, the outlawing of circumcision, and the encouragement to eat pork. "As is well known," one of the students said sarcastically, "pork is socialist, while *pilaf* [a Central Asian rice dish] is not."[20]

Among other reasons, the Uzbek students, as well as many other citizens of Central Asian nations, abhorred Russian colonialism because their own Altaic cultural and ethnic heritage is tied to Turkey (and Iran, in the case of Tajikistan) rather than to Russia. At one time, in fact, Central Asia was the cultural seat of an Islamic empire that controlled Russia, and the history of the region is clouded by the competition for dominion between Turkic Muslims in the south and Christian Russians in the north. In the early centuries of the common era, the kingdom that the ancient Greeks knew as Bactria fell under a variety of influences from the west and south. Along the Silk Road, which flowed through India and the Middle East, were Buddhists, Zoroastrians, Manicheans, and Nestorian Christians. The cultural identity of Central Asia was affected by all of them.

Islam also came to the region from the southwest, arriving from the Middle East in the seventh century.[21] By 639 C.E. Arabs had conquered Azerbaijan, and by 642 Dagestan was Arab territory. In 673, the Arabs crossed the Amu Darya River and laid siege to the city of Bukhara, now in Uzbekistan. During the first decades of the next century the conquests were completed, although it took several hundred years for Islam to take root among the Central Asian people. From the ninth to the sixteenth century, Central Asia's largest cities were among Islam's most prestigious cultural centers. The city of Samarkand—today in Uzbekistan—flourished during the Abbasid dynasty, and the great mosques and madrassas of Samarkand and Bukhara were Islam's easternmost outpost. From there, Islam traveled north along the Volga River, and east via the Silk Road into China. Although the region fell under the hegemony of the Mongol Empire in the thirteenth and fourteenth centuries, the Buddhist Mongols were not able to shake the Central Asians' dedication to Islam, which survived in part through Sufi brotherhoods and lay activities. In the late fourteenth century, Mongol sovereigns of the Golden Horde and the Chagatai Khanate had become Muslim themselves, and Islam again flourished throughout Central Asia and beyond. From the thirteenth to the sixteenth century, Russia was under Tatar domination—and to this day Russia is the only major Christian nation besides Spain to have been under prolonged Muslim rule.

In the mid-fourteenth century, Moscow began to fight back against the Golden Horde, and by the sixteenth century the Russians were sufficiently free from external domination to attempt to purge the region of Muslim influence. From 1565 on, Muslims began to be forcibly converted to Christianity. The major departure from this anti-Muslim policy of Russian rulers was taken by Catherine II, who in the eighteenth century protected the Volga River Tatars from persecution and encouraged the spread of Islam in the outlying regions, where, she felt, it helped to civilize such people as the Bashkir and Kazakhs. Most areas of Central Asia, including the regions around Chimkent, Tashkent, and Bukhara, were brought under Russian control in the latter half of the nineteenth century, but there was no significant attempt to Christianize or Russify the population at that time. The region became known as Russian Turkestan.[22]

After the Bolshevik Revolution, leaders of the region's territories sought freedom from Russian control, and in 1918 they declared a new state, the Turkestan Independent Islamic Republic. Needless to say, the new Communist government had no intention of letting any republic in the union, much less an Islamic one, remain autonomous, and by 1925 the independence movement was crushed. The region became firmly a part of the Soviet Union, and Russian Turkestan was split into the five republics of Soviet Central Asia.[23]

Initially, many Muslim leaders joined the Communist cause, but after 1928, when antireligious policies were promulgated throughout the Soviet Union, Islam and Marxism parted ways, and Muslim clergy were imprisoned. During the Second World War, when Stalin relaxed his repression of religion, Islam experienced a temporary revival. From 1959 to 1964, however, Khrushchev's offensive against religion was a serious blow to Central Asian Islam. The number of mosques dropped to fewer than five hundred in 1968—from more than six thousand in 1912. From 1982 to 1985, Central Asian Muslims suffered yet another wave of anti-Islamic sentiment because of the Soviet Union's war in Afghanistan. The end of the war and Mikhail Gorbachev's presidency in 1985 brought significant changes. From 1988 on, Islam underwent an enormous revival throughout Central Asia, spurred on by the breakup of the Soviet Union and the creation of new independent states in Central Asia in 1991–92.[24]

The expansion of Islam after 1988 was built on an Islamic organizational framework created during the Soviet era. During the 1940s, two spiritual directorates were created to lead Muslim religious organizations throughout the Soviet Union. One was established in Ufa (in Bashkir) to cover European Russia, and the other in Tashkent (in Uzbekistan) for Central Asia. A few years later, two more directorates were created: one in Baku (in Azerbaijan) for Transcaucasia (administering both Sunni and Shi'a congregations), and another in Makhachkala (in Dagestan) for the northern Caucasus region. Each of these directorates was led by a mufti—or, in the case of Baku, a sheikh. The mufti of Tashkent was the de facto leader of them all. In 1956 a *madrassa* was opened in Bukhara, in Uzbekistan; and in 1971 another was opened in Tashkent.

By 1992, the revival of Islam had turned into a torrent of new Islamic activities: the establishment of mosques, seminaries, Islamic courts, and political parties. In Uzbekistan in 1988 there were only eighty mosques in the whole of the country. By the end of 1991 there were several thousand—over a thousand in one of the country's twelve regions alone. According to some estimates, on average ten new mosques were opened every day in 1991 throughout Central Asia.[25]

The official spiritual directorates, however, have not fared well in this revival. In Tashkent, a new chief mufti of the directorate developed a television show in 1990 to promote Islamic teachings,[26] but he was accused of selling for profit some of the one million Qur'ans that had been donated to his office by Saudi Arabia for free distribution.[27] His fellow mullahs attempted to oust him from office, and the *qazi* of Almaty in Kazakhstan defied his authority and declared himself the nation's grand mufti.[28] The Communist government in Uzbekistan, fearing the rise of more militant new Islamic leaders, kept the Tashkent mufti in office.

Government support, however, did little to shore up his credibility among the masses, who already regarded many of the old-guard Muslim officials as colonial Russian errand-boys.

A Muslim leader in Tajikistan referred to the efforts of the secular government—led by reformed Communist leaders—to keep Islamic political parties from seizing power as an "ideological struggle" between Islam and communism.[29] Indeed, Islam poses a serious threat to the secular governments of Central Asian nations, for without the ideological underpinnings of Marxist theory and the military and economic support of the Soviet Union, they have little on which to base their political authority. Some of the former Communists have turned to nationalism as a basis of support, but the boundaries of the five nations of Central Asia were loosely drawn and encompass a variety of ethnicities. For that reason it is difficult to establish what is specifically Uzbek about Uzbekistan, for example, as opposed to what is Tajik or Kyrgyz.

Islam appears to unite all Central Asians, though there are variations in the pattern. National identities are linked to particular forms of religious identities—Shi'ite, Sunni, Sufi—all of them Muslim. Even some of the old Communists claim to have renewed their affiliations with their Muslim heritage. "In the past," a Muslim leader in Kyrgyzstan complained, "they lectured on atheism, but now they wear turbans and have become mullahs."[30] Most Islamic leaders in the region were Muslims before they became politicians, however, and their religious politics are extensions of their anti-Communist and anti-Russian attitudes. Most are also ethnic nationalists, and they are not necessarily rushing to re-create the old, united Turkestan. Instead, the Muslim activists of Central Asia have attempted to use their new political power to build a nationalist constituency in each of the five emerging nation-states.

In Uzbekistan, the most populous country in the region, the government has taken the threat of Islamic activists seriously and from its inception as a post-Soviet nation banned all religiously based political parties from participating in elections.[31] Although Uzbekistan's president, Islom Karimov, sought Muslim support by allying himself with the discredited head mufti of Tashkent, the Muslim masses largely rejected this attempt at cooptation. Instead, many supported the popular Birlik (Unity) movement, which regarded itself as an Islamic democratic movement, and the Islamic Renaissance Party, which called for the creation of an Islamic republic. According to one of its members, it sought to establish "a theocratic state run by the clergy" but also insisted that it, like the Birlik Movement, favors "an Islamic democracy."[32] Since the 1970s, underground Islamic groups have been organizing against the government, but they remained outlawed until the end of the Soviet Union in 1991, when independent Uzbekistan relaxed the ban slightly, allowing the Birlik Movement and other groups to register as religious—but not political—organizations. The government still prohibited it and the Islamic Renaissance Party from running candidates for office. For that matter, Uzbekistan banned all clergy of whatever faith from running for office regardless of which party endorsed them.

Between 2000 and 2002, thousands of suspected members of the most extreme Muslim movement in Uzbekistan, the Hizb ut-Tahrir, were rounded up and jailed as political prisoners. The movement was the largest jihadi organization in Central Asia until its members were decimated in their efforts to support the Taliban following the 2001 United States military invasion of Afghanistan. The group survived, however, and provided training camps for international jihadi activists.[33] In May 2005, hundreds of Muslim protesters were killed by police in political demonstrations organized by Islamic groups in the city of Andijan. The government of Uzbekistan seemed determined to prohibit the kind of Islamic rebellion that erupted in nearby Tajikistan and led to a virtual civil war between 1992 and 1997.

In Tajikistan during the Soviet era Islamic political parties were banned.[34] The Communist leader, Rakhman Nabiyev, a party boss during the Brezhnev era who was edged out of power in 1985, returned to leadership in 1990 and was again hounded out of office in September 1991—this time by means of public demonstrations in front of the parliament involving the building of a tent city with materials supplied by the central mosque. Two months later open elections allowed a variety of parties, including some Islamic groups, to contend for the first time: among these were the secular Democratic movement, a moderate Muslim movement known simply as the Renaissance, and Tajikistan's version of the radical Islamic Renaissance movement. The Islamic Renaissance received support from militant mujahadin leaders across the border in neighboring Afghanistan.[35] Despite accusations of voter fraud, Nabiyev was re-elected by a 57 percent majority; some election observers speculated that his victory was the result of a deal with the Islamic parties.[36] Whether he did or not, the Muslim politicians were biding their time for a more propitious moment to strike for political power.

Their time came in May 1992, with a wave of public demonstrations against the government. A Muslim guerrilla band was formed to counter the Tajik army, and a majority of Nabiyev's own Council of Ministers abandoned him for the opposition. The triumphant rebel coalition, led by the Islamic Renaissance Party and secular democrats, hastily formed a revolutionary council. But as the year wore on, the confrontation between Islam and Communism grew into a civil war in the southern part of the country.

The Islamic revolution in Tajikistan turned out to be short-lived. By December 1992, pro-communist leaders associated with the Kulyab region took control and purged the capital of Islamic political activists. In 1993 the backlash against the Islamic opposition was so violent that Muslim leaders, fleeing to Russia and Afghanistan, described it as "genocide."

One of the key leaders in Tajikistan's brief Islamic revolution was Qazi Hajji Akbar Turadqhonqoda, a thirty-seven-year-old activist who operated out of his office in the main mosque of Dushanbe with a cell phone and a fax machine.[37] A pragmatist, the qazi stated that although Islam would play a role in the new government, it would be a limited one; he did not want Tajikistan to become a new Iran. Even though Tajiks are ethnically linked with Persians, the qazi explained, they are Sunni rather than Shi'a, which means that it is "very difficult for a Khomeini-style figure to impose his views on everyone else."[38] Moreover, he said, he wanted to work in harmony with "the entire free world."[39] On an earlier occasion he explained that he did not want "the same thing to happen to the Islamic revolution that happened to the Communist revolution." By that, he meant that he did not want his state to become "isolated" from the rest of the world.[40]

The pro-Islamic parties formed a coalition in the United Tajik Opposition, which entered into a power-sharing arrangement that brought peace to the country by the year 2000. A Muslim political organization, the Islamic Rebirth Party, was allowed to run candidates for parliamentary seats. A third of the government positions have been allocated to government workers affiliated with the Islamic-leaning United Tajik Opposition, including several former UTO officials in senior cabinet-level positions. The government tolerates a moderate form of Islamic politics, which helps to undercut support for more militant Muslim parties. The collapse of the Taliban in 2001 in neighboring Afghanistan also reduced the influence of hard-line Muslim ideology in Tajikistan.

In the other three Central Asian nations, Islamic politics have been largely suppressed. In the vast region of Kazakhstan in the north, where almost as many residents are ethnically Russian as are Kazakh, and the old Communist Party (now called the Socialist Party) have held the preponderance of seats in parliament, one small Islamic political party, Alash, was dedicated to forming a government based on Islamic law.[41] Although it was not banned, it was barred from running candidates for office, and seven of its leaders were arrested in March 1992 for "insulting" Kazakhstan's president, Nursultan Nazarbayev.[42]

In Kyrgyzstan, near the Chinese border, the reformed branch of the Communist Party, led by President Askar A. Akayev, dominated politics during the 1990s. It was outspokenly in favor of the democratic system and joined forces with moderate Muslims in the Democratic Movement to defeat Communist hardliners.[43] A more radical Islamic movement remains in the background: the outlawed Sufi order known as the Hairy Ishans, who live in the lush Fergana Valley of Kyrgyzstan, and who resisted communist influence in the region for most of the twentieth century.[44] Islamic parties supported the so-called Tulip Revolution in 2005 that brought an end to Akayev's increasingly dictatorial regime.

In Turkmenistan, the desert region of western Central Asia, Islam is a potent force in the countryside, but during the Soviet era the prevailing Communist Party contained all efforts, Islamic or otherwise, at organizing opposition to its rule. In the post-Soviet period, Islamic movements continued to be suppressed. Because the country shares a long border with Iran, it has reason to be concerned about the potency of religious politics, and with that danger in mind Turkmenistan's president, Sapurmarad Niazov, attempted to coopt Muslim political opposition by embracing Islam. He also organized religious elders in projects touted as improving the social mores of the Turkmenistan population.[45] Niazov, who ruled with an iron hand, called himself Turkmenbashi ("leader of all Turkmen"), and imposed a cult of personality throughout the country. His picture adorned posters and commercial products, and watches and clocks had his image imprinted on the dial. His book was required to be revered like a sacred text. After his death in December 2006, he was replaced by his deputy prime minister, Gurbanguly Berdimuhammedow, who has ruled with similar severity. No political parties were allowed to run against his party, and political rallies were illegal. A carefully controlled election in February 2007 gave Berdimuhammedow almost 90 percent of the votes. In this climate no political opposition, Islamic or otherwise, could flourish, but religion has remained in the wings, ready to be tapped as a resource in political rebellion.

Throughout Central Asia the stage has been set in a post-Soviet era for confrontation between secular politicians, many of them former communists, and popular new Muslim leaders. However, the diverse Muslim political sentiments have not coalesced into a single Islamic position in any one of the five republics, much less throughout the whole region.[46] The Islamic Renaissance parties of Uzbekistan and Tajikistan and the Alash Party in Kazakhstan called for a theocratic state run by the clergy, as did the Muslim seminary students in Tashkent. Other Muslim activists have advocated an Islamic democracy. Some wanted to follow the Iranian model of Islamic revolution; others did not. Moderate Islamic leaders, such as the *qazi* in Tajikistan, called for Islamic social mores and Islamic nationalism in a non-theocratic state and, citing pragmatic considerations and ethnic differences within the Central Asian region, have rejected the goal of a transnational Turkestan.

Yet a great many Muslim activists, spurred on by a revival of Turkish influence in the region, yearned for the union of Central Asia under the banner of an Islamic Republic of Turkestan. It is this specter, more than any other potential effect of Islamic domination, that secular nationalists in the region fear, for it would not only undercut their own power but also have ramifications outside the region: it would alter relationships with neighboring China, Afghanistan, and Iran. But although there have been attempts at economic cooperation in the region— including the short-lived "Islamic Common Market" that was formed by Iran, Turkey, Pakistan, and Azerbaijan and four of the Central Asian countries, Uzbekistan, Kyrgyzstan, Tajikistan, and Turkmenistan—it is doubtful that an Islamic supernation will rise in the region. Still, despite the many differences within and among Central Asian nations, a deep cultural kinship persists within these independent Islamic nations.

HINDU NATIONALISM

In India, religious politics is sometimes violent, sometimes peaceful. The strategies of separatist religious activists have often been desperate and militant. Some Hindu activists have also taken extreme measures, but because the constituency to which they appeal is the majority community in the country, they have had recourse to a different form of power: the ballot box. The most successful religious-leaning party in India—and perhaps the largest religiously based political movement in the world— is the Hindu nationalist movement, the Bharatiya Janata Party (the BJP, or Indian People's Party), which was founded in 1980 and which led India's national government from 1998 to 2004.

The most significant boost in the movement's rise came in 1991 when it made a strong showing in opposition to what the BJP leader, Lal

Krishna Advani, called the "pseudosecularism" of secular politicians. The BJP gained more than 120 seats, making it the largest opposition party in India's parliament, and it gained control of several state governments, including that of India's most populous state, Uttar Pradesh. These gains were the result of almost a century of Hindu nationalist efforts, including protest movements; militant encounters with Muslims, minority leaders, and secular politicians; and the development of sophisticated mass-based organizations.

One of the reasons India has been vulnerable to the influence of Hindu nationalists is that "Hinduism" has come to mean so many things—an acceptance of particular religious beliefs and practices or a kind of broad cultural homogeneity. It is both the name for India's traditional culture and the title of a specific religious community. In traditional India there was no clear distinction between religion and the social mores of a region: even the words *India* and *Hindu* are etymologically linked, coined by outsiders to refer to the land and the people along the Indus River.[47] Today the term "Hindu" refers to someone associated with one of several religious communities in India; the most recent census states that 83 percent of the population is Hindu, 11 percent Muslim, 2.6 percent Christian, and slightly more than 1 percent Sikh, with small communities of Jains, Parsis, and Buddhists. Yet Hindu culture has traditionally embraced all people and aspects of life in the Indian subcontinent.

In classical Hindu social thought, religion and politics were linked. Each economic or political role in society, including kingship, had its own dharma (moral responsibility), and the prime duty of the king, as enunciated in the *Artha-sastra* by the Hindu political theorist Kautilya in the fourth century B.C.E., was to maintain power and uphold the *dharma* of the social whole.[48] In the great Hindu epics, the gods are portrayed playing regal roles. During most of India's history, however, there has not been a single centralized monarchy. Instead there have been hundreds of small princedoms and a pattern of local governance involving representative committees, called *panchayat* (a council of five).[49] The vacuum of leadership at the center made it possible for Muslim rulers from Central Asia and Persia, including the Mogul dynasties that ruled from the sixteenth to the nineteenth century, to establish great empires. The Moguls and their British successors formed alliances with local kings and left traditional Hinduism largely untouched. Hinduism remained independent of its cultural contacts in part because of its "tolerance"—a stance that is, in fact, an ability to absorb an opposition and ultimately to dominate it. What Ainslie Embree calls the "Brahmanical ideology" of high-caste Hinduism has a way of swallowing up other points of view and making them its own.[50]

Hinduism has not remained unchanged over the years however. One interesting development was the popularity of the *bhakti* (devotional) movements led by northern Indian poet-saints of the fifteenth to seventeenth centuries and by southern Indian bards who lived centuries before. The saints are portrayed as uninvolved in politics, but because their poetry ascribes little spiritual value to ritual or social status, they are sometimes advanced as prophets of social as well as spiritual reform. Whether or not India's religious groups were socially involved in an earlier period, they certainly became so in the eighteenth and nineteenth centuries, in part because of the stimulus of outsiders. Mogul military might and Muslim religious organization became models for the Sikh community in the Punjab. British civilization and Christian missionaries challenged Hindu movements, including the Brahmo Samaj and the Arya Samaj, in the nineteenth century throughout northern India. These movements promoted a socially engaged form of Hinduism and championed such social causes as mass education, rights for women, and the improvement of conditions for Untouchables. Although not overtly political, they were the first modern efforts to link Hindu religious values to public life and were predecessors of the groups that eventually formed the BJP.

In the twentieth century new forms of religion and new forms of politics began to interact more directly than they had before. Although officially secular, India's independence movement preached nationalist loyalties in terms that echoed the Hindu notion of dharmic obligation, and its espousal of devotion to "mother India" incorporated some of the characteristics of worship of Hindu goddesses. Mohandas Gandhi attempted to forge a compromise between the religious and secular wings of the independence movement by applying Hindu ethical values to the nationalist movement. He adhered to a form of Hinduism that had wide appeal beyond its sectarian origins and applied religious concepts to political tactics by using what he called *satyagraha* (the force of truth) and *ahimsa* (nonviolence) in political conflict.

Not all Indian political leaders were enthusiastic about Gandhi's compromise with religion: Jawaharlal Nehru and other secular nationalists, for example, felt uncomfortable with it, while Muslim leaders felt betrayed by it. Mohammed Ali Jinnah and his Muslim League, suspicious of what they regarded as Gandhi's Hinduization of the nationalist movement, demanded that the British create a separate nation for Muslims. When the British withdrew from India in 1947, they carved Pakistan out of portions of Bengal in the east and sections of Punjab, Sindh, and other areas in the west. Jinnah was named Pakistan's first governor general. Not all Muslims in the remainder of India moved to the areas designated as Pakistan, but eight million people did shift from one side of the borders to the other, and as many as a million lost their lives in the communal rioting that occurred during the transition. Gandhi strongly protested the partition of the country and the communal hatred it unleashed. Militant Hindus felt that he had capitulated to the Muslims, and a former member of a radical Hindu organization, the Rashtriya Swayamsevak Sangh (RSS), assassinated Gandhi in 1948.

The RSS was founded in 1925 by middle-class Hindus in Maharashtra and Madhya Pradesh, many of whom had been associated with the Arya Samaj movements. The main mission of the RSS was to train young Hindu men to resist the temptations of secular society and to revive the traditional values of Hindu India.[51] For years its main activities consisted of weekly meetings in urban homes and summer camps that were similar to Boy Scout outings except for their nationalist-religious ideology and training sessions in self-defense. Despite their Hindu rhetoric, the leaders of the movements were laymen, and the RSS did not—until much later—become a part of mainstream Hindu culture.

Nonetheless, the RSS set the standard and defined the terms of Hindu nationalism so effectively that they remain in force today. The ideas were shaped by the writings of Vinayak Damodar Savarkar, who had once debated Gandhi on the utility of using terrorism in the Indian national struggle against British rule.[52] He called on "the undying vitality of Hindu manhood" to assert itself "so vigorously as to make the enemies of Hindudom tremble."[53] Savarkar advanced the concept of *hindutva,* the idea that virtually everyone who has ancestral roots in India is a Hindu and that collectively they constitute a nation.[54] On the basis of this idea the RSS, in its constitution, called on all Hindus to "eradicate differences" and realize "the greatness of their past" in the "regeneration of Hindu society."[55] The RSS joined the Indian National Congress in opposing British rule but became increasingly disenchanted with Nehru and his emphasis on secular nationalism.

When India became independent in 1947, Nehru proclaimed it a secular state and exhorted India to "lessen her religiosity and turn to science."[56] But the tension between secular and religious nationalism remained.[57] Nehru was succeeded by his daughter, Indira (who had married a man named Gandhi and took his name, though neither he or she was directly related to Mohandas Gandhi). Indira Gandhi sustained her father's policies of secularism and was criticized by liberal as well as conservative wings of the Hindu religious community.

A liberal Hindu, Jayaprakash Narayan, who had succeeded Mohandas Gandhi as leader of his Sarvodaya movement for village-based social development, organized one of the first religious movements in recent history that attempted to topple a secular state. Narayan launched a massive campaign against what he regarded as political corruption within the Indian government in general and Indira Gandhi's Congress party in particular. In 1974 he proclaimed a "total revolution" against the Indian government; in response, in 1975 Indira Gandhi suspended the federal legislative bodies in India and declared a political emergency. Narayan was arrested and spent years in jail. When Indira Gandhi reinstituted electoral politics, she and her party were quickly voted out of office.

Even though the Indian government was criticized by Hindu religious leaders as being too secular, members of minority communities feared that it was becoming too Hindu. The gnawing suspicions about the political influence of Hindi religious leaders persisted among Sikhs, Muslims, and members of other minority communities. The Indian constitution requires the government to treat all religions equally: to protect and maintain religious institutions of all faiths; allow colleges sponsored by Sikhs and Muslims, as well as by Hindus, to be incorporated into state universities; and permit aspects of traditional Islamic law pertaining to marriage, divorce, and inheritance to apply to members of Muslim communities.

Despite the secular government's claims of impartiality, however, the leaders of the ruling Congress party have been accused of pandering to religious minorities, and the claim of the Hindu nationalist Advani that the Congress government was only "pseudosecular" was perceived by many Hindus to be correct. In an Indian context, the term "secularism" means treating all religious communities equally, and the government was viewed by many in the Hindu majority as too accommodating in its support of Muslims, Sikhs, and other minorities to the detriment of corresponding Hindu social groups.

Members of minority religious communities, however, saw the situation the other way around: they felt that the government was implicitly Hindu. From 1987 to 1989, for instance, the government television network, Doordarshan, sponsored a serialized presentation of one of the great Hindu epics, the *Ramayana,* followed in 1988–89 by the other

great Hindu epic, the *Mahabharata*. In both cases the government justified its support with the claim that these were traditional stories and not
religious myths. In fact, these televised epics may have worked against
secular politicians because their enormous popularity—they were the
most widely watched programs in India's history—was credited with fu-
eling the revival of religious politics.[58] Even members of the secular parties attempted to appease the Hindu religious right, and during the 1980s
many Sikhs regarded Mrs. Gandhi and her Congress Party as bending to
the interests of Hindu religious figures. The rise of militant Sikhism was,
in part, a response to what many Sikhs saw as the increasing Hinduization of Indian politics.

Hindu nationalism has always been strongest in northern India's "saffron belt" running from Rajasthan to Bihar and encompassing India's
most populous state, Uttar Pradesh. There, religious parties such as the
Jan Sangh labored for thirty years to build a political base on the interests of conservative Hindus, but for most of those years it was not able
to make a significant dent in the popular support given the dominance
of the Congress Party. The Jan Sangh's successor in the Hindu political
lineage, the BJP, became enormously successful, not only in the saffron
belt but throughout the country.[59]

The BJP achieved its success partly by default: the 1980s were not a
good time for the Congress and other secular parties, and at least half the
voters who cast their ballots for the BJP in 1991 did so out of unhappi-
ness with the other choices and "to give the new party a chance."[60] But
the BJP succeeded for other reasons as well: the popularity of its ideology of Hindu nationalism and its alliances with other, more strident,
movements for the creation of a Hindu state. Among these was an old
one—the RSS—and a potent new coalition of Hindu activists.

The RSS supplied the dedication, energy, and staff to make the new
party work. Its network of several thousand *pracharaks*—full-time, educated, unmarried staff workers—was put at the service of the BJP, giving the party overnight an effective political apparatus. Yet the RSS had
a mixed image in the Indian public eye. Many regarded it as a fascist
group of nationalist fanatics. It gained respectability and a link with traditional Hinduism through its association with the Vishva Hindu
Parishad (World Hindu Council, or VHP).

The VHP did not begin as a political organization, and its ties to the
RSS were at first unclear.[61] It was founded in 1964 when 150 Hindu
leaders were invited to a religious retreat center near Bombay (present-
day Mumbai), Sandeepany Sadhanalaya, by its leader, Swami Chinmaya-

nanda.[62] The swami, who had a large following in urban areas of India and abroad, including the United States, was in many respects a modern Hindu, but he and the other leaders who founded the movement—including the Sikh leader Master Tara Singh—were concerned about what they regarded as the relatively slight influence their religious groups had on the social values of Indian society.[63] They were determined to make a difference. Chinmayananda was elected the first president of the VHP, and Shivram Shankar Apte was elected its general secretary. Apte was a longtime leader of the RSS. The RSS may have been behind the organization from the very beginning, or it might have gained control gradually through the involvement of its *pracharaks* in the VHP organization. The VHP offered the RSS—and Hindu political parties such as the Jan Sangh and BJP—not only the legitimacy of connections with large religious groups but the manpower of the celibate *sadhu*s (holy men) and other workers who were connected with it.

The politicization of the VHP occurred largely in the 1980s. It first came into national prominence by organizing protests against mass conversions of lower-caste Hindus to Islam at Meenakshipuram in southern India in 1981. Islamic states in the Persian Gulf were alleged to have sent large sums of money to India to encourage religious raids on Hindu society. The secular government became a target for the Hindu leaders' wrath because they saw the state's policy of religious neutrality on conversion as protecting these Muslim assaults. In 1983, a great "Procession for Unity" organized by the VHP brought over a million people to New Delhi in one of the largest gatherings of its type in history.

The VHP's momentum increased with another issue: control over the purported birthplace of the god Ram. In a situation reminiscent of the Temple Mount dispute in Jerusalem, this issue involved a contest over certain sacred sites. For some time, conservative Hindus had objected to the government's protection of a number of mosques built on the sites of Hindu temples during the Mogul period. In 1984 the VHP called for a reassertion of Hindu control over a dozen of these. Chief among them was the Babri Mosque, built in the sixteenth century by a lieutenant of the Emperor Baber on the location of a Hindu temple in the city of Ayodhya, which is traditionally identified as the home and capital of the god-king Ram. At some point in history—exactly when is a debated issue—the site of the Babri Mosque was identified as Ram's birthplace. Soon after India's independence, during a time of Hindu/Muslim tensions, an image of Ram was reported to have magically manifested itself in the mosque, so some Hindus insisted on worshiping there. Riots broke out between Muslims and Hindus over the use of the site, and the government barred both groups from the mosque. In 1986, after the VHP demanded that Ram be liberated from what they called his Muslim jail, a judge again opened the site for worship. Violent encounters between Muslims and Hindus soon ensued, with the VHP calling for the mosque to be destroyed or removed and a new temple built in its place.

The VHP was linked in 1985 to a new all-India organization, the Dharma Sansad. Based in Karnataka in southern India, it consisted of nine hundred representatives of a variety of Hindu sects and orders of *sadhus* who vowed to fight for Hindu purification and the propagation of Hindu nationalism. It also forged ties with another potent movement, the Shiv Sena, which had organized protest rallies in Maharashtra, Gujarat, and Punjab over what it regarded as the government's pro-Muslim and pro-Sikh policies. By 1986 the VHP claimed to have over three thousand branches throughout India and over a million dedicated workers. It targeted for defeat politicians who it felt were unfaithful to the Hindu cause and lobbied for pro-Hindu legislation.

The VHP also continued to agitate on the Ayodhya issue, even though the Archeological Survey of India published a report in January 1989 concluding that it was unlikely that the mythical figure of Ram was born on the site, but report did not quell the strong feelings of the Hindu public. According to national polls in 1991, Ayodhya rivaled economic issues as one of the most important concerns of India's voters.[64] Over three hundred were killed in incidents related to the struggle, including a communal clash in Meerut during the week of May 18, 1987, that led to over a hundred deaths, possibly many more.[65]

Largely through the Ayodhya issue the BJP became directly linked with the VHP. There had been a relationship between the two parties for years through the RSS, whose workers supplied the organizational energy for both the party and the movement. The old Hindu political party, the Jan Sangh, had merged with the Janata party in a united front against the Congress in 1977. When the Janata party broke up, the leaders of the Jan Sangh regrouped in 1980 to form the BJP. The president of the party was Atal Behari Vajpayee, a former leader of the Jan Sangh; the vice-president was Vijaye Raje Scindia, a rather remarkable and outspoken woman who was a member of the former ruling family of the princely state of Gwalior; as general secretary the BJP named Lal Krishna Advani.

Advani's background indicates much about the character of the BJP. He was born in 1928 and was raised in Karachi but was forced to flee in 1947, when Pakistan was created. He was educated in Catholic schools, worked as a lawyer and a journalist, and was a member of the RSS. He seldom worshiped in a temple or performed Hindu religious rites, and at one time he ate meat, contrary to the usual upper-caste Hindu preference for vegetarianism. When asked why the BJP had become so phenomenally popular, he said it had nothing to do with religious sentiment; it was purely a matter of "nationalism" or, rather, as he put it, "patriotism."[66]

Initially the BJP's appeal was modest. In the first national election in which it participated, in 1984, the BJP won only two seats out of a total of 545 in the lower house of parliament (for all practical purposes the sole legislative body of the national government). In the 1989 elections the BJP won eighty-six seats and was a supporter of the new prime minister, V. P. Singh (although it was technically not part of his coalition). In the 1991 elections the BJP won 120 seats—compared with only 220 seats for the leading Congress party.

The BJP's electoral success in 1991 was due partly to the tragic assassination of the Congress party's leading candidate, Rajiv Gandhi.[67] The BJP leaders could claim that theirs was now the party of stability—one of the claims that Rajiv Gandhi had made about the Congress. Yet even before Rajiv Gandhi's death, bookies in Mumbai who were placing bets on the election had given odds in favor of the BJP's winning over a hundred seats.[68] The main reason was Ayodhya and all that it had come to symbolize.

The year before the election, in October 1990, Advani joined the VHP's call for faithful Hindus throughout the country to make bricks and bring them to Ayodhya to rebuild the temple at the site of the Babri Mosque. Advani himself attempted to march to the site, and he called on the government to relocate the mosque "with dignity and honor" a short distance away.[69] Long before Advani got near Ayodhya, however, the government arrested him and twenty thousand Hindu volunteers (including the vice-president of the BJP, Scindia) who were preparing to march to the mosque. The BJP immediately withdrew its parliamentary support from Prime Minister V. P. Singh, whereupon his national-front government collapsed. At the Ayodhya site the protest continued, and over thirty Muslims and Hindus were killed in the clash. "My conscience is clear," Prime Minister V. P. Singh said in a television interview broadcast after his government's collapse, claiming that he had "sacrificed the highest office for the cause of the unity of the country and the oppressed."[70]

Ayodhya had become a symbol for both sides. For V. P. Singh, it was a test of the will of the secular state to stand up for its policy of neutrality on religious issues. Behind this policy, however, was an even more fundamental cause: the nature of India as a modern state. In a speech made during the crisis, Prime Minister V. P. Singh recalled Mohandas Gandhi's struggle for Hindu/Muslim unity at the time of India's independence and said that he, like Gandhi, was fighting for the survival of "India as a secular nation."[71] Several scholars, in a book rushed into print soon after the event, evoked the image of Nehru in concurring with V. P. Singh that Ayodhya was ultimately about the ability of politics to stay free of the dangers of religion.[72]

On the other side, the leaders of the VHP and the BJP saw Ayodhya as the symbol of the government's inability to stand up for the Hindu majority and its tendency to seek to placate the interests of religious minorities. From the BJP's point of view, this stand was tantamount to selling the nation's interests for the sake of Muslim votes. Behind their position was the desire for India to be a Hindu, rather than a secular, state. In a curious way, Advani seemed to agree with V. P. Singh and the other secular nationalists about the importance of unifying India. The fundamental difference is that V. P. Singh thought that secularism was the sole possible unifying force, whereas Advani and his colleagues maintained that only India's Hindu culture could provide the cement to hold the nation together and form the basis for modern progress. For this reason Advani could state that in India "politicians do not command respect," for they are only "opportunists." Instead, he claimed, because his followers were motivated by principle, only his party was truly disciplined; only it held a truly "nationalist viewpoint."[73] Invoking Mohandas Gandhi, the party in its May 1992 meetings claimed that it embraced Gandhi's "holistic" approach to politics and economics, "different from capitalism and communism."[74]

Yet once the Hindu nationalists came to power in several states in 1991, they found how difficult it could be to hold onto both their religious ideals and the reins of power. In Uttar Pradesh, one of the states in which the BJP was victorious, the symbol for their political dilemma was, once again, Ayodhya. The city, which is located in Uttar Pradesh, became the beneficiary of one of the BJP government's efforts at urban renewal: it bought the land around the site of the disputed mosque in order, it claimed, to construct facilities for tourists and pilgrims—an action that angered Muslims and moderate Hindus who saw it as a ploy to take over the mosque. Meanwhile, some of the BJP's radical Hindu followers—the "boys," as the leaders called them—grew impatient with this slow strategy of encroachment, and they launched their own campaign to seize the mosque immediately. The attack failed, but the incident embarrassed the government and divided the Hindu nationalist movement.[75] In 1992 the government transferred the land to the VHP and began building a temple.

On December 6, 1992, an angry mob of Hindu activists broke through the police cordon, and the mosque was destroyed. Hundreds were killed in riots throughout India, and BJP leaders were briefly jailed. In part because it was ostracized, however, the party's popularity increased. In subsequent years the BJP made significant gains in state elections, but it continued to be plagued by internal quarrels. Beneath a struggle over leadership lay a deeper tension: whether the BJP was just a political party or the vanguard of a Hindu revolution.

The subsequent electoral successes demonstrated the efficacy of the BJP's choice of a broad-based moderate position. In the 1996 national elections, the BJP received a majority of votes, but were unable to maintain a stable coalition. After thirteen days in power, the government collapsed and was replaced by a left-secular coalition. In new elections two years later, a BJP-led front was more successful. But the fragile coalition broke down the following year, and the subsequent elections brought the BJP into firm control of the Indian parliament with 183 seats. This government would last until 2004. The BJP installed the seasoned political leader Atal Bihari Vajpayee as prime minister, and his old friend Lal Krishna Advani was appointed deputy prime minister and home minister.

The policies of the BJP were generally conservative but not extreme. Its foreign policy took a hard line, especially toward Pakistan, though at the same time Vajpayee sought to bring about a détente between the two countries. Nonetheless, he asserted that India should negotiate from a position of strength. One of the BJP's first acts when it came to office was to carry out a series of nuclear tests in a remote site in Rajasthan, thus bringing India into the nuclear camp. Pakistan soon responded with nuclear tests of its own. The BJP also took a hard line on what it regarded as terrorists in Kashmir. Following the December 13, 2001 terrorist attacks on the Indian parliament, the BJP supported the passage of the Prevention of Terrorist Activities Act in 2002, which increased the powers of police authorities and intelligence agencies in an effort to curb subversive political activities.

On the domestic economic front, Vajpayee's economic team supported the privatization of government-owned corporations, the liberalization of trade, foreign investment and ownership, and the creation of

"Special Economic Zones" for industrial development. The BJP catered to the rising information technology industry, and lowered taxes for the expanding middle class. So in many ways the BJP functioned like any other political party in responding to the needs and wishes of its constituency and attempting to maximize its influence.[76]

The BJP's adherence to a Hindu nationalist ideology was perhaps most evident in its attemps at overhauling the educational curriculum—especially its efforts to rewrite history textbooks to make them comform to conservative Hindu ideas—and its attitude towards India's Muslim minority. During the 2002 Gujarat riots, which led to the deaths of two thousand people, most of them Muslims, the chief minister of the state of Gujarat, Narendra Modi, who was a member of the BJP, was accused of supporting Hindu mobs. BJP activists and party members were accused of orchestrating the violence. In 2005 the U.S. government denied him a visa to enter the country on the grounds that he was responsible for ". . . severe violations of religious freedom."[77]

The question remains regarding to what extent the BJP can be considered to be a religious political movement. It has acted like any other political party in its organizational calculations, often to the frustration and disappointment of some of its more religious supporters. At the same time the BJP has not entirely shied away from defining itself as a religious party: it adopted the lotus as its symbol—with the rich religious significance that this image has in India—and defined the preservation of Hindu culture as one of its main missions. The website of the BJP lists two concepts under the party's philosophy: "integral humanism" and *hindutva,* which it describes as "cultural nationalism."[78] The concept of "integral humanism" was coined by Pandit Deendayal Upadhayaya, a leader of two of the BJP's predecessor organizations, the RSS and Jan Sangh party. It suggests that spirituality is an important component of social order and civic duty. Though the BJP website states that *hindutva* refers only to cultural unity and identity and is not limited to particular religious beliefs or theological concepts, many Muslims have interpreted it as a cultural identity that marginalizes them. From an Islamic and secular point of view, the idea of *hindutva,* the organizational ties of the party to overtly religious Hindu groups, and the prejudices of the BJP leadership are sufficient evidence to brand the party as a religious political movement. If so, its millions of followers in the Indian subcontinent and in diaspora Hindu communities around the globe confirm that it is indeed the largest religious nationalist movement in the world.

Outside of India, there are large Hindu communities in the West Indies islands of Trinidad and Tobago, where they constitute 25 percent of the population, and in the Pacific island of Fiji, where the Indo-Fijian community has been in a narrow majority. The success of political parties supported largely by Indo-Fijians in national elections in 1987 and again in 2000 created a series of ethnic political crises. In 2006 a military coup rejected the coalition arrangement that would have granted the Indo-Fijians a power-sharing role. But in neither Trinidad nor Fiji has Hindu religion been a political factor. Nor has Hinduism as a religion played a major role in the Tamil movement for ethnic separatism in northern Sri Lanka, where the largely secular ethnic movement is supported by Tamil Christians as well as Tamil Hindus.

In Nepal, which has a higher percentage of Hindus than does India, Hindu ideology and identity does play a role in domestic politics. Hindu religious activists influenced the committee assigned in 1990 to draft a new democratic constitution following King Birendra's agreement to relinquish political power in the face of popular revolt. The committee's chairman made public assurances that Nepal would not be described as secular. "The moment we declare a secular state," he said, "we would have religious riots."[79] A Nepal branch of the Shivsena, a Hindu nationalism movement based in the Indian state of Gujarat, agitated for the government to embrace a national Hindu identity and support policies favorable to Hindus.

After King Birendra and his family were massacred in 2001, he was succeeded by his nephew, King Gyanendra, who attempted to regain political control for the monarchy by disbanding the parliament.[80] He tried to shore up his monarchial powers by claiming to be a descendent of a Hindu god. He was forced to relinquish his authority (including his religious titles) in response to massive protests and civil unrest in 2005–2006, and parliamentary rule was re-established in April 2006. The title "His Majesty's Government" was replaced by "the Government of Nepal," and Nepal was no longer an absolute monarchy. The new parliament asserted in 2006 that Nepal was also no longer a Hindu state. Hindu movements launched a protest to attempt to restore the former monarchy's religious identity.

SIKHISM'S SUPPRESSED WAR

In northern India the Sikh religious community has launched its own religious rebellion, marked by a decade of bloody encounters between militant Sikhs and the armed forces of the secular state. Though their target

was largely the secular government led by Congress Party prime minister Indira Gandhi, members of the movement also attacked the Hindu
nationalist party, the BJP. On one occasion when the BJP had organized
a convoy of buses in what it proclaimed to be a unity march from India's
far south to its far north, hoping to demonstrate popular support for its
message that India was united in a single culture, this assertion of unity
collapsed in a violent encounter with the Sikhs. When the buses reached
the Punjab city of Phagwara, they were set upon by Sikh militants, and
five of the Unity Marchers were killed on the spot; sixteen others were
wounded.[81] From the militants' point of view, the BJP form of Hindu
unity was precisely what they were against: it appeared to them to be a
variation of the Congress Party's idea of a unified nation that excluded
the Sikhs' political identity. To these Sikhs, both Hindu activists and secular politicians were equally foolish and equally dangerous: both threatened their nationalist aspirations for a Sikh state.[82]

Often, however, the Sikh rhetoric was strikingly similar to the language of Hindu nationalists. I heard one example of this in a dark and
sparsely decorated room behind one of the main centers of Sikhism in
New Delhi, where a group of intense young men were explaining to me
why their hero—the fiery preacher Jarnail Singh Bhindranwale, who was
assassinated in 1984—was thereafter venerated as a martyr to the Sikh
cause. They were attracted not merely by his politics but by his religious
commitment as well: "He went to his death for what he believed."[83]
Other leaders are just politicians, they implied, and ultimately they are
looking out only for themselves. This same criticism—that secular politics was a cynical and self-serving business—had been made by the members of the Hindu movements, the RSS and the BJP.

Sikh leaders, like their Hindu counterparts, maintained that religious
politics offered a positive alternative. "Politics can be beautiful," I was
told by a former head priest of Sikhism's central shrine.[84] "But it must
be the right kind of politics," which he meant a politics fused with religion, where "religion dominated politics," rather than the other way
around.[85] He felt that Sant Jarnail Singh Bhindranwale represented this
sort of religion-dominated politics. For this reason, he explained, young
men throughout the Punjab carried crumpled pictures of the preacher
alongside their automatic weapons as they moved from village to village
under cover of night.

Bhindranwale is sometimes portrayed in the press and by secular Indian politicians as a bigot, his message nothing more than the poison of
intercommunal hatred. Yet during his heyday in the 1980s, Bhindran-

wale claimed that he had nothing against Hinduism as such. "I preach Hindu-Sikh unity," he proudly proclaimed.[86] What he disdained—indeed loathed—were "the enemies of religion." These included "that lady born in a house of Brahmans"—the phrase he used to describe Indira Gandhi—and heretics who had fallen from the disciplined Sikh fold and sought the easy comforts of modern life.

Bhindranwale's epithet for Indira Gandhi was an indictment against both secular and Hindu politicians—secular because of her party, Hindu because of her caste—and, in fact, he often regarded the two as twin enemies. He was reflecting a belief of many Sikhs: that secular politics in India was in fact a form of Hindu cultural domination. So conscious were many Sikhs of what they regarded as the oppressiveness of Hindu culture that they were uneasy when scholars located the origins of their tradition in a medieval Hindu milieu. The founder of Sikhism, Guru Nanak, was one of the introspective and devotional saints of the medieval *bhakti* movement.[87] But many Sikhs would like to think of him as having no significant theological connections with the Hindu tradition that preceded him.

Whether or not Guru Nanak himself formulated Sikhism as a radical departure from Hinduism, the movement that survived him has defined itself a distinctly separate community, in part because the Mogul military leaders regarded it that way and in part because of the cultural influence of the Jats, an ethnic group that joined the Sikh community at the end of the sixteenth century and became the dominant landholding caste of the Punjab. The Jats were great warriors, and they imposed their martial values and symbols on the whole of the Sikh community.[88] The tenth and final teacher in the historical lineage of Sikh masters, Guru Gobind Singh, presided over an army of considerable size, and martyrdom was the supreme honor. The symbols that he is said to have required his followers to display in 1699 and that are still meaningful to the faithful include such emblems of militancy as a sword and a protective bracelet worn on the wrist. The most frequently displayed symbol of Sikhism today is a double-edged blade, surrounded by a circle and surmounted by a pair of swords.

Thus the Sikh community grew from a small group of devotees of an introspective spiritual teacher into an army, and eventually into several separate armies, that protected kingdoms led by Sikh rulers. Early in the nineteenth century the land and the military forces of the Sikhs were consolidated by Maharaja Ranjit Singh, whose kingdom spanned most of the Punjab and lasted until the middle of the century; it was one of the last independent regions in India to fall to the British, conquered only after a series of wars.

The British colonial period initially saw a decline of the Sikh community until a reform movement in 1873 began reviving the tradition and imposing standards of faith and practice. This movement, the Singh Sabha, was especially exercised about what it regarded as the display of Hindu artifacts in the Golden Temple and in other Sikh shrines and *gurdwara*s (religious meeting places). In 1920, groups of Sikhs began agitating for reforms in the management of its *gurdwara*s, calling for the ouster of those who had been in control of the shrines, including the Udasis (a sect that traced its origins to the son of Guru Nanak, revered Hindu gods and texts, and venerated Guru Nanak to the exclusion of the other nine founding gurus of Sikhism).

The British government capitulated to these demands in 1925 and established a board of control, the Shiromani Gurdwara Parbandhak Committee (the SGPC, or Central Gurdwara Management Committee), consisting of elected representatives. The SGPC became an arena for Sikh politics. One group of partisans in the reform movement, the Akali Dal (the Band of the Immortal One), later became a political party, and after independence they successfully contested elections for legislative seats, sharing with the Congress Party the authority to form ruling governments in the state.

Sikh politicians, like other minority religious leaders, supported India's fight for independence from Britain, but like Jinnah and other Muslims, they were suspicious of the influence of Hindu nationalists in the independence movement.[89] When Gandhi talked about the importance of cultural and moral values in politics, they thought he was talking about creating a religious state—a Hindu state. Moreover, the creation of Pakistan for India's Muslim minority had planted the idea in the minds of many Sikhs that there should be a state for them as well.

India's independence disillusioned many Sikhs who had supported the struggle against the British and now felt outside the mainstream of national politics. They did not even have control of their area of India because they constituted less than half the electorate in the state of Punjab. In the 1950s they formed a new political movement that called for a redrawing of the boundaries of the Punjab to include only speakers of the Punjabi language, a demand that was tantamount to calling for a Sikh-majority state. The charismatic leader of the time, Sant Fateh Singh, went on a well-publicized fast in support of the idea and threatened to immolate himself on the roof of the Golden Temple's Akal Takhat (the Throne of the Immortal One, a building that housed the main Sikh organizations) if his demand was not met. The Indian government, led by prime minister Indira Gandhi, conceded, and in 1966 the old Punjab state was carved into three to produce Haryana and Himachal Pradesh, states with Hindu majorities, and a new, smaller Punjab with a Sikh majority.

The violent movement that erupted in the 1980s had some ties to these earlier campaigns for Sikh autonomy and political power, but it was in many ways more fanatical, more religious.[90] The movement began during a clash in 1978 between a group of Sikhs and the Nirankaris, a small sect that had splintered from the Sikh tradition and followed its own lineage of gurus. The leader of the Sikh group attacking the Nirankaris was Jarnail Singh, a young rural preacher who at an early age had joined the Damdami Taksal, a religious school and retreat center founded by the great Sikh martyr Baba Deep Singh. When Jarnail Singh joined the ashram, the leader was a master who had come from the village of Bhindran and was hence named Bhindranwale. It was a name that Jarnail Singh adopted out of respect when he became the ashram's leader after the master's death. Jarnail Singh Bhindranwale found the Nirankaris' worship of a living guru to be presumptuous and offensive, and in the escalating violence between the two groups, lives were lost on both sides. In 1980 the Nirankari guru was assassinated. Bhindranwale was accused of the crime but was found not guilty.

Soon Bhindranwale became busy with a new organization, the Dal Khalsa (the Group of the Pure), which was supported by the prime minister's younger son, Sanjay Gandhi, along with other Congress Party leaders, including the president of India, Zail Singh. They supported the group in hopes that it could replace the rival party, the Akali Dal, as the leading faction in the SGPC, but the plan never succeeded. Instead, it encouraged the growth of a new form of Sikh militancy. In 1981 the publisher of a chain of Hindu newspapers in Punjab who had been a critic of Bhindranwale was shot dead. Again, Bhindranwale was implicated. In response to his arrest and the destruction of his personal papers, Bhindranwale turned against the government. Bands of young Sikhs began indiscriminately killing Hindus, and later that year a group of Sikhs hijacked an Indian Airlines plane in Pakistan. The violence had begun.

The sermons of Bhindranwale offer clues to his religious sensibilities and their political implications.[91] In a rambling, folksy manner, he called on his followers to maintain their faith during a time of trial, and he echoed the common fear that Sikhs would lose their identity in a sea of secularism or, worse, in a flood of resurgent Hinduism.[92] One of his more familiar themes was the survival of the Sikh community; for *community* he used the term *qaum*, which carries overtones of nationhood.[93] As for the idea of

Khalistan, a separate Sikh nation, Bhindranwale said he "neither favored it or opposed it."[94] He did, however, support the Sikh concept of *miri-piri,* the notion that spiritual and temporal power are linked.[95] He evoked the image of a great war between good and evil waged in the present day: "a struggle . . . for our faith, for the Sikh nation, for the oppressed."[96] He implored his young followers to rise up and marshal the forces of righteousness. "The Guru will give you strength," he assured them.[97]

By 1983, Bhindranwale's power and the fear of it had grown to such an extent that Mrs. Gandhi suspended the Punjab government and was ruling it directly from Delhi. Bhindranwale had set up an alternative government of his own in the protected quarters of the Sikhs' most sacred shrine, the Golden Temple, in Amritsar. The Akali leader, Sant Harchand Singh Longowal, was also sequestered in the Golden Temple but in separate quarters because he and Bhindranwale had had a falling out that led to a series of killings in both camps. From time to time lists of demands to be presented to the government would be drawn up by one group of Sikhs or another, but the groups could seldom agree among themselves on which items to include. Besides, the larger issue was one of political legitimacy for Sikh identity—religious nationalism—so the specific demands were, in a sense, irrelevant. Government officials who focused on these demands in trying to negotiate a settlement were invariably frustrated. In 1984, shortly before she gave the command to the Indian army to invade the Golden Temple, an exasperated Indira Gandhi itemized everything she had done to meet the Sikh demands and asked, "What more can any government do?"[98]

The situation came to a head on June 5, 1984, when Mrs. Gandhi sent troops into the Golden Temple in a venture code-named Operation Bluestar. In a messy military operation that took two days to complete, two thousand or more people were killed, including a number of innocent worshipers. Bhindranwale was one of the first to die. Longowal was taken into custody. Even moderate Sikhs throughout the world were horrified at the specter of the Indian army stomping through their holiest precincts with their boots on, shooting holes in the temple's elaborate marble facades. Later that year, two of Mrs. Gandhi's Sikh bodyguards avenged the desecration of the Golden Temple by turning their automatic weapons on her as she walked through the garden from her home to her office in an adjacent bungalow. She died on the spot.[99] On October 31, 1984, the day after she was assassinated, over 2,000 Sikhs were massacred in Delhi and elsewhere by angry mobs.[100] Rajiv Gandhi, who became prime minister after his mother's death, entered into an agreement with Longowal in July 1985 to bring the violence to an end. But Longowal was killed, presumably by members of Bhindranwale's camp, later that year. (Some years later Rajiv Gandhi's life would also come to an explosive end when a Tamil militant, angry with the Indian government's support of Sri Lanka's efforts to quell the Tamil separatist movement, ignited the bomb she was wearing when she greeted the prime minister with flowers at a rally in 1991.)

The "Rajiv-Longowal accord" was never completely implemented, nor did the violence in the Punjab quickly abate. The followers of Bhindranwale became more strident, targeting the Longowal faction of Akalis that was led by Punjab's chief minister, Surjit Singh Barnala, and other moderate Sikhs. Despite this, the moderate leaders of the Akalis attempted a daring strategy of accommodation by appointing several religious leaders who were sympathetic to the extremists' cause to the five-member council that has traditionally made decisions regarding religious matters in Sikhism. (These are often misleadingly referred to in the press as the "five priests" of Sikhism—a misnomer because Sikhism is a lay community and the religious function of *granthi*, the word rendered here as *priest*, is primarily liturgical, similar to the role of a Jewish cantor.)

The newly appointed council declared its support of Khalistan and excommunicated Chief Minister Barnala. The least radical of the five religious leaders took "a leave of absence" from his position, and Jasbir Singh Rode, nephew of the martyred Bhindranwale, became the leader *(jathedar)* of the Akal Takhat. Radical organizations such as the Khalistan Commando Force, the Khalistan Liberation Force, and extremist factions of the All-India Sikh Students Federation had direct control of the official Sikh leadership. Violent assaults in the villages increased, and during 1987 over a hundred people a month were killed by extremists.

The Golden Temple again became a hideout for militants seeking protection from the police, and again the Indian security forces entered the temple to rout the militants. This spurred the Indian parliament to enact a law prohibiting religious shrines from being used for political and military purposes. Although the law applied to all religious institutions throughout the country, it had immediate applicability to the Sikh situation. Meanwhile, the moderate Akali leaders broke with the militants and dismissed the five leaders of the Golden Temple. In response, bombs were thrown in the major cities in the Punjab, killing seventy-three. To ameliorate the situation, the popular musician Darshan Singh Ragi was appointed *jathedar* of the Akal Takhat, and he allowed Chief Minister

Barnala to undergo acts of penance, including cleaning the shoes of Sikh worshipers, in order to reverse his excommunication from the faith.

In May, 1987, Rajiv Gandhi, claiming that Barnala was not able to control the problem, ousted him from office, suspended parliamentary government in the state, and again ran the state's affairs from the central government. As chaotic as Barnala's rule had been, the situation that year deteriorated even further. After the national elections in November 1989 removed Rajiv Gandhi and his Congress Party from control of the government, the new prime minister, V. P. Singh, inaugurated his rule with a ceremonial visit to the Golden Temple. Unfortunately, neither he nor his successor, Chandra Shekar, was able to handle the communal difficulties of the country any better than their predecessors had done.

In 1991, over three thousand people were killed in the Punjab's triangular battle among the police, the radicals, and the populace.[101] Accompanying the increase in violence was a general collapse of law and order, especially in rural areas of the state. This collapse was due in part to the erosion of idealism in the Sikh movement; increasingly it degenerated into roving bands of thugs. The anarchy in the villages was also caused by the failure of the Sikh movement to achieve its political goals, leaving a cynical and demoralized public in its wake. In that sense the public disorder proved what the Sikh religious nationalists had been saying all along: without a government legitimized by religion, there can be no credible government in the state at all. It was not surprising, therefore, that few Sikhs bothered—or dared—to vote in the 1992 elections.

In the absence of a legitimate government in the Punjab, the rural area became a no man's land in the battle between militants and armed police. The war was exacerbated by caste: the militants were largely young members of the dominant farming caste in the Punjab, the Jats. The leaders of the police and central administration of the Punjab were often urban Hindus and Sikhs from merchant castes—traditional rivals of the Jats. The armed police waging the war in the villages on the urban Hindus' behalf were often members of the lower castes, many of whom had been serfs of Jat Sikhs. Thus young Jats had to bear both the injury of being dominated by urban Hindus and the insult of being controlled by young police whom they regard as being of lower status than themselves.[102]

In a poignant attempt to break through this vicious cycle and reestablish a leadership to which the central government could maintain ties, Rajiv Gandhi, in virtually his last act of office, released the Akali leader, Simranjeet Singh Mann, from prison. This was an extraordinary act on the prime minister's part: Mann was in prison awaiting trial for his role—which according to some published accounts was central—in the plot that had led to the murder of Rajiv Gandhi's mother. Rajiv claimed that his pardon was an eleventh-hour effort to "heal wounds."[103] Following his release from prison, Mann served as a member of parliament until October 11, 1990; in January 1991 all the major factions of the Akali party united under his leadership. His was a short-lived success, however, since it was based on the support of militant cadres whose political grip on the Punjab would soon come to an end.

The Punjab state government finally gained an upper hand over the militants in 1992. The Congress Party leaders who came to power in the February elections used their mandate to unleash the police in search-and-destroy missions that literally eradicated the militant network. Several thousand were killed—dedicated revolutionaries, thugs, and innocent bystanders—in what amounted to a government-led massacre. Perhaps more important than the police action, however, was the complicity of villagers in the government's operations. They had had enough of all of the violence and bullying from both sides, especially as the high moral purposes of the Sikh militants had degenerated into gang warfare. Increasingly the villagers regarded them as thugs. The result was a state of calm in the Punjab that most residents had not experienced in over ten years.[104] By October the police barricades were dismantled in the streets of Amritsar and other urban areas, and by the spring of 1993, it was possible to move freely through the countryside, even at night.

As public order was returning to the region, a few of the militants survived the annihilation, and sporadic acts of violence continued. A car bomb was detonated in New Delhi in September 1993. On August 31, 1995, a massive explosion rocked the parking lot in front of the modernistic secretariat building in Punjab's state capital, Chandigarh. In the blast that shuddered through the impressive complex of government buildings designed by the French architect Le Corbusier, the chief minister of the state, Beant Singh, was literally blown to pieces. Fifteen of his aides and security guards were also killed, and several cars were demolished in the conflagration that followed. In the smoldering heap that minutes before was his official vehicle, only Beant Singh's Sikh bracelet (kara) remained to identify the chief minister.[105]

Among the mangled and limbless bodies was one believed to belong to the bomber himself. The car that brought him to the site stood empty nearby; the accomplice who was supposed to drive it away had apparently panicked and fled. By tracing the license plate, the police were able to identify and apprehend several of the alleged conspirators. All were members of one of the Sikh movement's deadliest guerrilla cells, the Babbar Khalsa. They were the last of the several groups, including the Bhindranwale Tigers and the Khalistan Commando Force, that had been both victims and perpetrators in the reign of terror in Punjab since the early 1980s.

The assassination of Prime Minister Beant Singh was the last gasp of the Sikh separatist movement. To a large extent the Sikh war against the secular state was over. The secular state had won.

How did the Indian secular government triumph over a movement of religious violence? One of the lessons that can be learned from this experience is that after the tragic attempt to quickly root out the militants through an armed invasion of the Golden Temple—an event that triggered the assassination of Prime Minister Indira Gandhi in response—the Indian government became more patient. The government relied on the police rather than the army. Moreover, after the end of the conflict the government did not ostracize the more moderate elements of the Sikh community. Within months, Sikhs were welcomed back into the political process. Some elements of the Sikh Akali Dal party joined forces with the Hindu BJP. Others rejoined the Congress Party. When the Congress Party defeated the BJP to regain control of the national government in 2004, it was a Sikh—the distinguished economist, Manmohan Singh— who was named prime minister.

Part of the reason that the Indian government was patient with the Sikh movement was that it wanted to set a model for other fissiparous groups. Any excessive force used against the Sikhs would certainly have been noticed by the Kashmiris, who had mounted their own separatist movement. During the same week that Punjab's chief minister Beant Singh was assassinated in 1995, for example, the Indian government was involved in delicate negotiations for the release of foreign hostages in Kashmir and could not have afforded to renew hostilities with the Sikhs.

The tensions between the Sikh community and the secular government were not completely resolved. The government won the war against the militants not because it persuaded the Sikh masses that it was right, but because the public and the moderate Sikh leadership had grown weary of the militants' posturing. They were ready to accept the restoration of law and order at any cost. A great number of Sikhs continue to hope for a public order that gives greater recognition to the authority of their religious community, and many continue to wage their own small wars against the secularism of society, including what they regard as the insidious influence of Western-style scholarship on Sikh history and texts. The ingredients of religious rebellion have remained.

BUDDHIST REVOLTS IN ASIA

Sri Lanka

The island nation of Sri Lanka, like India, was once part of Britain's vast South Asian empire. Today both countries are ruled by largely secular parties that are caretakers for the political apparatus the British left behind. In both countries voices protest these vestiges of Western secular nationalism and demand a national identity more in touch with the nation's cultural past. In Sri Lanka, as in India, these demands have come from two directions: separatist minority movements and religious nationalists from the majority community. Unlike India, in Sri Lanka the Hindus are in the minority. They regard themselves as oppressed. But then, in a way, so does the Buddhist majority.

On August 17, 2006, an interfaith peace rally in Colombo, Sri Lanka's capital, was disrupted by a group of Buddhist monks. The rally, calling for an end to the twenty-year war between Sri Lanka's northern Tamils and southern Sinhala groups that has left over sixty-five thousand dead, was led by Buddhist monks, Hindu priests, Christian clergy, and Muslim mullahs. Suddenly a large band of saffron-clad Buddhist monks associated with the extreme pro-Sinhala Buddhist movement, the Jathika Hela Urumaya, attacked the rally. The two groups fought, shoving each other, with the pro-war monks telling the protesters to take their banners and rallies to the northern part of the island, where the Tamil separatists were in control. The specter of Buddhist monks breaking up a peace rally, proclaiming that peace was not an appropriate response to Tamil separatism, is dramatic testimony to the fact that not all Buddhists are pacifists, and that many Sinhalese Buddhists in Sri Lanka are engaged in what they regard as defensive warfare.

A politically active *bhikkhu* in the highlands of Sri Lanka near the sacred city of Kandy explained to me why he was so protective of his cultural tradition. "Look at the map," he implored, "and see how tiny, how fragile Sinhalese Buddhist society is." Other cultures, the bhikkhu explained, including Muslim, Christian, Hindu, and even other Buddhist cultures, are "enormous and secure, but our Sinhala society is only a teardrop, a grain of sand, in an enormous sea." And, he concluded, lowering his voice, "it is in danger of being forever dashed away."[106]

The bhikkhu did not feel that the presence of Tamils in the north and east of Sri Lanka was in itself a threat to Buddhism, nor did he fear the Tamils' Hinduism, which he regarded as part and parcel of Buddhist heritage. Rather, the bhikkhu blamed his country's nominally Buddhist but largely secular politicians for what he regarded as too soft an attitude toward Tamil demands and too negligent a response to the Sinhalese. "They are attempting genocide," he proclaimed, for they are "deliberately" trying to annihilate Sinhalese Buddhist culture.[107]

The bhikkhu's politics are emblematic of the second of two rebellions that the government of Sri Lanka has faced: one, a popular uprising in the rural Sinhalese area of the central and southern provinces, and the other, a better known, well-organized movement for Tamil separatism in the northern and eastern sections of the country. The Sinhalese movement is in some ways more threatening to the secular government because it challenges the state's legitimacy on a fundamental level and because it touches a sensitive nerve in all quarters of the 70 percent of the Sri Lankan population that is Buddhist.

The Sinhalese rebellion was fueled by the sentiments of many Buddhists, including the bhikkhu, who felt that independence from the West has yet to be won on a cultural and ideological level. "Those politicians who use English language and British customs and force the British political system on us," the bhikkhu explained, "continue colonialism in Sri Lanka as surely as if the British never left."[108]

It is easy for some Buddhists in Sri Lanka to feel this way because their form of Buddhism has been associated with Sinhalese culture and kings throughout Sri Lanka's history. (The term *Sinhalese*, of which the word *Ceylon* is a variation, derives from an ancient name for Sri Lanka, *Sinhala*, meaning lion.) Theravada Buddhist dynasties have ruled Sri Lanka—or have struggled with contending Tamil kings to do so—ever since the time of Mahinda, the son of the great Indian king Asoka. He is said to have journeyed to Sri Lanka and established the first Buddhist throne there in the third century B.C.E., bringing with him an offshoot of the Bodhi tree (under which the Buddha was enlightened) and the Buddha's tooth, a sacred relic that is housed in Sri Lanka's most important shrine, the Dalada Maligawa (Temple of the Tooth) in Kandy. From a Sinhalese perspective, the governments established by the Portuguese, Dutch, and British from 1505 to 1948 were all merely interruptions in the overall course of Sinhalese Buddhist history.[109]

Sri Lanka never had much of a nationalist movement, although a small number of the country's Western-educated leaders attempted to introduce to Sri Lanka some of the same modern secular nationalism that they saw Nehru and the other leaders of India's Congress Party bringing to their large neighbor to the north. When the British suddenly offered independence to Sri Lanka in 1948, these people were prepared to rule. They had little time to develop an ideology of secular nationalism, however, and even in the nationalist movement, such as it was, a sizable contingent of religious leaders had no use for the rhetoric of secularism. The first person to carry a flag in support of the country's freedom was a Buddhist monk, and today a statue in front of the Dalada Maligawa celebrates his patriotic act.

After independence, there was a great deal of controversy over the role of Buddhism in the country's symbols of nationalism. In 1972 the name of the country was changed from the Anglicized form of Sinhala—Ceylon—to a less specifically Buddhist one, Sri Lanka (the name given to the island nation in the great Hindu epic the *Ramayana*). The symbol chosen for the national flag, however, was the Sinhalese lion. The suggestion that it would be more appropriate to have on the flag an ethnically neutral symbol such as Adam's Peak—the mountaintop in the central part of the island that is venerated equally by Hindus, Sinhalese, and Muslims—was rejected.[110] Many Sinhalese felt that the time had come to restore Buddhism as the national religion, and in 1953 a popular tract, *The Revolt in the Temple,* urged the populace to reject the emerging secular nationalism; another claimed that Buddhism had been "betrayed."[111] Political leaders found it increasingly useful to employ the rhetoric of Buddhism to buttress their own power.[112]

An emphasis on Buddhist culture and Sinhalese language was the vehicle on which Bandaranaike and his Sri Lanka Freedom Party (SLFP) rode to power. In 1956 they even supported legislation that made Sinhala the sole official language of the nation. As soon as the bill was passed, they backed away from its extreme implications in order to protect Tamil minority interests, but in doing so they alienated some of their Buddhist supporters (such as the wily political activist and monk, Mapitigama Buddharakkhita Thero) and left an opening for political rivals—including one of Bandaranaike's successors, J. R. Jayawardene—to gain Sinhalese support by claiming that the SLFP had reneged on its promises. On September 25, 1959, Bandaranaike was killed by a Buddhist monk in a conspiracy allegedly masterminded by Buddharakkhita, who among other things was unhappy with the pace of Bandaranaike's efforts to make Buddhism the state religion.

The idea of Buddhist nationalism, even in the tepid form proposed by Bandaranaike, did not sit well with minority communities. The largest of them, the Hindu Tamils, had lived for centuries in the northern and eastern sections of the island, and claimed it as a Tamil homeland. According to one Tamil writer, his community stemmed from the "aboriginal people of Sri Lanka," who had lived in the island long before the Sinhalese arrived.[113] Tamil unrest in the north led to a severe backlash in the south. In 1983 a storm of violence was unleashed against Tamils living in Colombo and elsewhere; hundreds—some say thousands—were killed in the riots.[114] Soon after, a Tamil separatist movement began in earnest.

The Tamil position was not explicitly religious. The movement was directed toward creating a separate Tamil nation, Thamil Eelam, in which religious identities—specifically Hindu and Christian—were not immediately apparent. As one separatist writer explained, "The original link between Tamil ethnicity and the Hindu religion has come to be severed."[115] Instead, Tamil ethnicity replaced Hinduism as the focal point of nationalist pride among Tamils. As a result, some of the most active participants in the Tamil separatist movement have been Christians, even Christian clergy. The cyanide capsules that dedicated members of the Black Tigers—the most militant Tamil movement—wore around their necks were suspended from the same black rope necklaces that Tamil Christians have worn in displaying the crucifix. The fanaticism of the Tigers led one Western writer to describe them as "the Asian guerrilla equivalent of the Rev. Jim Jones and his Guyana suicide cult."[116] Yet Tamil rebels seldom have chosen religious targets. Although Buddhist monks were sometimes caught up in the violence—in 1987, twenty-nine monks were dragged out of a bus near the ancient Buddhist capital, Anuradhapura, and systematically gunned down—the Tamil movement's main enemy was the secular government. Perhaps paradoxically, the favorite target of Buddhist militants was the government as well.

The growth in Sinhalese Buddhist militancy during the 1980s was in part a response to the Tamil separatist movement and in part a response to the government's purported secularism and neutrality in the face of communal conflict. The Sinhalese militants were bitterly opposed to the pact between Sri Lankan president Jayawardene and India's Rajiv Gandhi in May 1987 to bring in Indian troops to quell the Tamil uprising in the northern and eastern sections of the island. The pact gave increased political autonomy to the Tamils, which many Sinhalese viewed as capitulation to Tamil demands. Moreover, the pact did not quiet the most extreme of the Tamil separatists, the Liberation Tigers of Thamil Eelam, who persisted in fighting to the death, and who turned against Rajiv Gandhi, bringing about his death in 1991 in a suicide attack. The occupation troops of the Indian Army Peacekeeping Force, for their part, did not quickly leave. Rather, their numbers swelled to over sixty thousand—more soldiers than the British had in India even at the height of the empire.[117] Fear spread throughout Sri Lanka that Rajiv Gandhi's gift of peace was a Trojan horse and that even when the Indian army left, the military and political ties to India would remain.

The antipathy to Sri Lanka's pact with the Indian military greatly boosted support for the Janatha Vimukthi Peramuna (JVP)—the People's Liberation Front.[118] The JVP was a revival of an earlier movement of the same name that in 1971 attempted an abortive coup against Sirimavo Bandaranaike, the widow of the slain leader, who succeeded him in office. Both stages of the movement were said to have been led by Rohana Wijeweera, until he was captured and killed in police custody in 1989. Wijeweera was a secular radical with Marxist credentials—he once attended college in Moscow—and he was never fully accepted by many of the religious activists who followed the JVP banner, especially those in its later incarnation. Yet the movement was not so closely organized as to require strict obedience to any single leader, and Wijeweera himself claimed to have no influence over many aspects of the Sinhalese movement, including its most violent wing, the Deshapremi Janatha Viyaparaya.

Taken as a whole, the Sinhala movement could be described as one of cultural nationalism; it was in many ways a Sinhalese Buddhist revolt. Leaders of the movement recalled Sir Lanka's glorious Buddhist past, and they regarded the secular, democratic government of Colombo as an enemy of Buddhism and an obstacle to social progress. But although the new JVP was more Buddhist in its rhetoric than its predecessor party, it was perhaps even more savage. Some estimates put the number of villagers killed in the thousands. In many cases, the killings took the form of gangland slayings, as old rivalries were brought into the open and old grudges were avenged. In other cases, the violence was an attempt to assert the militants' own control over rural areas and to undercut the legitimacy of the government.

Though the JVP movement has been a fixture of Sri Lankan politics for over twenty years, it has consistently been a "youthful revolt."[119] The most active members of each generation of the movement are young men aged eighteen to twenty-six.[120] Thus, its constituency in the 1990s and the first decade of the twenty-first century was entirely different from that of its 1971 predecessor. Members of the earlier movement had become middle-aged and in some cases they were targets of the wrath of the new JVP youth.[121] Many of the most active supporters of the new generations of the movement have been unemployed villagers in the southern part of the island; some observers told me that a majority of the young people there were sympathetic to or at least did not resist JVP activities.[122] Fieldworkers in the Sarvodaya relief and development agency reported difficulties in carrying out their activities owing to JVP interference: they were harassed and their vehicles were stolen.[123] The main targets of the JVP, however, were government officials.

In 1987, President Jayawardene was targeted for assassination. When shots fired at him during a parliamentary meeting missed, hand grenades were then tossed in his direction. They bounced across the table in front of him and exploded. Jayawardene escaped unscathed, but a member of his cabinet was killed and seventeen others were wounded. In 1988, a popular Sinhalese film star and politician, Vijaya Kumaranatunga, who was in the process of creating a new alliance among three Socialist parties, was shot dead by gunmen on a motorcycle as they sped past his house in Colombo. Later in the day two bombs that had been planted inside a crowded Hindu temple near the film star's home exploded while priests were chanting their evening prayers; seven people were instantly killed, and thirteen more were seriously injured. Although Reuters reported that "police could not say who was responsible," the JVP was widely blamed for the assassination and the bombing.[124]

The government was clearly the enemy in what amounted to a Sinhalese holy war. One indication of the JVP's antipathy to the government—and its influence in the countryside—was evident on Sri Lanka's Independence Day in 1988, when leaders of the JVP sent out word that no one was to display the Sri Lanka national flag; I happened to be in Sri Lanka at the time and could verify that in areas dominated by the JVP virtually no one did. Black flags were flown instead.[125]

One place in which black flags were prominently in evidence—with no national flags in sight—was the campus of Peradeniya University, near Kandy, where strongly worded antigovernment slogans were scrolled across the walls of classroom buildings. "JR [the President] is a monkey," some of the graffiti proclaimed, "a pest that should be destroyed!" Behind the pro-JVP activities at Peradeniya was a secret student action committee. Its membership was mixed: it included Muslims and even Tamil supporters, and some of the most active members of the committee were student Buddhist monks.[126] Only four hundred monks were enrolled at Peradeniya, but a disproportionately large number of them were political activists. The more established leaders of Buddhist monastic orders admonished the monks to resist the temptation to use violent means, but even elder monks had a great deal of sympathy for the JVP cause.[127]

The young monks in the rural areas were especially vulnerable to the appeal of the JVP and particularly impatient: "They don't listen to us," one of the *bhikkhu*s I interviewed said, referring to the admonition of the older monks to keep quiet and not be involved in movements for radical change.[128] There was a certain pride in his voice as he spoke about these young firebrands. He explained that the concerns behind movements such as the JVP were valid, even if some of their actions could be faulted. "What is the message of these people?" the *bhikkhu* asked, and then answered his own question: "They want jobs and fair elections, they want order to be restored, and a peaceful Buddhist rule." The image he presented was of a fair-minded but oppressed generation that had been pushed to its limit. It was reasonable, from this point of view, for socially concerned monks to join in the revolution: he said that they "struggle for *dhamma*" in their own way. Politicians, according to the *bhikkhu*, "are not interested in Buddhism" but "only in themselves."[129] By implication, this left only the younger, more strident, and more selfless leaders to take the interests of the Sinhalese Buddhist nation truly to heart.

By mid-1989, the JVP was entering one of its most active—and brutal—phases. Increasingly young Buddhist monks who had secretly supported the movement came out into the open. On April 7, over two hundred demonstrated in front of the Temple of the Tooth, protesting government policies in general and the government's attempts to crush the JVP in particular. They were assaulted by the police and a good number were injured.[130] One scholar estimates that a hundred monks were killed in police encounters during 1989.[131]

An important moment in the government's war with the JVP came after Ranasinghe Premadasa was elected president on December 19, 1988. Although some observers had hoped that he would be regarded as more sympathetic toward Buddhism and traditional Sinhalese culture than his predecessor, the JVP boycotted the elections and vowed not to relax their activities until all their demands—including the demand for a Sinhalese Buddhist state—were met. Between January 10 and 26, 1989, eight candidates for parliamentary seats were dragged from their homes and killed by JVP supporters. Further acts of violence occurred after the parliamentary elections on February 15, 1989. The JVP initiated a series of highly effective strikes, demanding higher wages for workers and the withdrawal of Indian troops, and on June 12, 1989, several people were killed when police broke up a JVP-sponsored demonstration in western Sri Lanka that called for a boycott of Indian goods and for the departure of all Indians—civilian and military—from Sri Lankan soil.

By 1990 some of the most vicious elements of the JVP were destroyed, though radical Buddhist opposition to the secular government persisted. By engineering the retreat of Indian forces from Sri Lanka in 1990, Premadasa removed one of the major sources of irritation that had fueled JVP discontent. He dealt with the Sinhalese movement both directly, through confrontation, and indirectly, by coopting the Buddhist leadership.

The government confronted the militants directly. The army let it be known that for every one of them killed it would kill twenty members of the JVP or their sympathizers. In one case an assault on an entire village near Kandy left over two hundred dead.[132] On June 20, 1989, President Premadasa declared a state of emergency and arrested thirty-two hundred suspected JVP sympathizers and other leftists; scarcely a week later he survived a bomb attack at a crowded religious festival. The JVP was implicated in the attempt.

For the rest of 1989 and throughout the first half of 1990, the army was unleashed to use whatever means it wished. One of its most terrifying tactics was to kill young JVP activists and leave their bodies on the main roads, sometimes for days, as public examples. A taxi driver in Colombo told me that he had counted forty-seven such bodies while driving the short stretch of road between the towns of Humbantota and Tangalle on one day in January 1990.[133] The total number of JVP members and their sympathizers killed is a subject of some dispute. Some put the numbers in the tens of thousands.[134] Most estimates are in the thousands, but even if the accurate number is somewhere between three thousand and six thousand, as many claim, that is a significant figure. It was sufficient to destroy the leadership and break the momentum of the movement.

By the middle of 1990, the most militant wing of the JVP was crushed. The main outcry against the government's brutal repression of the movement came from civil libertarians and liberal Buddhists, who feared that the government's reign of terror could not be contained. Yet even students in Peradeniya University, including those whose friends had "disappeared" as a result of the army's action, seemed relieved that the JVP was no longer around to intimidate them. They claimed that the "excesses" of the government are sometimes necessary to maintain law and order.[135]

One of the reasons that there was not more of an outcry against the government's actions is that the Buddhist leadership had been coopted. In 1991 and 1992 Premadasa spent an enormous amount of time visiting Buddhist temples and monasteries, and the newspapers became crowded with pictures of the president giving offerings at such Buddhist shrines as the Temple of the Tooth. Genuinely religious—even superstitious, in a traditional Sri Lankan-village way—the lower-caste, rural Premadasa traveled with a coterie of dancers and musicians who blessed the floor that he stepped on at official functions. He proclaimed that *raj-dharma* (the age of religious righteousness) had begun, ordered the construction of a gold-painted replica of the throne used by ancient Sri Lankan kings for his use at official functions, and appeared on television and elsewhere seated on a specially blessed chair with all the aura of a religious master.[136]

Perhaps Premadasa garnered the most Buddhist support by creating a new cabinet-level agency, the Ministry of Buddhist Affairs, of which he appointed himself the first minister.[137] The leaders of the four main monastic chapters were appointed as the ministry's council. Premadasa presented the council with some twenty-five million rupees to use in establishing an endowment for Buddhist causes. The council was also given the responsibility of adjudicating matters of Buddhist concern and suggesting appropriate government policies on religion and morality. It was instrumental in persuading the government to rescind its support for fish-breeding ponds (because the purpose of the ponds was to kill animate life). The monks felt that their voice was finally being heard. One of the members of the council, a leader of a monastic order that had previously been critical of the government, said in January 1991 that the government was now beginning to "reflect Buddhist values."[138]

Not all monks were impressed with Premadasa's new policies however. One of the most militant of the *bhikkhu*s that I had interviewed in the heyday of the JVP movement seemed despondent over the destruction of the movement and the wanton killing of so many young activists, including a good many idealistic Buddhist monks.[139] When I interviewed him again in 1991, he told me that all the efforts of the government to put on a Buddhist front were just that, a show designed to win public support. "Supporting things like temples and stupas does not make one a good Buddhist," he explained; "you have to be Buddhist inside."[140] Moreover, he did not believe that the Sinhalese movement had been entirely crushed. "You can kill people," he said, "but this does not kill their ideas or destroy the things that caused them to fight."[141] He speculated that a revived Sinhalese nationalist movement would rise again.

He did not have to wait very long. On May 1, 1993, during a May Day parade in Colombo, a bicyclist strapped with explosives rammed into President Premadasa, instantly killing him and a dozen members of his entourage. Although Tamil rebels were implicated in the attack, the political chaos that ensued encouraged the tattered remnants of the government's other political enemy, the Sinhalese nationalists, to regroup. They soon were able to capitalize on the absence of Premadasa's charismatic leadership and his uncompromising stance toward his opposition. The Sinhalese movement was also spurred on by the increasing severity of Tamil attacks on the capital and elsewhere in the Sinhalese region of the country. After an unsuccessful attempt at a ceasefire in 1995, the last half of that decade was the bloodiest of Sri Lanka's civil war.

In the twenty-first century, peace came to the island, at least for a time.[142] The Norwegian government had been invited to help broker a peace agreement, which promised semi-autonomy for the Tamil-held areas with the understanding that the region would remain a part of the country. The motivation for a negotiated peace was driven in large part by the lack of success by either the Tamil or government forces in forcing a military solution. In 2001, national elections brought to power Prime Minster Ranil Wickremasinghe, as well as members of his United National Front (UNF) party, who had campaigned on a peace platform. By the end of the year a ceasefire was in effect.

For five years the ceasefire persisted. From the start, however, extremists on both sides seemed determined to undo the fragile peace. The tensions were exacerbated when the Tamil and Sinhala regions competed for relief efforts after the tragic tsunami of December 2004 swept over the eastern and southern shores of the island. On the Sinhala side, the peaceful intentions of the UNF were contradicted by President Chandrika Bandaranaike Kumaratunga, who had lost an eye in a Tamil assassination attempt and whose husband had been assassinated, allegedly by a member of the JVP. She opposed concessions to the Tamils and tried to block Prime Minister Wickremasinghe's reforms. In the 2005 elections she was succeeded by an equally hard-line opponent of Tamil concessions, Mahinda Rajapaksa, who was supported by Kumaratunga's party in coalition with the JVP. By the end of the year violence had again returned to the island.

The breakdown of the ceasefire was accompanied—some say precipitated—by the rise of a new pro-Sinhala Buddhist movement, the Jathika Hela Urumaya (National Heritage Party). It was founded in 2004 with a strong religious strand of Sinhala nationalism in its ideology. From the beginning it was led by Buddhist monks. In the 2004 legislative elections, the party received 6 percent of the votes and was able to place nine representatives in the Sri Lankan parliament, all of them from monastic orders. In addition to opposing the peace agreement with the Tamil movement, the party opposed the practice of proselytizing by Christian missionaries. It was Buddhist monks associated with the JHU who disrupted the peace rally in Colombo in August 2006.

Within the JHU there has been considerable discussion about whether the movement should involve itself in electoral politics or continue protests from outside the government. Like Hindu and Sikh religious nationalists in India and elsewhere in South Asia, Sinhalese nationalists have regarded the secular parliamentary process—often touted in the West as the hallmark of freedom and democracy—with ambivalence. Sometimes it has been embraced as a vehicle for expressing the religious and moral will of the people, and at other times it has been denounced as a purveyor of Western cultural colonialism. Either way, it has been subordinate to a vision of religious social order that religious activists believe to be superior to the politics of secular modernism. At one time Marxism provided an alternative to those who were looking for an ideological base different from the American or Western European models. Increasingly, however, social rebels have looked to their own cultural traditions for a distinctive national identity

Mongolia

Much of the same spirit of ethnic pride has fueled Buddhist politics in Mongolia, where it is Soviet control rather than British colonialism that created a homogenous political identity. As in Sri Lanka, many Mongolians now reject secular rule imposed from outside in favor of something more local, more reflective of their culture and religion. "Communism tried to conquer religion," the founder of a new Mongolian religious party told me in Ulan Bator. "But now," he proudly asserted, "religion is replacing communism."[143]

This claim of S. Bayantsagaan, president of the Association of Mongolian Believers, is somewhat exaggerated because many of Mongolia's old Socialist leaders are still very much in power, and his own party thus far has only a limited following. But he is correct in stating that the old ideology has lost its force, and a post-Soviet public consciousness has emerged in Mongolia—one that compounds nationalism and religion, and replaces Marxism as the legitimizing force in public life. In this sense what is happening in Mongolia is a paradigm of what is occurring throughout the former Soviet Union and its client states.[144]

As elsewhere in the region, much of the force of new nationalism has been fueled by a pent-up hostility against what was regarded by many as a long period of Russian colonialism. In Ulan Bator, a research historian for the government archives who is a member of the ruling socialist party—the Mongolian People's Revolutionary Party—was adamant in claiming that her party was not communist. It was founded before it came under Russian communist influence, she told me, and now the truth could come out about how her party had been "exploited and controlled" by the Russians all these years.[145]

The colonial control of the Russians was a mixed blessing, she explained, offering the architecture of the city as an illustration of how the benefits of Russian economic support were purchased at the expense of Mongolian national identity and pride. In the middle of a barren, windswept valley that rises above the chilly emptiness of the Gobi desert is the new center of Ulan Bator. Row after row of massive Soviet institutional buildings line the broad streets, punctuated by statues of Lenin and Mongolian revolutionary heroes. Behind these mammoth concrete showcases are bland cinder-block apartment houses, and behind them the teepee-like *ghers,* also known by their Russian name, *yurts.* It is in these round tents—made of woolen felt and canvas covering a latticed wood frame—that most Mongolians live. A pictorial map of the city at the turn of the century shows that it once consisted mostly of *ghers* and magnificent complexes of Buddhist temples and monasteries. At the time of the Mongolian revolution in 1921, there were said to have been almost a thousand monasteries in the country and 120,000 lamas—roughly 40 percent of the mature male population at that time.[146] Because a fourth of the country's population lives in the major city, Ulan Bator, many of the temples were located there.

Almost all these magnificent old temple buildings—some constructed in a circular, Mongolian style, and others in an elaborate Tibetan fashion—came tumbling down as the entire downtown of Ulan Bator was leveled, and Soviet-style monoliths were constructed in their place. The only temple complex to escape the Soviet wrecking ball was the Gandan Tegchinlen Monastery, the center of Mongolian Buddhism, which is located on a knoll on the outskirts of the Ulan Bator valley. Even there, the population of monks shrank from several hundred to under a hundred, and during Stalin's most repressive assaults against religious institutions throughout the Soviet world, the monastery virtually closed its doors.

Now the Gandan Monastery is open again, packed with worshipers on weekends and holy days. The number of lamas grew from a hundred to two hundred fifty in fewer than two years. Many of the newcomers were "hidden lamas," men who had been lamas years ago and were forced to go back to ordinary society when their monasteries were closed, and young monks who had been ordained in secret. In fact, existing monasteries could not meet the demand for places, and newly organized neighborhood monasteries were springing up all over the country. These new lamas included women as well as men, although the authorities were undecided about whether to grant women full monastic ordination. A council was instituted to set standards for monastic life and to decide where new monasteries should be situated.[147]

The rise of monastic organizations and the resurgence of Mongolian nationalism were related to one another. "Mongolian identity and its religion cannot be separated," the deputy head lama of Gandan Monastery remarked to me in a matter-of-fact way.[148] Although none in Mongolia would doubt this assertion, it strikes the outsider as being a little odd: the religion of Mongolia, after all, is a form of Buddhism associated with another country, Tibet. Mongolians follow the "yellow-hat" school of Vajrayana, or Tibetan, Buddhism, and one of the standards of monastic life is the facility in Tibetan—the canonical language of the tradition. Every major temple in Mongolia has a throne reserved for Tibet's exiled leader, the Dalai Lama, and when he sits on it—as he has on three visits to the temple of the Gandan Monastery—the seat becomes blessed.

The highest spiritual authorities in Mongolia come from outside the country. In 1989, shortly before the political climate rapidly changed, the Indian government attempted to help the Mongolian Buddhist authorities bring a famous Tibetan spiritual leader into the country. He was an incarnate spiritual being, a *bakula*, and the last of a lineage of seventeen. He was living in India, and the socialist authorities of Mongolia would not allow him a visa. The Indian government officials hit on a clever scheme, however: they named him the Indian ambassador to Mongolia, which enabled him to enter the country with diplomatic privileges. He continued to live in Ulan Bator for years afterward, holding spiritual court every Saturday in the Indian Embassy and providing religious guidance to the country's Buddhist institutions.[149]

What has made the country's Buddhism distinctively Mongolian, therefore, is not the tenets of the faith but the history of its religious institutions, which have been intertwined with Mongolia's national history. The people of Mongolia are ethnically mixed, but their language, and probably their basic ethnic stock, is Altaic and can be traced to a culture that stretches from Turkey to Manchuria, a cultural band that separates the Euro-Russians in the northwest from the Han Chinese in the southeast. Their religion, however, they acquired on their own.

According to the traditional history as recalled by the monks in Ulan Bator, Mahayana Buddhism came to Mongolia via the Silk Road in the century before the common era.[150] Over the centuries, other religious influences followed the same route and each of these religious traditions—Manicheanism, Nestorian Christianity, and Islam—has left its mark. The arrival of Tibetan Buddhism in the thirteenth century is credited by the monks to the Mongolian ruler Genghis Khan (1162–1227), whose campaigns took him throughout Central Asia.[151] Later in the thirteenth century one of Genghis Khan's descendants, Kublai Khan, ruled from China to Russia and named a lama in Beijing as the head of the Buddhist faith for Tibet, Mongolia, and China.[152] In the seventeenth to nineteenth centuries, when the tables were turned and the Manchu Ch'ing dynasty dominated Mongolia, the Mongolians held to Tibetan Buddhist tradition as a bulwark against Chinese cultural influences.

The departure of the Manchu governor in 1911 from what was then called Urga (Ulan Bator) marked the beginning of modern, independent Mongolia.[153] It also marked the advent of Mongolia's brief experiment with theocracy. On December 16, 1911, Mongolia's hereditary Buddhist leader, Bogda Cegeen Javdzandamba Hutagt, was proclaimed the new khan of Mongolia. Like the Dalai Lama in Tibet, he was regarded as possessing both secular and spiritual authority. Although the local leaders of the section of Mongolia that lay to the southeast of Ulan Bator, across the Gobi Desert, preferred to unite with their kinfolk under the leadership of the Bogda Khan, both Russia and China wished to keep independent Mongolia as small as possible, and the southeastern part of Mongolia—Inner Mongolia—remained, as it does today, a part of China.[154]

In the northern, independent part of the country—Outer Mongolia—the Bogda Khan's theocratic rule was short-lived. It was preoccupied with a military threat from the Chinese, who in 1919 set up a command post in Ulan Bator. Help appeared to come from a White Russian cavalry unit, which entered Mongolia with Japanese support and attempted to oust the Chinese and reinstall the Bogda Khan. But the picture was complicated by yet another group of Mongolians attempting to defeat the Chinese and set up its own secular, working-class rule. These Mongolian revolutionaries, led by Sukhbaatar, were no friends of either the Bogda Khan or the White Russians; they were supported by the new Communist government in Moscow.

Ultimately the new group—the Mongolian People's Revolutionary Party (MPRP)—won this three-way tussle. However, the intervention of the Soviet Army was necessary. With its help, the MPRP drove the Chinese back across the Gobi, and the White Russian cavalry was defeated. On July 11, 1921, the new government came to power, and that date has been proclaimed Mongolian National Day. One of the first acts of the new government was to request that Russian troops remain in the country for a while to help restore order.

The Russian troops managed to extend their stay for another seventy years. At first the religious institutions of the country were respected, and the Bogda Khan retained his title, although little of his secular power. When the Bogda Khan died in 1924, his palace across the river from the center of Ulan Bator was turned into a museum, and the country was proclaimed a republic. The new leader of the MPRP, Choybalsan, was a more determined Socialist than his predecessor had been and began to turn the country in a distinctly Stalinist direction. The 1926 Law of Separation of Religion from the State called for protection of the Buddhist faith, but it also sought to "liberate the population from religious prejudice."[155] Mongolia became de facto a part of the Soviet Union. During the so-called Leftist Deviation of 1929–32, Choybalsan and his colleagues appropriated many of the huge monastic properties—*jas*—and suspended the operations of many other religious institutions as well. Atheism became state policy.

Choybalsan's long career came to an end at his death in 1952. He was succeeded by Tsendenbal, who enforced one aspect of Stalin's Russification program that had heretofore been resisted in Mongolia: the use of the Russian Cyrillic alphabet rather than the strange, vertical cursive script used for centuries by the Mongolians, who had borrowed it from the Uigurs in the thirteenth century. In other ways, however, Tsendenbal was a rather bland, bureaucratic leader, and although he carried out Khrushchev's antireligious campaigns in the 1960s, his focus was more on "superstitious" religious folk practices than on Buddhist organizations;

in 1979 he allowed the Dalai Lama to make a brief but triumphant visit to Ulan Bator.[156] By 1984, when Tsendenbal was succeeded by Batmonh, the leadership was facing a rising swell of nationalism and religious resurgence at home, and the beginnings of Mikhail Gorbachev's restructuring in the patron state to the north.

The old system began to crumble in December 1989.[157] Massive demonstrations on the main square in front of the parliament building in Ulan Bator were followed in February 1990 by hunger strikes by ardent young activists who demanded the democratization of Mongolia. In March 1990, to everyone's surprise, the government capitulated and called for open elections in June of that year. As the MPRP reorganized to meet the election challenge, it removed virtually every senior party leader and government official from power. The new leader of the party, D. Bayambsuren, who advocated democratic reform, economic opportunity, and human rights, was overwhelmingly elected.[158]

The party lived up to its promises. In the two years that followed, myriad new political parties were formed, newspapers were allowed to openly criticize the government, the old Mongolian script was back in fashion, and, most important, a new constitution guaranteed these freedoms and promoted democratic elections and private ownership. Long before the Russian government adopted the idea, the Mongolian government instituted a system of vouchers, which were distributed equally to all its citizens, allowing them to "purchase" stocks in formerly state-owned companies or in private businesses, thereby, as one of Mongolia's economists described it, "creating an economic system from nothing."[159]

In 1991, in a burst of democratic enthusiasm, a crowd of young people attacked and destroyed a statue of Stalin, replacing it for a time with a talismanlike stone, which some regarded as having spiritual powers. This act was symbolic in several ways. The most obvious was the replacement of the most vicious symbol of Russian colonialism with a natively Mongolian symbol. Two other nearby statues, however, were ignored. In the central square, the statue of Sukhbaatar, the founding leader of the MPRP, is unblemished. Directly in front of Mongolia State University—a particularly vulnerable location—the statue of Choybalsan, "Mongolia's Stalin," is largely untouched as well. From time to time, I was told by university officials, graffiti and spray paint marred the statue's base, but for the most part students left it alone.[160] Even though Choybalsan's rule was dictatorial, he was still a Mongolian, and for that reason, if for none other, he deserved respect.

This same spirit of nationalism pervaded the new constitution (the Yassa) ratified early in 1992. Its preamble contained some familiar phrases of universal citizenship, but it also carried a distinctively nationalist slant: "We, the people of Mongolia, cherishing human rights, freedoms, justice, and the national unity; inheriting the national statehood, the traditions of its history and culture; strengthening the independence and the sovereignty of the nation; respecting the civilization of mankind; and desiring to develop a humane and democratic society in the land of Mongolia, hereby proclaim the State Yassa as the Constitution of the State."[161]

The drafting committee considered including a clause in the constitution that would have proclaimed Buddhism the state religion but ultimately rejected the idea in favor of the more vague wording respecting "the traditions of [Mongolia's] history and culture." Despite this show of support for traditional religion, the constitution explicitly prohibited monasteries from assuming political power. Presumably this clause was intended to guard against the resumption of the sort of theocratic power once enjoyed by the Bogda Khan.

There was good reason to be concerned. A new Bogda Khan was identified some years ago by the Dalai Lama living nearby in New Delhi.[162] Quite a few Mongolians were ready to install him as the nation's leader and many demanded that the government allow him to take up residence in Ulan Bator. "We need a spiritual center," one Buddhist activist explained, "and even if he is not yet allowed to have political power, he will give spiritual direction to the nation."[163] The government, however, was not eager to deal with the potential political consequences of such a significant immigrant. It already had its hands full with the explosion of religious activity throughout the country.[164]

In the past, the government controlled religion by allowing a moderate expression of it in the Gandan Monastery and by setting up a showcase international Buddhist organization, the Asian Buddhist Conference for Peace (ABCP), the headquarters of which were located in the monastery. The general secretary of the organization, G. Lubsantseren, was a scholar of Buddhist philosophy and a member of the MPRP. He once wrote articles offering a Marxist critique of Buddhism.[165] In post-Soviet Mongolia, however, government funding for the ABCP has been drastically reduced, and its offices moved out of the Gandan Monastery. Lubsantseren, who claims that he was never really an atheist, became involved in new projects, such as founding an international institute of Buddhist studies.[166]

Government-sponsored Buddhist organizations like the ABCP became obsolete as the traditional centers of Buddhism flourished after
1990. They tended to support government policies and played a moderate role in the nation's Buddhist affairs. Choiyal, elected in 1990 as the
first lama in the Mongolian parliament, the Great Hural, was a member
of Gandan. He ran as an independent but was said to have had the ruling party's support.

The growth of new monastic organizations outside its authority has
tested the Gandan Monastery's authority more than the government has.
Many of these upstart monasteries were nothing more than small neighborhood clubs, the *gher* equivalents of storefront churches. A more serious challenge has come from the former deputy head lama of the Gandan
Monastery, C. Dambajav, who hurried back to Ulan Bator from Dharamsala, India, where he had been studying with the Dalai Lama during the
1989–90 uprising, to found his own separate monastic organization.

Dambajav located several old monastic buildings in the heart of Ulan
Bator that had escaped the Soviet wreckers. These round, tent-like
wooden buildings situated behind several high-rise apartment buildings
had fallen into disrepair. Two were used as storage facilities; a third had
become the training gymnasium for young aspirants to the Mongolian
circus. Dambajav set up an office adjacent to the circus gymnasium and
began transforming the storage buildings into Tibetan Buddhist temples.
His Tashichoeling Monastery soon had a hundred lamas, and he expanded the space to make room for more. Conveniently located in the
heart of the city and run in an enthusiastic, youthful style, the monastery
became popular among the urban faithful. It soon began to rival the
Gandan Monastery in size and popularity. Dambajav told me that Buddhism in Mongolia was "a sleeping giant" that was only beginning to realize its potential.[167]

Both the Gandan Monastery and government authorities have been
concerned about Dambajav's own political potential, however, and took
steps to channel his power. Through the mediation of the Indian ambassador *cum rinpoche*, various Buddhist leaders were brought together
late in 1991, including Dambajav and the Gandan hierarchy, to form a
governing council—or rather a series of regional councils, each of which
would be represented on a national council of Buddhist organizations.
Dambajav was appointed head of the Ulan Bator division, which thereby
gave him a seat on the national panel, of which the head lama of the Gandan Monastery was appointed chair. Thus both leaders received status
and a role in the country's Buddhist leadership.

Dambajav has been circumspect about the role that monasteries should play in secular politics. He told me that he has not ruled out political involvement for lamas. Ordinarily, however, he felt that Buddhism as a religion has only two roles to play in Mongolian political life: it provides "social values," and it gives a locus of "national identity."[168] Any sincere Buddhist layperson—even a member of the MPRP—can bring these characteristics to public life. As long as they support Buddhist nationalism, he said, there was no need for a separate Buddhist political party.

Other Buddhists, more radical than Dambajav, disagreed. Many of them could be found outside the main gate of the Gandan Monastery, where a rough wooden-plank fence demarcated a section of bare earth on which a cluster of felt and canvas-covered *ghers* had been constructed. These served as the headquarters of the Association of Buddhist Believers and its allied political arm, the Mongolian Buddhist Party. Their founder, Bayantsagaan, graduated from the monastery's seminary in the late 1970s, but because opportunities to become a monk were limited in those days, he became a research scholar in Buddhist philosophy for the Institute of Oriental Studies in the state's Academy of Sciences. In 1990, when Mongolia was undergoing its political changes, he heard reports of new Islamic and Christian religious parties being formed in other former Soviet states and felt that the time was ripe for a similar, Buddhist party to be established in Mongolia.[169]

Bayantsagaan claimed over a hundred thousand registered members in the association and its political party. In a nation of two million, this is not yet sufficient to constitute a serious electoral threat. Shortly before the June 28, 1992, elections, he told me that he hoped his party would gain three or four seats out of the seventy-six contested, but in fact the party failed to gain any at all. Despite this personal defeat, Bayantsagaan was pleased with the modest success of several democratic opposition parties with which he was allied; they won five seats.[170] And he had no regrets for the time spent campaigning. He felt that the 1992 electoral campaign helped him build an audience for his message, which, simply put, is one of Buddhist political power. Until the last vestige of the old secular Socialism is rooted out, he said, Buddhism would be in danger. That, he added, was the reason Buddhist politics were necessary.

When I asked him whether he longed for the restoration of the Bogda Khan, Bayantsagaan responded, "Of course." Realizing this was not an immediate possibility, however, he stated that as many religious people should be elected to parliament as possible: preferably "half the deputies in the Great Hural," he said, "should be lamas."[171] Eventually, however, a Buddhist state would not need such devices as parliaments. The lamas could rule directly. "This would not constitute a theocracy, however," he hastened to explain, in answer to my query, "because Buddhism is by nature democratic." When I pressed him on this point, he explained that democracy essentially means "respect of man for others," and in that sense "Buddhism is the highest form of democracy."[172]

Though the party did not prosper, Buddhism continued to play a role in Mongolian politics. In 2000, the election of Nambarin Enkhbayar was said to have benefited from the support of the Buddhist monastic community. Enkhbayar, who had formerly been a Marxist, proclaimed himself a devout Buddhist, and solicited the support of the Buddhist leadership. Enkhbayar is reported to have been introduced to Buddhist ideas during the Soviet years, when he was subjected to an attempted anti-Buddhist indoctrination by his Communist mentors. After the 1990 revolution, he converted to Buddhism, translated Buddhist texts into Mongolian, and created a cross-party Buddhist forum within the Mongolian parliament. He has also represented the Buddhist faith at the World Faiths and Development Dialogues in London. Though his Mongolian People's Revolutionary Party lost the 2004 elections, Enkhbayar was elected to the largely ceremonial role of president in 2005.

Tibet

Buddhism has also played a central role in Tibetan politics, most recently in the resistance to the Chinese control of the country. The political role of religion in Tibet has been a long tradition, for the successive incarnations of the Dalai Lama have provided temporal as well as spiritual rule over the region. The occupation of Tibet by the Chinese army in 1950 disrupted this pattern and the present Dalai Lama, Tenzin Gyatso, went into exile in India along with many of his supporters in 1959. Since then he has been based in the northern Indian mountain town of Dharamsala when he is not traveling on his extensive trips abroad. The Chinese established another Buddhist religious authority, the Panchen Lama, as a figurehead leader whose authority was limited to religious matters; he was said to have lived virtually under house arrest. After his death in 1989, a new Panchen Lama was selected by the Chinese authorities, a choice that was contested by supporters of the expatriate Dalai Lama.[173]

In the late 1980s several uprisings in Tibet opposed Chinese rule and supported a return to power of the exiled Dalai Lama and his Tibetan

Buddhist regime. The bloodiest encounter occurred in March 1989, leaving as many as seventy-five dead and scores wounded. Thousands of Tibetans in Lhasa poured into the streets for three days of protests at the central Jokhang Temple, led by young Buddhist monks and nuns. The protests escalated to rioting against Chinese and Chinese-owned businesses, and the Beijing government sent an estimated two thousand troops to quell the riots. The Dalai Lama, in a conciliatory gesture, announced from his government in exile in India that he deplored the violence and assured the Chinese government that he had no ambitions of returning to power in Lhasa. He did, however, propose a five-point basis for peace talks, which included semiautonomous political status for Tibet.[174] Though the Dalai Lama has accepted U.S. government support for training Tibetans to fight in a resistance movement against Chinese authority, in general he has advocated a nonviolent stance toward the Chinese occupation of Tibet. In 1989 he was awarded the Nobel Peace Prize. Thus the Dalai Lama has come to be a global symbol of nonviolence at the same time that he provides a model for Buddhist engagement and political protest.[175]

RELIGIOUS ACTIVISTS IN SOUTHEAST ASIA

The head of Indonesia's largest Islamic educational institution—Azyumardi Azra, the rector of the Syarif Hidayatullah State Islamic University of Jakarta—told me that violence was not characteristic of Indonesian Islam.[176] He said that the upsurge in acts of terrorism in the country was related to the larger tensions between political Islam and Western secular politics that came to the surface in the climate of the "war on terrorism" following September 11, 2001, and was a response to America's political and cultural presence in the region. As if to make his point, several weeks later a car bomb exploded in front of an American hotel near where we had been talking in downtown Jakarta. The perpetrators of the attack were alleged to have been members of the Jemaah Islamiya, the radical Muslim movement in Indonesia known familiarly as "JI."

Yet religious violence has been part of the politics of the region for some time. Southeast Asia is largely Buddhist and Muslim, and both religions have been politically active in the region during the latter part of the twentieth century and the beginning of the twenty-first. Some areas of conflict have involved yet another religious community: Southeast Asian Christians. Christian militants in both Indonesia and the Philippines have attacked Muslims in places where Christians were in the majority, including Sulawesi and Kalimantan, where poor Muslim laborers were slaughtered by members of a Christian militia in 1988.[177] The involvement of Roman Catholics in Philippine politics during the revolt against the regime of President Ferdinand Marcos received worldwide attention. The support of Cardinal Jaimi Sin for Corazon Aquino in 1986 was credited with having been a deciding factor in her election as president and further underscored the Catholic character of Philippine national identity in the northern islands.

Elsewhere, Buddhist activists have been involved extensively in politics. Buddhist monks in Myanmar (formerly Burma) have been among the leaders of a series of uprisings against the military government. Some twenty thousand monks and nuns participated in massive nonviolent pro-democracy demonstrations in 2007 and many have also supported the underground revolutionary movement that was based along the Myanmar-Thai border.[178] In the 2007 protests, police confined the Buddhist monks and nuns to their pagodas and monasteries in an attempt to limit their political influence, though many were among the injured and killed in the government crackdown. In Cambodia, the peace accord in 1991 ushered in a wave of Buddhist activism that enabled Prime Minister Hun Sen to reconcile his differences with his former rival, Prince Norodom Sihanouk. Later, however, in 1998, Buddhist monks were at the forefront of political protests against what they claimed was corruption in Hun Sen's regime. In Thailand, Buddhist monks were also involved in political movements, and Chamlong Srimvang, the leader of the 1992 rebellion that toppled a military dictatorship, was a member of an activist Buddhist sect that aimed at establishing a new national religion in the country.

The most vigorous movements of religious rebellion in Southeast Asia, however, have been Muslim. In the southern tip of Thailand, Islamic revolutionaries associated with the Pattani United Liberation Organization and Barisan Nasional Revolusi have fought for the independence of Pattani, Yala, Narathiwat, and Satun provinces.[179] In Malaysia, the Parti Islam Se Malaysia and other Islamic political groups have had considerable influence on Malaysian ethnic policy, usually at the expense of the Chinese minority community.

Indonesia

In Indonesia, a movement for Islamic nationalism, Darul Islam, has flourished since the country's independence in 1949. In the early 1990s,

Islamic protests mounted against the Suharto government's purported secularism, and in the 1992 elections the Muslim-based United Development Party made significant gains at Suharto's expense. In the Aceh region, Islam is part of an ideology of separatism. The tsunami that destroyed much of the oceanfront regions of Aceh on December 26, 2004, temporarily produced a calm in the hostilities, but the tensions reemerged within a matter of months.

The rise of religious violence in Indonesia at the start of the twenty-first century is said to be related to the old Darul Islam movement, which for some decades had been advocating Islamic law as the sole basis for Indonesia's political order.[180] A Muslim cleric, Abu Bakar Bashir, who was associated with the Darul Islam, was alleged to have been one of the leading figures in creating the clandestine Jemaah Islamiyah. Other leading JI figures included Abdullah Sungkar and Riduan Isamuddin—known as "Hambali" and sometimes described as "the Osama bin Laden of Southeast Asia." Hambali had joined the *mujahadin* in Afghanistan, where he became a part of an international circle of Muslim radicals. When he returned to Indonesia, he joined the JI and has been accused of orchestrating a series of terrorist acts between 2001 and 2003. The most deadly was a cluster of attacks on nightclubs in the resort town of Kuta on the island of Bali in 2002.

Bali was a likely target for Islamic extremists for two reasons. It is the sole area of the Muslim-dominated Indonesia that is Hindu, and it has catered to foreign tourists, many of them from nearby Australia. Shortly before midnight on October 12, 2002, a bomb ripped through Paddy's Bar, a popular night spot for young foreigners. The explosive device had been hidden in a backpack and brought to the site by someone who died in the blast. Seconds later an even more powerful explosion in a car bomb leveled another popular spot, the San Club. A third bomb detonated in front of the American consulate in Bali. Within minutes, the blasts had left over two hundred dead and another two hundred badly injured. Many of the casualties were young Australians on vacation. The bombings deeply affected two countries—Australia, which regarded the event as comparable to the September 11, 2001, attacks on New York and Washington, and Indonesia, which had always regarded itself as a hospitable and gentle culture. It was the deadliest act of terrorism in Indonesian history.

Soon after, several Indonesian nationals were arrested and eventually sentenced to death. They were alleged to have been associated with the underground JI movement, of which Abu Bakar Bashir was identified as the spiritual head.[181] Bashir denied any affiliation with the JI and claimed that no Indonesian Muslim could have been involved in the Bali bombings because of the sophisticated bomb-making techniques required to carry out the attack. In March, 2005, Bashir was found guilty of conspiracy in planning the attacks and was sentenced to prison. His release, on June 14, 2006, prompted a protest from the Australian prime minister.[182]

Indonesia's alleged al Qaeda operative, Hambali, moved from country to country to avoid detection, but was located in Thailand in August 2003, where he had reportedly gone to plan attacks against several Thai hotels and the meeting of the Asia Pacific Economic Cooperation Summit, which was to be attended by the leaders of twenty-nine countries, including U.S. president George W. Bush. Though he railed against Western cultural influence in the region, the 37-year-old Hambali was wearing a pair of jeans, a t-shirt and a baseball cap when he was arrested in a joint operation between the Thai police and the U.S. Central Intelligence Agency. After being interrogated in Jordan, he was sent to the U.S. government's detention facility in Guantanemo, Cuba.[183]

In addition to association of these Indonesians with other activists in their own country, rumors have circulated about possible connections between Indonesia's JI and militant Muslim groups elsewhere in Southeast Asia and throughout the Muslim world.[184] One associate of Bashir's, Aris Munandar, who allegedly assisted one of the Bali bombers in acquiring explosives, was alleged to have had ties to other Southeast Asian radical Muslim groups. According to some reports, Philippine intelligence agencies considered Munandar to be an associate of Mohammad Abdullah Sughayer, a Saudi national suspected of financing the al Qaeda-affiliated Abu Sayyaf group in southern Philippines. Though Munandar has never been apprehended, other arrests continued to be made years after the Bali attacks. In 2005, Indonesian police arrested twenty-four individuals suspected of involvement in the 2002 Bali bombing and the 2003 bombing of the Marriott Hotel in Jakarta. Some were believed to have been preparing to leave Indonesia and hide out with Abu Sayyaf in the Philippines.

Philippines

The Abu Sayyaf movement is a radical offshoot of the Moro movement, which has been agitating for a separate Islamic state in southern Philippines for decades.[185] The Moro National Liberation Front has been attempting to organize the large Muslim community on the island of Mindanao and the Sulu archipelago since 1970. In 1996 a settlement was forged with the Philippines government that provided for a semi-autonomous Muslim state, the Autonomous Region of Muslim Mindanao. The most militant of the Muslim activists, however, rejected this compromise as insufficient, and continued a series of violent protests against the government.

Part of the issue was the matter of religion: initially the Moro movement was largely secular in its ideology, though it sought separate political power for Muslims as an ethnic group. Increasingly, however, the ideology took on a religious tone, and a strident one at that. The most active of the extreme Muslim political groups was the Abu Sayyaf, which was founded in 1991 by Abdurajik Abdulbakar Janjalani, a teacher of Arabic and Islamic theology who had studied in Libya, Syria, and Saudi Arabia, and who joined the mujahadeen in Afghanistan. It was there that Janjalani was alleged to have been given several millions of dollars by Osama bin Laden to start a new movement for Muslim political power based in the Philippines. Its goal, however, was not just Muslim control of the island of Mindanao and nearby areas of the Philippines, but a united Muslim authority in Southeast Asia that would stretch from the Philippines to Indonesia and Malaysia. The scheme was allegedly hatched in conjunction with the JI movement in Indonesia and their militant comrades in Malaysia.[186]

In 1995, the Abu Sayyaf group launched a series of large-scale bombings and attacks in the Philippines. On December 18, 1998, the movement's founder and leader, Abdurajik Janjalani, was killed in a firefight with the Philippine National Police. He was replaced by his younger brother, Khadaffy Janjalani, who was 23 years old at the time. The young leader aggressively consolidated his leadership within the movement and adopted a more violent posture toward the Philippine government. He also increasingly relied on kidnappings and theft in order to secure funding for the movement. Among the kidnappings and murders of foreigners attributed to Abu Sayyaf's activities were the American Christian missionaries Martin and Gracia Burnham. In 2000 the movement shifted its operations to nearby Malaysia, kidnapping foreigners from two resorts. Although several members of the movement were captured, their strength was sufficient to create an explosion at a military base on Jolo island in February 2006. In the same month, the leader of the Abu Sayyaf movement, Khadaffy Janjalani, was indicted in absentia in a U.S. district court for his alleged involvement in terrorist activities, including the kidnapping and murder of American citizens. He was placed on the FBI list of most-wanted terrorists, and a five million dollar bounty placed on his head. In December, 2006, his body was found, thought to have been shot by Filipino marines earlier that year.[187]

Perhaps more significant than its activities in the Philippines is the connection that Abu Sayyaf forged with the global militant Islam movement. Members of the organization allegedly had ties to the notorious Pakistani operative Ramzi Youssef, and his uncle, Khalid Sheik Mohammed, who were associated with the radical transnational jihad movement linked with Osama bin Laden's al Qaeda. Youssef was convicted of conspiracy in planning the 1993 World Trade Center bombing, and is serving a life sentence in the United States. Youssef was also implicated in the 1994 bombing of Philippine Airlines Flight 434, which was said to have been a trial run for an even more ambitious plot, Project Bojinka, in which Youssef intended to bring down eleven commercial airplanes over the Pacific in a series of simultaneous bombings. Youssef, who had taken up temporary residence in Manila, was also alleged to have been plotting to assassinate the pope and to crash an airplane into the headquarters of the CIA in Langley, Virgina. He was captured in 1995 before the Bojinka Plot could be carried out.[188] His uncle and co-conspirator, Khalid Sheik Mohammad, who was implicated in planning the September 11, 2001, attacks on the World Trade Center and Pentagon, was captured in March 2003, and has been detained at the U.S. military base in Guantanamo, Cuba.

Abu Sayyaf's aspirations for a Southeast Asian Muslim political union that would stretch from Malaysia and Indonesia to the Philippines is consistent with the transnational ideology of al Qaeda. It is also related to the vision of the mid-twentieth-century South Asian Islamic writer, Maulana Maududi, who regarded the creation of the nation-state of Pakistan to be something of a mistake, and who conceived of Islamic social order as a transnational union. Other religious-political activists in the region have limited their goals to providing an element of religious ideology and identity to the national order of which they are a part. Thus a variety of religious traditions in South, Central and Southeast Asia— Muslim, Hindu, Christian, Buddhist, and Sikh—have been pressed into service for political causes that have been both peaceful and violent, democratic and authoritarian, and aimed at separatist, national, and transnational forms of political order. These cases describe a broad and remarkable range in the diversity of religious politics in what might be described as South and Southeast Asia's post-secular age.

CHAPTER 4

Post–Cold War Rebels: Europe, East Asia, and the United States

When the Alfred P. Murrah Federal Building in Oklahoma City was destroyed by a truck bomb on April 19, 1995, the assumption of many observers was that the act must have been instigated by the same Muslim activists who had attacked the World Trade Center in 1993. The perpetrators, however, turned out to be Christian terrorists. Timothy McVeigh, like other members of the loose network of activists on the extreme Christian right in the United States, saw the U.S. government as the enemy of religion in almost the same way as did the Muslim activists in global jihadi networks.

Though McVeigh has been consistently portrayed as a lone activist with a bizarre animus against the American government, he in fact ascribed to a certain Christian ideology that placed his terrorist act within the wave of religious rebellion that swept the industrialized world toward the end of the twentieth century. In Western Europe, a surge of anti-immigrant xenophobia reflected a nervous political and cultural response to the uncertainties of a post–Cold War world. In Japan, a new religious movement imagined an apocalyptic war that would be the culmination of all the evil trends of modern secular society. In the socialist world, religious ideologies had challenged the dogmatic power of the state; in the post-socialist world, religion was infused with new movements of nationalist fervor.

This religious rebellion in the most modern of Western societies is one of the more puzzling features of the contemporary era. In the developing world, politicized religion is more easily conceived as an appropriate response to a post-colonial era in which traditional culture became a resource for a revived sense of nationalism. What is less obvious is the way in which the same process has been part of the post–Cold War search for identity in the more developed parts of the world, including those societies that had the upper hand during the colonial era. In Europe, the United States, and elsewhere in the developed world, religious activism, associated primarily with Christianity, has surfaced with a vengeance at the same time that anti-colonial Buddhist, Hindu, and Muslim religious movements have been active elsewhere. The underlying causes may be similar: in each of these cases religion has provided a way of thinking about public virtue, collective identity, and world order in the face of a social reality that seemed to be losing its moorings.

Although the Cold War created an atmosphere of suspicion and danger—with the constant threat of nuclear annihilation—it also provided a secure way of looking at the world. The dramatic political and social changes of the late twentieth century, however, made world order seem vulnerable. In this context of global insecurity, the comforting values of religion and its certain notions of moral struggle provided an avenue to make society more secure. To understand how this came about, we begin with the collapse of state socialism at the end of the Cold War in Russia and Eastern Europe and the rejection of the transnational ideology of world socialism that came in its wake.

THE RELIGIOUS REJECTION OF SOCIALIST STATES

The demise of the Soviet Union in 1991 ended one form of secular transnationalism, but it also set the stage for a confrontation between secular and religious nationalism in the decades to come. In post-Soviet regions, religion became the expression of a nationalist rejection of secular socialist ideology and helped to force a competition between new religious activists and old socialist politicians. To complicate matters, some of the old communists switched sides and became leaders in new movements of religious politics. The relation of religious-nationalist movements to Marxist states and socialist ideology has thus been anything but predictable.

Russia

After the fall of the Soviet Union, some religious activists in Russia accused secular socialism of bringing the country to its ruin. In rallies held in Moscow during the failed coup against Boris Yeltsin in August 1991, bearded Orthodox priests bearing sacred icons were at the forefront of many of the protests against the Communist Party. The party was viewed as a vestige of a decrepit secular nationalism—in the guise of a communist internationalism—that needed to be overthrown. A nationalist politician in Tajikistan defined the "real struggle" as "the battle between two ideologies: Islam and communism."[1]

Marxist theory never envisaged such an outcome. Religious identities, as well as all other parochial forms of social organization, should have been subsumed under a relationship to the state that transcended national loyalties.[2] Marxist theory imagines large, international political identities based on working-class alliances rather than on local religious or ethnic allegiance. As for the practice of religion, Karl Marx himself regarded it, at best, as the expression of travail, "the sigh of the oppressed" and at worst as an "opiate"—a narcotic that exploiters used to ease their victims' pain.[3] In the Soviet Union ethnic and religious identities persisted, however, despite Marxist doctrine and the various attempts of Communist leaders to enforce it. In fact, Lenin's policy of "divide and rule" in the 1920s led to an increased sense of ethnic identity and a rigid demarcation of ethnic boundaries that, in turn, led to the unraveling of the Soviet Union in the 1980s and 1990s.[4]

When, in the late 1980s, Mikhail Gorbachev offered the Soviet people the possibilities of *perestroika* (restructuring) and *glasnost* (openness), he got more than he bargained for. He not only opened the doors for economic changes and political reform but also sprung the lid on a Pandora's box of resurgent ethnic and religious nationalisms. During the months immediately following the fall of the Soviet Union in January 1992, many Americans and Europeans focused on the economic and political changes resulting from the system's collapse rather than the social and cultural ones. Yet in the long run the citizens of former Soviet states will be as deeply affected by the rise of national states as by economic forces. In fact, in Russia and many of the Central Asian countries, a new nationalism and an expansion of religious freedom are virtually the only differences that the collapse of the Soviet Union and the death of communism as an ideology have wrought. Despite efforts at economic reform and democratization, the economic system and the political apparatus remain much as they were before, although some political leaders have abandoned their Communist Party membership cards in favor of new-found ethnic and religious identities.

In some ways, the situation in the last decades of the twentieth century resembles that of the century's early decades, when socialism initially appeared on the Russian scene as an economic alternative to tsarist feudalism and before it became the ideological ally of an international empire. In the years immediately following the October 1917 revolution, religion was relatively untouched by the new communist leaders. Lenin's 1918 decree on the separation of church and state took a laissez-faire position toward religious institutions. Neither he nor other Communist leaders were friends of religion, but for the first ten years of the regime their attitude toward it was relatively tolerant.

All that changed after Joseph Dzhugashvili, a former seminary student who had renounced his religious past and joined the Communist Party, ascended to its leadership under his assumed name, Joseph Stalin. Legislation that he crafted in 1929 limited religion to "performance of the cult"— rites and rituals—and barred the church from education and social matters.[5] During the same year, other acts of legislation imposed "freedom of antireligion propaganda." More than a decade of repression followed.[6] In the 1930s churches were closed, monastic communities were dissolved, and seminaries were abandoned. Perhaps the most vivid symbol of the antireligious mood of the time was the burning of icons on huge bonfires in public squares.

The Second World War to some extent distracted Stalin from his attacks on religion. He even sought the support of the Russian Orthodox Church in his attempt to culturally unify the whole of the Soviet Union. In 1943, Stalin signed a concordat with church officials that led to the party control of the Moscow patriarchate. In some areas of the Soviet Union, including the Ukraine, this takeover of the church resulted in even greater repression of regional religious communities, as their property was confiscated and given over to Russian Orthodox leaders, and local clergy were forced to give allegiance to Moscow.

When Nikita Khrushchev came to power after Stalin's death in 1953, he inaugurated a new campaign against religion, which in its most virulent stage lasted from 1958 to 1964. During this period, two-thirds of the Orthodox churches opened in the 1940s were again closed. Muslim and Buddhist institutions were also targeted. In 1961, a bishops' council organized and controlled by the state abolished the power of the clergy and allowed only lay leadership in religious congregations—in effect destroying the parish church. Leonid Brezhnev, who followed Khrushchev from 1964 to 1982, continued this policy, even establishing Scientific Atheist Clubs in abandoned churches. Brezhnev's successors, Yuri Andropov

(1982–84) and Konstantin Chernenko (1984–85), did little to ameliorate the situation.

The revival of religion came as the direct result of Gorbachev's policies. Soon after he came to power in 1985, he adopted a tolerant attitude toward religious organizations and called for the release of individuals imprisoned on religious grounds. In March 1988, a consultation between government officials and church leaders, which happened to coincide with the celebration of a millennium of Christianity in Russia, charted major changes for the churches, and in a historic meeting between Gorbachev and church leaders on April 29, 1988, the walls of government repression began to collapse. New rules allowed churches to run themselves democratically, through assemblies established on a parish, diocese, and national level. In 1989, for the first time since the 1917 revolution, Orthodox clergymen were elected to parliament.

The de jure restoration of religious freedom in the Soviet Union came in 1990 with the passage of the Freedom of Conscience and Religious Organizations Act on October 9. On November 10, 1990, the Russian Federation passed the even more comprehensive Law on Freedom of Worship. The election of a new patriarch in 1990 was accomplished without interference from the state for the first time since the Bolshevik Revolution, and the choice of sixty-one-year-old Metropolitan Aleksy of Leningrad over the acting patriarch, Metropolitan Filaret of Kiev, a hardliner widely regarded as a KGB puppet, was regarded as a victory for freedom and reform.[7]

The church had little time to enjoy its newfound freedom, however, for it was drawn into the turmoil of new nationalist movements with the breakup of the Soviet Union on New Year's Day 1992. In post-Soviet Russia, the relation of the Orthodox hierarchy to Russian nationalism has been complicated because of its compromised position in the communist state. The exploitation of the church by Stalin during his Russification campaign prevented it from becoming the symbol of Russian nationalism that religion became in other parts of the former Soviet Union.[8] In some former republics, such as Ukraine, the Orthodox church was seen as a symbol of the Soviet past. Even so, the church's association with nationalism and its concept of the Russian people as a homogenous religious community were exploited by the politicians who surfaced in the wake of Russia's independence in 1992.[9] One deputy in the Russian legislature predicted that the church would now play "a great economic and political role."[10] But this made minority communities apprehensive.

In Chechnya and elsewhere, Russia encountered the same spiritual wave that broke over other areas of the former Soviet Union, where religion enjoyed a two-fold revival. On the one hand, the free expression of religion was part of the burst of democracy that brought the citizens of former Soviet states closer to their counterparts in the West. On the other hand, their religious affiliations linked them with nationalist and transnational identities of a bygone era. Through religion, they were able to revive the past, but in doing so they also joined in the uncertainties of the post-secular future.

Eastern Europe and the Balkan States

In the Soviet republics of Eastern Europe and in the Eastern European nations under Soviet control, religion also played a role in the resurgence of national identities. When I asked the official in charge of religious affairs in the Ukrainian government why the nation and so many of its neighboring states had turned to religion in their rejection of Soviet control, he attributed it to "a failure of ideology." Marxist and other secular ideologies have "failed," he explained, because they were not able to "touch the heart" the way ethnic and religious identities do.[11]

What the Ukrainian did not say was that Marxism had indeed become associated with a nationalist sentiment, but it was Russian rather than Ukrainian. The liberalization of Soviet policies in the 1980s opened the floodgates for a lively expression of non-Russian regional and ethnic loyalties in Eastern Europe that only intensified after the demise of the Soviet Union. In such diverse locations as Lithuania, Armenia, East Germany, Poland, and Ukraine, religious movements were at the forefront of opposition to Soviet control and the emergence of new nationalisms. In a sense, these were old nationalisms; they traced their identities at least to the nineteenth century and in most cases much earlier. In their post-socialist form, however, these national identities were new: their combination of democratic populism and cultural nationalism was a distinctive feature of the modern age.

In the nations of Eastern Europe and the European republics of the former Soviet Union the patterns of religion and nationalism have varied. In Romania and Hungary, for instance, despite the involvement of some dissident young priests in nationalist movements, the compromised church was largely supportive of the Communist authorities, not the dissidents.[12] In Romania, it was a secular force that toppled Nicolae Ceausescu in December 1989. By 1991, however, Romanian nationalism was accused of being so closely identified with the Romanian Orthodox Church that members of the Catholic minority in the Romanian Uniate Church were suppressed; anti-Semitism was also on the rise.[13] In Czechoslovakia there was no religious nationalism, in part because there was no united Czechoslovakia, although religion has played a role in the newly divided country in both Slovakia and the Czech Republic.

In the former Yugoslavia, the confrontation among the Serbs, Croats, and Slovenes involved, among other things, a clash of religious loyalties. The Serbs are largely Orthodox Christian; the Croats and Slovenes, Roman Catholic.[14] Priests in the Croatian Catholic Church have been at the forefront of the separatist movement in Croatia. To further complicate matters, the region of Bosnia-Herzegovina comprised an incendiary mixture of Serbs, Croats, and Muslims, which ignited into a bloody conflagration in 1992. The capital, Sarajevo, was a Muslim outpost under siege by the surrounding Serbs, and Muslims throughout the region were targets of "ethnic cleansing" by Serbian forces. Serbian leaders claimed that if Bosnia were allowed to become independent, its 44-percent Muslim population would create a "fundamentalist state."[15] In nearby Kosovo, religion also was a factor in distinguishing the largely Albanian (Muslim) ethnic population from the Serbian (Christian minority) during the 1999 uprising in which NATO military forces sided with the Muslim majority.

National and religious identities have coalesced in other Eastern European countries as well. Muslim and Christian movements were part of the resurgence of an Albanian nationalist identity that began in 1990. In Latvia, a statue of Jesus Christ was installed in the space where a statue of Lenin had once stood; Lenin's statue had been smashed to pieces in a mass rally shortly after the failed Soviet coup in August 1991.[16] Latvians, along with Estonians, have traditionally been Lutherans. Lithuanians identify with the Western-rite Catholicism. The ambit of Eastern Orthodox Christianity contains many regional variations—the Georgian Orthodox Church, the Armenian Apostolic Church, and the like—and these have been involved in the nationalist movements in their home countries. In other areas, non-Orthodox Christianity has played that role. In Poland and Ukraine, for instance, local forms of Catholicism informed nationalist struggles against Moscow's hegemony.

In Poland, the Roman Catholic Church has historically been supportive of the Polish national cause—even more so after the Soviet occupation of Poland, when Polish nationalism and the religious rejection of socialism became allied. "Next to God," Poland's Stefan Cardinal

Wyszynski proclaimed, "our first love is Poland."[17] This affection is re-
ciprocated by the Polish people. When workers marched on the headquarters of the Communist Party in Poznan in 1956, they demanded
"God and bread."[18] Their desire for economic security and religious freedom often expressed itself in support for the church as a symbol of national independence and prosperity.

The Polish church was linked with Polish national identity virtually
from the beginning. It was founded in 966, when Duke Mieszko I, who
had married a Czech princess from a Christian dynasty in Bohemia, embraced the faith and used it as the means to unify the new entity of
Poland, which he had created by consolidating several tribes into a new
state. Significantly for the independence of the Polish church, it was directly related to the Holy See in Rome rather than being affiliated with
the Roman Catholic bishops in Germany. During the eighteenth and
nineteenth centuries, when Poland's territory was carved up and controlled by three neighboring powers, the Polish church was one of the
primary purveyors of Polish nationalism. Its central role was especially
evident during the tsars' attempts to Russify the areas of Poland they
controlled by forcing the churches to embrace the Orthodox faith. These
unsuccessful attempts reinforced the image of the Polish church as a bulwark of Polish nationalist culture.

After the Second World War, when Poland came under Soviet occupation, the state attempted to reduce the power of the church. In addition to limiting and controlling the clergy, the state rewrote textbooks to
play down the role of the church in Poland's history, an attempt that was
countered by the church in a series of pastoral letters, sermons, and public statements. Cardinal Wyszynski became a symbol of the resistance.
He was imprisoned for refusing to follow the dictates of the government,
and his refusal to capitulate strengthened the image of the church as the
guardian of Poland's independence.

At the outset of the Soviet occupation, the church overtly supported
opposition parties. It endorsed the Labor Party of Karol Popiel and supported attempts to create a confessional political party in opposition to
the Communists. These attempts were stifled by the government, which
sought to limit the church's influence to matters of individual faith. The
church for its part was forced temporarily to retire from politics, and it
concentrated instead on matters of faith and worship.

The election of a Polish bishop as the Roman Catholic pope in 1978
was the occasion for a renewed emphasis on the political importance of
the Polish church. Almost at the same time, the Solidarity labor movement

emerged as a new mass base of power against the government. Although the church was clearly supportive of Lech Walesa and his Solidarity movement, its independence allowed it to play a mediating role between the movement and the government during critical moments of confrontation. The government increasingly relied on the church as a buffer against the most severe of the labor movement's actions; the labor movement, for its part, relied on the church as its interpreter and defender vis-à-vis the government.

After Solidarity became established as an official party in 1980, Walesa and his colleagues became the primary vehicle of political opposition. The church continued to support Solidarity, however, and it developed new forms of resistance to what it regarded as an occupying Soviet colonial government. Outside Poland, Pope John Paul II worked with U.S. president Ronald Reagan to keep Solidarity alive and to destabilize the Communist government.[19] Inside Poland, new movements for liberation were forming within the church. One of these, Wolnosc i Pokoj (Freedom and Peace), was founded in 1985 to encourage a new generation of Catholics to reject Soviet influence. It began with the refusal of a young Catholic to take the military oath, which included a pledge of loyalty to the Soviet Union. A band of his friends undertook a hunger strike at a church near Warsaw, and the new organization was formed. It based its ideas on the teachings of Pope John Paul II and in addition to opposing Soviet control put forward a broad platform of social reforms and pacifist ideals.

The liberalization of Soviet policies, the withdrawal of the Soviets from Poland, and democratic elections in 1990 were rewards for the church's patience. One of the leaders of Solidarity, Bogdan Cywinski, described the Polish church as a "Julian church," drawing a parallel with the Christian community that survived the persecutions of the Roman emperor Julian the Apostate.[20] After 1990, however, the church became part of the establishment. The new government that swept into power with Walesa's victory voiced its indebtedness to the church and pledged to support the church's central role in Poland's national life. The church has pressured the government to fulfill its social objectives, including a church-supported bill that would ban all forms of abortion. The government has also enacted a requirement that public schools teach courses in religion, and in the first decade of the twenty-first century government policies adopted strict moral guidelines, especially targeting the public expression of homosexuality.

Ironically, once the nationalist aspirations of the church were realized, the institution itself became more controversial in public life.[21] The church

faced rising anticlericalism and the implicit suggestion that with the triumph of nationalism, it had shifted its allegiance from the oppressed to the
new authorities. Yet the very openness of the new politics meant that the
church was not the sole vehicle in Polish society for expressing feelings of
nationalism and opposition to oppression. It retains that potential, however, and awaits an opportunity to again play that role.

Christianity also played a role in Ukraine's rejection of Russian domination and Soviet control, though the several strands of Christianity in
the country exhibit contradictory attitudes toward Ukrainian nationalism. The statement declaring Ukraine's independence on August 24,
1991, claimed "a thousand-year-old tradition of building statehood,"
which originated in the tenth century, when Vladimir the Great created
a separate Ukrainian Orthodox Church.[22] Christianity had come to the
region in 988, when Vladimir the Great became Christian, and in the great
division between Rome and Constantinople, the Ukrainian region fell on
the Orthodox side. For that reason the Christian churches in the two
western regions of Ukraine—Galicia and Transcarpathia—were largely
Orthodox in its practices and beliefs. Its clergy were allowed to marry,
for instance, as Orthodox clergy are. In 1596, a union between the Orthodox Church in Ukraine and the Roman Catholic Church resulted in
a new Ukrainian Uniate Church. Its practices were Orthodox, although
it obeyed the Roman pope and asserted its independence from the Russian Orthodox tradition.

When Ukraine was made a part of the Soviet Union in 1923, the role
of the Uniate Church became uncertain. The Marxist government, especially under Stalin, had no use for religion of any sort, but in its efforts
to undercut the Russian Orthodox Church it at first tolerated regional
forms of the faith, such as the Uniate Church. During the Second World
War, however, Stalin felt that latent nationalist sentiments in Ukraine
were being encouraged by the Uniate Church and were keeping Ukrainians from supporting the war effort. When the war ended, therefore,
Stalin attempted to make Ukraine in every way a seamless part of Russia. In the Synod of Lvov in 1946 the Uniate Church was abolished. The
property of some three thousand churches was transferred to the Russian
Orthodox Church, and the Uniate clergy were forced to obey Russian
Orthodox bishops. Many Uniate clergy abandoned their posts, and some
who stayed remained true to the Uniate confession but practiced their
faith in secret. Nuns who adopted civilian clothes and worked as teachers and nurses were often displayed wearing their identifying religious
habits only when they were laid to rest in their coffins.

This link between Ukrainian nationalism and religion was revived in the post-Soviet period, especially in western Ukraine. The eastern part of the country comprised a large percentage of ethnic Russians, most of whom were nominally Russian Orthodox.[23] During the years of Soviet repression of Ukrainian nationalism, Ukrainians in the western part of the country resisted not only the secular state but also the Russian Orthodox Church, which was perceived by many Ukrainians to be an agent of Russian colonialism. An uprising against the church in Ukraine in 1990 was regarded by the hierarchy as motivated by "an underlying nationalist cause," as one Russian Orthodox archbishop put it.[24] The Russian Orthodox Church's metropolitan of Kiev warned that "a handful of people" were trying to use Gorbachev's "democratization process" to establish a "national church" in the Ukraine that would "estrange Ukrainians from Russians."[25] Many western Ukrainians agreed. They felt, however, that their estrangement from Russians occurred decades—even centuries—ago and that the responsibility for the schism was as much Russian as Ukrainian.

In 1988, with the expansion of religious freedom throughout the Soviet Union, a new movement developed in western Ukraine to reestablish the Uniate Church. It became fashionable in some urban intellectual circles to join the Uniate confession largely for nationalist reasons.[26] By 1990 several hundred Orthodox churches had been converted back to Uniate congregations, in some cases by force, and in 1991 the Uniate Church's seventy-six-year-old head, Cardinal Miroslav Lubachivsky, returned in glory to the cathedral of Lvov from an exile that had been imposed on him since 1938. Cardinal Lubachivsky had spent many years abroad as a parish priest in Cleveland, Ohio. Between 1988 and 1991 over a thousand clergy professed to be Uniate rather than Russian Orthodox. The Orthodox patriarch in Moscow vigorously protested these conversions, claiming that the churches had been Russian Orthodox congregations for half a century and that many, if not most, of the members were now truly Orthodox in belief rather than Catholic. Moreover, he argued, the prime motive of most of the Uniate leaders in reclaiming their churches was political, not spiritual: they wanted to reestablish the cultural base for an independent Ukraine. The Russian Orthodox patriarch's contempt for Ukrainian nationalism, however, did not prevent him from changing the name of the Orthodox Church in Ukraine from the Russian Orthodox to the Ukrainian Orthodox Church.

In 1989, the Orthodox/Uniate controversy was further complicated by a group of formerly Russian Orthodox clergy and laity in Ukraine who wanted to revert to the "true Ukrainian church." They had in mind, however, not the Uniate Church but an earlier form of Ukrainian Orthodoxy that had existed before the union of 1596 and that answered to neither the pope nor the patriarch of Moscow nor the patriarch of Constantinople. It had its own head and was therefore known as the Ukrainian Autocephalous Orthodox Church. (Autocephalous means "independent"—literally, "self-headed.") It had been reestablished in 1921 as a nationalist movement, and Stalin allowed it to flourish briefly before crushing it in 1930. By 1991, the revived form of the Autocephalous Church had attracted few clergy and had small congregations, but it created a great deal of public controversy. It was virulent in its attacks on the Russian-related Ukrainian Orthodox Church and was even more nationalist than the Uniate Church, disputing which form of religion truly represented the Ukrainian nationalist cause. The Uniate Catholics claimed that because the adherents of the Autocephalous Church were Orthodox, they were somehow identified with Russia, and the Autocephalous Church claimed that because the Uniates were Catholic, they were somehow linked with Poland.[27] In December 1991 members of the Autocephalous Church staged a hunger strike in the Cathedral of Saint Sophia in Kiev to reclaim the Byzantine church they said was theirs.[28] In January 1992, Metropolitan Archbishop Mstislav Skrypnyk, who lived in the United States for more than forty of his ninety-three years, returned to Kiev to take up his post as patriarch of the Ukrainian Autocephalous Orthodox Church. Patriarch Skrypnyk stated that he intended to live half of each year in Kiev and the other half in his home in South Bound Brook, New Jersey.

The fact that the heads of both the Uniate and Autocephalous Ukrainian churches had lived in the United States was taken as a symbol of the independent spirit of the religious movements. A priest who supported the Autocephalous cause compared his leaders with "the founding fathers of America." Like them, he said, the Autocephalous leaders have "embarked upon the difficult road leading to self-determination which sooner or later must be accepted and recognized."[29] He went on to say that the members of his church desire nothing more than "their inalienable, divinely given rights of life, dignity, liberty and the pursuit of happiness."[30]

It is something of an irony that the Russian Orthodox Church, which suffered greatly under Stalin and Khrushchev, came to be regarded as the persecutor in Ukraine. But, as the minister of religious affairs in Ukraine explained to me, the leaders of the newly independent Ukrainian churches were young and remembered only the recent history of attempts to Russify Ukrainian culture through the imposition of the Russian Orthodox faith.[31] These members of a new generation saw the Uniate Church and the Ukrainian Autocephalic Orthodox Church as pioneers in a renewed cultural nationalism aimed at establishing an independent Ukraine. The Ukrainian churches had quarreled bitterly with one another, but they were united in their support for a Ukrainian nationalism free from any latent cultural ties to the old Soviet state with its secular socialist ideology and its colonial rule.

China, Vietnam, and North Korea

China, the other great socialist imperial power, has survived into the present century with its Marxist ideology at least superficially intact. Perhaps because it is still officially atheist, religion poses a threat to the socialist state.[32] In China, as in the former Soviet Union, movements for regional autonomy often have had a religious dimension. On the border between China and Kazakhstan, the Kirghiz and Uigur people of Kashgar in Xinjiang, who rioted against the Chinese authorities in 1990, have sought to establish an independent Islamic Republic of East Turkestan. Muslim communities in China have an ambivalent relationship to Beijing. Though they constitute less than 2 percent of China's population, these twenty million Chinese Muslims form a sizable presence. They are associated with a variety of ethnic communities, but the largest group of Muslim Chinese are the Hui, who are closely related to the Han, China's dominant ethnic group. Chinese Muslims have clashed with the government in different ways.[33] Whereas the Uighur and other ethnic Muslims in western China have been associated with movements of political autonomy, the Hui, who are dispersed throughout China, are more concerned about issues of religious liberty.

The Chinese government has banned Falun Gong, a transnational religious movement also known as Falun Dafa. It was founded in the 1990s by Li Hongzhi, who set up a Chinese expatriate center in New York City. The teachings of the movement are based on traditional Chinese Buddhist concepts and practices. The movement, whose membership worldwide numbers several million (Falun Gong itself claims to have 200 million followers), includes many non-Chinese in Europe and America, although most of its followers are in China. In 1999 the movement used the Internet to quickly organize a rally of some ten thousand members, who protested outside the offices of several Chinese leaders.

The Chinese government, alarmed by the organizational power of the movement, permanently banned it from the country and has blocked access to its websites from within China.[34]

Chinese Christianity has also presented a challenge to the Chinese authorities. Though there have been Christians in China for centuries—Nestorians arrived in China in the seventh century CE, and Catholic Jesuits were producing converts in the seventeenth century—the majority of Chinese conversions came as a result of missionary activity in the late nineteenth and early twentieth centuries. After the Communist government came to power in 1947, the Christian churches were banned, and, especially during the Cultural Revolution, Christians were severely repressed. After the end of the Maoist period, when religious restrictions were lifted, membership in Christian churches expanded seemingly exponentially. At the end of the twentieth century there were 10 million Catholic and 20 million Protestant Christians in China, and the country was experiencing one of the greatest rates of growth of Christianity in the world.[35] Much of the growth has been among the uprooted newly urban masses, but Christianity has also been eagerly accepted by members of tribal groups who find in the religion a way of distancing themselves from the ethnic Han majority in China.

One source of tension between the government and Chinese Christians comes from the requirement that all religious groups, including local churches, be registered with the government. Since the government limits the number of religious groups allowed on the approved list, many Christian groups meet illegally in warehouses, vacant lots, or private homes.[36] In some cases the leaders of these groups are arrested and punished; in other cases the authorities turn a blind eye. Another source of tension is over the appointment of bishops in the Catholic Church. Though the pope has insisted on his right to appoint Catholic bishops in China, a government committee asserts its own right to ignore the pope and make the appointments itself. Hence the Roman Catholic Church in China does not have full Vatican approval. Implicit in the Chinese government's insistence on making ecclesial appointments and registering religious groups is its fear that religion is a potent force that needs to be coopted and controlled or it might become a challenge to the authority of the state.

In Vietnam also, religion has been a threat to the socialist authorities. During the 1960s both Buddhist and Catholic leaders played a role in the civil war that developed into one of the more tragic conflicts of the Cold War. Catholics fled to the south, which is alleged to be one of the reasons why the Roman Catholic president of the United States, John F. Kennedy, committed U.S. troops to protect South Vietnam in the 1960s. Soon after, Buddhist monks protested the rising violence in the country and what they regarded as the oppression of Buddhists by the regime of the U.S.-supported president, Ngo Dinh Diem. Several of them, most famously Thich Quang Duc, doused themselves with gasoline and immolated themselves publicly in protest. In post-war Vietnam, several religious groups have accused the Marxist government of suppressing religion, especially Catholicism and Protestant evangelicalism. In Vietnamese expatriate communities in France, the United States, and elsewhere, religion has informed social identity.[37]

In North Korea, Buddhism and Christianity are closely controlled. In a visit to the North Korean capital of Pyongyang in the early 1990s, I found only one Protestant and one Roman Catholic church functioning in the city. Both were filled to capacity. In many ways the ideology of the late leader, Kim Il Sung, has taken on a religious character. Kim's doctrine of self-reliance, *Juche* thought, contains elements of Marxism, Confucianism, and Korean shamanism, and North Koreans told me proudly that *Juche* thought is superior to orthodox Marxism.[38] As uniquely Korean ideology, it separated North Korea culturally and intellectually from its powerful Chinese and Soviet patrons. In North Korea, as in other parts of what remains of the socialist world, religion has been either coopted by the state or suppressed for fear that it will be a base for insurrection. In either case, religion is perceived by authorities as the local foe of transnational Marxism.

Latin America

In many other parts of the world, capitalism rather than socialism is the main transnational ideology. In some of these regions, opposition religious movements have joined with socialist ones in protest against the culture of secular capitalism. This was the case in Sri Lanka, where Buddhist monks who abhorred the secular nationalist policies of the government advocated "Buddhism socialism" and aligned with Marxists in the antigovernment Janatha Vimukthi Peramuna (JVP) movement.[39] The monks regarded the Marxists, who identified with rural communities and poorer sections of the cities, as closer to grassroots Sinhalese society than the urban secular elite.

This has also been the case in parts of Latin America, including El Salvador, Guatemala, and especially Nicaragua, where American political influence and economic domination had so closely bound the Somoza government to the United States that the movement against it was perceived largely as an attempt to liberate the country from foreign domination. It was an anticolonial struggle with both cultural and political elements, and for a while it welded together popular religion and socialist revolution. "The Revolution and the Kingdom of God," proclaimed Ernesto Cardenal, a priest and cabinet member in Daniel Ortega's revolutionary government, "are the same thing."[40] This point of view was echoed by many other devout Christians who took part in Nicaragua's decade of revolution, which lasted from the overthrow of the Somozan dictatorship in 1979 to the election of Violeta Chamorro in 1990.

Although Ortega and his Sandinista party were portrayed in the American press as Marxist and were excoriated by Nicaragua's archbishop, Miguel Obando y Bravo, as hostile to the Catholic hierarchy, the revolution was to a remarkable degree a religious movement. It was conducted not only with a religious zeal but also with specifically Christian imagery. Moreover, it appealed to a large number of socially concerned clergy and other devout Christians, who often regarded their participation in the revolution as a religious act.[41]

When I was in Nicaragua during the Sandinista period, I talked with a priest in Managua who told me that he was so impressed with the revolution's call for social service that he turned his church into a grain warehouse and held mass on the streets.[42] One of the leaders of the Sandinista movement declared that she was in the revolution because of her Christian faith, explaining that it helped her to "live the gospel better."[43] Carlos Tuennermann, minister of education in the Ortega cabinet, also joined the revolution as the result of "a Christian decision."[44] Ortega himself claimed to have embraced Christianity years after his party had been voted out of office, and his renewed ties to the church were credited as one of the reasons for his return to power in 2006. In a sense, however, his charisma always had a touch of religious zeal.

One of the reasons the revolution had such a religious character—and a specifically Catholic one at that—is that the Nicaraguan national identity has always in some measure been linked with the church. A visit to the great cathedrals at Granada and Leon is like a visit to a national museum, and the walls of churches bear the scars of great moments in Nicaragua's history, often violent ones. Nicaraguan nationalism is characteristic of both the church's conservative leadership and its rebels.[45] For this reason, a genuine Nicaraguan nationalist revolution, one advertised as by and for the people, as the Sandinistas claimed theirs to be, had to be in some sense linked with the church. Thus, in Nicaragua the socialist revolution was also a religious revolution.

Religious movements opposed to the secular state are, therefore, both pro-socialist and anti-socialist. Dissident Catholics allied themselves with socialism in Central and Latin America, and numerous faiths opposed it in Eastern Europe and Central Asia. Religion has joined forces with nationalism in each of these locales as it has elsewhere in the world, but what is striking is how many religious politicians—be they Christians in Eastern Europe, the former Soviet Union, and Latin America, Muslims and Jews in the Middle East and Central Asia, or Sikhs, Hindus, and Buddhists in South and Southeast Asia—reject Western-style secular nationalism, in part because they reject its antireligious bias and its claims of universality. By implication, a transnational ideology—not just secular nationalism but international socialism as well—denies the value of what is unique in particular cultures. To counteract the loss of identity associated with a bland universal secularism, proponents of religion offer a powerful antidote: the symbols and communal pride related to particular people in particular places. Even the great religious traditions that seem transnational by nature, such as Christianity and Islam, are reduced to particular allegiances in particular places: it is the Ukrainian Church and Algerian Islam that Ukrainians and Algerians, respectively, embrace. For that reason socialism has been an ally of religion when it joins forces with it against a transnational foe—but socialism has been religion's enemy when it is itself transnational.

CHRISTIAN AND SECULAR XENOPHOBIA IN EUROPE

At the end of the twentieth century Europe was roiled by social changes, including the fall of the Berlin Wall and the dismantling of the iron curtain between Eastern and Western Europe, the rise of regionalism and the political transformation of nations associated with the European Union, a remarkable economic recovery in the era of globalization, and a new transnational social phenomenon: migration and the global diaspora of ethnic cultures. New ethnic communities were the locus of social tensions at the start of the twenty-first. Increased mobility and a labor shortage in economically expanding Western Europe had created the conditions for an influx of new immigrants. In France, residents of former French colonies such as Algeria flooded the country, and by the year 2000, 5.6 percent of France's population consisted of foreign-born residents; over 10 percent of Germany's residents were foreign-born, many of them immigrant laborers from Turkey. In England many of the new immigrants were Indian or Pakistani.

The appearance of new immigrants often produces tensions wherever it occurs, and religion need not have anything to do with it. In Europe, however, most of the new immigrants have been Muslim. The established communities in Europe are largely Christian. Symbolic and ideological elements of religion have become a component of both sides of the divide.[46] The efforts to control or suppress the new immigrants have taken the form of protecting Christian values and European customs, and they increasingly have targeted the religious symbols and practices of the newcomers—such as the attempt to ban the *hijab* (veil or head-scarf) in France. The immigrant communities' response to the indignities they have experienced can take the form of protecting religious values, as it did during the outcry that followed the September 2005 publication by a Danish newspaper of cartoons widely viewed as anti-Muslim.[47]

Some of the first signs of ethnic tension during the 1990s surfaced in Germany with the rise of neo-Nazi movements—especially in the former East Germany after the country's reunification in 1990. The rise of National Socialism in Germany earlier in 1930s and 1940s, while not explicitly religious, carried overtones of millenarian Christianity. Heinrich Himmler and other formulators of Nazi ideology relied on a mixture of quasi-religious images and ideas, including symbols associated with the Knights Templar; nature worship from the German Volk movement of the 1920s; the notion of Aryan superiority from, among others, the Theosophists; and a fascination with the occult from a particular strand of German Catholic mysticism. To the degree that the Nazi movement was religious, then, one could consider the Second World War as a war of (or from the Allies' point of view, against) Nazi religion.[48] It was also a war against the religious intolerance of the Nazis, especially against the Jews. Adherents of the neo-Nazi movement, while young and largely ignorant of the ideology of their namesakes, nonetheless also mimicked religion in their symbols and rituals and opposed what they regarded as alien religion—in their case not just Judaism, but also the Muslim religion of the Turks and other immigrants.[49]

Though in Germany the anti-immigrant movement never gained significant electoral strength, the situation in nearby Austria was quite different. There the fear of Muslim immigration propelled right-wing politician Jorg Haider into the headlines in 1999, when he and his Austrian Freedom Party (FPO) received 27 percent of the votes in the national elections. But their electoral support then sharply diminished, in part because of infighting within his organization. In 2005 Haider founded a new party, the Alliance for the Future of Austria, which split the followers of the FPO into two camps and diluted its electoral strength.

In France, another right-wing politician, Jean-Marie Le Pen, received the second-largest number of votes in 2002 presidential elections after Jacques Chirac, beating out the leader of the Socialist Party, Lionel Jospin. Le Pen made immigration an electoral issue, and his public statements were unapologetically anti-Muslim. Though Le Pen's surprising electoral showing was regarded as something of a fluke, tensions between conservative anti-immigrant elements and the expatriate Muslim community in France came to a head in the years following.

In 2004 France banned the wearing of "conspicuous religious symbols" in public places. The law prohibited the display of large jewelry crosses and Jewish skullcaps, and it applied to courts and government offices as well as to schools. Though crafted as religiously neutral in its application to all faiths, the law was widely regarded as an effort to keep immigrant Muslim schoolgirls from wearing the *hijab*. Although the practice of wearing the *hijab* is more custom than religious requirement, many Muslims viewed the ban as an insult to their religion.[50]

In the following year, a series of riots broke out throughout France. Young Muslim immigrant men, largely of North African ancestry, torched cars and public buildings in a display of anger at the French authorities that was based in part on the *hijab* controversy and in part on recent incidents of police brutality. The uprising began when two immigrant Muslim youths were chased by the police and took refuge in an electrical power station, where they were accidentally electrocuted. In twenty nights of fiery protests, almost nine thousand cars were burned.

Hundreds of cars were again burned in May 2007 across France, this time in protest against the election of Nicholas Sarkozy as president of the republic. Sarkozy—who is the descendent of Hungarian immigrants— ran on a platform that included a strong stand on immigration laws and a tough attitude toward the rebelliousness of immigrant youth. In 2005, when Sarkozy was minister of the interior, he described the young Muslims in housing projects who were burning cars and rioting in the streets as *racaille,* an insulting term that has been translated in the English language press as "rabble" or "scum."[51] Many in France's North African expatriate communities feared that in his new role as president, Sarkozy would regard them all as scum and ignore their concerns. Some feared that his opposition to Turkey's request for membership in the European

Union was for anti-Muslim cultural reasons. Yet Sarkozy's statements toward the immigrant Muslim communities since the elections have been conciliatory, and he has supported affirmative action efforts at including them in schools and government employment. One of his first cabinet appointments was Rachida Dati, a daughter of illiterate Algerian and Moroccan parents, as minister of justice.[52]

Ethnic tensions in the Netherlands came to a head in 2004 after a Muslim youth, the Dutch son of a Moroccan immigrant, responded to a film that he thought offensive to Muslims by killing the filmmaker, Theo van Gogh. Van Gogh had earned a reputation as an iconoclast, having previously insulted Jews as well as Muslims. He befriended an articulate Muslim woman, Ayaan Hirsi Ali, who was an outspoken critic of what she regarded as repressive and patriarchal attitudes of immigrant Muslim men in the Netherlands. Together they made a film that excoriated what they believed to be the Muslim attitude toward women.

Their brief film, *Submission,* includes scenes of presumably Muslim women kneeling in prayer, telling stories of their abuse by Muslim men as verses from the Qur'an are projected onto their veiled but otherwise naked bodies. The Muslim community was incensed, and on November 2, 2004, the 26-year-old Mohammed Bouyeri attacked van Gogh as he was riding through the streets of Amsterdam on his bicycle. Bouyeri shot the filmmaker eight times with a pistol, instantly killing him. The assassin then mutilated his body with knives, leaving two of them in Van Gogh's chest, one with a five-page note attached. The note condemned both the filmmaker and secular governments for allowing the Islamic faith to be publicly disrespected. The assassin was sentenced to life imprisonment.

The incident prompted public discussion about the immigrant Muslim communities in the Netherlands. Some thought that it showed how insufficiently they had been integrated into the Dutch community and called for a stricter enforcement of laws against blasphemy. The loudest voices, however, expressed the opposite opinion: that there were too many immigrants in the country and that they needed to be carefully controlled. Some advocated the monitoring of sermons given in mosques; others proposed a moratorium on new immigration.[53]

The traditional Scandinavian reputation for tolerance was also tested in Denmark in the uproar protesting the publication of a group of cartoons in 2005 that were viewed as mocking the Islamic faith. As in the Netherlands, the tensions between the immigrant Muslim communities in the country were already strained prior to the incident. In Denmark, no permits have been granted for the construction of new mosques or Muslim graveyards, though some fifty mosques are functioning in the country in converted buildings. When I visited one of these storefront mosques in 2007, the Pakistani mullah said that they were not allowed to broadcast the calls to prayer or to post religious slogans outside the building. Other Muslim immigrants complain that they have difficulty gaining access to jobs and that women wearing headscarves have been denied entry to supermarkets and public buses. The conservative Danish People's Party proposed a ban on wearing the *hijab* in schools and other public places. As in France, the ban would prohibit any "culturally specific" headgear, but the Danish law would exempt Christians and Jews. The party claimed that the Muslim dress has a "disturbing" impact on "ordinary people" and inhibited assimilation. In 2004 a public debate began over whether the threats of reprisals from the Muslim community had intimidated newspapers and magazines from publishing anything that might be provocative to Muslims, and thereby had placed de facto limits on free speech.[54]

It was in this context of this discussion that a series of cartoons was published in the Copenhagen newspaper *Jyllands-Posten* in September 2005. One of the cartoons portrayed the Prophet Mohammad wearing a turban in the shape of a bomb, the fuse lit and sputtering. Most of the men were shown with large noses, wearing beards and turbans. Leaders of the Muslim community in Denmark protested what they regarded as a blatant insult against them and their faith. As a result of widespread press coverage, the cartoons were reprinted in some fifty countries, thereby vastly enlarging the potential audience.

Around the world Muslim communities responded to the cartoons with outrage. They were widely viewed as deliberate attempts not only to insult the Islamic faith but also to defame and humiliate Muslim people. In February 2006, protests erupted in such disparate locations as Pakistan, Indonesia, Nigeria, Libya, and Afghanistan. Danish embassies were set on fire in Syria and Lebanon. Over 130 people were killed in the uprisings. A boycott of Danish goods in Muslim countries reduced exports to those countries by 15 percent, costing over 130 million euros in sales. The prime minister of Denmark declared it the worst international crisis involving his country since the Second World War.[55]

Other Scandinavian countries had experienced their own tensions with immigrant communities. In 2006 an anti-immigration party gained electoral strength in Sweden; in the preceding year a mosque in the city of Malmo had been firebombed by an anonymous arsonist. Though the local newspapers blamed factions within the Muslim community for the attack on the mosque, a mullah who practiced in the mosque told me in 2005 that he was convinced that his mosque was torched by Swedes who sought to drive the immigrant community out of the country. The Malmo mosque was frequented by immigrants from Albania as well as North Africa and the Middle East; the mullah with whom I spoke was Palestinian.[56]

The fear of the rising tide of Islamic politics is, somewhat paradoxically, a major issue in Turkey as well. Many of the new Muslim immigrants who have challenged cultural sensibilities in other parts of Europe are Turks. Yet Turkey itself is pledged to the form of secular politics advocated by the leader of the modern Turkish nation, Kemal Ataturk, at the time of the founding of the Turkish republic in 1923 after the fall of the Ottoman Empire. Over the years a series of Islamic-oriented political parties have arisen, though they have often been removed from the electoral process by Turkish judges who cite the country's ban on religiously based political parties.[57] In the 1995 parliamentary elections, for instance, the Islamic-leaning Refah Partisi (Welfare Party) garnered the largest number of votes, allowing its leader, Necmettin Erbakan, to become prime minister. He served in office from June 1996 until 2000, when the party was disbanded by Turkey's Supreme Court of Constitution for allegedly undermining the secular principles of the country. A new party, the Adelet ve Kalkinma Partisi (AKP, Justice and Development Party), received most of the Welfare Party's old supporters, although the AKP was careful to proclaim its support for the secular constitutional system of Turkey and its willingness to work within that framework. Nonetheless, when the AKP won 34 percent of the votes in the 2004 elections and its leader, Recep Tayyip Erdogan, became prime minister, a widespread protest from secular forces in the country initially prevented him from taking office. Erdogan did become prime minister, however, and led a government that focused primarily on economic reforms that benefited the country financially; virtually no policies were instituted that would have unduly favored Islam or changed the secular nature of the government.

In April 2007, the government was scheduled to elect a new president. Though the position was largely ceremonial, it carried considerable symbolic importance as head of state. Turkey's president is selected not by a general election but by votes cast by the parliamentary assembly. Since the AKP was the largest party in the assembly, it assumed that the position would go to its candidate, Abdullah Gul, who had served as the

country's foreign minister. As the election drew near, a large public outcry erupted over what was perceived as the encroaching Islamicization
of Turkey's politics. Pictures of Gul's wife wearing a headscarf were
prominently displayed in the press. On April 14 over three hundred
thousand pro-secular protesters marched through the streets of the capital, Ankara, and in other major cities in the country. Two weeks later
another pro-secular rally drew a crowd of over a million, the largest
protest in Turkish history. Again the crowds chanted the slogan,
"Turkey is secular and it will remain secular." Military leaders issued a
statement indicating that they were pledged to be the "absolute defender
of secularism" and would be willing to act, if necessary, to protect the
nation's secular principles of the country.[58] The assembly elections,
however, were not held at that time, due to a boycott of opposition parties that prohibited it from establishing a quorum. The rules of Turkey's
constitution required that if an assembly was not able to select a president, new general elections for the assembly members would have to be
held. On July 22, 2007, new elections resulted in a resounding confir-
mation of the AKP's leadership. The AKP received 46 percent of the
votes, more than 10 percent more than in the previous election; they received 340 seats in the assembly, a significant increase from the 252 in
the previous assembly, thus assuring their ability to select a member of
their own party as president. Yet the AKP leaders continued to be faced
with the challenge of assuring the vocal pro-secular elements of the country that they were pledged to the secular political process and nationalist ideals that have been the hallmark of the country's recent past. They
also were aware that Turkey's judiciary and its military had intervened
before under the pretext of making certain that the political process followed the country's secular principles, and they did not want to provoke
a military intervention again.

The pro-secular forces in Turkey were concerned that their country
would be adversely affected by the rising tide of Islamic activism in other
countries in the region—not only in the Middle East but also in Europe.
Militant Islamic movements in Europe, for example, posed challenges to
the secular politics of their countries that could spill over into the entire
region. The terrorist attacks on Madrid's trains in 2004 and the London
subway attacks in 2005 are usually attributed to the far-flung jihadi network often associated with Osama bin Laden and his al Qaeda organization. (They are discussed in that context in the next chapter.) But these
incidents also reflect Muslim immigrant unrest and the marginalization
of Islamic communities in Europe, since the perpetrators of these attacks

were not outsiders but Muslim residents of Spain and the United Kingdom.[59]

On March 11, 2004, four commuter trains were heading towards the Atocha station in Madrid. A total of thirteen improvised explosive devices had been packed on board the trains. Ten of them exploded, killing almost two hundred commuters. After an intensive investigation, twenty-nine suspects were charged with conspiracy in the attacks. Most were originally from Morocco but resided in Spain. Occurring three days before general elections in which one of the most contested issues was Spain's military support for the American-led coalition forces in Iraq, the attacks were widely interpreted as an attempt to force Spain to withdraw its troops from the country. Some speculated that the suspects were also motivated by resentment over the treatment of Muslims in Spain and a lingering sense of the loss of Moorish Spain from the Muslim world.[60]

The 2005 attacks on the London subway system were also home-grown, conducted by British citizens of Pakistani origin. During the morning rush hour on July 7, 2005, four bombs concealed in backpacks were ignited by suicide bombers. Three were detonated on underground subway trains within fifty seconds of one another, the fourth an hour later on a bus near Tavistock Square. Over fifty commuters were killed. The four young men were all raised in Britain but had visited *madrassa*s in Pakistan, and according to a videotape released by al Qaeda lieutenant Ayman al-Zawahiri they had also attended al Qaeda training camps in Afghanistan.

Two of the bombers made statements videotaped before the attack in which they described the causes for their actions. Mohammad Sidique Khan accused the British government of involvement in anti-Muslim activities and held Britain and other "democratically elected governments" responsible for "atrocities against my people all over the world." Khan concluded by saying that "we are at war and I am a soldier," warning the British public that "now you too will taste the reality of this situation."[61]

Another statement released the following year showed a second suicide bomber, Shehzad Tanweer, again speaking directly to the British public. "Tell all you British citizens," Tanweer said, "to stop your support to your lying British government and to the so-called war on terror." He concluded with this warning to the British public: "You will never experience peace until our children in Palestine, our mothers and sisters in Kashmir, and our brothers in Afghanistan and Iraq feel peace."[62]

In August 2006, British officials arrested dozens of Muslim activists involved in an elaborate plot to bring down British and American passenger planes. British and U.S. investigators described the plot as similar in scope to the September 11, 2001, attacks. The planners had intended to use common electronic devices such as cell phones and iPods to detonate liquid explosives that would have brought down as many as ten planes. As in the subway attack in London in the previous year, all of those involved directly in the plot were British citizens of Pakistani origin.

The statements of the attacks' perpetrators associate their anger with their experience of being marginalized. Though the stated intentions of the attackers were to punish Britain for its participation in the war in Iraq and other international campaigns that they regarded as anti-Muslim, the perpetrators also accused the British people of complicity in the humiliation of Muslims.[63]

The phenomenon of ethnic anger played out internationally is not unique to the contemporary experience of Muslim communities in Europe and the United Kingdom. In the early the twentieth century Indian immigrants in the United States directed their frustration and experiences of humiliation toward an international effort to end British colonialism in India.[64] Their organization—the Ghadar movement—was composed of Indian immigrants living in Northern California. The movement loaded five boats with munitions and a volunteer militia and set sail for India in 1915. The boats were intercepted by the British and the plot was foiled, but the incident is remembered in Indian history as the first armed attempt to overthrow colonial rule. The Ghadar volunteers even designed a flag—the first expressly created for an independent India—which first flew over the Ghadar headquarters at 5 Wood Street in San Francisco.

Similar movements of expatriate activism were waged by Chinese living abroad who supported the revolution of Sun Yat Sen, Irish immigrants who contributed to the Irish freedom movement, and Vietnamese abroad—including Ho Chi Minh—who planned the overthrow of French colonial control in their country. Ayatollah Khomeini was part of an expatriate group in France that orchestrated the Islamic revolution in Iran, and Sikhs around the world contributed significant support to the Khalistani movement in India. Expatriate Tamils have financed the Tamil separatist movement in Sri Lanka. In all of these cases, much of the incentive for international activism was fueled by marginalized immigrant communities far from their homelands.

Hence religion has played a role in the ethnic tensions of new immigrant communities on both sides of the conflict—assertions of privilege by the dominant culture and protests by minority groups. This is a common pattern found around the world. In South Africa, for example, Bishop Desmond Tutu led protests in support of Christian justice and reconciliation at the same time that South African Christian nationalism was promoted by the Reconstituted National Party.[65] In recent decades, however, new waves of Muslims immigrants have placed Europe on the front lines of ethnic religious conflict.[66]

A PEACEFUL RESOLUTION IN NORTHERN IRELAND

The immigrants involved in the "troubles" of Northern Ireland were a community of long standing—Scottish Protestants had resided in Ulster County since the seventeenth century—yet the intensity of the conflict with the native Irish was even more ferocious than the immigrant tensions elsewhere in contemporary Europe. Religious ill-will between Protestants and Catholics flared into conflict in the early twentieth century with the rise of Irish nationalism and gained new momentum toward the end of the century as nationalist sentiments around the world were increasingly defined in cultural terms. In Northern Ireland the religious culture was divided between Protestant and Catholic Christians, while nationalist affinities leaned, respectively, toward the United Kingdom and the Irish state.

Although one might trace the troubles of Northern Ireland back to the British invasion of Ireland in 1603, the most recent round of violence began after the Irish Free State was established in 1921. On one level, the troubles were an ethnic conflict between two groups that claimed the region as their home, but since the ethnic groups were divided by religion the tension was also on some level religious.[67] Catholics in Northern Ireland felt marginalized in what they claimed to be Irish territory. Protestants feared that Irish nationalism would deprive them of what they regarded as a part of Britain. One leader of the Catholic Sinn Féin party in Belfast even noted differences in the "thought processes" of the two groups: Irish Catholics tended to be more hierarchical and respectful of authority, Protestants more decentralized and individualistic.[68] For these and other reasons (including the political aspirations of the groups' leaders), violence erupted in the summer of 1969 in the Bogside area of the city of Londonderry. Following the clash, Protestants revived an old militia, the Ulster Volunteer Force, and militants of Roman Catholic background created a "provisional" version of the Irish Republican Army (IRA) more militant than the old IRA. In 1971, the Northern Ireland government began rounding up Catholic activists whom they regarded as potential terrorists and detained them without charges. Within hours, rioting and shooting broke out in the Catholic neighborhoods of Belfast and adjacent towns. The government, rather than retreating from its hard line, pressed on, declaring a war against terrorism. The suspects were beaten and tortured in an attempt to elicit information. They were forced to lie spread-eagled on the floor with hoods over their heads and subjected to disorienting electronic sounds.

The government's tactics backfired. The Catholic community united solidly behind the insurgency, and the violence mounted. Later the home minister who sanctioned the crackdown conceded that the hardline approach was "by almost universal consent an unmitigated disaster." The conflicts of the early 1970s came to a head on what came to be called "Bloody Sunday" when a peaceful protest march against the internment of Catholic activists turned ugly. British troops fired on the crowd, killing thirteen. For over twenty years the violence continued. Eye-for-eye acts of terrorism became a routine affair. The British embassy in Dublin was burned, British soldiers were attacked, police stations were bombed, and individual Catholics and Protestants were captured by opposing sides and sometimes hideously tortured or murdered.

In 1988 an internal dialogue began to take place within the Catholic side between a moderate leader, John Hume, and IRA leader Gerry Adams. In 1995, former U.S. senator George Mitchell was invited to Northern Ireland to help broker the peace talks. Initially they were unsuccessful, but Mitchell subsequently returned for eight months of intensive negotiations. The talks involved members of the Irish and the British government and eight political parties on both Catholic and Protestant sides of the Northern Irish divide. Agreement was reached on April 10, 1998—a day that happened to be Good Friday, the Christian solemnity that precedes Easter.

The Good Friday Agreement is a remarkable document. It attempted to provide structural resolutions to several different problems at the same time. To respond to the public mistrust and insecurity brought on by years of violence, the agreement established human rights and equality commissions. It called for an early release of political prisoners, required the decommissioning of paramilitary weapons, prescribed reforms of the criminal justice system and police policies, and established funds to help victims of violence. It also addressed the problem of

balanced governance by setting up a parliament with proportional representation, an executive branch that guaranteed representation from both
communities, and a consultative civic forum that allowed for community
concerns to be expressed directly. The agreement also dealt with relations among the three key governments involved—Ireland, Great Britain,
and Northern Ireland—by establishing councils and mediating bodies.

Prior to the agreement, the positions of the British government and
the paramilitary forces on both the Protestant Unionist and Catholic IRA
sides had been staked out in extreme and uncompromising terms, and
the methods used by all sides were so harsh as to be virtually unforgiv-
able. Ultimately they were able to break through this impasse by employing several basic nonviolent techniques, including the following: attempting to see the other side's point of view; not responding to violence
in kind (even as severe an incident as the Omagh terrorist bombing on
August 15, 1998, did not elicit retaliatory attacks); letting moderate
voices surface; isolating radical voices—they did not waste time in trying to reason with the militant Protestant leader Ian Paisley, for instance,
who had opted out of the negotiations; and setting up channels of communication. These channels involved an outsider—Senator Mitchell—
playing a mediating role, and the establishment of impartial frameworks
of communication for the two sides that had been deeply mistrustful of
one another.

Peace in Northern Ireland was not a forgone conclusion, and there is
no assurance that the agreement will last. In 2007, however, to the surprise of many, Ian Paisley appeared on the same podium with the IRA
leader Gerry Adams to jointly pledge their support for a peaceful settlement to their differences. Hence the Irish resolution provides at least one
case in recent political history where a form of violence related to religion has come to an end through nonviolent means.[69]

IMAGINED ARMAGEDDON IN JAPAN

In Japan as well religion has taken on elements of resurgent nationalism.
In the Japanese case, however, the nation's most notorious violent incident in the late twentieth century was aimed not at immigrants but at the
Japanese population itself. On March 20, 1995, members of the Aum
Shinrikyo, a new religious movement based loosely on Buddhist teaching, released vials of nerve gas in the Tokyo subway to fulfill its leader's
prophecy of a great catastrophic war that would destroy what the members of the movement regarded as Japan's degenerate society. Although

the movement's ideas were mythic and bizarre, the social context for the movement's actions was the experience of modern alienated society. The same element of discontent led to the rise of religious activism in modern Japan and elsewhere.

Religious nationalism in Japan figured prominently during the Second World War, when the Japanese emperor was regarded as both a political and a spiritual leader. In postwar Japan, forms of religious nationalism have surfaced in the revival of veneration for the emperor and in new religious movements that carry strongly nationalist overtones. One of these movements was the Institute for Research in Human Happiness led by Ryuho Okawa, which claimed to have sold thirty million copies of its anti-American and pro-Japanese books of prophecy and spiritual mysticism. Okawa, evoking the Prophet Moses, asserted that the Japanese were the new chosen people.

Taking the success of this and similar movements as its model, the members of Aum Shinrikyo formulated an even grander vision. Its leader, Shoko Asahara, predicted that the world as we know it would end in an apocalyptic encounter between the forces of light and darkness that would propel Japan into global leadership, and Asahara and his movement would emerge from this cosmic battle as the dominant force in world affairs. Asahara based his teachings on Buddhism while invoking eclectic elements of other religions: images of the Hindu god Ganesh were combined with prophecies from the Christian Bible. The movement was organized as a global government-in-exile, a remnant of society that was waiting for the coming conflagration—Asahara used the New Testament term, Armageddon, to describe it—that the followers expected to occur around the time of the new millennium in 2000.

In 1995, news of a nerve gas attack on Tokyo's subways that killed twelve people and injured five thousand other passengers stunned the Japanese public. When one of the members of the movement first heard about the event, he recalled in a conversation with me some months later that he knew exactly what it meant. He thought that "the weird time had come."[70] When I asked what he meant, he whispered, "Armageddon."

At the core of Shoko Asahara's prophecies was a world catastrophe unparalleled in human history. Although the Second World War had been disastrous for Japanese society, this destructive conflagration—including the nuclear holocausts at Hiroshima and Nagasaki—was nothing compared with what Asahara described as the coming Third World War. Asahara took the prophecies of the Book of Revelation and mixed them with apocalyptic Old Testament imagery and sayings of the

sixteenth-century French astrologer Nostradamus (Michel de Nos-
tredame). It was from Nostradamus that Asahara acquired the notion
that Freemasons have been secretly plotting to control the world. To
these fears Asahara added the paranoid delusions of Jewish international
conspiracies advanced by Christian Identity extremists. Inevitably, the
U.S. Central Intelligence Agency was also thought to be involved. Asahara also incorporated Hindu and Buddhist notions of the fragility of life
into his prognosis for the world. "Armageddon," Asahara said, must
occur because "the inhabitants of the present human realm do not recognize that they are fated to die."[71]

When Armageddon came, Asahara said, the evil forces would attack
with the most vicious weapons: "Radioactivity and other bad
circumstances—poison gas, epidemics, food shortages—will occur."[72]
The sole survivors would be those "with great karma" and those protected by the Aum Shinrikyo organization. "They will survive," Asahara
said, "and create a new and transcendent human world."[73]

One of the things that convinced Ashara's followers that the nerve gas
attack was the forerunner of the dreaded Armageddon was the location
of the attack: not just the subway system but trains converging at the Kasumigaseki station in downtown Tokyo. Since the deep underground station was located in the heart of Tokyo's government district, many journalists at the time concluded that the site had been chosen as an attack
on the Japanese government. But inside the Aum Shinrikyo movement's
headquarters in Tokyo, the members—those who were not informed
that their own leaders had been implicated in the plot—offered somewhat different scenarios. Several told me that the assault might indeed
have been an attack on the Japanese government, albeit a deceptive one.
They suggested that the government officials had attacked themselves to
deflect the public's attention from what the Aum members thought had
really occurred: a Third World War had begun, and the Japanese government had been secretly captured by America. The use of nerve gas
seemed to them to confirm this theory, since the Aum members had been
told by their leaders that only the American army in Japan possessed
such a weapon.[74]

A book of Asahara's prophecies published by the movement a few
months before the subway attack indicated another—and perhaps a
more important—reason why the Kasumigaseki station was targeted.
Among the predictions of the great conflagration at the end of the twentieth century was one that nerve gas would be used against the populace.
The Japanese government, he claimed, could not sufficiently protect

them; it had prepared "a poor defense for the coming war," Asahara said.[75] He went on to say that the government had constructed only one subway station of sufficient depth and security to be used as a haven in time of nuclear or poisonous gas attack. "Only the Kasumigaseki subway station, which is near the Diet Building, can be used as a shelter," and even it was vulnerable.[76]

The concept of Armageddon also justified murder. Once one is caught up in cosmic war, Asahara explained, the ordinary rules of conduct do not apply. "The world economy will have come to a dead stop," he said. In the mid-1990s, he identified this event as occurring somewhere around August 1, 1999.[77] "The ground will tremble violently, and immense walls of water will wash away everything on earth. . . . In addition to natural disasters," Asahara prophesied, "there will be the horror of nuclear weapons."[78] Nerve gas—sarin gas, specifically—would also be used in that horrific war.[79]

In a perceptive analysis of the Aum Shinrikyo movement, Ian Reader linked Aum's concept of cosmic war to a history of rejection experienced both by Asahara and by members of his movement. This sense of alienation led to conflict with the society around them, and these encounters in turn led to greater rejection and ultimately to a paranoid attitude of "Aum against the world."[80] According to Susumu Shimazono, a professor of religion at Tokyo University, these traits reflect an uneasiness shared by many Japanese about the future, a nervousness about Japanese identity in a global society, and a lack of trust in their political leaders to provide moral vision and social solidarity during times of economic and social disarray.[81]

Perhaps because they reflect some of the deepest concerns that Japanese have about their society, new religious movements such as Aum Shinrikyo have been quite popular. Not even the infamy of Aum Shinrikyo dampened the public's interest in such movements. Following Asahara's trial in the late 1990s a resurgence in Aum membership—under a new name, Aleph—has been documented not only in Japan but also in Russia and other parts of the world where it had previously enjoyed a sizable following.[82] Although the Japanese government had considered whether to use its authority to outlaw the Aum movement entirely, it backed away from such measures. New religious movements in Japan, including Aum, enjoy considerable government leniency in their freedom of action and range of public expression. They are successful in part because they provide a religious haven for those who have felt battered by a loss of purpose and identity in urban society and the excesses of secular modernity.

THE MILITANT CHRISTIAN RIGHT IN THE UNITED STATES

Recent movements of religious activism in the United States also respond
to a perception of secular society's moral deficiencies. At times this religious dimension has taken a turn toward politics. Politicized religion in
the United States is not, in itself, a new thing. American patriotism has
often been fused with biblical images and Protestant Christian rhetoric,
creating a "civil religion" that has been as nationalist in its own way as
the Muslim Brotherhood in Egypt or the Rashtriya Swayamsevak Sangh
in India. Periodically in American history, separatist movements have
created their own ideal societies; native peoples have used symbols from
their religious heritage to define an identity of their own that insulates
them from absorption into the dominant society.[83]

What was new about American religious politics in the late twentieth
century was the way that religion became infused into a radical critique
of the secular political order. Though Christianity has always contained
the idea of a kingdom of God that contrasts with the worldly human
order, the notion of a catastrophic moment in history in which this
godly kingdom intersects with the human order is peculiar to Evangelical Protestant Christianity. It began to take shape in the modern era with
the theology of John Nelson Darby, a nineteenth-century British theologian, who believed that the time of the kingdom would be at hand when
pious Christians experienced the "rapture" of being united with heavenly existence. This vision reemerged with remarkable popularity in the
United States after the end of the Cold War. It has provided the framework for the *Left Behind* novels of Tim LaHaye and Jerry Jenkins, which
have sold tens of millions of copies. Many of the sixteen volumes in the
series made the *New York Times* best-seller list.[84]

The evangelical Christian movement in the United States that is the
audience for the *Left Behind* books has had a profound impact on
American politics. It required American political society to take on a
Christian character in order to fulfill society's role in the coming of
Christ.[85] Even though there were two branches of millenarian thinking
about the return of Christ's kingdom to earth—premillennarian and
postmillenarian, the first envisioning Christ to come again to reign on
earth for a thousand years and the other imagining the return of Christ
at the end of a thousand-year period—both posited the need for a virtuous political order in order to make possible the expected messianic
return. Thus Christian politics was not only desirable; it was a theological necessity.

At the end of the Cold War the talk of a "new world order" alarmed many evangelical Christians, who took this to mean the global domination of secular government. Some conservative Christians interpreted it as opening up American society to a variety of religions, races, and sexual orientations, all of which they regarded as contrary to their desire for a Christian nation that would fulfill the messianic expectations of the coming of Christ. As a result, many evangelical Christians turned to electoral politics to increase their power, and in the late twentieth century, their efforts bore fruit.[86]

One branch of postmillennial evangelical thought that had considerable political impact was Dominion Theology. This theological position maintained that Christianity had to assert the dominion of God over all creation, including secular politics and society, in order for messianic expectations to be fulfilled. This point of view—articulated by such right-wing Protestant evangelicals as Jerry Falwell and Pat Robertson—led to a burst of social and political activism in the Christian right in the 1980s and 1990s. It also corresponded with the thinking of many Christians who had become politically active in their efforts to prohibit abortion in the United States.

The Christian movement opposing abortions is permeated with ideas from Dominion Theology.[87] Randall Terry, founder of the militant Operation Rescue organization and a writer for the Dominion magazine *Crosswinds*, helped craft the magazine's "Manifesto for the Christian Church." The manifesto asserted that America should "function as a Christian nation" and opposed such "social moral evils" of secular society as "abortion on demand, fornication, homosexuality, sexual entertainment, state usurpation of parental rights and God-given liberties, statist-collectivist theft from citizens through devaluation of their money and redistribution of their wealth, and evolutionism taught as a monopoly viewpoint in the public schools."[88]

At the extreme right wing of Dominion Theology is a relatively obscure theological movement, Reconstruction Theology, whose exponents seek to create a Christian theocratic state. Leaders of the Reconstruction movement trace their ideas, which they sometimes called "theonomy," to Cornelius Van Til, a twentieth-century Presbyterian professor of theology at Princeton Seminary who followed the teachings of the sixteenth-century Reformation theologian John Calvin regarding the necessity for presupposing the authority of God in all worldly matters. Followers of Van Til, including his former students Greg Bahnsen and Rousas John Rushdoony, and Rushdoony's son-in-law, Gary North, adopted this "presuppositionalism," with all its implications for the role of religion in political life, as a doctrine.

Reconstruction writers regard the history of Protestant politics since the early years of the Reformation as having taken a bad turn, and they are especially unhappy with the Enlightenment formulation of the separation of church and state. They feel it necessary to "reconstruct" Christian society by turning to the Bible as the basis for a nation's law and social order. To propagate these views, the Reconstructionists established the Institute for Christian Economics in Tyler, Texas, and the Chalcedon Foundation in Vallecito, California. They published a journal and a steady stream of books and booklets on the theological justification for interjecting Christian ideas into economic, legal, and political life.[89]

According to the most prolific Reconstruction writer, Gary North, it is "the moral obligation of Christians to recapture every institution for Jesus Christ."[90] He regarded this as especially so in the United States, where secular law as construed by the Supreme Court and defended by secular politicians has been moving in what Rushdoony and others regarded as a decidedly un-Christian direction, particularly in matters regarding abortion and homosexuality. What the Reconstructionists ultimately wanted, however, was more than the rejection of secularism. Like other theologians who invoked the biblical concept of "dominion," they reasoned that Christians, as the new chosen people of God, were destined to dominate the world.

One of the followers of Reconstruction thought was Michael Bray, a Lutheran pastor in Maryland who was convicted and served prison time for bombing clinics that performed abortions on the East Coast. Bray had studied the writings of Reconstruction Theology authors extensively and owned a shelf of their books. He and his friend Presbyterian pastor Paul Hill regarded their political actions as sanctioned by the Bible and Christian history as interpreted by Reconstruction theologians. Hill had once studied with a founder of the movement, Greg Bahnsen, at the Reformed Theological Seminary in Jackson, Mississippi.[91]

In my conversations with Michael Bray, he maintained that the idea of a society based on Christian morality was not a new one, and he emphasized the "re-" in "reconstruction."[92] Although Bray rejected the pope's authority, he valued much of the Roman Catholic Church's social teachings and greatly admired the tradition of canon law. Only recently in history, he observed, had political order in Europe and America not been based on biblical concepts. Opposed to the disestablishment of the political role of the church, Bray labeled himself an "antidises-tablishmentarian."

Bray was serious about bringing Christian politics into power. He said that it is possible, under the right conditions, for a Christian revolution to sweep across the United States and bring in its wake constitutional changes that would make biblical law the basis of social legislation. Failing that, Bray envisaged a new federalism that would allow individual states to experiment with religious politics on their own. When I asked Bray what state might be ready for such an experiment, he hesitated and then suggested Louisiana and Mississippi, or, he added, "maybe one of the Dakotas."

Bray justified violence as an appropriate response to what he regarded as the secular captivity of American society. In an arresting book, *A Time to Kill,* Bray used biblical references and theological justifications for warfare—including those propounded (or so Bray believed) by liberal Protestant theologians Dietrich Bonhoeffer and Reinhold Niebuhr—to justify his position.[93] His friend Paul Hill took this advice seriously. In 1994, Hill approached a medical doctor who was about to enter a clinic in Pensacola, Florida, that performed abortions and shot the doctor, John Britton, and his escort, killing them both. Hill said that in the days preceding the attack, he had opened his Bible and found verses that he thought were speaking to him and directing him to this action.[94] Hill was immediately apprehended, convicted of murder, and some ten years later was executed for the crime by the state of Florida.

Not all Reconstruction thinkers have endorsed the use of violence, especially the kind that Bray and Hill justified. As Reconstruction author Gary North admitted, "there is division in the theonomic camp" over violence, especially with regard to anti-abortion activities. Some months before killing Dr. Britton and his escort, Hill—apparently hoping for North's advance approval—sent North a letter, along with a draft of an essay justifying such killings in part on theonomic grounds. North ultimately responded, but only after the murders had been committed. North regretted that he was too late to deter Hill from his "terrible direction" and chastised Hill in an open letter, published as a booklet, denouncing Hill's views as "vigilante theology."[95] According to North, biblical law provides limited exceptions to the commandment "Thou shalt not kill" (Exodus 20:13), but in terms similar to just-war doctrine: when one is authorized to do so by "a covenantal agent" in wartime, to defend one's household, to execute a convicted criminal, to avenge the death of one's kin, to save an entire nation, or to stop moral transgressors from bringing bloodguilt on an entire community.[96]

Hill—joined by Bray—responded to North's letter. They argued that many of those conditions applied to the legal status of abortion in the United States. Writing from his prison cell in Starke, Florida, Paul Hill maintained that the biblical commandment against murder also "requires using the means necessary to defend against murder—including lethal force."[97] He went on to say that he regarded "the cutting edge of Satan's current attack" to be "the abortionist's knife" and that his actions therefore had ultimate theological significance.[98] Bray, in *A Time to Kill*, addressed North's concern about the authorization of violence by a legitimate authority or "a covenantal agent," as North put it. Bray raised the possibility of a "righteous rebellion."[99] Just as liberation theologians justified the use of unauthorized force for the sake of their vision of a moral order, Bray saw the legitimacy of using violence not only to resist what he regarded as murder—abortion—but also to help bring about the Christian political order envisioned by Reconstruction thinkers such as Gary North. In Bray's mind, a little violence was a small price to pay for the possibility of fulfilling God's law and establishing His kingdom on earth.

Another strand of radical religious thought—Christian Identity—had relatively few qualms about the use of violence. This strand of Protestant Christian thought is based on the notions of racial supremacy and biblical law and has had enormous influence on some of the most radical Christian movements in America.[100] It has been in the background of such extremist groups as the Posse Comitatus, the Order, the Aryan Nations, the supporters of Randy Weaver at Ruby Ridge, Herbert Armstrong's Worldwide Church of God, the Freeman Compound, and the World Church of the Creator. It is popular among many militia movements and motivated Buford Furrow in his 1999 assault on a Jewish center in Granada Hills, California. Christian Identity ideas were also in the background of the thinking of Timothy McVeigh, the convicted perpetrator of the 1995 Oklahoma City bombing, and Eric Robert Rudolph, who bombed the Olympic Park in Atlanta in 1996.

Timothy McVeigh was exposed to Identity thinking through the militia culture with which he was associated and through his contacts with the Christian Identity encampment, Elohim City, on the Oklahoma-Arkansas border. Although there is no evidence that McVeigh was ever affiliated with the commune, phone calls he made to Elohim City in the months before the bombing are a matter of record, including one made two weeks before the bombing.[101] McVeigh likely visited the site, since he once received a citation for a minor traffic offense ten miles from the commune on the only access road leading to it. McVeigh also imbibed Identity ideas, or similar concepts, through such publications as *The Patriot Report*, an Arkansas-based Christian Identity newsletter that McVeigh received, and perhaps most of all from *The Turner Diaries*.[102] According to McVeigh's friends, this was "his favorite book"; it was "his bible," some said.[103] According to one gun collector who saw McVeigh frequently at gun shows, he hawked the book at bargain prices, and it was always at his side.[104] More to the point, McVeigh's telephone records indicate that despite his denials, he had talked directly with the author of the novel on several occasions, including a conversation shortly before the Oklahoma City bombing.[105]

The author of McVeigh's favorite novel was William Pierce, who received a Ph.D. from the University of Colorado, once taught physics at Oregon State University, and for a time served as a writer for the American Nazi Party. Although he denied any affiliation with the Christian Identity movement—and in fact attacked the clubbishness of most Identity groups—Pierce's ideas are virtually indistinguishable from Identity thinking. In 1984 Pierce proclaimed himself the founder of a religious compound very similar to those associated with the Christian Identity movement. He called it the Cosmotheist Community.[106]

Pierce's novel, written under the pseudonym Andrew Macdonald, was the main vehicle for his Identity/Cosmotheist ideas. Published in 1978, it describes an apocalyptic battle between freedom fighters and a dictatorial American government. The novel soon became an underground classic, selling 200,000 copies in gun shows and through mail-order catalogues. It served as the blueprint for such activists as Robert Matthews, who was implicated in the 1984 assassination of a Jewish talk-show host in Denver. Matthews, like Timothy McVeigh, seems to have taken seriously the novel's predictions of the encroachment of government control in America and the resistance by a guerrilla band known as "the Order." Matthews called his own movement "the Order," and the modus operandi McVeigh used in destroying the Oklahoma City federal building was almost exactly the same as the one used by patriotic guerrillas to attack government buildings in Pierce's novel.

Although written almost eighteen years before the 1995 Oklahoma City bombing, a section of *The Turner Diaries* reads almost like a news account of the event. It recounts in chilling detail its hero's bombing of the federal office building with a truckload of "a little under 5,000 pounds" of ammonium nitrate fertilizer and fuel oil. Timothy McVeigh's own truck carried 4,400 pounds of the same mixture, packaged and transported exactly as described in the novel. In Pierce's novel, the bombing was directed against the perceived evils of the government and sought to arouse the fighting spirit of all "free men."[107] Such efforts were necessary, according to Pierce, because of the dictatorial secularism that had been imposed on American society as the result of an elaborate conspiracy orchestrated by Jews and liberals desperately seeking to deprive Christian society of its freedom and its spiritual moorings.

Pierce and Christian Identity activists yearned for a revolution that would undo America's separation of church and state; in fact, disdaining organized religion, they sought to merge "religion and state" in a new society governed by religious law. That aspiration may explain why so many Identity groups lived in theocratic societies such as Elohim City, the Freeman Compound, the Aryan Nations compound, and Pierce's Cosmotheist Community. Although these religious communalists believed in capitalism, many held property in common. They also shared an apocalyptic view of history and an even more conspiratorial view of government than the Reconstructionists. They believed that the great confrontation between freedom and a government-imposed slavery was close at hand and that their militant efforts might awaken the spirit of the freedom-loving masses. These ideas came to Timothy McVeigh from William Pierce *and The Turner Diaries* and indirectly from the theories of Christian Identity.

Christian Identity thought originated in the movement of British Israelism in the nineteenth century. According to Michael Barkun, who has written extensively about the movement, one of the founding fathers was John Wilson, whose central work, *Lectures on Our Israelitish Origin,* brought the message to a large British and Irish middle-class audience.[108] Wilson claimed that Jesus had been an Aryan, not a Semite; that the migrating Israelite tribes from the northern kingdom of Israel were in fact blue-eyed Aryans who somehow ended up in the British Isles; and that the "Lost Sheep of the House of Israel" were none other than present-day Englishmen.[109] According to later versions of this theory, people who claim to be Jews are imposters. Some versions of Identity thinking regard them as descendants of an illicit sexual act between Eve and Satan; other versions identify them as aliens from outer space. In either case, Identity thinking claims that the people known as Jews pretend to be Jews in order to assert their superiority in a scheme to control the world. According to Wilson, the Jews' plot is allegedly supported by the secret Protestant order of Freemasons.

British Israelism came to the United States in the early twentieth century through the teachings of the evangelist Gerald L. K. Smith and the
writings of William Cameron, a publicist for the automobile magnate
Henry Ford.[110] Ford himself supported many of Cameron's views and
published a book of anti-Semitic essays written by Cameron but attrib-
uted to Ford, *The International Jew: The World's Foremost Problem*.
Cameron conveyed such Christian Identity tenets as the necessity for the
Anglo-Saxon race to retain its purity and political dominance and the
need for Western societies to establish a biblical basis for governance.
The Christian Identity philosophy was promoted further by Bertram
Comparet, a deputy district attorney in San Diego, and Wesley Swift, a
Ku Klux Klan member who founded the Church of Jesus Christ-
Christian in 1946. This church was the basis for the Christian Defense
League, organized by Bill Gale at his ranch in Mariposa, California, in
the 1960s, a movement that spawned both the Posse Comitatus and the
Aryan Nations.[111]

British Israelism appealed to some members of the elite of
nineteenth-century British society, but by the time these ideas came to
the United States, the ideology had taken a more strident and political
turn. Most of the followers of Christian Identity were relatively benign,
and according to Jeffrey Kaplan, who has studied contemporary Christian Identity groups in the American Midwest and Northwest, their
ideas tended to be simplified in the public mind and the groups reduced
to the ranks of "monsters" in America's right-wing fringe.[112] Though
that may be true, the fact remains that the ideology underlay a strain
of violent religious activism in American society in the late twentieth
century.

In recent decades the largest concentration of Christian Identity
groups in the United States was in Idaho—centered on the Aryan Nations compound near Hayden Lake—and in the southern Midwest near
the Oklahoma-Arkansas-Missouri borders. In that location a Christian
Identity group called the Covenant, the Sword and the Arm of the Lord
(CSA) established a 224-acre community and a paramilitary school,
which it named the Endtime Overcomer Survival Training School.[113]
Nearby, Christian Identity minister Robert Millar and former Nazi
Party member Glenn Miller established Elohim City, whose members
stockpiled weapons and prepared themselves for "a Branch Davidian–type
raid" by the federal Bureau of Alcohol, Tobacco, and Firearms.[114] It was
this Christian Identity encampment that Timothy McVeigh contacted
shortly before the Oklahoma City bombing.

The American incarnation of Christian Identity incorporated many of the British movement's paranoid views, updated to reflect the social anxieties of many contemporary Americans. The United Nations and the Democratic Party were alleged to be accomplices in a joint Jewish-Masonic conspiracy to control the world and deprive individuals of their freedom. In a 1982 Identity pamphlet, Jews were described as "parasites and vultures" who controlled the world through international banking.[115] The establishment of the International Monetary Fund, the introduction of magnetized credit cards, and the establishment of paper money not backed by gold or silver were listed as the final steps in "Satan's Plan."[116]

Gun control is also an important issue to Christian Identity supporters, since they believe that this is how the "Jewish-UN-liberal conspirators," as they call them, intend to eliminate the last possibilities of rebellion against centralized power. These "conspirators" are thought to be intent on depriving individuals of the weapons they might use to defend themselves or free their countrymen from a tyrannical state. This obsession with gun control has made many Christian Identity followers natural allies with the National Rifle Association. The association's rhetoric has played a significant role in legitimizing Christian Identity members' fears of the evil intentions behind governmental gun control and has provided a public voice for their paranoid views.

By the last decade of the twentieth century, the Christian Identity movement had become publicly identified as one of the leading voices of America's radical right. At that time the dean of the movement was Richard Butler, a former Presbyterian minister sometimes described as "the elder statesman of American hate."[117] Butler's designated successor was Neumann Britton of Escondido, California. Although Butler's Aryan Nations compound in Idaho consisted of only a handful of supporters on a twenty-acre farm, its website received over five hundred hits a day. Moreover, the movement received an infusion of financial support from two Silicon Valley entrepreneurs, Carl E. Story and R. Vincent Bertollinni. Their organization, the Eleventh Hour Remnant Messenger, is said to have spent a million dollars promoting Christian Identity ideas as of 1999. It was also said to have had access to fifty million more. One of the projects they funded was the mass mailing of a videotape of Butler presenting his Christian Identity theory of "Adam's pure blood seed-line," and the alleged global conspiracy to destroy it.[118]

At the extreme fringes of the Christian Identity movement have been rogue terrorists. Some were closely linked to Identity organizations.

Buford Furrow—the man who attacked the Jewish day-care center in Los Angeles—once lived in Butler's compound and had married Matthews' widow. Benjamin Smith, the 1999 Fourth of July sniper in Illinois and Indiana, belonged to an Identity-like church that eschewed other Identity groups and, for that matter, all of Christianity. Others were like Timothy McVeigh, whose group was virtually an anti-organization: a nameless, close-knit cadre that shared Identity beliefs but did not have formal ties to organized Identity groups.

One of the most elusive of the lone-wolf Christian Identity terrorists was Eric Robert Rudoph, who was captured in 2003 after having successfully dodged a massive and well-publicized seven-year manhunt. In 2005 Rudolph pleaded guilty to a long list of charges, including bombing abortion clinics in Birmingham, Alabama, and Atlanta, Georgia and a lesbian bar in Atlanta, and exploding a bomb at the 1996 Atlanta Olympics that killed three and injured 150. What these incidents had in common is their relationship to what many Christian activists regard as sexual immorality: abortion and homosexuality. According to another Christian activist, Michael Bray, Rudolph's anger at the Olympic organizers came in part because the carriers of the Olympic torch, which passed through the southern United States on its way to Atlanta, skirted one county in North Carolina that had approved an ordinance declaring that "sodomy is not consistent with the values of the community." Rudolph is said to have interpreted this detour in the torch's journey as a pro-gay stance on the part of the Olympic organizers.[119]

In a broad sense, Rudolph was concerned about the permissiveness of secular authorities in the United States and "the atheistic internationalism" controlling one side of what Bray called "the culture war" in modern society.[120] These concerns are shared by many Christian activists, but in Rudolph's case they were associated especially with the ideas of the Christian Identity movement with which Rudolph became familiar in childhood. At one time he and his mother stayed at the American Identity compound led by Dan Gayman, and there are press reports that Rudolph knew the late Identity preacher Nord Davis.

The world as envisioned by Eric Robert Rudolph, Timothy McVeigh, Buford Furrow, Benjamin Smith, William Pierce, Richard Butler, and Michael Bray—by followers of both Christian Identity and Reconstruction thought—is a world at war. Identity preachers have cited the biblical accounts of Michael the Archangel destroying the offspring of evil to point to a hidden, albeit cosmic, war between the forces of darkness and the forces of light.[121] Reconstruction thinkers have also seen the world enmeshed in a great moral struggle. "There is murder going on," Mike Bray explained, "which we have to stop." In the Christian Identity view of the world, the struggle is a secret war between colossal evil forces allied with the United Nations, the United States, and other government powers, and a small band of the enlightened few who recognized these invisible enemies for what the Identity followers thought they were— satanic powers, in their view—and were sufficiently courageous to battle them. Although Bray rejected much of Christian Identity's conspiratorial view of the world and specifically decried its anti-Semitism, he valued its commitment to fight against secular forms of evil and its insistence on the need for a Christian social order.

As Mike Bray explained, his justification of violence against abortion clinics was not the result of a personal vendetta against agencies with which he and others had moral differences, but the consequence of a grand religious vision. His position was part of a great crusade conducted by a Christian subculture in America that considered itself at war with the larger society, and to some extent was victimized by it. Armed with the theological explanations of Reconstruction and Christian Identity writers, this subculture saw itself justified in its violent responses to a vast and violent repression waged by secular (and, in some versions of this vision, Jewish) agents of a satanic force.[122]

Mike Bray and his network of associates around the country saw themselves engaged in violence not for its own sake but as a response to the institutional violence of what they regarded as a repressive secular government. Those within his culture did not view his burning of abortion clinics as an assault on civil liberties or as a vengeful and hateful crime. Instead, Bray was seen as firing the opening salvos in a great defensive Christian struggle against the secular state, a contest between the forces of spiritual truth and heathen darkness, in which the moral character of America as a righteous nation hung in the balance.

CHAPTER 5

Transnational Networks: Global Jihad

When a truck bomb was detonated under the World Trade Center in New York City on February 26, 1993, most Americans were puzzled but not deeply alarmed. Unlike the catastrophic attacks some eight years later on September 11, 2001, only six people were killed (more than a thousand, however, were injured). Although the blast in a subbasement of the taller of the complex's two towers created a great deal of smoke and confusion, the offices in the buildings were back in operation within a few hours. Moreover, it was not clear why someone would want to do such a thing. A small group of Muslim activists living across the Hudson River in New Jersey was soon implicated. The impression given in the public media was that this was an isolated gang motivated by a paranoid strain of anti-Americanism. It would be some years later before the American public began to understand how widespread the group's beliefs were and how well connected this group was to a network of activists that stretched around the world.[1]

THE RISE OF JIHADI IDEOLOGY

The spiritual leader of the group, Sheik Omar Abdul-Rahman, had been preaching in a small mosque called El Salam ("the place of peace") located above a Chinese restaurant in Jersey City, New Jersey. The blind Islamic scholar had once been a professor of theology at the prestigious Al-Azhar University in Cairo, where he was linked with one of Egypt's most militant Islamic movements, al-Gamaa al-Islamiya ("the Islamic group"). Abdul-Rahman had been indirectly implicated in the assassination of Egypt's president, Anwar al-Sadat, and in a series of violent attacks on the government. His group was also believed to have been involved in two more killings in Egypt—the murders of the Speaker of the People's Assembly, Rifaat al-Mahgoub and a secular writer, Farag Foda—and assassination attempts on President Hosni Mubarak and the novelist Naguib Mahfouz, a Nobel laureate. With the government closing in on his circle, Abdul-Rahman fled to Sudan, then Afghanistan, and ultimately to New Jersey. He entered the United States presumably by error: visa officials at the American embassy in Khartoum overlooked his name on a State Department watch list. (Some commentators claim that the sheik had been favored by the Central Intelligence Agency because of his support of anti-Communist rebels in the war against Soviet control of Afghanistan during the 1990s and that he was allowed to enter the United States as a sort of reward.)[2]

In the United States, Abdul-Rahman preached against the evils of secular society both in the Middle East and in the United States. He singled out America for special condemnation because it helped create the state of Israel, supported the secular Egyptian government, and sent troops to Kuwait during the Gulf War, all of which he deemed "un-Islamic."[3]

Listening attentively to the words of Abdul-Rahman was a growing circle of Islamic activists in their thirties, mostly male, who had emigrated from several Middle Eastern countries to the United States. It included Muhammad Salameh, an unemployed Palestinian refugee; Siddig Ali, a Sudanese; several Egyptians, including Nidal Ayyad, who was trained as a chemical engineer; Ibrahim El-Gabrowny, the president of the Abu Bakr Mosque in Brooklyn and his cousin, El Sayyid Nosair, who would later be imprisoned on charges related to the killing of the Jewish activist Meir Kahane.[4] In contact with the group was a man known by various names, including Ramzi Ahmed Yousef, a Pakistani national said to have been born in Iraq and raised in Kuwait, who had masterminded some of most destructive attacks in recent terrorist history. It also included Mahmud Abouhalima, who for a time served as the sheik's chauffeur and bodyguard.

I interviewed Mahmud Abouhalima on two occasions at the federal penitentiary in Lompoc, California, where he was serving a prison sentence for conspiracy in the 1993 World Trade Center bombing. Abouhalima, a tall, freckled Egyptian with reddish hair, turned out to be an animated conversationalist. Though passionate about Islam's role in politics, he was reluctant to discuss his role in the World Trade Center bombings, since his case was on appeal.

I asked Abouhalima why Muslim activists such as Abdul-Rahman would consider the United States an enemy. Although he did not respond to that question directly—he in fact praised America for its religious freedom, claiming that it was easier for him to be a good Muslim in this country than in Egypt—he argued at some length that America's news media, financial institutions, and government were controlled by Jews. In that sense, Abouhalima explained, although the United States claimed to be a secular nation and tolerant of all religions, "it is involved in religious politics already."[5] Abouhalima maintained that America's involvement in religious politics—its support for the state of Israel and for "enemies of Islam" such as Egypt's president, Hosni Mubarak—was not a consequence of Christianity but due rather to the ideology of secularism, which Abouhalima regarded as generous toward Judaism, but hostile toward other religions, especially Islam. I asked him whether the United States would be better off under a Christian government. "Yes," Abouhalima replied, "at least it would have morals."[6]

Abouhalima's animosity toward the Justice Department (which he called the "Department of Injustice") was compounded by its swift prosecution, in several trials, of the case against him and his colleagues. The one that ended on March 4, 1994, focused on the anti-American motives for the attack; four were convicted for the bombing—Muhammad Salameh, Nidal Ayyad, Ahmad Muhammad Ajaj, and Abouhalima—and Ramzi Ahmed Yousef was indicted as a fugitive. Nine individuals were convicted in the second trial, which concluded on January 17, 1996 (Sheik Omar Abdul-Rahman received a life sentence) for their part in what the judge described as a "terrorist conspiracy" of a magnitude comparable with militant fascism and communism.[7] The prosecution offered evidence that the circle of Muslim activists associated with Abdul-Rahman had intended to blow up not only the World Trade Center but also the United Nations buildings in Manhattan, two New York commuter-train tunnels under the Hudson River, and the Manhattan headquarters of the Federal Bureau of Investigation.

A third trial, begun on May 13, 1996, focused on Ramzi Ahmed Yousef, who had been captured in Pakistan in a raid on his Karachi hotel room in February 1995 and extradited to the United States. Yousef, whose real name is thought to be Abdul Basit Mahmoud Abdul Karim, was implicated not only in the New York bombing but also in a plot to assassinate the pope during his visit to the Philippines in 1995 and the so-called Bojinka Plot, aimed at destroying U.S. passenger airplanes over the Pacific Ocean in 1995. The plot was allegedly bankrolled by Osama bin Laden, with whom Yousef was thought to be in contact. The trial ended on September 5, 1996, with Yousef's conviction for conspiracy in the Bojinka Plot; in August 1997 Yousef again stood trial in New York City, this time for his part in the bombing of the World Trade Center.

Yousef was one connection between Sheik Omar Abdul-Rahman's group and al Qaeda, but there were other ties between the two organizations as well. Abdul-Rahman had worked with Osama bin Laden in Afghanistan during the 1980s in the *mujahadin* resistance. What brought them together was a radical Islamic political ideology propounded by Sayyid Qutb and other leading Egyptian thinkers.[8] As I described earlier in chapter 2, Qutb, in books such as *Milestones* and *This Religion of Islam,* articulated an idea of Islam's political relevance that went far beyond private belief. He saw Islam as a social ideology that was directly competitive with secularism and a basis for a political order that challenged the Western notion of the secular nation-state. Qutb's arguments were invoked as justification for an Islamic nationalism in Egypt, but they were also the basis for a concept of Islamic political society that transcended national boundaries. Like the Pakistani Islamic thinker Maulana Maududi, Qutb faulted the European creation of nation-states such as Pakistan, Egypt, and the Arab states out of the old Indian Raj and Ottoman Empire, thus attacking the very premises of secular nationalism in the Muslim world. In Egypt, during the early days of the republic, these arguments were regarded as treasonous, and Qutb was imprisoned during most of the 1950s and executed in 1966.

One of Qutb's junior colleagues, Abd al-Salam Faraj, an electrical engineer by training, wrote several influential tracts on political Islam. He picked up where Qutb left off and mapped out how the struggle against the secular political order was to be waged. According to Faraj, "modern values, Women's Rights, Human Rights, Secularism, the separation of church and state, Democracy and Tolerance" were fundamentally anti-Islamic.[9] Faraj set forth a carefully argued brief for waging war against the political enemies of Islam in the pamphlet "Al-Faridah al-Gha'ibah" (The Neglected Duty), justifying acts of terrorism on religious grounds.[10] According to Faraj, it is permissible in Islam "to make a raid on the disbelievers whom the call of Islam has reached without prior warning."[11]

These are interesting ideas: the approval of force for the defense of Islam can be expanded to include struggles against perceived political and social injustice, and the traditional limitation of violence to a defensive posture can be extended to preemptive strikes that take the form of terrorist acts. The true soldier of Islam, under Faraj's reading (based largely on the Qur'an and the *hadith*) is allowed to use virtually any means available to achieve a just goal.[12] Deceit, trickery, and violence are specifically mentioned as available options.[13] In other words, Faraj set the Islamic struggle in the context of a form of warfare in which military obligations and religious duties are identical. The Egyptian government regarded these ideas as seditious, and Faraj was executed in 1982.

The circle of young Islamic activists in Egypt during the 1970s found these ideas exhilarating. The fading public confidence in European and American models of secular politics for Egypt made these ideas credible. Theological scholars such as Sheik Omar Abdul-Rahman joined forces with activists such as Osama bin Laden and Ayman al-Zawahiri to put these ideas into an active context. The result was an incendiary mix and the emergence of the contemporary jihadi movement.

EMERGING NETWORKS IN THE AFGHAN-SOVIET WAR

The jihadi movement spread from Egypt and took on an international character as a result of two developments. One was the influential role of Al-Azhar University as a center for Islamic discourse throughout the Muslim world. Ideas that were discussed there had repercussions from Morocco to Indonesia, and students from these regions returned home and shared their learning with others. Jihadism was broadcast as well by the exile of Egyptian Islamic radicals after the trial of the Anwar al-Sadat's assassins. Many ended up in Afghanistan, where they joined the *mujahadin*. In the milieu of a multinational fighting force of Islamic activists, they became the jihadi battlefield soldiers that their ideology had encouraged them to be and forged a new network of activism in the process. Both these forms of jihadi expansion were exemplified in one person: Abdullah Azzam, a Palestinian intellectual who had studied at Al-Azhar University. He left Egypt after graduation and became a professor at King Abdul Aziz University in Jeddah, Saudi Arabia, where he influenced a new generation of Saudi activists. Later he would leave Saudi Arabia and come to Afghanistan to join the Egyptian radicals and other activists in the international Muslim resistance force.

One of Azzam's students in Saudi Arabia was Osama bin Laden, a young businessman from a wealthy family that traced its origins to Yemen. Osama's father moved to the Saudi port city of Jeddah and became a building contractor for the Saudi royal family during the 1950s.[14] Osama was born in 1957, one of more than fifty children of his father (the offspring of over twenty wives),[15] and one of the heirs to the multibillion dollar estate left by the father when he died in the late 1960s. Though Osama received only a fraction of the estate (his share is commonly estimated at $57 million), he was a millionaire many times over.

Osama enrolled in King Abdul Aziz University, studying economics and business administration. Abdullah Azzam was one of his professors, as was Muhammad Qutb—the brother of Sayyid Qutb. Osama's political philosophy blended Islamic puritanism from his Saudi Wahhabi background with radical Islamic political ideas from Egypt. These ideas intensified after the 1973 Yom Kippur war, when Osama became convinced that U.S. support for Israel had been the deciding factor in the defeat of Egypt and Syria.

Osama dropped out of college and went into his father's construction business, but he continued to take a deep interest in world affairs and what he viewed as the exploitation of Muslim countries by the West. His former professor, Abdullah Azzam, went to Afghanistan at the end of the 1970s to join the *mujahadin*, establishing his headquarters in the Pakistani city of Peshawar near the Afghan border. Bin Laden joined him in 1980. Azzam provided intellectual and organizational skills, and the young bin Laden provided financial support. Together in 1984 they founded an organization called Maktab al-Khadamat ("The Office of Order"), also known by its Arabic initials, MAK. Though it was not an armed unit, MAK provided money and weapons to the Afghan rebellion, and the organization recruited volunteers to fight in Afghanistan from throughout the Muslim world. In addition to funding a large portion of MAK's purchases of arms and airline tickets, Osama helped publish a magazine promoting jihad in Afghanistan. According to some reports, the guesthouse in Peshawar that trained foreign *mujahadin* recruits was called Sijill al Qaeda ("the register of the base"); it was bin Laden's first association with the name.[16] Bin Laden also set up a network of couriers to transfer supplies and manpower from Peshawar to Afghanistan, a network that would be useful years later as he went into hiding in the same region after the U.S. invasion of Afghanistan in 2001. Another connection that ultimately proved useful was the relationship between the Arab *mujahadin* and Afghan warlords, including Gulbuddin Hekmatyar. Hekmatyar served as prime minister of Afghanistan after the fall of the Soviet occupation government, and he went into hiding after the 2001 U.S. invasion of Afghanistan because of his support for the Taliban and al Qaeda. In an interview with a Pakistani television network in 2007, Hekmatyar admitted helping Osama bin Laden escape the U.S. military attack on the al Qaeda hideout at Tora Bora in 2001.[17]

In the midst of the *mujahadin* resistance of the 1980s, two of Azzam's Egyptian colleagues—the professor of Islamic law Sheik Omar Abdul-Rahman and the medical doctor Aymen al-Zawahiri, who was a leader in the Islamic Jihad movement—traveled to Afghanistan to join the resistance. Al-Zawahiri disagreed with Azzam and the MAK organization over tactics, and he encouraged bin Laden to join him in splitting from his former professor. Azzam conceived of the *mujahadin* volunteers largely as a support for the Afghan resistence, whereas al-Zawahiri and bin Laden were more eager to play a direct role in the military engagement. They left MAK and in 1988 created their own military headquarters—using the name *al Qaeda* ("the base")—as a training camp and a base of operations. Soon they were directly engaged in military confrontation. Among the foreign *mujahadin* who joined bin Laden and al-Zawahiri was a Pakistani, Khalid Sheik Mohammed, who had lived and worked in Kuwait; he would later admit to being the mastermind of the September 11, 2001, attacks on the United States.

In 1989—a year after the formation of al Qaeda and at the time that the Afghan-Soviet war was winding down—Azzam was assassinated. The murder was never solved, and the perpetrator's identity is disputed. Osama bin Laden himself has been suspected of involvment in the assassination of his former mentor.

Though Sheik Abdul-Rahman had supported Azzam and MAK, he continued to maintain ties with bin Laden and al-Zawahiri after Azzam's death. In the late 1980s, the United States had supported the *mujahadin* efforts, and Sheik Omar Abdul-Rahman was rumored to have received funding from the U.S. government through the Central Intelligence Agency.[18] In 1990, a year after the end of the Soviet-Afghan war, Abdul-Rahman and some of his Egyptian supporters flew to the United States and settled in New Jersey and the outer boroughs of New York City. They were soon associated with MAK activists tied to an Afghan war veterans group in Brooklyn. One of Abdul-Rahman's key Egyptian supporters, Mahmud Abouhalima—who had also traveled to Afghanistan to be part of the *mujahadin* resistance—was implicated in the assassination of a local Islamic cleric who was reported to have opposed the group's takeover of his mosque. Abdul-Rahman soon set up his own mosque in Jersey City above a Chinese restaurant, and it was members of this congregation, including Abouhalima, who carried out the plot to blow up the World Trade Center in 1993.

In the meantime, Osama bin Laden had left Afghanistan after the end of the Soviet-Afghan war and returned to Saudi Arabia. Almost immediately after returning in 1990, he found another cause. Saddam Hussein, the secular rule of Iraq whom most Muslim activists abhorred as an apostate, had invaded Kuwait. According to some reports, bin Laden volunteered to organize his *mujahadin* from Afghanistan against the invading Iraqis.[19] The Saudi rulers rejected bin Laden's offer and instead welcomed U.S. military efforts to counter Iraq's invasion of Kuwait. According to this account, bin Laden was incensed and turned against both the House of Saud and the Americans. He regarded as desecration the U.S. military presence in the "land of the sacred shrines," as he described Saudi Arabia, which is home to Islam's most sacred sites at Mecca and Medina.[20] Having publicly rebuked the Saud family for their pro-American stance, bin Laden was forced out of the country, and his Saudi passport was revoked. In 1991, he went to Sudan.

Bin Laden had reason to think that he would be welcomed in Sudan, since an Islamic group, the National Islamic Front (NIF), had gained control of the country in 1989. The founder and leader of the NIF, Hassan al-Turabi, advocated religious politics similar to those advanced by Sayyid Qutb, and for a time in the 1970s and early 1980s Turabi called his movement the Muslim Brotherhood, implying an ideological affiliation with the identically named Egyptian movement. In the Sudan, bin Laden established an import-export business and a construction firm that built a highway connecting Sudan's capital, Khartoum, with Port Sudan. He was also said to have set up training camps in Sudan for *mujahadin* operatives, including his former comrades, Saudi and Egyptian fighters in the Afghan-Soviet war. Aymen al-Zawahiri was among them.[21]

In 1993 another group of *mujahadin* veterans associated with bin Laden and Sheik Omar Abdul-Rahman plotted the destruction of the World Trade Center in New York City. Although the extent to which the plot was formulated by the al Qaeda group in Sudan is not clear, at least one of the conspirators, Ramzi Yousef, was in close contact with bin Laden and was said to have received financial support from him.[22] Two years later Youssef was in the Philippines, where he was involved in plots to assassinate the pope on his visit to that country and to explode American aircraft crossing the Pacific. Yousef was caught in Pakistan and extradited to the United States for his trial and conviction in the 1993

World Trade Center bombing. At that time, however, his ties to bin Laden were still unclear.

While in Sudan, bin Laden may also have had a hand in the resistance to U.S. forces in nearby Somalia. When American troops entered Somalia in 1993 to support United Nations famine-relief efforts, bin Laden was said to have financed the resistance and sent soldiers to counter the Americans. Bin Laden was also implicated in plots against the Saudi regime; in 1994 his citizenship was revoked, and his family publicly disowned him. Bin Laden responded with a public denunciation of the Saudi Muslim clerics' support for the Oslo peace accords, which he viewed as an endorsement of Israel and a blow to Palestinian interests.[23] When the Khobar Towers, a U.S. military residence in Saudi Arabia, was attacked by a car bomb in June 1996, bin Laden was named a suspect, although the plot seemed to implicate an Iranian-supported movement related to a Saudi branch of Hezbollah. Bin Laden's colleague, al-Zawahiri, was likely involved in an attempt to assassinate Egypt's president, Hosni Mubarak—successor to Anwar al-Sadat, who had been killed by Islamic militants—in 1995.[24] Egypt then joined the governments of Saudi Arabia and the United States in pressuring the Sudanese government to expel the jihadi activists, which they did in 1996. Bin Laden, al-Zawahiri, and some two hundred of their followers returned to their former base at Tora Bora in Afghanistan.

Afghanistan turned out to be a hospitable platform for bin Laden and al-Zawahiri to launch a campaign of global warfare. In 1996, the same year that bin Laden and his jihadi cadre arrived in the country, the radical Muslim party, the Taliban, established strict Islamic rule. Bin Laden soon ingratiated himself with the leader, Mullah Omar, showering him with gifts; he is reputed to have arranged the marriage of one of his daughters to the Taliban leader. Bin Laden and al-Zawahiri provided training for their cadres in the Tora Bora headquarters left over from the Afghan-Soviet war, communicating with their operatives and supporters throughout the world by radio telephones and the Internet. One of bin Laden's first acts in 1996 was to release a statement, "A Declaration of Jihad Against the American Occupation of the Land of the Two Holy Sanctuaries"—alluding to Mecca and Medina and to the presence of American military bases in Saudi Arabia.[25]

Two years later, in 1998, bin Laden and al-Zawahiri, along with Khalid Sheik Mohammed and other militants from Pakistan, Bangladesh, and Egypt, proclaimed a World Islamic Front against the "Crusaders and Zionists"—the United States, Europe, and Israel. Though the origins of the global jihad movement can be traced to the *mujahadin* struggle in the Afghan-Soviet war in the 1980s, it was the 1998 proclamation that launched an expanded international campaign of violence. The declaration, issued as a *fatweh*—a religious edict—implored Muslims "to kill the Americans and their allies civilians and military" as "an individual duty" in any country "in which it is possible to do it," in order to liberate the Dome of the Rock and the al-Aqsa mosque in Jerusalem, to free "the land of the holy places"—Saudi Arabia—from foreign forces, and to remove the American military from all Islamic lands, "defeated and unable to threaten any Muslim."[26] The *fatweh* was an ideological justification for an international network to respond to what it described as a global scheme of America and the West to control and humiliate Islamic society.

Within a few months of the proclamation, in August 1998, the al Qaeda network carried out a pair of bombings almost simultaneously on U.S. embassies in Kenya and Tanzania. Over two hundred were killed and many more injured, some speared by falling glass from high-rise buildings adjacent to the shattered embassies. Within days, U.S. president Bill Clinton announced that bin Laden and the "Islamic Army Organization" were responsible for the bombings.[27] He ordered a military raid on an al Qaeda camp in Afghanistan in an attempt to eliminate bin Laden and his inner circle. The attack was unsuccessful. Jihadi operations associated with bin Laden's network then launched an attack in October 2000 on the USS *Cole*. A suicide squad of jihadi activists steered its small boat loaded with explosives into the U.S. Navy guided-missile destroyer while it was docked in the harbor at Aden in Yemen.

The attacks of September 11, 2001, were the most dramatic of the jihadi assaults against the United States and a turning point in the global movement. The World Trade Center and Pentagon attacks were the culmination of years of planning, carried out by an international network. Nineteen activists—three teams of five and one team of four, each with a trained pilot—hijacked four commercial airliners. American Airlines Flight 11 and United Airlines Flight 175 were flown into the two tallest towers of the World Trade Center at 8:46 and 9:02 A.M., respectively; both towers collapsed about an hour afterward. Almost three thousand office-workers, visitors, and relief workers perished in the attacks. In the meantime a third plane, American Airlines Flight 77, hit the Pentagon building in Arlington, Virginia, near Washington D.C. at 9:37 A.M., and a fourth, United Flight 93, crashed in a field at 10:03 A.M. near Shanksville, Pennsylvania, about 150 miles northwest of Washington. The fourth plane's target is thought to have been the U.S. Capitol; the National Commission on Terrorist Attacks upon the United States determined that a mutiny of the captured passengers prevented the plane from carrying out its mission.

Almost immediately after the attacks, members of the jihadi movement in general and Osama bin Laden's al Qaeda network in particular were the prime suspects. Mohammad Attah, who was on the first plane to crash into the World Trade Center towers, was quickly identified as one of the leaders of the operation. Papers in his luggage, which missed the transfer from his earlier flight from Portland, Oregon, to Logan Airport in Boston, named all nineteen of the hijackers. Most were from Saudi Arabia. Attah, however, was an Egyptian who had studied in Germany. He is said to have come under the influence of radical Islam in Europe and to have met Osama bin Laden in 1999. He then received his mission to participate in what was called the "Planes Project" by jihadi leaders.

According to the report of the National Commission on Terrorist Attacks upon the United States (commonly known as the 9/11 Commission Report), the mastermind of the September 11 operation was Khalid Sheik Mohammed,[28] a Pakistani who had lived in Kuwait for much of his youth and studied in the United States for several years at a small Baptist College in North Carolina.[29] He returned to Pakistan and Afghanistan to fight with the mujahadin in the Afghan-Soviet war in the 1980s, where he crossed paths with Osama bin Laden, Ayman al-Zawahiri, and others who would later be identified with the global jihadi movement. Afterwards Khalid took up work as an engineer and exporter, living for a time in Qatar and the Philippines where he continued to promote the jihadi ideology he learned in Afghanistan. (At the same time, he is said to have indulged in a sensuous lifestyle involving alcohol and loose women.)[30] Though he had been associated with the Muslim Brotherhood in Kuwait as a teenager, his anger at the United States increased in the 1990s over U.S. support for Israel, and he began promoting the idea of a clandestine war against American influence in the Muslim world. In 1996, when U.S. intelligence agencies began to close in on him as a co-conspirator with his nephew, Ramzi Yousef, in the plot to blow up U.S. commercial aircraft over the Pacific, he quickly returned to Afghanistan. There, Khalid renewed his relationship with Osama bin Laden and became a member of the inner circle of the movement that became known to the world as al Qaeda. According to a confession made by Khalid under U.S. detention in 2007, he had a hand in some of the most significant jihadi plots: the September 11, 2001, attacks, the 1993 bombing of the World Trade Center, the Bojinka Plot, and later the Bali nightclub bombing and the murder of the *Wall Street Journal* reporter Daniel Pearl.[31] He is also said to have provided support to Muslim fighters in Bosnia and Chechnya. Khalid was captured in Pakistan in 2003 and was held in custody thereafter by the U.S. military.

In the Philippines, the group associated with Khalid's nephew, Ramzi Youssef, that formulated the failed Bojinka Plot had ties to the local radical movement, Abu Sayyaf, and an international network of activists. Among them was Jamal Khalifa, who had been a college classmate of bin Laden's in Jeddah and followed him to Afghanistan in the early 1980s. During the Afghan-Soviet war, he was said to have been a close friend and bunkmate of the al Qaeda leader, and he married one of Osama's sisters.[32] Khalifa founded the Benevolence International Foundation to raise funds for a variety of activities, including the Bojinka Plot and the 1993 bombing of the World Trade Center. He was arrested in Mountain View, California, in 1994 on suspicion of being involved in the 1993 bombing. The next year the U.S. government deported Khalifa to Jordan to stand trial for other charges, on which he was acquitted. Years later he was found in Madagascar, where he was killed in 2007 during what was presumed to be a robbery attempt.

The jihadi movement was organizationally complex, and there was considerable overlap among many of the jihadi activist groups and individuals that were involved in militant operations in the 1990s and the early 2000s. Some appear to have communicated with each other, especially with regard to large-scale operations such as the September 11, 2001, attacks. Yet the loose structure of these organizational connections raises the question of the extent to which the global jihadi struggle is a unified endeavor.

As best as I can tell, the answer is most likely "not completely." Though there were some ties among various groups and activities before 1998, the working relationship that was forged between the individuals who found themselves in Afghanistan between 1998 and 2001 was a rare moment in jihadi organization. For the most part, the jihadi movement was a loose confederation of disparate groups that occasionally worked together on large projects.

Before 1998 there were several strands of activists. Each group had experience in the *mujahadin* movement and was schooled in the radical jihadi ideology of Qutb and Faraj. Each had already carried out its own terrorist plots. The al-Gamaa al-Islamiya group, led by the Egyptian cleric Sheik Omar Abdul-Rahman, was involved in the 1993 World Trade Center bombings and a series of attacks on politicians and tourists in Egypt. Ayman al-Zawahiri's Egyptian Islamic Jihad group was implicated with Abdul-Rahman in the 1981 assassination of Anwar al-Sadat and the massacre of more than sixty Swiss, German, British, and Japanese tourists at Luxor in 1997. Khalid Sheik Mohammed was involved in anti-U.S. terrorist plots from the Philippines to New York City. Osama bin Laden's largely Saudi group was best known for the U.S. embassy attacks in Africa in 1998. The strands intertwined when Zawahiri, Khalid, and bin Laden found themselves in Afghanistan after 1996, and a "World Islamic Front" was proclaimed in 1998.[33] Plans for September 11 began in earnest soon after. Even then, according to Khalid's statements to his interrogators after his arrest in 2003, he went along with bin Laden's leadership but did not pledge loyalty to him.[34] For this reason it is questionable as to whether the name "al Qaeda" should be given to all of these groups, especially if the use of that term would imply a unified organization under a single individual's command. Rather, the groups should be regarded as part of a global jihadi movement, united in their common conception of a global struggle, although their methods and organizational channels differ. This entire confederation of jihadi groups probably involved not more than several hundred closely involved activists in various parts of the world. It lasted until shortly after the September 11, 2001, attacks, when the U.S. military invaded Afghanistan and the groups' leaders scattered and went into hiding.

GLOBAL JIHAD AFTER SEPTEMBER 11, 2001

After 2001, and especially after the U.S. invasion of Iraq in 2003, a resurgence of jihadi activism erupted around the world. Groups of self-proclaimed jihadi activists emerged in the Middle East, Southeast Asia, North Africa, Europe and the United Kingdom, though it is doubtful that they were orchestrated by central command. These new jihadi groups were stimulated by at least three factors: One was the dramatic character of the 2001 attacks, which had an impact around the world. To many Muslims it was a hideous crime unworthy of being associated with Islam. To others, however, it was impressive: it showed that Muslim activists could successfully undertake a mission of this magnitude, and do it with audacity and conviction. The jihadi videos that were compiled after 2001 as recruitment aids emphasize the courage of the nineteen hijackers.

A second factor in the growth of jihadi sympathy was related to U.S. foreign policy after 2001. The American military incursions in Afghanistan and especially in Iraq were perceived as motivated in large part by efforts to "control Muslim politics," as a mullah in Baghdad put it in a conversation with me after the U.S. invasion of Iraq.[35] Because the United States' stance during the administration of President George W. Bush was widely perceived in the Muslim world as being uncritically in favor of Israel, U.S. policies in the Middle East were often construed as being calculated to oppose Islam either directly or indirectly.

A third factor was the advent of new forms of communication that provided instant and intimate access to large numbers of young Muslims around the world. Internet sites provided both chat rooms for conversations and websites for information. Short propaganda and recruitment videos were produced that could easily be accessed through the Internet and downloaded on iPods and home computers. The theme of these jihadi videos was invariably valor in the face of repression. Often the videos would open with a multiplicity of images of oppressive American military operations and grieving Muslim families, and then turn to actual footage of attacks using improvised explosive devices and truck bombs. The images were accompanied by a narration that underscored the jihadi message of a cosmic war between Islam and the West, cast as a struggle between light and darkness, good and evil.[36]

Behind these three factors was a fourth, the major theme of this book: the loss of faith in the secular nation-state. Though this theme runs through all of the cases I have described, it has been exacerbated in the twenty-first century by globalization. The rise of the global jihad movement coincides with the increased pace of global social, economic, and cultural changes in the first decade of this century and the weakening of political authority in many parts of the world. Protests against what are perceived to be the moral failures of the state often take religious forms, and in the Muslim world they are easily fused with the rhetoric of global jihad. Hence assaults on individual states—including Indonesia, India, Morocco, Egypt, Spain, and the United Kingdom—appear as decentralized versions of transnational jihad. In many of these cases the organization and many of the grievances are local, but the rhetoric is that of global jihadi movement.

One of the first examples of this decentralized phase of the global jihadi movement came in 2002, when a series of car bombs in Bali leveled nightclubs and killed more than two hundred people, many of them young Australians on holiday. The Indonesian Jemaah Islamiyah leader

Riduan Isamuddin (popularly known as Hambali), who was implicated in the attacks, was said to have been a colleague of Khalid Sheik Mohammed and had met two of the September 2001 hijackers before they undertook their mission.[37] But the Indonesian activist and his co-conspirators had their own anti-Western momentum, encouraged by the radical Indonesian cleric Abu Bakar Bashir. For some years the Indonesian Muslim militants had condemned the secular authorities in Jakarta for pandering to the interests of the West.

This pattern of local anti-authoritarian Islamic activism that is loosely tied to the international jihadi movement also appears in other post-2001 terrorist incidents. It applies to attacks in India in the disputed northern region of Kashmir and Kashmir-related terrorist assaults in Delhi and Mumbai, including the December 2001 attack on India's parliament and the July 2006 train bombs in Mumbai, in which over two hundred were killed. In both cases local pro-Kashmiri Muslim activists were implicated and alleged to have received support from global jihadi connections in Pakistan and the Middle East.[38]

A critical turning point in the post-2001 growth of the global jihad movement came as a result of the war that followed the downfall of Saddam Hussein's regime by an American-led military coalition in March 2003. Iraq was important for the jihad movement in two ways. It presented a clear example of the jihadi claim that the United States was determined to control Muslim countries, and it provided a new center for global struggle, attracting jihadi activists from around the world. In an interesting way, Iraq in the first decade of the twenty-first century replicated the experience of Afghanistan during the 1980s. It is paradoxical that this was so, considering the role that the United States played in supporting the Muslim *mujahadin* in their attacks on the secular Soviet-supported Afghanistan regime; in Iraq, America became the secular foe of the new *mujahadin*.

The central figure in the Iraq theater of the global jihadi war was Musab al-Zarqawi. Al-Zarqawi came from the Jordanian city of Zarqa—hence his adopted name (his real name was most likely Ahmad Fadeel an-Nazal al-Khalayeh). According to Jordanian intelligence reports, he was born in 1966, grew up as a teen-age thug, and was briefly jailed on charges of drug possession and sexual assault.[39] Later in life he became a convert to militant jihad and traveled to Afghanistan in 1989 to join the last stages of the *mujahadin* struggle against the Soviet-supported government. Soon after he returned to Jordan and created a militant organization, al-Tawhid ("unity"), dedicated to fomenting a militant

Islamic revolution in the country. In 1992 he was arrested and served five years in prison for conspiracy to overthrow the Jordanian government. As soon as he was released in 1999, he attempted to blow up the Radisson SAS Hotel in Amman, Jordan's capital; the hotel was frequented by Americans, Israelis, and other foreigners. With the Jordanian government eager to place him back in prison, al-Zarqawi fled to Pakistan and Afghanistan. It was there that al-Zarqawi most likely met Osama bin Laden, Ayman al-Zawahiri, Khalid Sheik Mohammed, and other expatriate jihadis who were forming a global activist coalition. Though bin Laden is said to have been wary of the coarse and thuggish al-Zarqawi—and for his part al-Zarqawi was said to have resisted paying obeisance to bin Laden or anyone else—bin Laden reportedly provided him some monetary support.[40]

After the September 11, 2001, attacks and the subsequent U.S.-led military invasion of Afghanistan, al-Zarqawi for a time supported the remnants of the Taliban in their resistance struggle against the new government in Kabul. In 2002 he was in Iraq—according to some reports, for medical treatment of injuries sustained in the Afghan struggles.[41] He settled in the north, in the Kurdish region, which enjoyed semi-autonomous status with American military support. Al-Zarqawi joined an Islamic guerrilla movement, Ansar al-Islam, that aimed at resisting Kurdish nationalism. Hence at the time of the U.S.-led military coalition's invasion of Iraq in March 2003, al-Zarqawi and his cadre were well poised to join the resistance movement and to try to bend it in a transnational jihadi direction.

Al-Zarqawi's forces, organized under the banner of the al-Tawhid group, targeted a wide range of individuals and public institutions in order to destabilize and discredit the embryonic Iraqi government that was being established by U.S.-led reconstruction efforts. One of their first acts was a well-orchestrated suicide truck-bombing that demolished the United Nations headquarters in Baghdad on August 19, 2003, killing twenty-two, including U.N. special envoy Sérgio Vieira de Mello. The group found that their acts of violence drew more attention if they were performed in a particularly gruesome manner—hence the rash of televised beheadings, beginning with a young American, Nicholas Berg, in May 2004, and including British hostage Ken Bigley, who was kidnapped in Baghdad's upscale al-Mansour district and beheaded in September 2004. Al-Zarqawi's role in fomenting Sunni-Shi'a sectarian strife in Iraq, and his death as the result of an American military attack, are discussed in chapter 2.

Al-Zarqawi provided a model for ad-hoc acts of antiauthoritarian struggle that could be conducted by jihadi activists anywhere. In some cases he helped promote these acts; in other cases he served as an inspiration for makeshift terrorism. Increasingly small groups of jihadi activists—often young men—were involved in vicious attacks that were related both to local issues and global concerns. In Morocco, for instance, a series of bombings in 2003 on a tourist hotel, a Jewish-owned restaurant, a Jewish cemetery, and the Belgian consulate in Casablanca killed forty seven, including the fourteen young Moroccan activists. The targets of the attacks indicated their hatred of Jewish and foreign influences on Moroccan culture. The Moroccan militants were said also to have objected to the U.S. invasion of Iraq two months earlier, as well as to Israel's treatment of the Palestinians. The bombers who were part of the Salafia Jihadia group were alleged to have been in contact with al Qaeda and with al-Zarqawi.[42]

The Casablanca attacks occurred days after an incident in Saudi Arabia: the bombing of a housing complex populated by foreigners in the capital, Riyadh. Dozens were killed, including the six militants, who drove a convey of two cars, a truck, and a sports-utility vehicle into the gate of a housing compound owned by an American-based defense contractor that was training the Saudi National Guard. A Saudi group was implicated as perpetrators of the attack, which was aimed at removing the presence of foreigners—specifically Europeans and Americans—from the country. It was unclear to what extent the local Saudi group was connected to bin Laden, al-Zarqawi, or other leaders of the global jihadi movement.

Attacks in 2005 in the Egyptian resort of Sharm el-Sheik at the southern end of the Sinai Peninsula were also aimed at removing the presence of foreigners. In this case the bombs were directed at tourist hotels and restaurants visited by Israelis. An Egyptian group was implicated in the attack. It had named itself the Abdullah Azzam Brigade in honor of the Palestinian professor who was a colleague of Sayyid Qutb in Cairo and later became the teacher of Osama bin Laden in Saudi Arabia. But since bin Laden had distanced himself from Azzam (and some suspected him of involvement in Azzam's death), it is not clear whether the choice of Azzam's name was meant to link the group with transnational jihad or to highlight the Egyptian contribution to the Palestinian cause.

The perpetrators of a similar group of attacks on tourist hotels in Amman, Jordan in 2005—the Grand Hyatt, the Radisson SAS and the Days Inn—had ties to the international jihadi network, and in this case they were directly associated with al-Zarqawi. The Radisson explosion targeted a wedding party and was conducted by a husband-and-wife team of suicide bombers that al-Zarqawi had recruited from Iraq.

The jihadi-related attacks in Europe in the post-2001 anti-American climate have also been motivated by both local and transnational issues, as I discussed in chapter 4: disgruntled members of Muslim minorities in European nations have identified their local causes with that of global jihad, particularly with the role of the United States and European nations in the occupation of Iraq and the support for Israeli policies. In Madrid in March 2004, a cadre of expatriate Moroccans, supporters of the group that had been involved in the Casablanca blasts the year before, were implicated in a series of bombing attacks on commuter trains that were widely interpreted as a reprisal for Spain's support of the U.S. position in Iraq. Almost two hundred were killed. In London on July 7, 2005, three bombs exploded within a minute of one another on three underground subway trains, and a fourth was ignited an hour later on a double-decker bus. Over fifty commuters were killed. After the bombing, the Al-Jazeera television network aired a videotape in which one of the bombers professed his defense of Islam against the purported global aggression of the United Kingdom, the United States, and European nations.[43]

Though the al Qaeda headquarters in Afghanistan were destroyed soon after the U.S.-supported coup that toppled the Taliban government in 2001, bin Laden and al-Zawahiri survived. From secret hiding places along the Afghanistan-Pakistan border, they continued to send out a stream of audio and video messages to the wider world.[44] Al-Zawahiri wrote a book stating the al Qaeda position, *Knights Under the Prophet's Banner,* and issued written proclamations.[45] What is not clear is whether anyone was listening to the messages.

The relationship between al-Zarqawi's group in Iraq and the al Qaeda leaders in the mountains of Afghanistan and Pakistan is an interesting case in point. Though at one time bin Laden, in an audiotape broadcast on the Al-Jazeera television network, proclaimed al-Zarqawi the "prince of al Qaeda in Iraq," and al-Zarqawi returned the favor by publicly praising Osama bin Laden, their relationship seems to have ambivalent at best. Their association was marked by disagreements and deep mistrust. In 2005 al-Zawahiri sent a message of advice to al-Zarqawi that was intercepted and made public in the West questioning the Jordanian's strategy in Iraq.[46] Al-Zawahiri was concerned about the rebuilding of Iraq after the departure of the American occupation force, and he encouraged al-Zarqawi not to alienate the country's Shi'a population. Al-Zarqawi, however, regarded the Shi'a as apostates and ignored the message of moderation; indeed, the year following he orchestrated the catastrophic destruction of the Imam al-Isqari Mosque in Samarra, one of Shi'ite Islam's most sacred shrines.

The relationship between al-Zarqawi and the al Qaeda leaders indicates how tenuous were the ties within the global jihadi movement. According to some reports, Osama bin Laden took an immediate dislike to the crude, brash al-Zarqawi.[47] Bin Laden regarded the green tattoos on al-Zarqawi's hand as contrary to Islamic practice and was disturbed by al-Zarqawi's almost visceral hatred of Shi'ites. Bin Laden's own mother could be described as a Shi'ite, since she was from Syria and was most likely Alawite, a movement that is an offshoot of Shi'ite Islam. Bin Laden was raised in the Sunni tradition, but he had no particular animus against Shi'ism; moreover, he regarded internal squabbles as distractions from his jihad's principal target: American and Israeli influence in the Middle East. Nonetheless, al-Zarqawi was said to have received several hundred thousand dollars in funding from al Qaeda to set up jihadi training camps in Afghanistan, and in 2005 bin Laden and al-Zarqawi forged a kind of alliance that helped to promote the idea of al Qaeda as a centrally administered international organization.

This was a misleading impression, however. It seems likely that the global jihadi movement which spread rapidly throughout the world after September 11, 2001, was much like the earlier jihadi movement in lacking a unified organization. Ideological differences, internal power struggles, and competing groups weakened what otherwise might have been a significant political force. Yet as a social movement it was quite remarkable. Through the Internet and personal networks, a sizable number of Muslim youth throughout the world became excited by the notion that they could at least vicariously participate in a great struggle between the forces of good and evil, exemplified by the jihadi confrontation with the secular state. In the United States and Europe, an influential element of the political leadership saw the struggle in equally vaunted terms. Thus the global jihadi encounter with secular political authority has revived the idea of ideological enemies that propelled the Cold War between capitalism and communism over many decades in the twentieth century. It would be an almost poignant recapitulation of the crusty old global encounter of the Cold War—if the new religious incarnation of ideological confrontation had not been so bitterly violent.

CHAPTER 6

The Enduring Problems
of Violence, Democracy,
and Human Rights

One of the reasons why religious politics appear problematic is that in the long run they may lead to regimes like the Taliban that are repressive, undemocratic, and dismissive of human rights. In the short run, however, the concern is over terrorism and security: the possibility that religious rebels will use violence to convey their message and advance their goals.

Rebellions of any kind are often violent, so it is not surprising that religious rebellions are violent as well. Yet the ferocity of some of the acts of violence associated with religious activism is jarring: they seem more extreme than necessary to achieve strategic goals. Moreover, they are justified in the vaunted moral terms of religion. The issue addressed in this chapter is the character of religious politics: whether it is by nature violent, repressive, undemocratic, and resistant to human rights.

WHY RELIGIOUS CONFRONTATIONS ARE VIOLENT

No one who witnessed the televised images of the horrific attack on the World Trade Center and the Pentagon on September 11, 2001, could doubt the destructive power of religious confrontations. Yet the specter of religious violence is not exclusive to jihadi warriors in Sunni Islam. The rhetoric of warfare is evoked in virtually every religious tradition. The Sikh leader Sant Jarnail Singh Bhindranwale praised his young lieutenants for hijacking an airplane and called on India's political leaders to meet his demands or give up "their heads."[1] Iran's Ayatollah Khomeini said he knew of no obligation "more binding on the Muslim than the command to sacrifice life and property to defend and bolster Islam."[2] Christian militants in the United States recalled the slogans of the Crusades and the images of Armageddon in the Book of Revelation. A rightwing Jewish leader in Israel told me confidently, "Of course we have no problem with using force to win our religious goals."[3] Scores of political leaders have fallen at the hands of religious assassins in recent years, and thousands of religious rebels and their secular opponents have also been killed.

These violent acts seem uncharacteristic of religion. To be sure, every religious tradition teaches peace and tranquility and allows for violence only in the most extreme instances—in defense of the faith or to bring to an end an act of violence in progress. In Christianity, as in other religious traditions, warfare is allowed only for limited and just causes. A version of this theory of "just war" is also a part of Muslim ethics, and the very word *Islam* means "peace."

At the same time, religious symbols and historical narratives are steeped in blood. The brutal martyrdom of Hussain in Shi'ite Islam, the crucifixion of Jesus in Christianity, the sacrifice of Guru Tegh Bahadur in Sikhism, the bloody conquests detailed in the Hebrew Bible, the terrible battles celebrated in the Hindu epics, and the military engagements described in the Sinhalese Buddhist Pali Chronicles—all these episodes indicate that in virtually every religious tradition images of violence occupy a central place. For that reason, any attempt to understand the violence of contemporary religious rebels must begin with an understanding of the violence inherent in religious symbolism and tradition.

Elsewhere I have shown how the language of warfare—fighting and dying for a cause—is appropriate to the realm of religion and endemic to it.[4] Although it may seem paradoxical that images of destruction often accompany a commitment to realizing a harmonious form of existence, there is a certain logic at work that makes this conjunction natural. Since religion may be defined as the language of ultimate order, it has to provide those who use it with some way of envisioning disorder, especially the ultimate disorder of life: death. Believers need the conviction that death and disorder on an ultimate scale can be encompassed and domesticated. Ordinarily, as René Girard has eloquently argued, religion tames death and disorder through images projected in myth, symbol, ritual, and legend.[5] The cross in Christianity is not, in the eyes of most believers, an execution device but a symbol of redemption; similarly, the sword that is the central symbol of Sikhism is worn proudly by the most pious Sikhs not as a weapon but as a symbol of divine power.

Thus violent images can be given religious meaning and domesticated. But an awful thing can also happen: conceptual violence can be identified with real acts of violence. These acts, although terribly real, are then transformed by becoming symbols; they are stripped of their horror by being invested with religious meaning. They are justified and therefore exonerated because they are part of a religious template that is even larger than myth and history: they are elements of a ritual that makes it possible for people involved in it to experience the drama of cosmic war.

Osama bin Laden characterized his struggle in such cosmic terms: as a fight against evil. For ten years before the attacks on the World Trade Center and the Pentagon, his carnage left a trail of blood—not just the three thousand deaths on September 11, 2001, but also the many more who perished in the acts of terrorism around the world that were perpetrated by the jihadists associated with his cause. Bin Laden declared that President Bush's "war on terror" was really a "war against Islam."[6] After the September 11 attacks, President George W. Bush proclaimed a "war on terror," which he also described as a fight against evil. The image of warfare was not merely a metaphor for the pious American president: it was the justification for his invasion and occupation of two Muslim countries, Afghanistan and Iraq. In both cases, an imagined war of good versus evil—a cosmic confrontation—was associated with real military and paramilitary confrontations.

When the activist Sikh leader Sant Jarnail Singh Bhindranwale exhorted his followers to undertake real acts of violence, his rhetoric evoked the imagery of cosmic war, which he described as a "struggle . . . for our faith, for the Sikh nation, for the oppressed."[7] On the personal level, Bhindranwale's language pointed to a tension between faith and lack of faith; on the cosmic level, however, it described a battle between good and evil. Often his rhetoric was vague about the enemy's true identity. "To destroy religion," Bhindranwale informed his congregation, "mean tactics have been initiated," and they come from "all sides and in many forms."[8] But rather than explain what these forces are, who wields them, and why they would want to destroy religion, Bhindranwale concentrated instead on the appropriate response: a willingness to fight and defend the faith—if necessary, to the end. "Young men: with folded hands, I beseech you," Bhindranwale implored, reminding his audience that the ultimate decision for good or evil was up to them.[9]

Because the cosmic war is waged against disorder, the foes are amorphous; they are, in fact, symbols for amorphousness itself.

This link between the worldly and the cosmic struggle appears in the rhetoric of other religious activists as well. "Life is faith and struggle," said the Ayatollah Khomeini, implying that the notion of fighting is basic to human existence and on a par with religious commitment.[10] Khomeini's one-time associate Abolhassan Bani-Sadr wrote at some length about the notion of struggle in Islam, explaining how the monotheism of Islam envisions a struggle against duality at the same time that it denies the duality of world and spirit.[11] When Khomeini and Bani-Sadr talked about the struggle against evil and injustice in these amorphous terms, they were in accord with preachers in every religious tradition who describe the need to struggle against a generalized notion of falsehood and unbelief.

What made the language of Bani-Sadr and Khomeini different from the language used by many of their fellow preachers in Islam and elsewhere is that they situated the struggle in a social and political context. When Khomeini prayed to his "noble God for protection from the evil of every wicked traitor" and asked Him to "destroy the enemies," he had particular traitors and enemies in mind.[12] His list of the "satanic" forces who seek Islam's destruction included Jews but also the even "more satanic" Westerners, by whom Khomeini meant merchants, politicians, and corporate leaders (including the shah of Iran) with "no religious belief" who see Islam as "the major obstacle in the path of their materialistic ambitions and the chief threat to their political power."[13] Like the radical Sikhs' enemies, the ayatollah's foes were often elliptically described.[14]

One interesting aspect of the ayatollah's diatribes was that they identified American colonialism as a threat to the Islamic faith as well as to Muslim social and political interests: Iran's problems were due to the treachery of "foreign colonialists" but so were the problems of Muslims everywhere.[15] On another occasion, the ayatollah blended political, personal, and spiritual issues in generalizing about the cosmic foe—now described as Western colonialism—and about "the black and dreadful future" that "the agents of colonialism, may God Almighty abandon them all," envisaged for Islam and the Muslim people.[16]

Christians supporting the Sandinista revolution in Nicaragua also perceived their opponents as more than political enemies: they were cosmic foes (and often vaguely described). A fight against such a foe was not merely an ordinary political conflict, the Christian revolutionaries implied, but one with sacral dimensions. Ernesto Cardenal, a liberation theologian, characterized the opposition to Anastasio Somoza's regime as "totally different from the case of political parties that are all trying to come to power" in what he described as "a normalized, organized country." Cardenal searched for biblical metaphors in explaining what made the revolution in Nicaragua different: "We're taking sides, yes—with the good Samaritan." He went on to say that "here you have to take sides, you have to be partisan. Either you're with the slaughtered or you're with the slaughterers. From a gospel point of view I don't think there was any other legitimate option we could have made."[17]

In Sri Lanka, the metaphors of sacred struggle are drawn from Buddhist theology. "We live in a time of *dukkha*," a militant bhikkhu explained.[18] As he elaborated this point it became clear that he was not simply restating the first of the Four Noble Truths, that all life is suffering. For the bhikkhu, suffering—*dukkha*—had a definite social significance. "We live in an immoral world," he stated, using the term *adhammic*, which can also be translated as "disorderly" or "irreligious." Behind the notion is the conflict between *dhamma* and *adhamma*—order and disorder, religion and irreligion—and, by invoking that dialectic, he couched the political concerns of himself and other Buddhist activists in sacred terms.

Right-wing Jewish activists in Israel have also used the images of cosmic war to justify their actions. Meir Kahane, for instance, spoke of God's vengeance against the Palestinian Gentiles, which began with the humiliation of Pharaoh in the exodus from Egypt over three thousand years ago and continues in the present with the humiliation of the Gentiles that resulted in the creation of Israel.[19] "When the Jews are at war," Kahane said, "God's name is great."[20] An Israeli activist who had been arrested for his participation in a plot to blow up the Dome of the Rock in Jerusalem echoed Kahane's words, explaining that "God always fights against His enemies"; he added that activists such as himself "are the instruments of this fight."[21] Although he tended to blame secular Jews as much as Muslims for exacerbating the cosmic struggle, the identity of the enemy—like the cosmic foe itself—is beyond any easy description or demarcation.

Hence the language of cosmic struggle is easily exploited by political activists who want to give sacred legitimacy to worldly causes. Sometimes they do so only for the sake of public relations; in other instances, however, it serves a much more important purpose: empowerment. Because religion has the capacity to give moral sanction to violence, and because violence is the most potent force available to a nonlegal entity, religion can be a potent political tool.

The case of the Sikhs in India is an interesting example of religious legitimization. Among the Sikhs' concerns were several that most people in India would regard as perfectly legitimate—the inadequacy of political representation and the inequity of agricultural prices. These issues did not need the additional moral weight of religion to give them respectability. In fact, the Sikh businessmen and political leaders who were primarily concerned about such issues were seldom supporters of Bhindranwale and his militant followers, at least early on. Even when they were later drawn into his campaign, their relation to him and his strident religious language remained ambivalent.

One political demand, however, was not widely supported at the outset, and it desperately needed all the legitimization that it could get, including the legitimacy it could garner from religion. This was the demand for the creation of Khalistan as a separate Sikh nation. Although it was seen initially as a political solution to the Sikhs' desire for a separate identity, it soon became a religious crusade. Separatist leaders such as Jagjit Singh Chauhan appealed to Bhindranwale for support and were greatly encouraged when he said, "I have always expressed myself in favor of mobilising the entire Sikh world under one flag."[22] They cheered when he stated further that he would fight for a separate identity for the Sikhs, "even if it demands sacrifice."[23]

Despite these fighting words, Bhindranwale never explicitly supported Khalistan. "We are not in favor of Khalistan nor are we against it," he said, adding that "we wish to live in India" but would settle for a separate state if the Sikhs did not receive what he regarded as just respect.[24] Whatever his personal reservations regarding Khalistan, his appeal to sacrifice made his rhetoric attractive to the separatists. It also suggested another, potentially more powerful result of the sacralization of political demands: the prospect that religion could give moral sanction to violence.

Even though virtually all religions preach the virtues of nonviolence, it is their ability to sanction violence that gives them political power. The Sikh tradition, for instance, ordinarily celebrates nonviolence and proscribes the taking of human life.[25] Bhindranwale himself acknowledged that "for a Sikh it is a great sin to keep weapons and kill anyone." But he then went on to justify the occasional violent act in extraordinary circumstances and said that "it is an even greater sin to have weapons and not to seek justice."[26] Many other religious leaders, be they Christian or

Muslim or Buddhist, agree. They believe that the rule against killing may be abrogated in circumstances when social or spiritual justice is at stake.

Killing is often justified during a "just war"—a conflict that is deemed appropriate because the end merits it and the means to achieve it may in fact moderate the violence that existed before the conflict. First formulated by Cicero, the theory of just war was developed by Saint Ambrose and Saint Augustine into a Christian doctrine that was later refined by Thomas Aquinas. It has analogues in Jewish, Islamic, and many other traditions as well. Christians supporting the liberation struggle in Latin America have speculated that there can be a "just revolution" as well as a "just war."[27]

A similar question was raised by Kahane regarding his movement to establish a religious state in Israel and the West Bank. Jewish law allows for two kinds of just war: obligatory and permissible. An obligatory war is required for defense, while a permissible war is allowed when it seems prudent. The determination of when conditions exist for a just war made by the Sanhedrin or a prophet (in the case of permissible war) or a Halakhic state (in the case of obligatory war). None of these religious entities exists in the present day. In the absence of such authorities, the existence of the necessary conditions is to be determined by any authoritative interpreter of Halakha, such as a rabbi.[28] Kahane was himself a rabbi and perhaps for that reason felt that he was capable of judging the morality of his own movement's actions.

Kahane called on the people of Israel to rise up and reclaim the West Bank. He argued that defense was not the sole religious basis for warfare: national pride was also a legitimate reason.[29] He traced Israel's claim to the West Bank to a two-thousand-year-old vision that originated when the Jews came "out of the fear and shame of exile" and were led by Moses to the Promised Land. And now, Kahane asked them, "what about our national pride?"[30] He pointed out that Jews were afraid to go to the Mount of Olives on the Palestinian side of Jerusalem, much less to Judea and Samaria—the biblical names for the West Bank. He urged them to fight to retain their self-esteem and pride, and to reclaim the biblical lands.

Kahane also justified acts of violence as expressions of what he regarded as a hidden war for the reestablishment of a Jewish state, whose enemies he identified as both Arabs and secular Jews. "Every Jew who is killed has two killers," Kahane posited: "the Arab who killed him and the government who let it happen."[31] This logic justified Kahane's use of force not only against Arabs but against the secular Israeli state as well.

In using violence against cosmic foes, the lives of individuals are not important. "We believe in collective justice," a right-wing Jewish leader explained,[32] meaning that any individual who was part of a group deemed to be the enemy, even innocent bystanders, might justifiably become the object of a violent assault. In a cosmic war, innocence is moot; all individuals are potentially soldiers. "War is war," Kahane explained,[33] and he justified violence against civilian Arabs as a tactic to dissuade them from believing that they could live in Israel peacefully or normally.[34]

Some of Kahane's Arab opponents made precisely the same argument in justifying their struggle against the Israelis. When I interviewed the Hamas leader Sheik Yassin, he defended the *intifada* as necessary to demonstrate to the Israelis that the Palestinian situation is intolerable and should not be treated as ordinary. "There is a war going on," the sheik told me, implying that the *intifada* is simply an expression of a larger, hidden struggle.[35]

Sheik Yassin justified the violence of the *intifada* as self-defense, but he expanded the notion of self-defense to include the defense of personal dignity.[36] The leader of the political wing of Hamas, Dr. Abdul Aziz Rantisi, told me that their struggle was "not about land, but about honor."[37] One of Yassin's colleagues, Sheik 'Odeh, explained that the Islamic *intifada* is different from the *intifada* waged by secular supporters of the Palestine Liberation Organization in that the Islamic struggle is a moral struggle as well as a political one and derives from religious commitment. It is also part of a tradition of Islamic protest against injustice.[38] The *intifada* is a "sign from God," the sheik proclaimed, indicating that "the people need Islam as a center."[39]

The *intifada* is sometimes, but not always, described as a holy war. The concept of jihad, although important, is not central to the thought of all Islamic activists. Defense of the faith—including the traditional mores of the faith—is a sufficient basis for political action. In Egypt, in part because of the influence of the writings of Muhammed Abd al-Salam Faraj, the "neglected duty" of jihad has increasingly been applied by Muslim activists to political and paramilitary struggle as well as to military combat. Even in a political context, however, they stress that jihad has a wider meaning than violent encounters with an enemy. At Cairo University, a supporter of the Muslim Brotherhood, Ibrahim Dasuqi Shitta, told me that the "neglected duty" is a call for a general engagement against the forces of evil in the world, a battle that can be waged through economic policies and social service as well as through political and revolutionary action.[40]

Most religious activists are able to find within their religious traditions an existing justification for violence that they then apply to their own revolutionary situations. Buddhist militants are in an unusual position in this regard because their tradition proscribes any form of violence, including the killing of animals. One might think that the doctrinal commitment to *ahimsa* would prevent both monks and the laity in Buddhist societies from approving or justifying violence as an act of sacred war. Members of the Aum Shinrikyo rationalized their use of poisonous gas in their attack on the Tokyo subways as a kind of karmic shortcut: the moral weight of living in such perverse times as the present was so onerous that being relieved of the burden of living was an act of generosity.

In Sri Lanka some bhikkhus also have justified the violence of Sinhalese activists in religious terms. Some monks told me that they actively participated in violence because there was no way to avoid violence "in a time of *dukkha*."[41] During such times, they said, violence naturally begets violence. Politicians who are enemies of religion and who resort to violence to achieve their ends might expect violence in return as a sort of karmic revenge.[42] During such times evil rulers are always overthrown. "We believe in the law of karma," one of the bhikkhus added. "Those who live by the sword die by the sword."[43]

The murder of Sri Lanka's prime minister by a Buddhist monk in 1959 underscores the seriousness of the monks' involvement and the degree to which they, like their clerical counterparts in every other religious tradition, justify violence on moral—or, rather, supramoral—grounds.[44] Like violent activists in Sikhism, Islam, and Christianity, Buddhist militants have identified their political targets as enemies of religion and believe they have been given the authority to take their lives. Those who seek moral justification for their use of violence seek sanction from a higher source: the metamorality that religion provides. By elevating a temporal struggle to the level of the cosmic, they bypass the usual moral restrictions on killing. If their struggle is part of an enormous battle of the spirit, then it is not ordinary morality but the rules of war that apply.

EMPOWERING MARGINAL PEOPLES

The empowerment granted by religious violence is especially appealing to those who have not had power before. The Iranian revolution is a potent example. Beneath the clerical exclusivity of the ayatollah's regime was a genuine social revolution, one that has had an effect on all levels of Iranian society.[45] The Iranian revolution was not simply a reversion to an earlier form of Islamic government. Traditional Islamic government has often been monarchic: rule by a caliph, a king, or some other individual power-holder. The revolutionary government of Iran has a parliament and all the accoutrements of Western democracy. More to the point, it has the active participation of hundreds of lower-echelon mullahs throughout the country. These kinds of religious functionaries have never held power before—neither in Iran nor in any other Islamic regime.

Much the same can be said about many of the other movements of religious politics, including the one that received overwhelming electoral support in the Algerian elections in the 1990s. The Islamic opposition to the secular National Front Party was fueled by a 20 percent inflation rate, a 25 percent unemployment rate, and a young population—70 percent of which was under the age of twenty-five—who could not hope for marriage, an apartment, or a job given Algeria's economic circumstances.[46] In Sri Lanka, a similarly desperate situation prevailed, especially in the countryside. There, an antipathy to the relatively wealthy urban middle class was expressed in religious differences: the rural population rejected the middle-class "Protestant Buddhism"—which eschews traditional and folk forms of Buddhism and is ambivalent about the leadership of the monastic orders—and instead rallied around the monks.[47] They also provided the base of support for the Sinhalese nationalist involvement in the revolutionary Janatha Vimukthi Peramuna.

The phenomenon of marginal groups rising to power by means of violent religious nationalism was also a feature of the Sikh revolution in the Punjab. Bhindranwale's call to take up arms to defend the faith had a particular appeal to those who greatly wanted to be associated with a core group within Sikhism: Sikhs who were socially marginal to the community, including Sikhs from lower castes and those who had taken up residence abroad. Some of the most fanatical of Bhindranwale's followers, including Beant Singh, the assassin of Indira Gandhi, came from untouchable castes, and a considerable amount of money and moral support for the Punjab militants came from expatriate Sikhs in such faraway places as London, Houston, and Los Angeles.

From their identification with Bhindranwale, these Sikhs gained a sense of belonging. The large expatriate Sikh communities in England, Canada, and the United States were especially sensitive to his message that the Sikhs needed to be strong, united, and defensive of their tradition. Many of Bhindranwale's supporters in the Punjab, however, received a more tangible benefit from associating with his cause: politically active village youth and religious functionaries were able to gain a measure

of popular support. In that sense Bhindranwale was fomenting something of a political revolution, and his constituency was not unlike that
of the Islamic revolution in Iran. Insofar as Bhindranwale's message was
taken as an endorsement of the killings that some of these fundamentalist youth committed, the instrument of religious violence gave power to
those who had little power before. In the Punjab it was not the established leaders who encouraged violence but a lower level of leadership—
a younger, more marginal group for whom violence was enormously
empowering. The average age of Sikh extremists killed by police was
quite low. The largest group was young men in their twenties; most were
sons of small farmers with little education.[48]

The male composition of the violent Sikh cadres is noteworthy. This
gender bias is found in many other activist movements as well, including groups of Hindu nationalists and rural Sinhalese nationalists, and
Muslim movements in Egypt, Palestine, Algeria, and elsewhere.[49] The activists often refer to the need to properly clothe and respect women, and
to keep them in their place. During the 1991–92 Muslim uprising in Algeria, Ali Belhaj, one of the Islamic Front leaders said a woman's primary
duty was to "bear good Muslims"; and Sheik Abdelkhader Moghni, another Islamic Front leader, complained about women working and taking jobs away from men. Women, he said, just "spend their salaries on
makeup and dresses, they should return to their homes."[50] A business-
woman in Algiers responded by saying she feared that if the Islamic
Front succeeded, it would usher in a reign of "pig power." "They're
all male chauvinist pigs," she explained, adding, "believe me, we are
worried."[51]

In India, Bhindranwale addressed his congregations as if the men (especially the young men) were the only ones listening, encouraging them
to let their beards grow in the long Sikh fashion and describing their acts
of cowardice in the face of the government opposition as "emascula-
tion." One senses in this and other politically active religious movements
a longing for a recovery of virility—a strange, composite yearning that
is at once sexual, social, and political.[52] The marginality of such persons
in the modern world is experienced by them as a kind of sexual despair.
It could almost be seen as poignant if it were not so terribly dangerous.

Perhaps these men found that their power had eroded in modern society and for that reason were attracted to militant cadres. Violence is
empowering. The power that comes from the barrel of a gun is direct,
but the indirect, psychological dimension of this power may be even
more effective. As Frantz Fanon argued in the context of Algeria's war

of independence some years ago, even a small display of violence can have immense symbolic power by jolting the masses into an awareness of their own potency.[53] In this sense there are in the Punjab, as in Sri Lanka and elsewhere in the world, aspects of social revolution embedded in violence that at first glance seems to be only religiously inspired.

It can be debated whether Bhindranwale succeeded in jolting the masses in the Punjab into an awareness of their own capabilities, but the violent actions of the militants among them made the masses more appreciative than they were of the militants' power. Militants were treated as if they possessed an authority rivaling that of the police and other government officials. One of the problems in the Punjab was that villagers in the so-called terrorist zones around the towns of Batala and Tarn Taran were unwilling to report terrorist activities to officials. The radical youth even set up their own courts and governmental offices.

By being dangerous, these young religious radicals gained a certain notoriety, and by clothing their actions in the moral garb of religion they gave those actions legitimacy. Because their activities were sanctioned by religion, they were not just random acts of terror but political actions: they broke the state's monopoly on morally sanctioned killing. By putting the right to kill in their own hands, the perpetrators of religious violence have made a daring claim to power on behalf of those who previously had been impotent and ignored.

For these reasons it is not surprising that many radical movements of religious activism have been accompanied by violence. What is surprising is that there have not been more. Religious revolutionaries see a cosmic struggle between the old order they wish to bury and the new religious nations they are pledged to create, yet a sizable number of them subscribe so deeply to democratic procedures and human rights that the violent potential of their struggle is tempered.

DOES RELIGION CHALLENGE DEMOCRACY?

As I mentioned at the outset of this chapter, one of the widely expressed fears in the West is that, left unchallenged, most movements of religious activism will end up like the Taliban. It is this specter that makes civil libertarians wary of the prospects of politicized religion. A propensity toward violence may be the matter that most immediately alarms outsiders about religiously rebellious movements, but in the long run observers are often more concerned about the restrictions on freedom that might be imposed in religious states should they succeed. Because there have been so few successful attempts to create a religious state in modern times, it is easy to conclude that such an entity would be like the ones that have actually come to power: dogmatic, repressive, and intolerant. Accounts of the reign of the Taliban in Afghanistan and life in the Islamic Republic of Iran under the mullahs have shaped these impressions; and because Iran was the first religious state to have come into existence in this generation, it is often adduced as an example of what all religious nationalists purportedly want.

But not all religious activists see the Taliban or Iran as the ideal model. Only three Muslim countries granted diplomatic recognition to Afghanistan under Taliban rule, and Iranian leaders such as the Ayatollah Khomeini and Mahmoud Ahmadinejad have been criticized throughout the Muslim world, even by such militants as Sheik Yassin in Palestine and Qazi Turadqhonqodz in Tajikistan. And other post-revolution leaders in Iran, such as Mohammad Khatami and Akbar Hashemi Rafsanjani—both clerics—have been considerably more moderate. Yet the image persists of Iran in particular and religious nationalists in general being horribly out of step with modern times.

When the Bharatiya Janata Party (BJP) first ascended to power in India, many secular political observers predicted the nation's political collapse as a result. Several volumes critical of the BJP were rushed into print, lamenting the inability of Indian politics to stay free from the scourge of religion. The editor of one of the volumes, Sarvepalli Gopal, claimed that the very reputation of India as a modern nation was at stake. To his mind, "the separation of the State from all faiths" was a fundamental attribute of modernity and was characteristic of "a modern outlook anywhere." Only "secularism of this type," he claimed, was appropriate for "an egalitarian, forward-looking society."[54]

Are Gopal's assumptions correct? Let us, for the moment, put aside the question of whether a religious state can be "modern" and begin with the issue of whether religious activists have a propensity toward dictatorship. Since religion is an ideology of order, as I have described it in chapter 1, religious organizations assert that order in both social and spiritual realms. Movements with a strong religious vision indeed have a tendency toward authoritarian leadership and internal discipline. A Muslim leader in Algiers buttressed his opinion that the place of women is in the home with the statement, "It is not I who demand this, but God."[55]

Having a strong religious vision often also means settling on a single figure as the authority for the entire movement. In India, the Hindu nationalist movement, the Rashtriya Swayamsevak Sangh (RSS), claimed that its "skilled and efficient leadership" should not only be obeyed but also venerated, just as a guru in traditional Hinduism is revered, even worshiped.[56] In Iran, some believed that the Ayatollah Khomeini led his country under a divine providence. Even those who disagreed with Khomeini's ideology often admired his leadership abilities. Though the Palestinian Hamas leader Sheik Ahmed Yassin regarded the Iranian revolution as "an experiment that failed," he said that he "admired Khomeini."[57] From the opposite camp in Israel, Meir Kahane also professed an admiration for the Iranian leader and led his own movement as Khomeini led his—autocratically, with virtually no rivals.[58] A Christian activist in the United States pointed to Khomeini as the sort of leader that he wished conservative Christians could have in America. Muslim religious activists from Egypt to Indonesia have valued the clear religious vision and unchallenged authority associated with Khomeini's style of leadership.

Although religious movements tend to be authoritarian, the same is true of some secular nation-states, which, like religion, uphold ideologies of order and are pledged to maintain society's mores. In some cases the authoritarianism of secular nationalism has resulted in dictatorships as brutal as any that religious politics has produced, such as Stalin's Soviet Union and Hitler's Germany. Although one might argue that at times Communism and Nazism took on the character of religion, there have been fascist tendencies in many secular states. In most secular societies, however, strong central authority has devolved to systems of authority involving an elected parliament of representatives and an independent judiciary. Most secular nationalists refer to this system when they speak of democracy. The question, then, is whether religious nationalism can embrace a democratic system.

The rhetoric of many religious nationalists suggests that they place a high value on democracy. Even those activists most opposed to the secular state affirm the political importance of the democratic spirit. Sheik Yassin, for instance, told me that "Islam believes in democracy."[59] One of his Buddhist counterparts in Sri Lanka said that Buddhism also "is democratic by its nature."[60] A member of the Muslim Brotherhood in Egypt told me that "democracy was the only way" for an Islamic state.[61] A leader of Israel's Gush Emunim said that "we need democracy," even in "a religious society."[62] Central Asian religious nationalists have also echoed this desire for democracy in a religious state.[63] An international survey conducted by the Pew Foundation in 2006 revealed a surprising correlation between support for Muslim politics and a belief in democracy. In Jordan, Pakistan, and Palestine, even those respondents who approved of Osama bin Laden affirmed that their country could and should have a democratic future.[64]

Some of this enthusiasm for democracy is self-serving. If democracy simply means majority rule, then it means letting the people have what they want. If the people want a religious society rather than a secular one, then they should have it. "Since 80 percent of the people in Egypt are Muslims," one Muslim activist explained to me, "Egypt should have a Muslim state."[65] The same line of reasoning has been used in Sri Lanka and in Punjab, where Sinhalese and Sikh activists, respectively, treat democracy as the legitimization of rule by whichever camp has the preponderance of the population on its side. These arguments equate democracy with the will of the majority.

In some cases, religious activists conclude that the will of the majority can be discerned by an astute leader outside the mechanisms of elections and parliaments. In these cases, they affirm the general idea of democracy but reject its processes. Yet most religious activists—even those who interpret democracy solely as majority rule—stress that government should not rule by fiat. "The decision to have an Islamic state," Sheik Yassin affirmed, "should come about through democratic vote."[66]

Ultimately, however, it is not the will of the people that matters in a religious frame of reference but the will of God. For that reason, religious nationalists often define good leadership as the ability to discern what is godly and truthful in a given situation. But, as Meir Kahane said, "you don't vote on truth."[67] Most religious activists similarly regard the discernment of truth as ultimately beyond the democratic process.[68] Thus the normal way of maintaining in democratic states—through voting, political bartering, and the interplay of competing interest groups—is seen as irrelevant and perhaps even contrary to a higher morality. In an interesting moment during my conversations with a Buddhist bhikkhu in Sri Lanka, he cited as evidence of secular government's immorality its tendency to pander to the self-interests of contending parties. That, however, is precisely what democratic government in the United States and elsewhere in the West is supposed to do: respond to competing interests by distributing the largesse of the state as widely as possible and satisfying the greatest number of citizens. But this was a morally insufficient notion of government from the bhikkhu's point of view. He wanted the government to adopt a larger vision of ethical order and uphold *dhamma* (virtue).[69]

To a remarkable degree, the bhikkhu's position on democracy and truth echoed that articulated in Plato's *Republic*. There, Plato characterized democracy as a "charming form of government, full of variety and disorder," which leads naturally to tyranny.[70] Plato feared that if people were allowed to make decisions collectively, they would simply advance their own interests, which would result in policies that were nothing more than the lowest common denominator of individuals' greed and desire for personal security. What was needed, he maintained, was leadership that could rise above self-interest and provide a broad vision for the whole. Just government was embodied in the philosopher-king.

Democratic theory as propounded by John Locke and other eighteenth-century rationalists countered Plato's objections to democracy in two ways. First, proponents of democracy had considerable faith in the ability of individuals to rise above self-interest in their collective decisions and to vote for the welfare of the whole. Second, democratic theorists thought that elected representatives would have a dual role: they would be both mouthpieces of their constituencies and independent judges of what was appropriate for the welfare of the wider community.[71] These two roles might clash, of course, and much of the discussion at the time of the writing of the American Constitution had to do with structuring the Congress in such a way that these two roles were balanced. The creation of two houses of Congress, a House of Representatives to represent the people and a Senate to represent the states, was part of this compromise.[72]

Many religious nationalists, however, challenge Locke's assumptions, lacking the rationalists' faith that reason alone is sufficient for finding the truth, and unconvinced that unbridled self-interest is an adequate moral basis for a political order. This view puts the religious nationalists back in Plato's position: unhappy with the prospect of mob rule and eager to find a philosopher-king.

Religious nationalists have one advantage over Plato: they are more certain than he about where truth may be found. The tradition of most religious activists provides a framework of religious law that is considered normative for human activity. Because religious law is the only reliable repository of social and ethical truth, they reason, it should be the basis of politics. According to some activists, the establishment of religious law is the primary goal—some would say the sole aim—of religiously political movements. Religious leaders in Egypt, for instance, identified the main problem with the governments of Anwar al-Sadat and Hosni Mubarak as their elevation of secular law over *shari'a*. "Why should we obey Western laws when Muslim laws are better?" one of them asked me.[73]

This sentiment is echoed in Israel, where some Jewish nationalists felt that the Knesset gave more credence to gentile laws than to Jewish ones, even though, as one of them put it, "Jewish law was formulated long ago when the Gentiles were still living in the bushes."[74] The same speaker, on another occasion, told me that Israel should strive for "Torahcracy" rather than democracy.[75] He developed a constitution for the state of Israel based entirely on Halakhic laws; but for the slightly archaic language, it looked much like a modern constitution based on Western secular law. The Torah constitution, for example, granted individuals freedom of expression. The main deviation from a Western secular constitution was its provision for an ultimate arbiter of what is good for society: the council of judges, the Sanhedrin.

Yet democracy survives in even the most severe religious contexts.[76] To a remarkable extent, the constitution of the Islamic Republic of Iran resembles the constitutions of most modern Western countries. It contains guarantees of civil rights and minority rights and prescribes three branches of government—executive, judicial, and legislative. The president and the members of the legislature are elected by the people for fixed terms. The only unusual features of the constitution, from a Western secular point of view, are the centrality of Islamic law as the basis from which all principles of law derive and the role of Islamic clergy in telling the lawmakers when the judicial process, in their opinion, has stepped out of line. The constitution also defines the special office of Supreme Leader; initially this office was delegated specifically to the Ayatollah Khomeini and after Khomeini's death to Sayyed Ali Khamene. The leader appoints the council of clergy, who pass judgment on Islamic law, selects the Supreme Court, and the commanders of the army, leads the National Defense Council, and declares war and peace. Interestingly, the leader does not have the power to appoint the president of the country (an elected office), but he can withhold signing the decree approving the election of the president if he chooses. The leader can also dismiss the president, but only if the Supreme Court convicts the president of "failure to fulfill his legal duties," or the National Consultative Assembly testifies to "his political incompetence."[77] Similarly, the leader has the power to pardon convicts or to reduce their sentences, but only after receiving a recommendation to that effect from the Supreme Court. Thus the Iranian constitution has provided the country with an Islamic version of Plato's philosopher-king—but it has placed this religious monarch within a modern parliamentary system and with a number of checks and balances.[78]

Even in Iran, then, the power of the clergy is limited.[79] At the beginning of the revolution the mullahs were slow to become involved in politics, and a number of American scholars concluded that the clergy would "never participate directly in the formal government structure" because they lacked the capacity or the interest to do so.[80] Most of the mullahs would have been satisfied with a return to the democratic constitution of 1906, which provided a review process to ensure that laws were enforced according to Islamic principles. Khomeini, however, insisted on the more active involvement of the clergy and a more complete break from the old system of politics.[81] Some of the Western-trained politicians who led the government soon after the revolution, including Abdolhassan Bani-Sadr, Mehdi Bazargan, and Sadeq Qotbzadeh, were replaced with clergy who had little familiarity with Western democracy. But even with their involvement, Iran was far from being a theocracy, and following Khomeini's death the number of clergy involved in politics dropped dramatically. Some of the most vicious, including "Judge Blood"—Hojat-ol-Eslarn Sadeq Khalkhali—fell into disfavor. In October 1991 Khalkhali and several other radical clergy were barred from running for seats in the Assembly of Experts because the *ulama* jurists (doctors of Muslim religion and law) in the Council of Guardians gave them failing marks during what one scholar called a "humiliating examination in Shi'ite jurisprudence."[82]

In other movements of religiously inspired rebellion, the leadership of the clergy has also been quite limited. The main leaders of al Qaeda have been an engineer, Osama bin Laden, and a medical doctor, Ayman al-Zawahiri. In other movements, although the leadership has included rabbis, sheiks, and other religious authorities, they have not been the sole guardians of their organizations.[83] Sheik Yassin, for instance, maintained that the leadership of Hamas should be open to all and that the clergy should not be forced into political activity against their will.[84] In Buddhist and Christian movements, monks and priests have actively participated in movements of rebellion without being the primary leaders. A bhikkhu in Sri Lanka told me that it was not necessary to have monks in power so long as government officials consult with religious leaders: "They should seek their advice."[85] Religiously based political movements in Egypt and India are generally not led by clergy. In Egypt, a Muslim activist said that the clergy should be teachers of religious principles rather than politicians.[86] In India, where large numbers of sadhus (religious ascetics) worked to bring out the votes for the Hindu-nationalist

BJP, the leaders of the party gave public assurances that the sadhus would not exert a significant influence on party policy. Although the party allowed some sadhus to run for office under the BJP banner, they were not a significant bloc in the party leadership. In virtually every movement for religious nationalism, the idea of theocracy—rule by the clergy—has been rejected.

In fact, as long as religious law is affirmed as the basis for political action, the method for discerning that law and the procedure for choosing leaders who will carry it out can be democratic, relying on ballots and elections. "These days we expect our governments to be democratically elected," a bhikkhu explained to me in Sri Lanka, indicating that democracy is consistent with Buddhist principles as long as the leaders are mindful of their obligation to uphold *dhamma* (divine order).[87] In Egypt, some religious activists maintain that legitimate religious parties can succeed only through the democratic process.[88]

Most movements of religious activism also follow democratic procedures within their own organizations. Even though Rabbi Kahane advocated autocratic rule for Israel, he endorsed democratic procedures for the committee that he set up to establish an independent state of Judea.[89] The internal organization of radical religious movements from Sri Lanka to Algeria, and from Palestine to Montana, have been chosen by broad consultation of their members if not by vote.

The electoral process, as a means of choosing leaders and making decisions, has become well established internationally, including regions in which activist religious political movements are on the rise. To the degree to which elections are the hallmark of democracy, religious activists are as democratic as any secular politician. Religious nationalists and transnationalists are concerned not with the process but with the purpose: from their point of view, the political system exists ultimately only for divine ends, to make certain that human activity is consonant with its underlying moral order. Religious activists break with democratic theorists primarily over two issues. One is whether the democratic system can be legitimate without higher moral authority establishing it: religious politicians deny the possibility. A democratic gang of thieves, they argue, is still a gang of thieves. For the process to be morally valid it must be put to moral purposes, and that is why religious law must be the basis for any moral state. The other issue is the democratic principle of minority rights.

MINORITY AND INDIVIDUAL HUMAN RIGHTS

In many parts of the world, minority communities have watched the rising tide of religious activism with great apprehension. Their misgivings, often exacerbated by the warnings of secularists, center around the concern that a society commanded by proponents of one religion will favor the majority religious community at the expense of the minorities.

This apprehension is warranted, for at the very least religious nationalists want the symbols and culture of their own religious communities to be elevated as part of the nation's heritage. Most members of minority communities can live with reminders that they are residents of a nation dominated by another religion if it is simply a matter of putting up with the Sinhalese lion or the phrase *Allahu Akbar* ("God is Great") on their national flag, as they do in Sri Lanka and the Islamic Republic of Iran, respectively, or enduring a string of national holidays that celebrate someone else's faith, as Muslims and Jews do in the Christian-dominated culture of the United States. Minorities, however, are concerned about two more problematic possibilities: the potential for preferential treatment of majority community members in government hiring and policies, and the possibility that the minorities will be required to submit to religious laws that they do not respect. Beyond these concerns is a third, more apocalyptic, fear: that they will be driven from their homes or persecuted or killed if they remain.

Interestingly, the issue of minority rights is also discussed within politically active religious groups. Before I describe how religious nationalists deal with these problems, though, I should point out that issues surrounding minority rights and the assertion of minority identities are not exclusive to religious nationalists; they are the subject of debate in secular societies as well. In fact, secular nationalism is unable to deal easily with any kind of collective identity except that defined by geography. African Americans in the United States, for instance, constitute more than 10 percent of the nation's population but fewer than 10 percent of the representatives in the U.S. Congress because their populations are dispersed. A system that is intended to represent people on the basis of where they reside almost invariably fails to represent its residents equally, unless the minority groups happen to be coextensive with the geographical boundaries of a city or state.

In India, the British recognized this flaw in the Western system of democratic representation and tried to correct it with the device of "reserved constituencies"—a system that allowed only members of certain minority communities (people from formerly untouchable castes, for instance) to run as candidates in selected constituencies. In most cases, however, secular governments have dealt with the political representation of minority communities by denying that a problem exists—that is, they have held to the illusion propounded by democratic theory: that all people are equal, and that for that reason discrimination should not occur among groups. The illusion is reinforced by law: if people are, in fact, found to be discriminating on the basis of communal distinctions, they will be punished. Thus the myth of equality is enforced.

By using the phrase *the myth of equality* I do not mean that this ideological position of democratic theory is untrue or morally insufficient. Just the opposite may be the case: as with religious myth, secular myth envisages the moral potential of humanity. The term *myth,* however, suggests that equality is an ideal condition—one that is desired but not necessarily realized. The conviction of religious activists that people are defined fundamentally by their affiliation with cultural groups is also a myth, and the competition between religious and secular nationalists is to some measure a contest to see which myth will prevail. In the Europeanized West, to a large extent the myth of equality has won, as public attitudes have been molded by the laws established to enforce it and by the political, economic, and social structures designed to promote it.[90]

Yet communal identities continue to exist in Europe and the Europeanized countries of the Western world, just as they continue to exist elsewhere. What makes religious nationalists shockingly out of step with most secular governments is their recognition that communal identities persist and that secular politics has failed to change what they would regard as natural religious loyalties. Their recognition of these loyalties makes them both dangerous (if one feels that communal identities are immoral in a healthy society) and honest (if one believes that these identities exist, whether or not one wants them to).

Some religious nationalists believe that honesty about communal identities is an advantage in dealing with minority groups. In India, for example, the BJP claimed that tensions between the government and the Muslim and Sikh minorities were eased under BJP rule because government leaders valued communal identities and sought to find a way of integrating Muslims and Sikhs into society as Muslims and Sikhs rather than as individual members of a secular state. For this reason, Lal Krishna Advani, the BJP leader, claimed prior to the BJP electoral victories that when his party came into power, "the Muslims will be happy" within "a couple of months."[91] Their happiness, however, was short lived if it was experienced at all, since communal violence between Muslims and Hindus increased after the BJP victory. In Israel, similarly, Rabbi Kahane told me that when his group fought for its own religious rights, it became more sensitive than it had been to Muslim groups who were fighting for theirs.[92] Nonetheless, Kahane said, the Arabs should leave what he regarded as Jewish sacred land. In Iran, one of the early leaders of the revolution, Bani-Sadr, argued that every group should have rights—minority groups as well as majority ones. "Considering one's identity and rights as one's own and someone else's as his own is an Islamic idea," he claimed; "therefore, we have no quarrel with those who say: our rights belong to us."[93]

The question, then, is how religious nationalists should deal with the issue of minority rights if and when a religious state is established. In general, they have proposed two solutions. One is to provide a separate status (or even a separate state) for minority communities—similar to the British solution of providing reserved constituencies for minorities in India. The other solution is to accommodate the communities within the prevailing ideology—primarily by regarding the dominant religious ideology as a general cultural phenomenon to which a variety of religious communities are heir. This is the approach of the BJP in India, which claimed all of Indian tradition—including Sikhism, Buddhism, and Jainism—to be Hindu tradition and allowed religions from outside India, such as Christianity and Islam, to be affiliated with Hinduism as syncretic Christian-Hindu and Muslim-Hindu branches. In Sri Lanka, efforts were made to create a Buddhist "civil religion" that would incorporate various strands of the country's religious traditions.[94]

The first solution—separate status—is problematic in that it requires finding an appropriate status or place for the minority groups. Whereas the British could provide separate electoral positions in parliament, most religious nationalists have been obligated to come up with a much more substantial peace offering for minorities: land. The issue of land is significant because religious nationalism is often rooted in a particular place. Judaism is intimately connected with biblical locations, many of which are on the West Bank of the Jordan River in Palestine. The religious nationalists of Sri Lanka insist on the political integrity of the island in its entirety; and the Hindu nationalism of the BJP is defined by all of India. There is not much room in these positions for granting separate territory to minority communities. For that reason, religious nationalists who want to solve the minority problem through separatism

might be forced to compromise their claims or return to the British solution of separate political representation.[95]

The second solution—accommodation of cultural differences—allows
minorities rights within an undivided national or political process. This
solution has its problems, but it provides a more flexible range of options. One of the more promising is an idea that I first heard discussed
by Muslim activists in Egypt, and then again in an entirely different context, among Muslim leaders in Gaza.[96] These Muslim leaders insisted
that Egyptian and Palestinian nationalism should subscribe to Islamic
shari'a, but they indicated that there are two kinds of *shari'a*, or rather
two levels of it: at a general cultural level there are social mores that are
incumbent on all residents of the nation, regardless of their religious affiliations. This general level of *shari'a* is much like what passes for law-
abiding, civilized behavior everywhere. At a more particular level, however, are detailed personal and family codes of behavior that are required
only of Muslims. This formulation is similar, they said, to patterns they
had experienced while traveling abroad. When in England or North
America they were expected to obey the laws and standards of Western
civilization in public, but privately they followed Muslim, rather than
Western, customs.[97] They would expect Christians to return the favor
when visiting, or living in, Muslim countries.

The two-level-*shari'a* solution is a promising one and has parallels in
other traditions. In India, as I have mentioned, the leader of the BJP, Lal
Krishna Advani, maintains that on one level Hinduism is simply another
name for India's national cultural identity, and one of his party's slogans
is that while other parties play castes and ethnic groups against one another, the BJP "unites the country with its cultural heritage."[98] In Sri
Lanka, proponents of the Jatika Chintanaya movement claim that Sinhala Buddhist culture is all-embracing and that Tamils are Sinhalese Buddhist Tamils and Muslims are Sinhalese Buddhist Muslims. Even some
Christian leaders have described the Sinhalese culture as part of the background of all religious traditions represented in the country, including
their own. Anglican and Catholic priests in Colombo have encouraged
Christians to embrace with the Buddhist dimension of their culture in
order to be true Christians.[99] The two-level-*shari'a* solution also has
parallels in earlier periods of Islamic history. The Delhi sultanate in
fourteenth-century India, for instance, tolerated the practice of other religions, including the maintenance of Hindu temples and priests, as long
as Islam was recognized as the state religion.[100] The Mogul emperor
Akbar is fabled for his tolerance of non-Muslim religions, and although

scholars dispute just how open-minded he was, Akbar is familiarly portrayed in art surrounded by religious counselors of various faiths, including a Jesuit.

The two-level-*shari'a* solution will not work, however, if it implies that members of minority communities are second-class citizens. If members of minority communities feel that they are treated badly, leaders of religious states may face the same sorts of political strategies that they themselves have used against the secular state. There is reason to hope that a form of the two-level-*shari'a* solution might work in some of the cases discussed in this book; in others one wonders whether a solution to longstanding ethnic and cultural differences will ever be found.

In Iran, there is some reason for hope. The leaders have allowed a limited number of minorities to operate under their own domestic codes of behavior as long as they behave with a propriety consistent with Muslim standards in public. The constitution of the Islamic Republic of Iran guarantees "equal rights" not only to every "ethnic group or tribe" but to "Zoroastrian, Jewish, and Christian Iranians" as "recognized minorities."[101] Some groups, such as the Baha'is, however, are regarded as heretical Muslims rather than as genuine minorities, and they have only two options: to revert to the true faith or leave. Those that have done neither have been persecuted.[102]

The Coptic Christian community is Egypt's largest religious minority and can claim a more ancient link with Egyptian culture than Islam. It traces its roots to the fifth century, when a central tenet of the Monophysite branch of Christianity—that Christ had a single, divine nature, not two, a human and a divine one—was rejected by the Council of Chalcedon, and the Eastern rite churches split. The patriarch of Alexandria, a Monophysite, led his branch of the church in its own direction, relying on a liturgy written in the Coptic language. Today most Copts still live in Egypt, where they constitute a small percentage of the population. They tend to reside in urban areas, and they have prospered as businessmen and professionals. Their prosperity is a cause for some resentment among their Muslim neighbors, and the perception that they were favored during the regime of Gamal Abdel-Nasser has been the cause of some hard feelings as well. Nonetheless, the antiquity of their tradition brings them respect, and even members of the Muslim Brotherhood acknowledge that the Copts are as Egyptian as any Muslim citizen.[103]

For that reason, any plan for Muslim nationalism in Egypt invariably provides exceptions for the Copts, such as in the two-level-*shari'a* solution. Some Muslim leaders have suggested that the Copts be given their own representation in parliament. If they were, the Muslim leaders told me, the Copts would be "better off" than they are under the secular government, which does not recognize religious differences and does not provide political concessions for religious minorities.[104] Other Muslims say that the Copts should wear distinctive clothing, or some other sign, that would indicate that they were allowed to keep their own customs. The Copts themselves are suspicious of these suggestions, however. Although they confirm that many Muslim leaders are trying to find a way of including them, they fear "Muslim fanatics."[105] One scholar in Cairo said that, with the rise of Islamic nationalism, Copts have been made to feel "less Egyptian."[106]

In Israel, the Palestinian Muslim minority is less easily accommodated than the Coptic community in Egypt. The secular Jewish state gives citizenship to Muslims but on secular terms: the state tolerates Muslim nationalists even less than they abide Jewish ones. Jewish nationalists have no problem with Muslim nationalism—as long as it is not practiced in Israel, including especially the wider Eretz Yisra'el described in the Bible, which includes most of the West Bank. For that reason, the most extreme Jewish nationalists in Israel call for a direct solution to "the Arab problem": they should leave. Jordan and Saudi Arabia are the most frequently suggested destinations. If they wish to stay, Rabbi Kahane told me, they could be treated as "resident guests" but not as full citizens.[107] At the same time, Kahane said, he could not imagine why self-respecting Muslims would want to stay in a place where they were treated as second-class citizens. Out of "respect for them" and not wanting them to "live in disgrace in an occupied land," Kahane explained, he felt that "they should go."[108]

Jewish nationalists such as Kahane have not been willing to accept the idea that Palestine is as sacred to Muslims as it is to Jews, and they regard the Muslim veneration for the Dome of the Rock and other sites in Palestine as "recent affectations" professed "for political reasons."[109] As a result, it is unlikely that a Jewish state along Kahane's lines could easily accommodate its Muslim minority. The solution of a separate location—an independent Palestine—may in time prove to be the only viable one.

Separation is a solution that is increasingly accepted throughout the world as large, unwieldy nations have fragmented into federations of smaller, more ethnically homogeneous ones. The idea that India might break into smaller units was unthinkable during the Nehru era, when large national units such as the United States and the Soviet Union were the models for modern nation-states. Now that the Soviet Union has broken into smaller, ethnic-based entities, the fissiparous ethnic tendencies of the Sikhs and other groups in India do not seem so ominous. The same can be said of Sri Lanka. Even though Buddhist leaders there have invited the Tamils to remain a part of a united Sri Lanka—as long as they accept the condition that Sri Lanka is culturally a Sinhalese Buddhist nation—many Tamils want a separate homeland of their own. Increasingly many Buddhists in Sri Lanka see this as a viable solution. The separatist solution works best when the minority community resides in a distinct region that can be given a measure of autonomy in a federal state. When the minorities are dispersed throughout society—as the Copts are in Egypt and the Muslims are in India—the accommodation approach is more viable.

Could the accommodation approach work with secular minorities? Even in traditional religious cultures there are people who were raised in religious households but who, through travel, education, or association with modern urban culture, have lost interest in religion. Should there not be a safe cultural haven for such people in a religious society, just as the cultures of Copts and other minorities are maintained as islands in seas of religiosity? From most religious nationalists to whom I posed the question, the answer was a resounding no.[110] They could accept the idea that other religious traditions provide valid alternatives to their own religious law but not secular culture: it has, in their eyes, no links with a higher truth. From their point of view, it is simply antireligion. Some religious nationalists found it difficult to accept secularism even in Europe and the United States, where, they felt, Christianity failed to keep its backsliders in line.[111] Still, it seems to me that the logic of the two-level-*shari'a* admits at least the possibility of islands of different cultures within a religious state.

Yet behind the question of minority rights is a more fundamental issue: the protection of individuals. Terms such as *separate status* and *accommodation* ultimately are important only insofar as they define how persons are treated. If a separate status for minority groups leads to new political positions or a semiautonomous state through which individuals may express their needs and concerns, that is one matter. If it leads to oppression and ostracism, that is quite another.

The term that has evolved in the West to indicate resistance to oppression and respect for people is *human rights*. It has come to have a host of meanings, from legal due process to equal opportunities for women to freedom of the press. At the very least it means the right that Amnesty International and Human Rights Watch seek to encourage: to live free from physical intimidation and incarceration on account of one's political positions or ethnic and religious affiliations. At the very most it means a liberal attitude toward any expression of an individual's tastes, feelings, or desires.

Before we can ask whether traditional religions embrace human rights, we have to be clear about what we mean by the term.[112] Not only is the concept vaguely defined in English, it does not easily translate into other languages. The minimum definition of human rights—that people should be able to reside peacefully alongside each other in dignity and with personal security—is embraced by virtually every religion, albeit in its own terms. For example, one might find, as one Western scholar has, "deep and surprising parallels" between Islamic notions of religious tolerance and one's own.[113] The problem that Islam and many other religious traditions have is with the notion that individuals have inherent characteristics that do not come from the community or from God.[114]

Some religious activists feel that a definition of rights as being held by individuals rather than groups connotes the unacceptable idea that a society is composed of persons who are granted authority and independence—*their* rights—at the expense of the integrity of the communal whole. Rather than using the term *rights,* then, most religious activists would rather describe the relationship between the individual and society as one of moral responsibility. As one of them put it, "We have no rights, only duties and obligations."[115]

This reluctance to embrace the term *rights* and the individualism that is perceived as standing behind it is not confined to religious critics in non-Western societies. Their concerns are echoed by some clergy in the United States and Europe, and increasingly by liberal intellectuals. Robert Bellah and other sociologists who coauthored the popular critique of American individualism, *Habits of the Heart,* see the commitment and communal identity of religion as a vital counterbalance to the isolation and competitiveness of American individualism.[116] In a similar vein, Alasdair MacIntyre has suggested a recovery of virtue in the classical sense as the antidote to what he regarded as an excessive preoccupation with individual rights.[117]

In a way the controversy over rights makes little difference as long as societies respect the personal security and dignity that is at the heart of both human rights and the moral values of all religious traditions. In Egypt, for instance, Muslim nationalists speak ardently about the "uplift of the oppressed."[118] In Sri Lanka, religious nationalists insist that one of the prime purposes of a nation is to uphold free expression and personal dignity—the sorts of "rights" listed in the United Nations' Universal Declaration of Human Rights—but they describe them as Buddhist values rather than as secular humanistic ideals.

The constitution of the Islamic Republic of Iran affirms that one of the purposes of an Islamic republic is to protect the "exalted dignity and value of man, and his freedom, joined to responsibilities, before God."[119] The constitution describes the protection of this dignity in terms that echo constitutions everywhere: the language of human rights. These are, however, the rights of "the people" rather than of individuals. The constitution contains a whole chapter—some twenty-one articles—devoted to the "rights of the people," including equal protection under the law, the equality of women, freedom to express opinions, freedom from torture or humiliation while in incarceration, and freedom to hold "public gatherings and marches," with the condition that "arms are not carried and that they are not detrimental to the fundamental principles of Islam."[120] The constitution also goes beyond the usual list of human rights and includes the right to being provided with "basic necessities," including housing, food, clothing, healthcare, education, and employment.[121]

The only part of the Iranian constitution's list of rights that might give a Western advocate of human rights pause is the occasional use of the phrase "subject to the fundamental principles of Islam." This wording, for example, accompanies Article 24, freedom of the press. It also accompanies the last article of the constitution, regarding mass media: Article 175 guarantees that the media, especially radio and television, will be dedicated to "the free diffusion of information and views" but "in accordance with Islamic criteria."[122]

Is this caveat about Islamic principles the loophole through which massive violations of human rights can enter Iranian society? The answer to that question depends on how much one trusts the Iranian leaders to be true to their word and on how much one believes that the fundamental principles of Islam are consistent with human rights. A good many Muslims outside of Iran think that the Ayatollah Khomeini and his "Judge Blood" comrades took liberties in interpreting Islamic principles and gave Islam the image of being narrow and intolerant. Even Sheik Yassin, the Palestinian Muslim leader, disapproved of taking Americans hostage and said that Khomeini "went too far" in bridling freedom of speech.[123] Sheik Yassin and other Muslim leaders thought that Khomeini's actions contradicted his own constitution, which on the face of it seems as dedicated to human rights as any created by a secular state.

The Islamic versions of human rights are seldom, however, the same as the humanistic secular versions. From the point of view of traditional religious cultures, stark individualism and a laissez-faire attitude toward personal expression run fundamentally counter to the collective loyalty and disciplined demeanor typically found in the religious life. It is unlikely, therefore, that religious nationalists will ever fully support a libertarian version of individual rights, even though in many other ways they may look and talk like human-rights advocates anywhere in the world. The fact is that most religious activists would carry the values of communal life to an extreme that would be uncomfortable even for the most sympathetic Westerner—a Bellah or a MacIntyre. This difference between the role of an individual in Western "individualistic" countries and in non-Western "communitarian" societies is basic, and underlies many of the controversies over the protection of human rights. That difference is so deep and abiding that it will not be easily resolved.

When critics cite religious nationalism as being out of step with modernity, they often have in mind this inability to enshrine individualism as an ultimate value. Or they may be thinking of a related matter: the familiar religious limitations on freedom of expression. Restrictions of this kind are also to be found in a secular nation when it is seized with a sense of ideological purpose—during a period of revolutionary change, for instance, or in the midst of war. The dismal American press coverage of the 1990s Gulf War and the limitations of "embedded journalists" in the U.S. military in the twenty-first-century Iraq war are ample testimony to that fact.

Yet although similar restrictions often accompany movements of religious nationalism, the logic of religious nationalism does not, in itself, require close-mindedness.[124] In fact, most movements of religious nationalism are remarkably unspecific about how far a government—even one that exemplifies moral virtue—can go in limiting personal freedom. Should government legislate morality? Most religious nationalists, like most morally concerned citizens around the world, would say "Yes, up to a point." But this point may vary. Most citizens of even the most liberal societies would accept government censorship of certain kinds of pornography. But only a few would limit the right of dissident religious groups to claim alternative sources of divine revelation—as the Baha'i do—in spite of the preferences of a dominant religious community. In Islamic Iran, the Baha'i claims entail severe criminal penalties.

In India, Hindu nationalists have made a distinction between nation and state, claiming that as long as the country has a clear sense of national

identity and moral purpose, the specific policies of the state matter little.[125] The policies undertaken by the Hindu BJP during its control of the
federal government from 1998 to 2004 were remarkably similar to those
of secular political parties. It stated that despite its affirmation of Hinduism as the ideological glue that holds the nation together, it had no
intention of "running a Hindu government."[126] In this case, the role of religion in the political process was primarily the formulation of a national
identity. Other religious activists have followed a similar position. An Israeli activist told me that there was no need for religion to control the
state, as long as government leaders are "in touch with the God behind
the justice and the truth that the government espouses."[127]

As religiously based political movements reach out to include a wider
constituency and a greater diversity of members, they become more tolerant. In Iran, as I have noted earlier, the influence of the clergy in the
government has both waxed and waned since the revolution in 1979.
Members of the Iranian legislature come from a wide spectrum of the
population, including a far greater percentage of women than are represented in the U.S. Congress. Some of the more conservative supporters
of the Iranian government believe that it has reached too far in trying to
be inclusive. In India, there was a tension between the Hindu extremists,
including the eccentric band of religious mendicants who helped get out
the vote for Hindu parties, and the middle-class urbanites who provided the intellectual leadership. Among the urban followers of the BJP
were those whom the Indian press referred to as Scuppies—saffron-clad
yuppies. They were successful businessmen and administrators who saw
in Hindu political parties a stabilizing influence on the country and not
a narrow dogmatism.[128]

In other movements of religious nationalism one can also find similar
patterns of an educated, urban religious elite somewhat uncomfortably
linked with a large, disenfranchised rural constituency. In Sri Lanka, for
instance, groups of uneducated rural youth have urban student allies. In
Sudan, where the Islamic regime is based on the support of the uneducated masses, the leadership is well educated; the Muslim leader, Hassan
Abdullah Turabi, studied in Paris at the Sorbonne. Many Palestinian
Muslim leaders were also educated and trained abroad. The same is true
of the Islamic Front in Algeria, where participants in the electoral surge
in the early 1990s included many highly educated doctors, scientists, and
university professors. According to one of them, Fouad Delissi, a forty-
year-old party leader in the Bab al-Oued district who worked as a maintenance director for Algeria's petroleum-products retailing company, "If

there are people who consider themselves democrats, . . . it's us." A majority of the Muslim leader's circle of comrades studied in the United
States or in France, and their interest in being involved in the Islamic political movement was to help "guide the country in a scientific, normal,
modern way."[129]

As they appear to have a broad outlook on their own society and its
role within the larger international context, can we take these Algerian
religious nationalists at their word and accept them as "modern"? The
answer to that question depends in large measure on what is meant by
the term. As I mentioned in the introduction to this book, a number of
scholars have insisted on distinguishing between *modernity,* largely defined as the acceptance of bureaucratic forms of organization and the ac-
quisition of new technology, and *modernism,* described as embracing the
ideology of individualism and a relativist view of moral values. This distinction allows us to observe that religious nationalists are modern without being modernists.[130] Although they reject what they regard as the perverse and alienating features of modernism, they are in every other way
creatures of the modern age.

In Anthony Giddens's frame of reference, their situation is perhaps inevitable. Nationalism, from his point of view, is a condition for entry
into a modern world political and economic system based on the building blocks of nation-states.[131] It is unthinkable that a political or economic entity can function without some relationship to large patterns of
international commerce and political alignment, and this relationship requires strong centralized control on a national level. Because movements
for religious nationalism aim at strengthening national identities, they
can be seen as highly compatible with the modern system.

According to Craig Calhoun, one of the hallmarks of the modern nation is the implicit violence of social coercion—creating "homogenous
and compliant national populations."[132] John Lie, in an interesting
study of the relationship between social identities and the state, argues
that the Enlightenment concept of the nation-state requires a homogenous social identity—"modern peoplehood," as Lie puts it—that makes
the modern nation possible.[133] In a curious way, as I mentioned in the
first chapter in this book, religion helps to provide that sense of community and buttress the concept of the nation-state.

New transnational religious movements are an accommodation to
yet another phase in the development of modernity, or perhaps post-
modernity: globalization. Transnational cultural networks provide a collective identity to peoples who are widely dispersed—a kind of Internet

ethnicity. At the same time, as al Qaeda has graphically shown, they can provide a cultural basis for challenging the social assumptions of an emerging global culture based on the economic and mass communication aspects of contemporary globalization.

Religious nationalism, then, may be viewed as one way of reconciling heretofore irreconcilable elements—traditional religion and modern politics. In the past, religious movements have often been apolitical and sometimes hostile to the nation-state. As Gerald Larson has suggested, they have legitimized the views of those who oppose the notion of a global nation-state system.[134] In a similar vein, Wilfred Cantwell Smith contended in the mid-1950s that there was a fundamental opposition between Islam and modernity, by which he meant not only the attributes of modernism that Bruce Lawrence has mentioned but also the fact that the transnationalism of Islamic culture has aligned against the nation-state in the manner suggested by Larson.[135] There are, however, new religiously based movements that in general have been particular to individual nation-states and provide a remarkable synthesis between traditional religious cultures and modern nationalism. The BJP and the Islamic Republic of Iran are examples. As one observer of the Iranian revolution remarked, it has "no precedent" in modern history.[136] Since the revolution, however, there have been a number of attempts in other parts of the world to achieve the kind of synthesis between traditional culture and modern politics to which the Iranian revolution aspires. It is ironic, but not entirely surprising, that such attempts would be dubbed anti-modern by secularists who have become accustomed to thinking of modern politics as their private domain.

Religious Rebellion and Global War

Religious challenges to secular politics in the last decades of the twentieth century had, by the beginning of the twenty-first, all the appearances of a global rebellion. The confrontation developed in stages, and at each stage the escalation of hostility was due both to the belligerence of new religious activists and to the obstinacy of their secular opponents. What once had seemed simply an anomaly or an annoyance to many secular leaders increasingly came to be seen as a global foe.

The First Stage: Uprisings

The first stage of the encounter was marked by isolated outbursts. It began in the 1970s with a variety of groups—Hindu, Buddhist, Sikh, and Muslim—rebelling against what they regarded as the moral failings of the secular state. One of the first of these religious rebellions was nonviolent—the movement in India led by one of Mohandas Gandhi's disciples, Jayaprakash Narayan, who called for a "Total Revolution" in 1974 against corruption in the Indian government. It threatened to bring the government to a standstill, and in 1975 Prime Minister Indira Gandhi responded by proclaiming a national emergency. Several years later, in 1979, the Ayatollah Khomeini led a revolt against the secular regime of the shah of Iran; though not entirely bloodless, the number of deaths directly caused by the coup probably did not exceed more than a few hundred. Soon after, the Khalistani Sikh separatist movement gained

momentum and unleashed an avalanche of violence in the northern Indian state of Punjab throughout the 1980s, in which tens of thousands
were killed by militants and government forces. At the same time Buddhist
activists violently resisted attempts by the Sri Lankan government to appease the growing Tamil separatist movement that arose in that island nation during the 1970s. The gathering power of Muslim extremists in Egypt
led to the brutal assassination of President Anwar al-Sadat in 1981.

The common element among all these incidents of Hindu, Sikh, Shi'ite,
and Sunni Muslim violence in the 1970s and early 1980s was an implicit
moral critique of secular politics. Though radical religious movements
had been at the margins of politics for much of the twentieth century—
the Muslim Brotherhood, for example, was formed in 1928—the movements did not gain strength until the last decades of the century. By that
time a revived anticolonialism had developed, opposing the cultural and
political legacies of European modernity in the Middle East and South
Asia, that gave the movements a new force. The modern secular governments in those regions that were fashioned in the mid-twentieth century in the image of the retreating European colonial powers were
deemed to be insufficient conveyers of social identity and moral purpose.
The opponents of these secular regimes used the power of religion not
only as a mobilizing force but also as an ideological basis of cultural
identity and moral critique.

Secular authorities treated these movements of religious rebellion simply as attempts to usurp power and did not address the substantive issues they raised. During the early months of the Iranian revolution, for
instance, some American scholars deemed it "an unfortunate interrup-
tion of the historical process," which they believed had been leading Iran
inexorably toward a Western-style liberal political democracy.[1] In India,
Indira Gandhi scoffed at the pretensions of the young Sikh leaders who
challenged her authority and refused to take them seriously. Yet at the
same time, many among the general public in South Asia, Iran, and Middle East began to accept some aspects of these movements' critique of
their governments as valid. In some cases, they regarded the new religious activists as Robin Hoods—extralegal but virtuous challengers to
the political status quo.

The Second Stage: Internationalization

The next stage of the developing warfare between religious and secular
politics was the internationalization of the conflict during the 1980s.

This stage is most clearly embodied in the ad hoc international coalition of jihadi Muslim radicals that developed during the Afghan war. It is hard to underestimate the formative power of their experience, shared by thousands of volunteer soldiers in the Afghanistan struggle against the Soviet regime in the 1980s. In one central theater of involvement, activists were brought together from throughout the Muslim world. The fighting force of *mujahadin* included former jihadi soldiers whose countries of origin spanned much of the Islamic world, from Pakistan to North Africa. It also included Egyptian militants linked to Sadat's assassination and Saudis who would later be identified with Osama bin Laden's al Qaeda movement. Afghanistan became the crucible for the international Muslim political networks that would dominate global politics for the next two decades.

Early in the 1980s international developments also informed the religious politics of Israel, which in turn spurred the growth of Muslim movements in the region. Israel's victory in the 1967 war with its Arab neighbors had been a point of pride for the young nation, and it stimulated new thinking about a broader role for Israel, both geographically and theologically. Meir Kahane's Kach Party came to symbolize the religious aspect of Israel's irredentist claims on adjacent territory. After Israel's invasion of Lebanon in the 1982 war, the Hezbollah Shi'ite movement was formed to oppose Israel and to resist the Westernization of Lebanon. At the end of the decade, the Palestinian resistance movement—which up to that time had been largely secular—took on a religious character in the formation of Hamas.

The Third Stage: Anti-Americanism

The third stage in the gathering confrontation between religious and secular politics was characterized by growing anti-American and anti-European sentiment during the 1990s. During this stage, the target of the religious activists' wrath shifted from local regimes to international centers of power. Increasingly the political and economic might of the United States and Europe were regarded as the cause of both local and global dysfunction. In Algeria, for instance, France became the target of religious violence soon after the Algerian elections were canceled by the military in 1991. Algerian activists regarded the French rejection of Islamic politics as resistance to what they regarded as the "march of history" away from Western-dominated society to a society based on indigenous cultures.[2]

The 1990s constituted a decade of social dissent linked with religions of various kinds: Christianity, Judaism, and Buddhism as well both Sunni and Shi'ite Islam. America, regarded as the fount of secularism, was often the target of protests. Many who attacked the United States or its symbols were incensed by what they regarded as its economic, cultural, and political oppression of other nations under the "new world order" of a secular, American-dominated, post–Cold War world. Some of the fiercest opponents of the United States' secular power were themselves Americans. The venom of the Christian militia and other extremist Christian groups in the United States led to a series of terrorist attacks, culminating in the 1995 bombing of a federal office building in Oklahoma City by Timothy McVeigh, a follower of William Pierce's racist Christian ideology, which he called "Cosmotheism." In the same year, in Japan, members of a Buddhist religious movement, the Aum Shinrikyo, imagined an apocalyptic and catastrophic world war in which American global military power would once again be directed at Japan. The group unleashed nerve gas in the Tokyo subways as a way of demonstrating the validity of their prophecies, dire predictions that condemned the power of both Japan and the United States as sinister and manipulative.

Many radical Muslim groups saw America's military and economic power the same way, albeit with a more realistic basis for their critique. The United States' economic interests in the oil reserves of the Middle East, and its unchallenged cultural and political influence in a post–Cold War world led many Muslim activists to see America as a global bully, a fitting target for their religious and political anger. It appealed especially to those whose resistance methods had been honed through the opposition to the Soviet occupation of Afghanistan, which also was seen as a fight against enemies of Islam. They had seen the strength of their forces grow as they rallied against an enemy—the Soviet Union. In the 1990s, they needed a new enemy, and the United States fit that bill.

In 1993, a group of Muslim activists in the New York City area who had been implicated in Sadat's assassination and had participated in the Afghan resistance attempted to blow up the World Trade Center. Some of the conspirators were linked to a new network of anti-American activism associated with Osama bin Laden and a global jihadi movement. In 1998, simultaneous explosions destroyed the American embassies in Kenya and Tanzania; and in 2000 a ship-based bomb hit the USS *Cole*, while it was docked in the harbor at Aden.

Because this new surge in anti-Americanism arose during the decade
following the collapse of the Soviet Union and the dismantling of the
Berlin Wall, one might legitimately ask whether there is any connection
between the end of the old Cold War and the rise of the new one. There
was certainly a direct relationship in the areas of the former Soviet Union,
where indigenous religious movements reawoke in part as reactions
against the homogenous secular ideology enforced during the Soviet era.
A burst of Christian cultural nationalism occurred in Eastern Europe and
the former Soviet Union in the 1990s. In the early 1990s, Buddhist nationalism emerged in Mongolia, and Muslim nationalism gained
strength in areas far from the Middle East: in Afghanistan, in Tajikistan,
and in other Central Asian members of the Commonwealth of Independent States. New leaders rode the crests of power provided by these
movements, and found in religion a useful support.

There was also an indirect relationship between the end of the old
Cold War and the rise of the new religious rebellions. The collapse of the
global polarity between communism and capitalism left the United States
as the sole remaining superpower, but it also left the perception that su-
perpowers were flawed bastions and could crumble and fall. At the same
time, America and Europe's economic superiority was being challenged
by the rise of the East Asian economies, and America's moral authority
had not recovered from the effects of the Vietnam War and the Water-
gate, Iran-Contra, and other government scandals. The perception that
the old order was weak and could be destroyed was the occasion for new
religious challenges to old secular European and American powers.
Times of social turbulence and political confusion—which the collapse
of the Soviet Union and the decline of American economic power and
cultural influence created around the world—are often occasions for new
ideological solutions to surface. It was inevitable that many of these
would involve religion, sometimes perceived as the only stable point in
a swirl of economic and political indirection.

Moreover, as nations rejected the Soviet and American models of nationhood, they turned to their own pasts and to their own cultural resources. Secular ideologies often lead to frustration because their material promises usually cannot be fulfilled in one's own lifetime; the
expectations of religious ideologies do not disappoint in the same way
because they are not fulfilled on the worldly plane. Religious nationalism raised new hopes, and it came along in time to rescue the idea of the
nation-state. The political organization of a modern nation must be
morally justified, and in many former colonial countries new generations

of leaders found it increasingly difficult to gain support from the masses for a vision of society that mirrored that of the failing old colonial powers. Many of these countries might have descended into anarchy, been conquered by neighboring states, or come under the hegemony of a large international power had it not been for the insulation provided by religious nationalism. In Eastern Europe and the former Soviet Union, religious and other forms of ethnic nationalism might well have blocked Mikhail Gorbachev's vision of a new secular, nonsocialist empire to replace the vast Soviet Union.

The Fourth Stage: Global War

The most recent stage in the development of the global religion rebellion occurred at the beginning of the twenty-first century, when contests between secular and religious forces began to be played out in a global context. The significant moment in this development was September 11, 2001. Though most of the nineteen hijackers who boarded the commercial airplanes that attacked the World Trade Center and the Pentagon on that day were Saudis, the planning for the conspiracy was global. It involved scores of activists in several countries from Afghanistan to Germany to the United States. Moreover, the goals of the jihadi networks were transnational. Originally jihadi leaders such as Khalid Shaikh Mohammad and Osama bin Laden had been fixated on local issues—in bin Laden's case, on Saudi Arabia. He took particular issue with U.S. support for the Saudi royal family and America's exploitation of the country's oil resources. He then adopted a broader critique of Middle Eastern politics, following the teachings of Maulana Maududi, Sayyid Qutb, and other Muslim political thinkers who rejected all forms of Western political and social influence in the region. Increasingly, bin Laden's goal, and that of other jihadi activists, was not simply to free Saudi Arabia from American influence but to liberate the entire Muslim world from U.S. hegemony. This meant a confrontation of global proportions on multiple fronts.

September 11 to that degree was just a signature moment in the series of jihadi terrorist attacks that sought to bring to public consciousness the notion that the world was at war. The attacks were bewildering to the surviving victims and to those who witnessed them since they did not seem motivated by any clear political objective. Although bin Laden had declared war on the United States in his famous *fatwa* of 1996, it was largely an invisible conflict, a great confrontation that lay largely within the imaginations of the jihadi activists, until September 11, 2001, brought it to public attention.

The response of America's political leaders following the September 11 attacks was dramatic and historically transformative. The televised statements of President George W. Bush on September 11 and even more decisively on the day following made clear how he and his administration were going to interpret the attack: they adopted the jihadi terms. Rather than viewing the terrorist acts as criminal deeds by a gang of thugs, the U.S. leaders adopted major elements of bin Laden's view of the world and saw the terrorist acts as skirmishes in a global war. The simmering new Cold War of the 1990s had boiled over into a real war, the first of the twenty-first century.

The new Cold War came to be known as the "War on Terror" by U.S. officials and the American news media. It was characterized as the "struggle against radical Islam," and indeed the encounter of Islam with the secular state became the sole concern of Western policymakers, despite the persistence of Christian militants in America, Hindu and Sikh activists in India, Jewish extremists in Israel, and violent Buddhists in Sri Lanka and Thailand. Only the Muslim activists, it seemed, shared an ideological perspective that was global in scale and transnational in its network of activists. Its actions were brutal and violent. So too were the American attempts to suppress it, and the heavy-handed approach spawned further cycles of violence.

Within a month after the September 11 attacks, the U.S. military bombarded Afghanistan, lending its support to an alliance of Afghan rebels that sought to topple the Taliban regime. Because the Taliban had harbored bin Laden, many observers saw this as a justified response to the attacks, although many in the Muslim world thought it an unwarranted military invasion directed more at the Taliban than at the transnational terrorists. At the same time, the U.S. involvement in the Philippines, Somalia, and elsewhere in support of the attempt to control radical Muslim groups were also perceived anti-Muslim military exercises.

Iraq became the most significant theater in the U.S. "war on terror" and the single largest catalyst for global anti-American anger. The invasion and occupation of the country in 2003 were initially justified as an attempt to locate and destroy weapons of mass destruction (although none were found). But throughout the Muslim world, the Iraq invasion was widely perceived as an attempt to control Middle East politics and its economic resources. Many who saw it as part of America's war on

Islam were receptive to al Qaeda's analysis vision of global war and the need to defend the Muslim faith—if necessary through violence.

Terrorist acts associated with jihadi Muslim activists increased dramatically around the world following the attacks of September 11, 2001, and the arena of terror became transnational. Some of the acts were indirectly aimed at Israel—such as an attack on a synagogue in Tunisia and on hotels patronized by Israelis in Egypt's Red Sea resorts. Other acts were directed at Western cultural influence in Muslim countries far from the Middle East, such as the assault on Bali resorts in 2002 and the 2003 bombing of the Marriot Hotel in Jakarta. Still others were directed at purportedly repressive governments—such as India with regard to its policies on the Muslim separatist movement in Kashmir, which were likely the pretext for the Mumbai train blasts in 2006.

But the most destructive attacks directly or indirectly targeted the coalition of American-led forces in Iraq. In addition to incidents in Iraq itself (including the bombing of the United Nations headquarters and sites sacred to Shi'a Muslims) were those far from Baghdad—the Madrid train bombings in 2004, for instance, which killed almost two hundred, and the London subway and bus bombings in 2005, which took the lives of over fifty commuters. Another plot was intercepted in 2006 that might have killed thousands of passengers on commercial airplanes flying from London to the United States. When the conspirators were apprehended, most turned out to be British citizens—expatriate Pakistanis and other Muslims living in the United Kingdom.

Many of the Muslim activists in Europe were equally angry about European attitudes toward the Muslim immigrant community. Among the more troubling moments were the tensions following the assassination of the Dutch filmmaker Theo van Gogh in November 2004; the riots by North African and Arab youth in France in 2004; and the protests over the French attempt to ban the wearing of the *hijab* by Muslim women in France. An international outcry followed a Dutch newspaper's publication of cartoons that many Muslims deemed offensive.

The actions of Muslim militants associated with Hamas in Palestine and Hezbollah in Lebanon continue to roil the Middle East. Though their activities are not transnational in scope, their ideology and much of their support have come from kindred Muslim supporters in other parts of the Shi'ia world (in the case of Hezbollah), or from Sunni regions (in the case of Hamas). By the middle of the decade, many supporters of the largely local Hamas movement had began espousing the rhetoric of global jihad. The Hezbollah victory in the 2006 war with Israel in southern Lebanon was hailed throughout the Muslim world. In Iraq the violence against the U.S.-led occupation forces and the new government (operating under American support) also became much more than a resistance struggle against a foreign occupation. Under the leadership of Abu Musab al-Zarqawi, the movement forged an alliance with al Qaeda that sought to destroy Shi'a political power in Iraq.

The Internet has become a new arena for radical religious activism. Through password-protected sites and publicly accessible chat rooms, the ideological net of radical jihad was cast around the world. New acts of violence emerged from small cells of activists mobilized through the Internet but not controlled or coordinated by any single command. Thus the virulence of religious radicalism metastasized throughout the planet through cyber-networks. Among a diversity of groups—from minority immigrant communities in London to prison converts in California— jihadi rhetoric became a vehicle of social protest. The new Cold War was waged not only on a geographical battlefield but also in the intellectual terrain of cyberspace. Yet, like the old Cold War, the ideological confrontation always carried the threat of bloodshed.

WHAT DOES RELIGION HAVE TO DO WITH IT?

How will this violence end, and how will the global rebellion come to a peaceful conclusion? The answers to these questions depend in part on what created the tension in the first place. If the confrontation has been largely about religion, it will never disappear, since religious expression is central to culture and has endured over the millennia.

But is the conflict essentially about religion? There is no question that many of the movements against secular states at the turn of the twenty-first century have been expressed in religious terms, but this does not make them movements essentially "for" or "about" religion. In a widely discussed book, *Dying to Win*, Robert Pape examined the most brutal form of violence associated with religious activism—suicide bombing— and argued that in these cases religion is not the motive.[3] Looking at a broad swath of incidents at the end of the twentieth century, Pape concluded that suicide activists are not motivated by religious fervor as much as by calculated politics. The primary motive has been to defend territory. Pape accurately pointed out that until 2003, most suicide bombings were conducted not by religious groups but by a secular ethnic movement, the Tamil Tigers in Sri Lanka.

Pape based his conclusions on an analysis of a database profiling 462 suicide terrorists (primarily, although not exclusively, male), compiled by the Chicago Project on Suicide Terrorism. They are not, he argued "mainly poor, uneducated, immature religious zealots or social losers," as they have sometimes been portrayed. What they have in common is the sense that their territory or culture has been invaded by an alien power that cannot easily be overthrown. In this desperate situation of social survival, they turn to the simplest and most direct form of militant engagement, using their own bodies as bombs. Contrary to the perception of many observers, suicide bombers are not religious loners but are usually part of large militant organizations with well-honed strategies aimed at ousting foreign control from what they consider their own territory. The concessions made in the past to such organizations by the governments who opposed them have given them the confidence that their strategies work and are worth repeating. Rather than seeing these activists as religiously motivated madmen, Pape sees them as strategists making rational calculations for political gain.

I think that Pape is largely correct. Yet, though religious ideas do not initially provoke the conflicts, as the case studies in this book make abundantly clear, they play an important role. The conditions that lead to conflict are typically matters of social and political identity—what makes individuals cohere as a community and how they are defined. Often this is manifested as a defense of the homeland, as Pape describes it, a protection of territory or culture that is perceived to be under control by an outside power. At some point in the conflict, however, usually at a time of frustration and desperation, the political and ideological contest becomes "religionized." Then what was primarily a worldly struggle takes on the aura of sacred conflict. This creates a whole new set of problems.

All of the groups described in this book—including Sikhs in the Punjab, Muslim separatists in Kashmir, Buddhist antigovernment protesters in Sri Lanka, the Aum Shinrikyo movement in Japan, the Islamic revolution in Iran, Sunni jihadi movements in Egypt, Palestine, and elsewhere in the Middle East, messianic Jewish movements in Israel, Catholic and Protestant militants in Northern Ireland, the Christian militia in the United States, and the transnational movement of jihadi activists around world—share some common characteristics. Though each group was responding to its own set of local issues, in all cases these were communities that perceived themselves to be fragile, vulnerable, and under siege.

They also shared an ideological component: the perception that the modern idea of secular nationalism had let them down. They were convinced that the secular state was insufficient to protect their communities or provide the moral, political, economic, and social strength to nurture them. They had lost faith in secular nationalism, as I described it in the first chapter of this book. In many cases the effects of globalization were in the background, as global economic and communications systems wiped away the identities of the nation-state. In some cases, the hatred of the global system was overt, as in the American Christian militia's contempt for the "new world order" and the jihadis' targeting of the World Trade Center. Underlying their political activism was a motivating "cause"—if such a term can be used—that was not a yearning for a specific political goal but a gnawing sense of a loss of identity and control.

This sense of social malaise is not necessarily a religious problem, but it is one for which religion provides a solution. In each of the cases I examined, religion has become the ideology of empowerment and protest. Particular religious images and themes have been marshaled to resist what were imagined to be the enemies of traditional culture and identities: the global secular systems and their secular nation-state supporters.

There are other similarities among these cases. In each the supporters of radical religious ideologies perceived the secular state as an oppressive agent. They experienced this oppression as an assault on their pride, and felt insulted and shamed as a result. The failures of the state—although economic, political, or cultural—were often experienced in personal ways as humiliation and alienation—as a loss of selfhood.

It is understandable then, that the men (and they are usually men) who experience this assault on their identity lash out violently—as men often do when they feel frustrated and humiliated. Such expressions of power are meant at least symbolically to enable these individuals to regain their sense of manhood.[4] In each case, however, the activists channeled these feelings through images of collective violence borrowed from their religious traditions: the idea of cosmic war.

The idea of cosmic war is a remarkably consistent feature among all of these cases. It is a powerfully restorative image for social malaise. Those whom we might think of as terrorists often think of themselves as soldiers. They are engaged in attempts to restore their sense of power and control in what they imagine to be sacred battles. Acts of religious terror serve not only as tactics in a political strategy but as symbolically empowering sacred deeds. These are performances of violence, enacted to create a moment of spiritual encounter and personal redemption. Religious violence is especially savage and relentless since its perpetrators see it not merely as part of a worldly political battle but as part of a scenario of divine conflict.

So although religion may not be the problem, the religious response to the problem of identity and control in the modern world is often problematic. When antimodernism, anti-Americanism, and antiglobalization are expressed in the drama of religious struggle, religion brings in a whole new set of elements. For one thing religion personalizes the conflict. It provides *personal rewards*—religious merit, redemption, the promise of heavenly luxuries—to those who struggle in conflicts that otherwise have only social benefits. It also provides *vehicles of social mobilization* that embrace vast numbers of supporters who otherwise would not be mobilized around social or political issues. In many cases, it provides an *organizational network* of local churches, mosques, temples, and religious associations from which patterns of leadership and support may be tapped. It gives the legitimacy of *moral righteousness* in political encounter. Even more important, it provides *justification for violence* that challenges the state's monopoly on morally sanctioned killing. Using Max Weber's dictum that the state's authority is always rooted in its capacity to enforce its power through the use of socially approved bloodshed—in police authority, capital punishment, and armed defense—religion is the only other entity that can give moral sanction for violence; it is therefore inherently at least potentially revolutionary.

Religion's images of *cosmic war* further complicate a conflict that has become hardened by positions reinforced with religious authority. The notion of cosmic war is by definition an *all-encompassing worldview*. Supporters of Christian militia movements, for instance, described their "aha" moment when they discovered the worldview of the totalizing ideology that helped them make sense of the modern world, their increasingly peripheral role in it, and the actions they can take to set the world right. It gives them roles as *religious soldiers* who can literally fight back against the forces of evil. When the template of spiritual battle is implanted onto a worldly conflict, it dramatically changes how those engaged in it perceive that conflict. It *absolutizes the conflict* into extreme opposing positions and *demonizes opponents* by imagining them to be satanic powers. This absolutism makes compromise difficult to achieve and holds out the promise of *total victory* through divine intervention. A sacred war that is waged in a godly span of time need not be won immediately, however. The *time line of sacred struggle is vast,* perhaps even eternal.

I once had the occasion to point out the futility—in secular military terms—of the Islamic struggle in Palestine to Abdul Aziz Rantisi, the late leader of the political wing of the Hamas movement. It seemed to me that Israel's military force was such that a Palestinian military effort could never succeed. Dr. Rantisi assured me that that "Palestine was occupied before, for two hundred years."[5] He explained that he and his Palestinian comrades "can wait again—at least that long." In his calculation, the struggles of God can endure for eons. Ultimately, however, they knew they would succeed. In the religious frame of reference, a defeat is never really a defeat since in the vast time line of sacred warfare ultimately the righteous side will succeed.

So religion can be a problematic aspect of contemporary social conflict even if it is not *the* problem, in the sense of the root cause of discontent. Much of the violence in contemporary life that is perceived as global terrorism is directly related to the absolutism of conflict. The demonization of enemies allows those who regard themselves as God's soldiers to kill with impunity. In many cases they feel that their acts will give them spiritual rewards.

Curiously the same kind of thinking has crept into some of the responses to terrorism. The "war on terrorism" that was launched by the United States government after September 11, 2001, is a case in point. To the degree that the war references are metaphorical, implying an all-out effort in the manner of previous administrations' "war on drugs" and "war on poverty," they are strategies to marshal public support for security measures and police surveillance. The September 11 attacks were, after all, hideous acts that deeply scarred the American consciousness, and one could certainly understand that a responsible government would want to concentrate efforts to hunt down those culpable and bring them to justice.

But among some public commentators and politicians who espoused a "war on terrorism" the militant language was more than metaphor. God's blessing was imagined to be bestowed on a view of confrontation that was, like all images of cosmic war, all-encompassing, absolutizing, and demonizing. It led to the invasion and occupation of two Muslim countries, and justified the curtailing of civil rights for the purposes of obtaining information from detainees suspected of being terrorists. What is problematic about this view is that it is intolerant of the slow procedures of systems of justice—even if these are ultimately more effective in locating those believed to be terrorists and provoke fewer acts of violence. The war rhetoric demanded instead the quick and violent responses that simplified the confrontation and lent a sense of divine certainty to its resolution. Alas, as the arc of violence in Iraq bore testimony, such a position fueled the flames of retaliation, leading to more terrorism instead of less.

The role of religion in this literal "war on terrorism" in a curious way resembles religion's role in the cosmic war imagined by those perpetrating the terrorism. In both cases religion was a problematic partner of political confrontation. Religion brought more to conflict than simply a repository of symbols and the aura of divine support. It problematized the conflict through its abiding absolutism, its justification of violence, and its images of warfare that demonize opponents and cast the conflict in transhistorical terms.

THE FUTURE OF RELIGIOUS REBELLIONS

What will happen next? The trajectory of religious activism over the years does not give any simple answers. The political movements based on religion that have entered the public arena from the late 1970s through the beginning of the twenty-first century trace a complex and diverse history. Several religious revolutions have been attempted—including the Taliban's regime in Afghanistan and the Islamic Courts Council's brief rise to power in Somalia—but Iran remains the only long-term example of a successful attempt to establish a religious state. It has founded a political order based on religious ideology, fanned the fires of nationalism with religious zeal, enacted laws that privilege particular religious ideas and practices, and brought into the sphere of political influence clerics whose only credentials are their knowledge of theology. Even in Iran, though, the main business of government is the same as anywhere else—providing a stable and just political order and supporting economic development. These aspects of mundane politics have no particular religious claim. Moreover, the influence of the clergy and religious ideology in Iran has waxed and waned since the 1979 revolution.

In other countries, religious movements have been assimilated into the political process in a nonrevolutionary way. They have become political parties or used their political support to back particular candidates. The Hindu religious nationalist movement that supported the Bharatiya Janata Party in India scored huge electoral successes in both state and national parliaments. In Palestine, the Hamas movement transformed itself into a political party and soared to victory in the 2006 parliamentary elections. In Algeria, the Islamic Salvation Front (or FIS, after the French *Front Islamique du Salut*) continued to be politically influential even after it was outlawed following the military crackdown that terminated its electoral success in 1991. In Egypt, the Muslim Brotherhood has also often been outlawed though it sometimes fielded de facto candidates by supporting individuals sympathetic to its cause, as it did in the 2005 parliamentary elections, when candidates it supported formed the largest opposition bloc in the parliament. In general, when religious movements turn to electoral politics they abandon violent tactics, and if they are banned the level of violence rises again. Compromise with the secular political order, however, may lead to divisions within the movement and the formation of extremist splinter groups that are even more violent than the mainstream movement.

In other cases religious rebellions have been brutally suppressed before they have had a chance to take the reins of power. The Sinhalese arm of the radical Janatha Vimukthi Peramuna movement in Sri Lanka was essentially killed off in the 1990 military action against the movement but later resurfaced. In India, rebellious Sikhs were killed in the thousands along with large numbers of armed police in a protracted ten-year war. It ended early in the 1990s, as much from exhaustion and infighting as from the government's militancy. Eventually, many villagers who were weary of all the violence refused to give the Sikh militants safe shelter.

Elsewhere factionalism weakened a good number of other movements, including the Christian militia in the United States, opposition nationalist churches in the Ukraine, Shi'a factions in Lebanon, and rival Muslim groups in the resistance movement in Palestine. In Iraq, extremist groups of Shi'a and Sunni Muslims have set about killing one another in a violence that shifted the pattern of militancy in the post-Saddam era from antioccupation insurgency to civil war. These developments give rise to the possibility that infighting might destroy some of the movements from within.

In other cases the violence of rebellious religious movements has been contained through legal means. In Japan, after the 1995 nerve gas attacks in the Tokyo subways, the Aum Shinrikyo was placed under extensive government surveillance. The major participants were arrested and after lengthy trials were sentenced to long prison terms. The leader of the movement, Shoko Asahara, was sentenced to death by hanging in 2004. Though the movement resurfaced under a new name, Aleph, it was nonviolent. In China, the government outlawed religious movements it regarded as potentially dangerous, including Falun Gong. Although the group protested that it was being persecuted by the Chinese, there has been little bloodshed on either side.

Perhaps the most successful conclusion to movements of terrorism through nonviolent means was the Good Friday Agreement in 1998 that brought the troubles of Northern Ireland onto a path of peace. The Northern Ireland solution brought an end to decades of violence that terrorized London, Belfast, and other cities. It showed the value of not responding in kind to provocative terrorist attacks and letting the slow process of patient negotiation and compromise work out a solution of accommodation. The agreement called for both Protestant and Catholic communities in the region to have guaranteed representation through a commission supported by both the state of Ireland and the United Kingdom.

Could other violent situations be settled in a manner similar to Northern Ireland's Good Friday Agreement? It would not take a huge stretch of imagination to think that they could, especially when the issue is largely over contested land. The Kashmir situation is similar to that of Northern Ireland, in that two religious communities occupy and lay claim to the same territory. India and Pakistan could join in a settlement similar to the Good Friday Agreement. The Israeli-Palestinian conflict is more complex, but like Northern Ireland it is essentially a squabble over territory in which both sides have a moral and political claim. Since the Oslo Agreement in 1993, a negotiated settlement in the region has seemed a realistic though still elusive possibility. The Annapolis accord in 2007 affirmed the principle of a two-state solution.

In yet other cases, moderate members of the movements were assimilated into the public arena after the extremists were isolated. In Northern Ireland the radical positions of activists such as the Protestant Ian Paisley were largely ignored, and negotiations were conducted with more moderate members of the Protestant and Catholic communities. In Sri Lanka, the most radical of the Sinhalese Buddhist supporters of the anti-government movement could be marginalized and destroyed in part because moderate religious nationalists had been appeased by the government's policies.

Yet other movements have abandoned political activism altogether as the futility of their efforts encouraged their leaders to turn toward other ventures. In the case of the Christian militia in the United States, there is some indication that the enormity of the violence perpetrated by Timothy McVeigh in bombing the Oklahoma City Federal Building in 1995 had a sobering effect on the right-wing Christian movement in the rest of the country. Yet another factor in diminishing the role of the violent religious right after the Oklahoma City bombing was the fact they were largely ignored by the public authorities and the news media. Neither the prosecution or his defense in Timothy McVeigh's much-publicized trial made any effort to link McVeigh with the larger underworld of the Christian militant movements in the United States. The absence of media attention has further marginalized them.

By contrast, when a similar sort of terrorist attack resulted in the catastrophic collapse of the World Trade Center and damage to the Pentagon on September 11, 2001, the connections to radical Islam became the central issue. Within days, the al Qaeda network became identified as America's most vicious foe and Osama bin Laden the protagonist in a new world war. When American leaders adopted bin Laden's rhetoric of religious war and elevated him to the level of the nation's global foe, they inadvertently promoted his image and ideas throughout the Muslim world. It is possible that this might have further emboldened al Qaeda. As I mentioned earlier, the paradoxical effect of the "war on terror" might well have been the increased proliferation of terrorism. The popularization of jihadi ideology as an anti-American posture of protest may be due in no small part to the fact that the United States has cast it in the role of a global enemy.

Hence to a large degree the future of religious rebellions against the secular state depends not only on the rebellious religious movements but also on the way that government authorities respond, especially in Europe and the United States. Much of the passion underlying religious activists' positions is a response to what they have perceived as the West's arrogance and intolerance. If they could perceive the West as changing its attitude—respecting at least some aspects of their positions—perhaps their stance would be less vindictive. It is this sensitivity that has been behind some of the more cautious moments in European and U.S. responses to acts of terrorism. In Spain, for instance, one response to the Madrid bombings was an attempt by the Spanish government to be more hospitable to the Muslim minority living in the country.

Attitudes are difficult to sway, however, and the frequency of acts of terrorism associated with the radical jihadi movement has led to a certain Islamophobia in Europe and the United States. Like the old Cold War, the perception is one of Western civilization under siege, attacked by a hostile and alien force. This, in turn, has led to the notion that all Muslim activists—or even all Muslims—are the same. Policies based on this perception widen the gulf between the two sides, just as they did during the Cold War, and even more violence is the result. As one U.S. State Department official put it, "We have to be smarter in dealing with Islam than we were in dealing with communism thirty or forty years ago."[6]

For Americans and Europeans who are comfortable with the tenets of secular society, the difficulty is a matter of accepting not only a non-Christian or non-Jewish religion, but also a form of political religion. Even if the religious activism is Christian or Jewish, it is still suspect for many. Most Westerners are not used to the notion that religion has a role to play in defining public order and in stating its basic values. Although religion is historically part of the background of Western secular nationalism, that heritage is largely neglected. If religion were a more vital force in Western societies in ways that were seen as facilitating public life and promoting the common welfare, perhaps it would be easier to accept religion's public presence in other parts of the world.

From time to time one hears calls for a more active role for religion in American public life.[7] One of the reasons that figures such as Bishop Desmond Tutu, Mother Theresa, and Mohandas Gandhi appeal so much to the Western imagination is that, without being aggressively religious, they have brought a moral and spiritual consciousness into the public sphere. The poet T. S. Eliot lamented the "waste land" of empty spirituality in the West, and Gandhi once described the absence of spirituality in Western civilization as a "sickness." In a treatise titled *Hind Swaraj, or Indian Home Rule*—arguably his only sustained writing on political theory—Gandhi observed that the West's materialism separated it from its spiritual soul.[8] Many Westerners have agreed. Among them is Reinhold Niebuhr, the American Protestant theologian who influenced the Roosevelt government in the 1940s and who has been quoted by American politicians at distant ends of the political spectrum.[9] One of Niebuhr's central theses had to do with the limited moral ability of nations. They cannot be selfless, Niebuhr claimed, because they are by nature nothing more than a collection of the self-interests of all the individuals contained within them. He added, however, that religion can help transform political organizations and make them more like communities: it can temper some of the harsher characteristics of self-interest and draw people together through a common recognition of "profound and ultimate unities."[10]

Yet both Gandhi and Niebuhr can be faulted for not providing adequate models for the fusion of religion and public responsibility. Gandhi, according to some critics, went too far: as Ainslie Embree suggests, "Gandhi's use of a religious vocabulary—inevitably Hindu in origin"—may have exacerbated relations between Hindus and Muslims, and in any event his form of cultural politics cannot be transposed easily to the West.[11] Niebuhr may not have gone far enough: despite his appreciation of the values that religion provides, politically Niebuhr was the consummate secular liberal. His greatest fear was that nations would become too religious and become absorbed with their own illusions of power.[12] Niebuhr was deeply concerned about the destructive role that the "illusions" of religion and other moral ideals could play. "Illusion is dangerous," Niebuhr said, because it "encourages terrible fanaticisms." It must, therefore, "be brought under the control of reason."[13] Even so, Niebuhr cautioned against overreacting: keeping religion too far from political life can obscure the positive images of a perfected society that the religious imagination is capable of producing. "One can only hope," he added, "that reason will not destroy it before its work is done."[14]

More than seventy years after Niebuhr wrote those words, religion is not at the brink of being destroyed by reason. Yet it is possible that Niebuhr's dark vision has come to pass, and reason and religion have begun to war with one another on a global plane. Because there is ultimately no satisfactory ideological compromise between religious and secular views of the grounds for legitimizing public authority, mutual suspicion and sporadic violence have intensified into widespread hostility approaching the dismal climate of the old Cold War. One can foresee the emergence of a united religious bloc stretching from Southeast and Central Asia through the Middle East to North Africa. In this worst-case scenario, one can envision popular movements of jihadi rebellions toppling fragile governments (as one did in Somalia). Saudi Arabia and Egypt seem particularly vulnerable. One could imagine a wave of Islamic revolutions from Morocco to Indonesia, creating an arc of anti-American power dominating global politics. With an arsenal of nuclear weapons at its disposal and a youthful populace fueled by a hatred of the West and an American fear of Islam, it might well replace the old Soviet Union as a united global enemy of the secular West.

Such a conflict might be compounded by the rise of new religious radicals in Europe and the United States, including members of new immigrant communities whose religious pride is stoked by the anger of social marginalization. The Internet offers a whole new arena for networking and the illusion of involvement in an imagined war. Such connections can promote decentralized bands of activists engaged in acts of sabotage and terrorism in almost any part of the world. The new Cold War could truly be a global confrontation.

Barring this apocalyptic vision of a worldwide conflict between religious and secular nationalism, we have reason to be hopeful. It is equally likely that most religious activists—even those who share the same religious tradition—are incapable of uniting easily with one another. It is also clear that when they have positions of real political influence, they seek some kind of economic and political accommodation with the secular world. In this event, a grudging tolerance might develop between religious activists and secular nationalists. Under the best circumstances, each might be able to value what the other provides: communitarian values and moral vision on the one hand, individualism and rational rules of justice on the other. After all, both are responses to, and products of, the modern age.

In Sri Lanka, India, Iran, Egypt, Algeria, Afghanistan, Indonesia, Central Asia, China, Japan, the United States, Eastern and Western Europe, and all other places where groups of religious activists have rebelled against the secular state and experimented with forms of politics related in some way with religion, they have done far more than resuscitate archaic ideas of religious rule. They have created something new: a synthesis of religion and modern politics. In some cases this has led to a merger between the cultural identity and legitimacy of old religiously sanctioned monarchies and the democratic spirit and organizational unity of modern industrial society.

This combination can be incendiary, for it blends the absolutism of religion with the potency of modern politics. Yet it may also be necessary, for without the legitimacy conferred by religion, the authority of political order cannot easily be established in some parts of the world. In some of these places, even the essential elements of democracy have been conveyed in the vessels of new religious politics. In a curious way, at the same time that politics have embraced religious ideologies, religious values have buttressed some of the ideals of the modern state. The revival of tolerant forms of religion may therefore be a part of the cure for the excesses of its rebellious and intolerant extremes.

Notes

INTRODUCTION: THE RISE OF RELIGIOUS REBELLION

1. Interview with Sheik Muhammad al-Kubaisi, deputy secretary general, Association of Muslim Clerics, at the Mother of All Battles Mosque, Baghdad, May 5, 2004.

2. Interview with Dr. Muhammad Ibraheem el-Geyoushi, dean of faculty of Dawah [Preaching, or Call to Islam], Al Azhar University, in Cairo, May 30, 1990.

3. Interview with Rev. Michael Bray, Reformation Lutheran Church, Bowie, Maryland, March 20, 1998.

4. Francis Fukuyama, "The End of History," *The National Interest* 16 (Summer 1989): 3–18; and *The End of History and the Last Man* (New York: Free Press, 1992), xi–xxiii.

5. Quoted in Kim Murphy, "Islamic Militants Build Power Base in Sudan," *Los Angeles Times,* April 6, 1992, A9.

6. Editor's introduction to Conor Cruise O'Brien, "Holy War against India," *Atlantic Monthly* 262 (August 1988): 54.

7. Imam Abu Kheireiddine, quoted in Kim Murphy, "Islamic Party Wins Power in Algeria," *Los Angeles Times,* December 28, 1991, A1.

8. For an analysis of Bhindranwale's sermons, see Mark Juergensmeyer, "The Logic of Religious Violence," in David C. Rapoport, ed., *Inside Terrorist Organization* (London: Frank Cass, 1988), 172–93.

9. See Mark Juergensmeyer, "What the Bhikkhu Said: Reflections on the Rise of Militant Religious Nationalism," *Religion* 20, no. 1 (1990): 53–75.

10. Dru Gladney, *Muslim Chinese: Ethnic Nationalism in the People's Republic* (Cambridge, Mass.: Council on East Asian Studies, Harvard University, 1991), 113–15 and passim.

11. Umar F. Abdallah, *The Islamic Struggle in Syria* (Berkeley: Mizan Press, 1983), 23, quoted in Bruce B. Lawrence, *Defenders of God: The*

Fundamentalist Revolt against the Modern Age (San Francisco: Harper & Row, 1989), 96.

12. This objection to the comparative use of fundamentalism is also voiced by David Martin, "Fundamentalism: An Observational and Definitional *Tour d'Horizon*," *Political Quarterly* 61, no. 2 (April–June 1990): 129–31.

13. Lawrence, *Defenders of God,* 2. As an alternative *to fundamentalism* I once proposed *heretical modernism* because religious activists challenge the principles of secularism enshrined in the ideology of modernism (panel, "Does Fundamentalism Exist Outside of Christianity?", annual meeting of the American Academy of Religion, Kansas City, Missouri, November 25, 1991). John Hawley proposed the phrase *militant antimodern religious activism* before accepting the term *fundamentalism*. See his introduction to his edited volume *Fundamentalism and Gender* (New York: Oxford University Press, 1994). For a discussion of the issues, see my essay "Antifundamentalism," in Martin E. Marty and R. Scott Appleby, eds., *Fundamentalisms and the State* (Chicago: University of Chicago Press, 1995), 353–66.

14. Lawrence, *Defenders of God,* 27.

15. The literature on religion and modernity is rich and interesting. See, for instance, Talal Asad, *Formations of the Secular: Christianity, Islam, Modernity* (Stanford, Calif.: Stanford University Press, 2003); Peter Berger, ed., *The Desacralization of the World: Resurgent Religion and World Politics* (Grand Rapids, Mich.: Eerdman's, 1999); José Casanova, *Public Religions in the Modern World* (Chicago: University of Chicago Press, 1994); and Richard Madsen et al., *Meaning and Modernity: Religion, Polity, and Self* (Berkeley and Los Angeles: University of California Press, 2001).

16. Interview with Sheik Ahmed Yassin, leader, Hamas, in Gaza, January 14, 1989.

17. Similar definitions are given in other studies of nation building and nationalism. See, for instance, Anthony D. Smith's introduction to his edited study *Nationalist Movements* (New York: St. Martin's Press, 1977) 1–2; and Hugh Seton-Watson, *Nations and States: An Enquiry into the Origins of Nations and the Politics of Nationalism* (Boulder, Colo.: Westview Press, 1977), 1–5. In a similar vein, Anthony Giddens defines a *nation* as an entity with a political system that administers and has ultimate authority over a distinct territory, and *nationalism* as the subscription of individuals to "a set of symbols and beliefs emphasizing communality among the members of a political order." Anthony Giddens, *The Nation-State and Violence,* vol. 2 of *A Contemporary Critique of Historical Materialism* (Berkeley: University of California Press, 1985), 215–16.

18. Eric Hobsbawm explains that *nationalism* as a term emerged in the late nineteenth century, replacing *principle of nationality*. I use the term in this nineteenth-century sense, as the theoretical base on which the concept of a nation rests and with it, a sense of identity. Hobsbawm, however, refers to it in an even more subjective manner as the emotional identification of peoples with "their nation" and the ability to be "politically mobilized" under such a rubric. Eric J. Hobsbawm, *The Age of Empire, 1875–1914* (New York: Pantheon Books, 1987), 142. The *nation* he calls "the new civic religion of states" (149). What he calls *nationalism* I might call "extreme nationalism" or

xenophobia; what I call nationalism he might call "national identity" or "national ideology."

19. By *secular* I mean in this context principles or ideas that have no direct reference to a transcendent order of reality or a divine being. This concept will be discussed in chapter 1 of this book.

20. Interview with the Rev. Uduwawala Chandananda Thero, member of Karaka Sabha, Asgiri Chapter, Sinhalese Buddhist Sangha, in Kandy, Sri Lanka, February 2, 1988.

CHAPTER 1: THE RELIGIOUS CHALLENGE TO THE SECULAR STATE

1. Quoted in Kim Murphy, "Islamic Party Wins Power in Algeria," *Los Angeles Times,* December 28, 1991, A1. In February 1992, after the Islamic Party was crushed, an underground movement called the Faithful to the Promise vowed a jihad against the government that would be "in continuation" of Algeria's 1954 war for independence from France. Kim Murphy, "Algeria Cracks Down, Targets Islamic Front," *Los Angeles Times,* February 10, 1992, A10.

2. Hans Kohn, *Nationalism: Its Meaning and History* (Princeton: D. Van Nostrand, 1955), 89.

3. Ibid., 16.

4. Ibid.

5. Jawaharlal Nehru, *The Discovery of India* (New York: John Day, 1946), 531–32.

6. Donald Eugene Smith, *India as a Secular State* (Princeton: Princeton University Press, 1963), 140.

7. Ibid., 141 (italics in the original).

8. Nehru, *Discovery of India,* 531.

9. Kohn, *Nationalism,* 9 (italics supplied).

10. Ibid., 4.

11. Rupert Emerson, *From Empire to Nation: The Rise to Self-Assertion of Asian and African Peoples* (Boston: Beacon Press, 1960), 158.

12. Ibid.

13. Ibid., vii.

14. Giddens, *Nation-State,* 2:215–16.

15. Ibid., 2:4.

16. According to Joseph Strayer (*Medieval Statecraft and the Perspectives of History* [Princeton: Princeton University Press, 1971], 262–65), secular nationalism was promoted in thirteenth-century France and England in order to buttress the authority of secular rulers after the clergy had been removed from political power earlier in the century. In the fourteenth and fifteenth centuries, there was a reaction against central secular-national governments; the next great wave of laicization occurred in the sixteenth century.

17. Giddens, *Nation-State,* 4. The situation in India prior to the twentieth century was remarkably similar to that in pre-eighteenth-century Europe. See Ainslie T. Embree, "Frontiers into Boundaries: The Evolution of the Modern State," chap. 5 of *Imagining India: Essays on Indian History* (New Delhi and New York: Oxford University Press, 1989), 67–84.

18. Giddens, *Nation-State,* 25ff. This world economic pattern, which Immanuel Wallerstein calls the "modern world-system," has its roots in the sixteenth century. *The Modern World-System: Capitalist Agriculture and the Origins of the European World-Economy in the Sixteenth Century* (New York: Academic Press, 1974); and *The Modern World-System, 2: Mercantilism and the Consolidation of the European World-Economy, 1600–1750* (New York: Academic Press, 1980). For the importance of the economic market system in European nation building, see Sidney Pollard, *Peaceful Conquest: The Industrialization of Europe, 1760–1970* (New York: Oxford University Press, 1981).

19. Challenges to the divine right to rule in Europe reach back at least to the twelfth century, when John of Salisbury, who is sometimes regarded as the first modern political philosopher, held that rulers should be subject to charges of treason and could be overthrown—violently if necessary—if they violated their public trust. Along the same lines, William of Ockham, in the fourteenth century, argued that a "secular ruler need not submit to spiritual power." See Sidney R. Packard, *Twelfth-Century Europe: An Interpretive Essay* (Amherst: University of Massachusetts Press, 1973), 193–201; and Thomas Molnar, "The Medieval Beginnings of Political Secularization," in George W. Carey and James V. Schall, eds., *Essays on Christianity and Political Philosophy* (Lanham, Md.: University Press of America, 1985), 43.

20. Because humans are "equal and independent" before God, Locke argued, they have the sole right to exercise the power of the Law of Nature, and the only way in which an individual can be deprived of his or her liberty is "by agreeing with other Men to joyn and unite into a community, for their comfortable, safe, and peacable living one amongst another." John Locke, "Of the Beginnings of Political Societies," chap. 8 of *The Second Treatise on Government* (New York: Cambridge University Press, 1960), 375.

21. According to Rousseau, a *social contract* is a tacit admission by the people that they need to be ruled and an expression of their willingness to relinquish some of their rights and freedoms to the state in exchange for its administrative protection. It is an exchange of what Rousseau calls one's "natural liberty" for the security and justice provided through "civil liberty." Rousseau implied that the state does not need the church to grant it moral legitimacy: the people grant it a legitimacy on their own through a divine right that is directly invested in them as a part of the God-given natural order. Jean-Jacques Rousseau, "On the Civil State," chap. 8 of *The Social Contract* (New York: Pocket Books, 1967), 23.

22. Strayer, *Medieval Statecraft,* 323.

23. Although the churches supported a number of secular reforms in the nineteenth and twentieth centuries, religion in the West largely fit Whitehead's description: it was what "an individual does with his own solitariness." Alfred North Whitehead, *Religion in the Making,* reprinted in F. S. C. Northrup and Mason W. Gross, eds., *Alfred North Whitehead: An Anthology* (New York: Macmillan, 1961), 472.

24. Alexis de Tocqueville, *The Old Regime and the French Revolution,* translated by Stuart Gilbert (New York: Doubleday, Anchor Books, 1955), 11. See

also John McManners, *The French Revolution and the Church* (Westport, Conn.: Greenwood Press, 1969).

25. Ernst Cassirer, *The Philosophy of the Enlightenment* (Boston: Beacon Press, 1955), 171. Among the devotees of deism were Thomas Jefferson, Benjamin Franklin, and other founding fathers of the United States.

26. Robert Bellah, "Civil Religion in America," *Daedalus* 96, no. 1 (Winter 1967): 1–22.

27. Tocqueville, *The Old Régime,* 13.

28. Liberal politicians within the colonial governments were much more insistent on imparting notions of Western political order than were the conservatives. In the heyday of British control of India, for instance, the position of Whigs such as William Gladstone was that the presence of the British was "to promote the political training of our fellow-subjects," quoted in H. C. G. Matthew, *Gladstone, 1809–1874,* vol. 1 (Oxford: Clarendon Press, 1986), 188. Conservatives such as Benjamin Disraeli, however, felt that the British should "respect and maintain" the traditional practices of the colonies, including "the laws and customs, the property and religion." From a speech delivered after the Sepoy Rebellion in India in 1857, quoted in William Monypenny and George Buckle, *The Life of Disraeli,* 1: *1804–1859* (London: John Murton, 1929), 1488–89. In the end the liberal vision caught on, even among the educated Indian elite, and the notion of a British-style secular nationalism in India was born.

29. Not all missionary efforts were so despised however. The Anglicans were sometimes seen as partners in the West's civilizing role. Activist, evangelical missionaries were considered more of a threat.

30. Gerald Larson describes the relation between religion and nationalism as mutually destructive. According to him, the global system relies on autonomous nation-states that need religion for their legitimacy—as long as religion stays in its place. But as religion is drawn into the public arena, the debate over public values is opened up, and religion can then impose itself on political decisions. This "religionization" of politics is a blow to secular nationalism and calls into question the global nature of the nation-state system. Gerald Larson, "Fast Falls the Eventide: India's Anguish over Religion" (Paper presented at a conference, *Religion and Nationalism,* University of California, Santa Barbara, April 21, 1989).

31. Wilfred Cantwell Smith, *The Meaning and End of Religion* (New York: Macmillan, 1962).

32. Anderson, *Imagined Communities;* Smith, *The Meaning and End of Religion;* and Ninian Smart, *Worldviews: Crosscultural Explorations of Human Beliefs* (New York: Scribner's, 1983).

33. See Karl Marx and Friedrich Engels, *The German Ideology,* edited by R. Pascal (New York: International Publishers, 1939); and Karl Mannheim, *Ideology and Utopia* (New York: Harcourt, Brace & World, 1936). For a discussion of the contemporary meaning of ideology, see David Apter, ed., *Ideology and Discontent* (New York: Free Press, 1964); and Chaim I. Waxman, ed., *The End of Ideology Debate* (New York: Simon & Schuster, 1964).

34. Richard H. Cox, *Ideology, Politics, and Political Theory* (Belmont, Calif.: Wadsworth, 1969).

35. Quoted in Cox, *Ideology,* 17.

36. Anthony Giddens, *Central Problems in Social Theory: Action, Structure and Contradiction in Social Analysis* (Berkeley: University of California Press, 1979), 184.

37. Clifford Geertz, "Ideology as a Cultural System," in David Apter, ed., *Ideology and Discontent* (New York: Free Press, 1964).

38. Karl Deutsch, *Nationalism and Social Communication* (Cambridge, Mass.: MIT Press, 1966).

39. Ernest Gellner, *Nations and Nationalism* (Oxford: Basil Blackwell, 1983), 140.

40. Anthony D. Smith, *Nationalism in the Twentieth Century* (Oxford: Martin Robertson, 1979), 3. See also L. Doob, *Patriotism and Nationalism* (New Haven: Yale University Press, 1964).

41. Max Weber, "Politics as a Vocation," in Hans H. Gerth and C. Wright Mills, eds., *From Max Weber: Essays in Sociology* (New York: Oxford University Press, 1946), 78. Regarding the state's monopoly on violence, see John Breuilly, *Nationalism and the State* (Manchester: Manchester University Press, 1982); and Anthony D. Smith, *Theories of Nationalism* (London: Duckworth, 1971).

42. Giddens, *Nation-State,* 219.

43. Lawrence (*Defenders of God,* 90–101), for example, describes fundamentalism as a "religious ideology" that emphasizes the maintenance of traditional values.

44. The notion of religion as a conceptual mechanism that brings order to the disorderly areas of life is a theme of such structuralists as Claude Lévi-Strauss and Mary Douglas, and the adherents of René Girard's mimetic theory. For mimetic theory, see Jean-Pierre Dupuy, *Ordres et désordres: Enquêtes sur un nouveau paradigme* (Paris: Éditions du Seuil, 1982); and Paisley Livingston, ed., *Disorder and Order: Proceedings of the Stanford International Symposium (Sept. 14–16, 1981),* Stanford Literature Studies 1 (Saratoga, Calif.: Anma Libri, 1984).

45. Geertz defines religion as "a system of symbols which acts to establish powerful, pervasive and long-lasting moods and motivations in men by formulating conceptions of a general order of existence and clothing these conceptions with such an aura of factuality that the moods and motivations seem uniquely realistic." "Religion as a Cultural System," reprinted in William A. Lessa and Evon Z. Vogt, eds., *Reader in Comparative Religion: An Anthropological Approach,* 3d ed. (New York: Harper & Row, 1972), 168.

46. Robert N. Bellah, "Transcendence in Contemporary Piety," in Donald R. Cutler, *The Religious Situation: 1969* (Boston: Beacon Press, 1969), 907.

47. Peter Berger, *The Heretical Imperative* (New York: Doubleday, 1980), 38. See also Peter Berger, *The Sacred Canopy: Elements of a Sociological Theory of Religion* (Garden City, N.Y.: Doubleday, 1967).

48. Louis Dupré, *Transcendent Selfhood: The Loss and Rediscovery of the Inner Life* (New York: Seabury Press, 1976), 26. For a discussion of Berger's and Dupré's definitions, see Mary Douglas, "The Effects of Modernization on Religious Change," *Daedalus* 111, no. 1 (Winter 1982): 1–19.

49. Durkheim describes the dichotomy between the sacred and the profane in religion in the following way: "In all the history of human thought there exists no other example of two categories of things so profoundly differentiated or so radically opposed to one another. . . . The sacred and the profane have always and everywhere been conceived by the human mind as two distinct classes, as two worlds between which there is nothing in common. . . . In different religions, this opposition has been conceived in different ways." Émile Durkheim, *The Elementary Forms of the Religious Life,* translated by Joseph Ward Swain (1915; reprint, London: Allen & Unwin, 1976), 38–39.

50. Although I use the term *religion* (as in "the Christian religion"), in general I agree with Smith, who suggested some years ago that the noun *religion* might well be banished from our vocabulary because it implies a thing—a codified structure of beliefs and practices. He suggested that we restrict ourselves to using the adjective *religious.* Smith, *The Meaning and End of Religion,* 119–53.

51. Weber, "Politics as a Vocation," 78.

52. Stanley J. Tambiah, *World Conqueror and World Renouncer: A Study of Buddhism and Polity in Thailand against a Historical Background* (Cambridge: Cambridge University Press, 1976). For a useful overview of Theravada society, see Donald K. Swearer, *Buddhism and Society in Southeast Asia* (Chambersburg, Pa.: Anima Books, 1981). For the role of monks in Thai politics, see Somboon Suksamran, *Buddhism and Politics in Thailand: A Study of Socio-political Change and Political Activism of the Thai Sangha* (Singapore: Institute of Southeast Asian Studies, 1982); and Charles F. Keyes, *Thailand: Buddhist Kingdom as Modern Nation-State* (Boulder, Colo.: Westview Press, 1987).

53. For the background of religious nationalism in Burma (Myanmar), see Donald Eugene Smith, ed., *Religion and Politics in Burma* (Princeton: Princeton University Press, 1965); E. Sarkisyanz, *Buddhist Backgrounds of the Burmese Revolution* (The Hague: Martinus Nijhoff, 1965); and Heinz Bechert, "Buddhism and Mass Politics in Burma and Ceylon," in Donald Eugene Smith, ed., *Religion and Political Modernization* (New Haven: Yale University Press, 1974), 147–67. For a somewhat opposing point of view—that there is relatively little Buddhist influence on Burmese nationalism—see the chapter on Burma in Fred R. von der Mehden, *Religion and Nationalism in Southeast Asia: Burma, Indonesia, the Philippines* (Madison: University of Wisconsin Press, 1963), and "Secularization of Buddhist Polities: Burma and Thailand" in Smith, *Religion and Political Modernization,* 49–66.

54. Donald Eugene Smith, ed., *Religion, Politics, and Social Change in the Third World: A Sourcebook* (New York: Free Press, 1971), 11.

55. See Walter H. Capps, *The New Religious Right: Piety, Patriotism, and Politics* (Columbia: University of South Carolina Press, 1990); Randall Balmer, *Mine Eyes Have Seen the Glory: A Journey into the Evangelical Subculture in America* (New York: Oxford University Press, 1989); and Lawrence, *Defenders of God.*

56. Arlie J. Hoover, *The Gospel of Nationalism: German Patriotic Preaching from Napoleon to Versailles* (Stuttgart: Franz Steiner Verlag, 1986), 3.

57. Carlton J. H. Hayes, *Nationalism: A Religion* (New York: Macmillan, 1960).

58. Talal Asad, *Formations of the Secular: Christianity, Islam, Modernity* (Palo Alto, Calif.: Stanford University Press, 2003).

59. Ninian Smart, "Religion, Myth, and Nationalism," in Peter H. Merkl and Ninian Smart, eds., *Religion and Politics in the Modern World* (New York: New York University Press, 1983), 27. For another comparison of nationalism and religion, see Hoover, *Gospel of Nationalism*, 3–4.

60. Benedict Anderson, *Imagined Communities: Reflections on the Origin and Spread of Nationalism* (London: Verso, 1983), 18.

61. W. Howard Wriggins, *Ceylon: Dilemmas of a New Nation* (Princeton: Princeton University Press, 1960), 169.

62. Arend Theodor van Leeuwen, *Christianity in World History: The Meeting of the Faiths of East and West,* translated by H. H. Hoskins (New York: Scribner's, 1964), 331.

63. Ibid., 332.

64. Ibid., 334.

65. Ibid., 331.

66. Ibid., 333.

67. Ibid., 418.

68. Ibid., 333.

69. Ibid.

70. Robert N. Bellah, "Civil Religion in America," *Daedalus* 96, no. 1 (Winter 1967): 1–21, reprinted in Robert N. Bellah, *Beyond Belief* (New York: Harper & Row, 1970).

71. Jaroslav Krejci, "What Is a Nation?" in Peter Merkl and Ninian Smart, eds., *Religion and Politics in the Modern World* (New York: New York University Press, 1983), 39.

72. Ibid.

73. Interview with Leila el-Hamamsy, director, Social Research Center, American University in Cairo, in Cairo, January 10, 1989.

74. Interview with Saad Ibrahim, professor of sociology, American University in Cairo, in Cairo, January 10, 1989.

75. See Smith, *India as a Secular State,* which details the many concessions the government has made.

76. Ainslie T. Embree, *Utopias in Conflict: Religion and Nationalism in Modern India* (Berkeley: University of California Press, 1990), 88.

77. Abolhassan Bani-Sadr, *The Fundamental Principles and Precepts of Islamic Government,* translated by Mohammed R. Ghanoonparvar (Lexington, Ky.: Mazda Publishers, 1981), 40.

78. Interview with Essam el-Arian, medical doctor, member of the National Assembly, and member of the Muslim Brotherhood, in Cairo, January 11, 1989.

79. Interview with Ibrahim Dasuqi Shitta, professor of Persian literature, Cairo University, in Cairo, January 10, 1989.

80. Ibid.

81. To some, including Ibrahim Shitta, *Christendom* and *Western civilization* are interchangeable terms.

82. Samuel Huntington, "The Clash of Civilizations?" *Foreign Affairs,* Summer 1993, 22–49. The essay was revised, expanded, and published as a book,

The Clash of Civilizations and the Remaking of World Order (New York: Simon and Schuster, 1996).

83. The terms *Westomania* and *West-toxification* (and also sometimes *Occidentosis*) are translations of the Farsi word *gharbzadegi,* coined by Jalal Al-e Ahmad. It is discussed in Michael C. Hillmann's introduction to Jalal Al-e Ahmad, *The School Principal,* translated by John K. Newton (Minneapolis: Bibliotheca Islamica), 1974.

84. Imam [Ayatollah] Khomeini, "Anniversary of the Uprising of Khurdad 15," in Khomeini, *Islam and Revolution: Writings and Declarations,* translated and annotated by Hamid Algar (Berkeley: Mizan Press, 1981; London: Routledge & Kegan Paul, 1985), 270.

85. Interview with Uduwawala Chandananda Thero, in Kandy, Sri Lanka, February 2, 1988.

86. Bani-Sadr, *Fundamental Principles and Precepts of Islamic Government,* 40.

87. Interview with Rabbi Meir Kahane, former member, Knesset, and leader, Kach Party, in Jerusalem, January 18, 1989; and an article by an anonymous author in the pamphlet *Islam and Palestine,* Leaflet 5 (Limassol, Cyprus, June 1988).

88. Bernard Lewis, *The Political Language of Islam* (Chicago: University of Chicago Press, 1988), 3.

89. Ibid.

90. Interview with Yoel Lerner, director, Sanhedrin Institute, in Jerusalem, January 20, 1989.

91. Interview with Sheik Yassin, Gaza, January 14, 1989.

92. *Islam and Palestine.* The meaning of this term was pointed out to me by Dr. Ifrah Zilberman, research scholar, Hebrew University, in Jerusalem, May 25, 1990.

93. Interview with Uduwawala Chandananda Thero, Kandy, Sri Lanka, February 2, 1988.

94. Ibid.

95. Ibid.

96. Quoted from comments of leaders of Egypt's Islamic Labor Party in Gehad Auda, "An Uncertain Response: The Islamic Movement in Egypt," in James P. Piscatori, ed., *Islamic Fundamentalisms and the Gulf Crisis* (Chicago: Fundamentalism Project, American Academy of Arts and Sciences, 1991), 116. The Muslim Brotherhood and Islamic Jama'at voiced similar suspicions about U.S. intentions in the Gulf War. Ibid., 119–20.

97. Hamas communiqué, January 22, 1991, quoted in Jean-François Legrain, "A Defining Moment: Palestinian Islamic Fundamentalism," in Piscatori, *Islamic Fundamentalisms,* 76.

98. Ayatollah Sayyed Ruhollah Mousavi Khomeini, *Collection of Speeches, Position Statements,* translated from "Najaf Min watha'iq al-Imam al-Khomeyni did al-Quwa al Imbiriyaliyah wa al-Sahyuniyah wa al-Raj'iyah" ("From the Papers of Imam Khomeyni against Imperialist, Zionist, and Reactionist Powers"), 1977, Translations on Near East and North Africa 1902 (Arlington, Va.: Joint Publications Research Service, 1979), 3.

99. Khomeini, *Islam and Revolution,* 28.

100. I explore further this process of satanization in my *Terror in the Mind of God* (Berkeley: University of California Press, 2003), 174–89.

101. Interview with el-Arian, January 11, 1989.

102. Interview with Uduwawala Chandananda Thero, Kandy, Sri Lanka, February 2, 1988.

103. Interview with Kahane, Jerusalem, January 18, 1989. A similar remark was made by Rabbi Moshe Levinger, a leader of Gush Emunim, in my interview with him in Jerusalem, January 16, 1989.

104. Interview with Levinger, Jerusalem, January 16, 1989.

105. Jürgen Habermas, *Legitimation Crisis,* translated by Thomas McCarthy (Boston: Beacon Press, 1975), passim.

106. D. C. Vejayavardhana, *The Revolt in the Temple: Composed to Commemorate 2,500 Years of the Land, the Race, and the Faith* (Colombo: Sinha Publications, 1953), reprinted in Donald Eugene Smith, *Religion, Politics and Social Change in the Third World: A Sourcebook* (New York: Free Press, 1971), 105.

107. Ibid.

108. Giddens, *Nation-State,* 71. Giddens goes on to deny that most religions outside the West have much to do with day-to-day morality and the social order (73). He seems unaware, however, of the importance of such ethical and social notions as *dharma* in Hindu tradition, *shari'a* in Islam, and *li* in China.

109. Interview with Abdullah Schleiffer, director, Communications Center, American University in Cairo, in Cairo, January 7, 1989.

110. Lewis, *Political Language of Islam.* In a large nation-state such as China, it is "the nation-state apparatus itself" to which minority ethnic groups find themselves in opposition (Gladney, *Muslim Chinese,* 81). When an ethnic group is in the majority, however, it more easily accepts the nation-state.

CHAPTER 2: THE FRONT LINE OF RELIGIOUS REBELLION: THE MIDDLE EAST

1. See Michael Walzer, *The Revolution of the Saints: A Study in the Origins of Radical Politics* (New York: Atheneum, 1974).

2. A stasis-disequilibrium model of society is presumed in the models of revolution developed by social scientists in the 1950s and 1960s. See, for example, Crane Brinton, *The Anatomy of Revolution,* rev. ed. (New York: Random House, Vintage Books, 1957), 16–17; and Chalmers Johnson, *Revolutionary Change* (Boston: Little, Brown, 1966), *passim.* Hannah Arendt (On *Revolution* [New York: Viking Press, 1963], 36) maintains a different view of revolutions, arguing that they must always be "something new," aiming at "freedom." She concludes that revolutions are always, therefore, secular.

3. Gary Sick, *All Fall Down: America's Tragic Encounter with Iran,* rev. ed. (New York: Penguin, 1986), 187.

4. I saw this picture in the home of Sheik Ahmed Yassin in Gaza, January 14, 1989.

5. Kalim Siddiqui, "Nation-States as Obstacles to the Total Transformation of the *Ummah,*" in M. Ghayasuddin, ed., *The Impact of Nationalism on the Muslim World* (London: Open Press, Al-Hoda, 1986), 1.

6. Ira M. Lapidus, A *History of Islamic Societies* (Cambridge: Cambridge University Press, 1988), 887.

7. Siddiqui, "Nation-States as Obstacles," 11.

8. Ibid., 6.

9. Some observers maintain that the Gulf War was the final nail in the coffin of the pan-Arab movement. See Auda, "An Uncertain Response," 122.

10. Nejla Sammakia, "Egypt's No. 2 Man Slain by Assassins," *San Francisco Examiner*, October 13, 1990, national edition, A16.

11. For the rise of the Muslim Brotherhood in Egypt, see Charles Wendell, trans., *Five Tracts of Hasan al-Banna (1906–1949)* (Berkeley: University of California Press, 1978), 40–68, 133–62; Bernard Lewis, "The Return of Islam," in Michael Curtis, ed., *Religion and Politics in the Middle East* (Boulder, Colo.: Westview Press, 1981), 14–16, 55–67, 77–128; Richard P. Mitchell, *The Society of the Muslim Brothers* (London: Oxford University Press, 1969); and Emmanuel Sivan, *Radical Islam: Medieval Theology and Modern Politics* (New Haven: Yale University Press, 1985).

12. Interview with Ibrahim, Cairo, January 10, 1989.

13. Faraj's tract was also published in *Al-Ahrar*, an Egyptian newspaper, on December 14, 1981. An English translation, accompanied by an extensive essay about the document, is in Johannes J. G. Jansen, *The Neglected Duty: The Creed of Sadat's Assassins and Islamic Resurgence in the Middle East* (New York: Macmillan, 1986). I have also found helpful the analysis of this document by David Rapoport in "Sacred Terror: A Case from Islam" (paper delivered at the annual meeting of the American Political Science Association, Washington, D.C., September 1–4, 1988). Its political implications are discussed in Mohammed Heikal, *Autumn of Fury: The Assassination of Sadat* (London: André Deutsch, 1983).

14. Faraj, para. 84, in Jansen, *Neglected Duty*, 199.

15. In the description often given by Sunni theologians, jihad in a military sense is allowed only for defense of Islam when it is under direct assault. See Rudolph Peters, *Islam and Colonialism: The Doctrine of Jihad in Modern History* (The Hague: Mouton, 1979), 121–35; David Cook, *Understanding Jihad* (Berkeley: University of California Press, 2005); and Michael Bonner, *Jihad in Islamic History* (Princeton: Princeton University Press, 2006).

16. Faraj, paras. 102 and 109, in Jansen, *Neglected Duty*, 210–11.

17. Faraj, para. 113, in Jansen, *Neglected Duty*, 212–13.

18. According to an Egyptian scholar who interviewed imprisoned members of the group responsible for Sadat's assassination, the writings of Maududi were "important in shaping the group's ideas." Saad Eddin Ibrahim "Islamic Militancy as a Social Movement: The Case of Two Groups in Egypt," in Ali E. Hillal, Dessouki, ed. *Islamic Resurgence in the Arab World* (New York: Praeger, 1982), 125.

19. For a discussion of the significance of Sayyid Qutb's life and work, see Richard C. Martin, "Religious Violence in Islam: Towards an Understanding of the Discourse on *Jihad* in Modern Egypt," in Paul Wilkinson and A. M. Stewart eds., *Contemporary Research on Terrorism* (Aberdeen: Aberdeen University Press, 1987), 54–71; Gilles Kepel, *Muslim Extremism in Egypt: The Prophet and*

Pharaoh (Berkeley: University of California Press, 1986), 36–69; Yvonne V. Haddad, "Sayyid Qutb: Ideologue of Islamic Revival," in John L. Esposito, ed., *Voices of Resurgent Islam* (NewYork: Oxford University Press, 1983); and Ronald L. Nettler, *Past Trials and Present Tribulations: A Muslim Fundamentalist's View of the Jews* (New York: Pergamon Press, 1987).

20. Qutb studied in Washington, D.C., and California from 1949 to 1951. Haddad, "Sayyid Qutb," 69.

21. Sayyid Qutb, *This Religion of Islam (Hadha 'd-Din),* translated by Islamdust (Palo Alto, Calif.: Al-Manar Press, 1967), 87.

22. Interview with A. K. Ashur, dean of the faculty of education, Al-Azhar University, in Cairo, May 27, 1990.

23. Ibid.

24. These points are summarized in Marius Deeb, "Egypt," in Stuart Mews, ed. *Religion in Politics: A World Guide* (London: Longman, 1989), 64.

25. Initially the Muslim Brotherhood condemned Iraq for invading Kuwait; when the United States became involved, it shifted its condemnation to the United States. This confusion "induced deep ideological and behavioral uncertainty in its ranks." Auda, "An Uncertain Response."

26. Shahrough Akhavi, "The Impact of the Iranian Revolution on Egypt," in John L, Esposito, ed., *The Iranian Revolution: Its Global Impact* (Miami: Florida International University Press, 1990), 138. For a comprehensive analysis of the separation between Sunni and Shi'a radical groups, see Sivan, "Sunni Radicalism."

27. Interview with el-Arian, Cairo, January 11, 1989.

28. The Iranian revolution is described as an example of the worldwide development of Islamic political consciousness in articles in the Egyptian Muslim political journal *Al-Hilal,* July 1987, translated into French and summarized in *Revue de la presse égyptienne,* no. 27 (1987).

29. Shaul Bakhash, for example (*The Reign of the Ayatollahs: Iran and the Islamic Revolution* [New York: Basic Books, 1984], 4), implies that the Iranian revolution provides a roadmap for Muslim radicals in Egypt and elsewhere.

30. Interview with Ayatollah Khomeini by Hamid Algar on December 29, 1978, at Neauphle-le-Chateau, France, in Khomeini, *Islam and Revolution,* 323.

31. Ibid.

32. Lewis, *Political Language of Islam,* 2.

33. Ayatollah Ruhullah Khomeini, "Muharram: The Triumph of Blood over the Sword," in Khomeini, *Islam and Revolution,* 242. For a general assessment of Khomeini's politicization of Ashura, see Emmanuel Sivan, "Sunni Radicalism in the Middle East and the Iranian Revolution," *International Journal for Middle East Studies* 21 (1989): 16–17.

34. Sivan, "Sunni Radicalism," 8–11 and 29 n.11.

35. Hamid Algar, foreword to Khomeini, *Islam and Revolution,* 10.

36. Quoted in Sivan, "Sunni Radicalism," 12.

37. A. Ali-Babai, "An Open Letter to Khomeini, *Iranshahr,* June 15–July 16, 1982, quoted in Ervand Abrahamian, *Radical Islam: The Iranian Mojahedin* (London: I. B. Tauris, 1989), 19.

38. Khomeini, *Islam and Revolution,* 334.

39. Ibid., 335.

40. For the U.S. State Department's perspective on the crisis, see the revealing study by Sick, *All Fall Down.*

41. Ibid., 229–30.

42. The early years of the revolution and the mullahs' ascension to power are chronicled Bakhash, *The Reign of the Ayatollahs.*

43. Supporters of the moderate Islamic revolutionary movement, the Mojahedin, were especially targeted for repression because of the considerable power and popularity they had gained after the revolution. See Abrahamian, *Radical Islam.*

44. Said Amir Arjomand, "A Victory for the Pragmatists: The Islamic Fundamentalist Reaction in Iran," in James P. Piscatori, ed., *Islamic Fundamentalisms and the Gulf Crisis* (Chicago: Fundamentalism Project, American Academy of Arts and Sciences, 1991), 52.

45. Nick B. Williams Jr., "Iran's Rafsanjani, Guarding His Political Flanks, Steers a More Militant Course," *Los Angeles Times,* January 13, 1992.

46. Robin Wright, "Iran Extends Reach of Its Aid to Islamic Groups," *Los Angeles Times,* April 6, 1993.

47. For interesting accounts of life in postrevolutionary Iran, see Robin Wright, *In the Name of God: The Khomeini Decade* (New York: Simon & Schuster, 1989); John Simpson, *Inside Iran: Life under Khomeini's Regime* (New York: St. Martin's Press, 1988); and Roy P. Mottahedeh, *The Mantle of the Prophet* (New York: Pantheon, 1986).

48. For the theological history of the concept, see Abdulaziz Abdul-Hussein Sachedina, *The Just Ruler (al-sultan al-'adil) in Shi'ite Islam: The Comprehensive Authority of the Jurist in Imamite Jurisprudence* (New York: Oxford University Press, 1988).

49. Khomeini, *Islam and Revolution,* 342.

50. Ibid., 343.

51. Akhavi, "Impact of the Iranian Revolution," 144.

52. Interview with Kahane, Jerusalem, January 18, 1989.

53. Ibid. See also an interview with Kahane published in Raphael Mergui and Philippe Simonnot, *Israel's Ayatollahs: Meir Kahane and the Far Right in Israel* (London: Saqi Books, 1987), 40–41.

54. Carl E. Schorske, *Fin-de-Siècle Vienna: Politics and Culture* (New York: Knopf, 1980), 165.

55. The best analysis of the new religious politics in Israel may be found in Ehud Sprinzak, *The Ascendance of Israel's Radical Right* (New York: Oxford University Press, 1991). See also Ian S. Lustick, *For the Land and the Lord: Jewish Fundamentalism in Israel* (New York: Council on Foreign Relations, 1989).

56. Alter B. Z. Metzger, *Rabbi Kook's Philosophy of Repentance: A Translation of "Orot Ha-Teshuvah,"* Studies in Torah Judaism 11 (New York: Yeshiva University Press, 1968), 111. See also Jacob B. Agus, *Banner of Jerusalem: The Life, Times, and Thought of Rabbi Abraham Isaac Kuk* (New York: Bloch, 1946).

57. There have been several biographies of Kahane, including Robert Friedman, *The False Prophet: Rabbi Meir Kahane—From FBI Informant to Knesset Member* (London: Faber & Faber, 1990). For a comprehensive study of the religious right in Israel that puts Kahane's movement in context, see Sprinzak, *The Ascendance of Israel's Radical Right.*

58. Quoted in John Kifner's obituary of Kahane, "A Militant Leader, Fiery Politician and Founder of Anti-Arab Crusade," *New York Times,* November 7, 1990.

59. H. K. Michael Eitan's speech to the Knesset Rules Committee in 1984, quoted in Gerald Cromer, *The Debate about Kahanism in Israeli Society, 1984–1988,* Occasional Papers 3 (New York: Henry Frank Guggenheim Foundation, 1988), 37–38.

60. Yair Kotler, *Heil Kahane* (New York: Adama Books, 1986).

61. Interview with Kahane, Jerusalem, January 18, 1989.

62. According to Sprinzak (*The Ascendance of Israel's Radical Right,* 225), Kahane did not make the usual nationalist argument that the Jews deserved the land because it was their ancient birthplace; rather, the Jews "*expropriated* it in the name of God and his sovereign will" (italics in the original).

63. Kahane made this point during a function proclaiming a new state of Judea—one that would be established on the West Bank if and when the Israeli army retreated from those areas (from my notes taken at the event in Jerusalem, January 18, 1989).

64. Interview with Kahane, Jerusalem, January 18, 1989. See also similar comments made by Kahane in the interview published in Mergui and Simonnot, *Israel's Ayatollahs,* 43, 44, 68, 76–77, 150.

65. Sprinzak, *The Ascendance of Israel's Political Right,* 220.

66. Interview with Levinger, Jerusalem, January 16, 1989.

67. See Ehud Sprinzak, "Fundamentalism, Terrorism, and Democracy: The Case of Gush Emunim Underground" (Colloquium paper given at the Woodrow Wilson International Center for Scholars, Washington, D.C., September 16, 1986), published in revised and expanded form as "From Messianic Pioneering to Vigilante Terrorism: The Case of Gush Emunim Underground," *Journal of Strategic Studies* 10, no. 4 (December 1987): 194–216 (a special issue titled "Inside Terrorist Organizations," edited by David C. Rapoport) and reissued as a book: David C. Rapoport, ed., *Inside Terrorist Organizations* (New York: Columbia University Press, 1988).

68. The idea that the rebuilding of the Temple will be a part of the messianic age is a common theme in Jewish history. See, for example, George W. Buchanan, *Revelation and Redemption: Jewish Documents of Deliverance from the Fall of Jerusalem to the Death of Nahmanides* (Dillsboro: Western North Carolina Press, 1978); and Jonathan Frankel, ed., *Jews and Messianism in the Modern Era: Metaphor and Meaning,* Studies in Contemporary Jewry 7 (New York: Oxford University Press, and Jerusalem: Institute of Contemporary Jewry, Hebrew University of Jerusalem, 1991), 197–213 and 34–67. I am grateful to Richard Hecht of the University of California, Santa Barbara, for bringing to my attention these and other references on Jewish nationalism.

69. Interview with Lerner, Jerusalem, January 20, 1989.

70. Interview with Gershom Salomon, head, Faithful of Temple Mount, in Jerusalem, May 25, 1990.

71. I am grateful to Prof. Hecht for pointing out that the calendar has long been a critical element in clashes between Jews and Muslims at Temple Mount and that conflicts between groups of religious nationalists often involve a skirmish over sacred space. See also Bernard Wasserstein, "Patterns of Communal Conflict in Palestine," in Ada Rapoport and Steven J. Zipperstein, eds., *Jewish History: Essays in Honour of Chimen Abramsky* (London: Peter Halban, 1988), 611–28.

72. Although the American television news reports routinely described the incident as unprovoked rock-throwing by Palestinians aimed at Jewish worshipers gathered at the Western Wall (directly below the scene of the clash in the Temple Mount area), a fairly full and accurate report of the incident, including the provocation by Salomon and his group, may be found in the October 9, 1990, editions of the *New York Times,* the *Los Angeles Times,* and the *Washington Post.* One of the most complete accounts is Jackson Diehl, "The Battle at Temple Mount: Neither Palestinian nor Israeli Version Tells Full Story," *Washington Post,* October 14, 1990, A1, A23; and "Special File: The Haram al-Sharif (Temple Mount) Killings," *Journal of Palestine Studies* 20, no. 2 (Winter 1991): 134–59.

73. John Kifner, "Suspect in Kahane Case Is Muslim Born in Egypt," *New York Times,* November 7, 1990, B13.

74. "The Legacy of Hate," *New York Times,* November 7, 1990, A30.

75. Interview with Yochay Ron, Kiryat Arba settlement, Hebron, August 18, 1995.

76. Interview with Leah Rabin, Tel Aviv, March 2, 1998.

77. Yitzhak Rabin, quoted in Serge Schmemann, "Rabin Assassinated in Jerusalem," *New York Times,* November 5, 1995, 1.

78. Yigal Amir, quoted in Joel Greenberg, "Rabin's Assassin," *New York Times,* November 5, 1995, A1.

79. Schmemann, "Rabin Assassinated in Jerusalem," *New York Times,* November 11, 1995, A1.

80. See the essay by Elie Rekhess, "The Iranian Impact on the Islamic Jihad Movement in the Gaza Strip," in David Menashri, ed., *The Iranian Revolution and the Muslim World* (Boulder, Colo.: Westview Press, 1990). An excerpt from this article, under the title "The Growth of Khomeinism in Gaza," was published in the *Jerusalem Post Magazine,* January 26, 1991, 12.

81. Legrain, "Defining Moment," 72.

82. Interview with Sheik Yassin, Gaza, January 14, 1989.

83. Ibid.

84. Ibid.

85. Though they feared the power of Hamas, many leaders of the PLO coalition have used the ideology of Islam to their own advantage. See, for instance, Matti Steinberg, "The PLO and Palestinian Islamic Fundamentalism," *Jewish Quarterly* 52 (Fall 1989): 37–54.

86. Interview with Fathi Arafat, president, Palestine Red Crescent Society, Cairo, May 30, 1990.

87. Ibid.

88. Though a poll conducted in 1991 claimed that Hamas was supported by only 18 percent of the residents in Gaza, Hamas leaders described it as "nonsense" and claimed 60 percent support in Gaza and 50 percent on the West Bank. "Surveys Show Support for Moslem Hardliners Weaker Than Believed," *Mideast Mirror,* May 7, 1991, 3.

89. Interview with Saleh Zamlot, student leader, Fatah, Palestine Liberation Organization, at Al-Azhar University, Cairo, May 27, 1990.

90. Interview with Sheik Yassin, Gaza, January 14, 1989.

91. See Jean-François Legrain, "Islamistes et lutte nationale palestinienne dans les territoires occupés par Israel," *Revue française de science politique* 36, no. 2 (April 1986): 227–47; and Ifrah Zilberman, "Hamas: Apocalypse Now," *Jerusalem Post Weekly,* January 12, 1991, 11. Book-length studies include Shaul Mishal and Avraham Sela, *The Palestinian Hamas: Vision, Violence, and Coexistence* (New York: Columbia University Press, 2006); and Zaki Chehab, *Inside Hamas* (New York: Nation Books, 2007).

92. Jean-François Legrain, "The Islamic Movement and the *Intifada,*" in Jamal R. Nassar and Roger Heacock, eds., *Intifada: Palestine at the Crossroads* (New York: Praeger, 1990), 177, and "Defining Moment," 72–73. Legrain identifies Fathi Shqaqi, a pharmacist from Rafah, as the military commander of the Islamic Jihad and 'Odeh as the movement's spiritual leader.

93. Legrain, "Islamic Movement," 177.

94. Ibid.

95. Ibid., 176. I am grateful to Ifrah Zilberman of Jerusalem for showing me a number of copies of *Islam and Palestine,* which he has in his possession.

96. Legrain, "Islamic Movement," 182.

97. Quoted in ibid.

98. Ibid., 183.

99. Reuven Paz, *Ha-'imna ha-islamit umichma'utah 'iyyon rechoni utargum* (The Covenant of the Islamicists and Its Significance—Analysis and Translation) (Tel Aviv: Dayan Center, Tel Aviv University, 1988).

100. These rumors were reported to me by Dr. Ifrah Zilberman, research scholar, Hebrew University, in my interview with him (Jerusalem, May 25, 1990). See also Legrain, "Islamic Movement," 185. During the first months of 1989 Sheik Yassin was allowed to talk to journalists and foreigners, including myself.

101. This ritual, in which the young men were required to sleep beside the Dome of the Rock all night, was described in the newspaper *Al-Sabil,* April 1989.

102. Communiqué no. 66, October 31, 1990, quoted in Legrain, "Defining Moment," 83.

103. "Israelis Round Up Palestinians in Hunt for Killers," *New York Times,* December 16, 1990, international edition. This article quoted an Israeli army spokesman describing Palestinian estimates of the numbers of those arrested as "terribly exaggerated."

104. Ibid.

105. In the year before the Gulf War, Kuwait gave $60 million to Hamas and only $27 million to the PLO. Legrain, "Defining Moment," 79.

106. See "Three Hurt in Muslim-PLO Clash as Internal Feud Turns Violent," *Los Angeles Times,* June 3, 1991, A10. Clashes between Hamas and Fateh occurred in the Jabalya refugee camp in Gaza and in Nablus on the West Bank. At the same time, Hamas began to require women in Gaza to wear the Muslim head scarf *(hijab).*

107. Joel Brinkley, "A West Bank Business Chamber Votes for Islamic Fundamentalists," *New York Times,* June 20, 1991, international edition, A10.

108. Daniel Williams, "Arab Revolt: From Rocks to Revenge," *Los Angeles Times,* May 5, 1992, H4.

109. Daniel Williams, "The Quiet Palestinian," *Los Angeles Times Magazine,* June 7, 1992, 53.

110. Interview with 'Odeh printed in *Islam and Palestine,* Leaflet 5 (Limasol, Cyprus, June 1988).

111. Interview with Sheik Yassin, Gaza, January 14, 1989.

112. Interview with Abdul Aziz Rantisi, leader of the political wing of the Hamas movement, Khan Yunis, Gaza, March 1, 1998.

113. Ibid.

114. Ibid.

115. Ibid.

116. Ibid.

117. Interview with Muhammad al-Kubaisi, Association of Muslim Clerics, in Baghdad, May 6, 2004.

118. Jeffrey Gettleman, "Enraged Mob in Falluja Kills Four American Contractors," *New York Times,* March 31, 2004.

119. David Barstow, "Killed Contractors were Ambushed," *New York Times,* April 10, 2004.

120. Jeffrey Gettleman, "Enraged Mob in Falluja Kills Four American Contractors," *New York Times,* March 31, 2004.

121. Ibid.

122. United Press International report by P. Mitchell Prothero, quoted on the *Washington Times* website (www.washingtontimes.com), April 2, 2004.

123. Patrick McDonnell, "Outgoing Marine General Faults Fallouja Strategy," *Los Angeles Times,* September 13, 2004.

124. See Nir Rosen, "Letter from Falluja," *The New Yorker,* June 28, 2004; Robert Kaplan, "Five Days in Fallujah," *Atlantic Monthly,* July 2004; and Bing West, *No True Glory: A Frontline Account of the Battle for Fallujah* (New York: Bantam, 2006).

125. Interview with Muhammad al-Kubaisi, Baghdad, May 6, 2004. I discuss this theory further in my article "Dateline Baghdad: The Saddam Conspiracy Theory," *The Globalist,* September 24, 2004.

126. Interview with Dr. Isam Al-Rawi, professor of geology at Baghdad University and member of the Association of Muslim Clerics, Iraq, in Cairo, March 12, 2005. In 2007 an unknown assassin killed Dr. Al-Rawi on the grounds of the university.

127. Interview with Jawad al-Maliki (also known by his birth name, Nouri Kamel Mohammed Hassan al-Maliki), deputy director, Islamic Dawa Party, and

later prime minister of Iraq from May 2006 to the present, in Baghdad, May 5, 2004.

128. Raymond A. Hinnebusch, "The Islamic Movement in Syria: Sectarian Conflict and Urban Rebellion in an Authoritarian-Populist Regime," in Dessouki, *Islamic Resurgence*, 138–69.

129. Quoted in R. Stephen Humphreys, "The Contemporary Resurgence in the Context of Modern Islam," in Dessouki, *Islamic Resurgence*, 80.

130. The Jordanian government uncovered a cache of weapons allegedly being held for an armed rebellion. See Nick B. Williams Jr., "Chasm Widening between Amman, Fundamentalists," *Los Angeles Times*, August 8, 1991.

131. Youssef M. Ibrahim, "Saudi Rulers Are Confronting Challenge by Islamic Radicals," *New York Times*, March 9, 1992.

132. Kim Murphy, "Islamic Militants Build Power Base in Sudan," *Los Angeles Times*, April 6, 1992, A1.

133. Ibid., A9.

134. Abdelkadir Hachani, quoted in Kim Murphy, "Algerian Election to Test Strength of Radical Islam," *Los Angeles Times*, December 26, 1991, A18. The first stage of the national elections, on December 27, 1991, gave the Front 40 percent of the parliamentary seats, and a total of more than 60 percent were expected if the runoff elections had been allowed in 1992. The Islamic movement has been a thorn in the side of Algerian nationalists since independence. See John P. Entelis, *Algeria: The Revolution Institutionalized* (Boulder, Colo.: Westview Press, 1986); and Hugh Roberts, *The Battlefield: Algeria, 1988–2002. Studies in a Broken Polity* (London: Verso, 2003).

135. Quoted in Robin Wright, "Muslims under the Gun," *Los Angeles Times*, January 28, 1992, B1.

136. Kim Murphy, "Revolution Again Echoes through the Casbah," *Los Angeles Times*, March 15, 1992, A15. The leader of the Islamic Salvation Front, Abdelkadir Hachani, urged his followers to respond nonviolently to the military and to confine their protests to attendance at mosques. The protests swelled significantly after Hachani was jailed on January 22, 1992. Wright, "Muslims under the Gun."

137. Jonathan C. Randall, "Algeria Leader Assassinated during Speech," *Los Angeles Times*, June 30, 1991, A1. Boudiaf, a hero of Algeria's war of independence, had openly supported the separation of religion and politics in Algeria and had defended the ban on the Islamic Salvation Front. He was killed in a complicated attack involving bombs and automatic-weapons' fire as he was giving a speech in the Mediterranean port city of Annaba. On July 2, he was succeeded by Ali Kafi, another civilian member of the Council of State.

138. Conversation with Moulay Hicham, prince of Morocco, in Isla Vista, California, February 7, 2007.

139. François Soudan, *Jeune Afrique / L'Intelligent,* Paris, France, August 12–15, 2002; English translation in *World Press Review* 49, no. 11 (November 2002).

140. See Jeff Haynes, *Religion and Politics in Africa* (London: Zed Books, 1996); and John Lonsdale, *Religion and Politics in Kenya*, Henry Martyn Lectures (Cambridge: Henry Martyn Centre, 2005).

CHAPTER 3: POLITICAL TARGETS OF REBELLION: SOUTH,
CENTRAL, AND SOUTHEAST ASIA

1. For an excellent overview, see Ahmed Rashid, *Taliban: Militant Islam, Oil and Fundamentalism in Central Asia* (New Haven: Yale University Press, 2001); and Peter Marsden, *The Taliban: War, Religion and the New Order in Afghanistan* (London: Zed Books, 1998).

2. Quoted in Bob Drogin, "Democracy Takes Hold in Himalayan Kingdom," *Los Angeles Times*, August 5, 1990, A6.

3. Interviews with Massoud by a Canadian journalist in 1998 are recorded in A. R. Rowan, *On the Trail of a Lion: Ahmed Shah Massoud, Oil Politics and Terror* (Oakville, Ontario: Mosaic Press, 2005).

4. Owen Bennett Jones, *Pakistan: Eye of the Storm* (New Haven: Yale University Press, 2003).

5. For the impact on Pakistan of Afghanistan's militant religious politics, see Rizwan Husain, *Pakistan and the Emergence of Islamic Militancy in Afghanistan* (Aldershot, Hampshire [U.K.]: Aldersgate Press, 2005).

6. For background on religious politics in Pakistan, see Anwar Syed, *Pakistan: Islam, Politics, and National Solidarity* (New York: Praeger, 1982); Aziz Ahmad, "The Ulama in Politics," in Nikki R. Keddie, ed., *Scholars, Saints, and Sufis: Muslim Religious Institutions in the Middle East since 1500* (Berkeley: University of California Press, 1972); and Mumtaz Ahmad, "Islamic Fundamentalism in South Asia: The Jama'at-i-Islami and the Tablighi Jama'at," in Martin E. Marty and R. Scott Appleby, eds., *Fundamentalisms Observed* (Chicago: University of Chicago Press, 1991), 457–530.

7. For background on the Kashmir conflict, see Sumit Ganguly, *The Crisis in Kashmir: Portents of War, Hopes of Peace* (Cambridge: Cambridge University Press, 1999); Victoria Schofield, *Kashmir in Conflict* (London: I. B. Tauris, 2000); and Sumantra Bose, *Kashmir: Roots of Conflict, Paths to Peace* (Cambridge Mass.: Harvard University Press, 2005).

8. *The New Islamist International: A Report of the Task Force on Terrorism and Unconventional Warfare of the House Republican Research Committee, U.S. House of Representatives*, February 1, 1993.

9. Anuj Chopra, "India Train Blasts Echo Madrid Attacks," *Christian Science Monitor*, June 12, 2006.

10. For background on Islamic politics in Bangladesh, see Craig Baxter, *Bangladesh: From a Nation to a State* (Boulder, Colo.: Westview Press, 1997); and Sufia M. Uddin, *Constructing Bangladesh: Religion, Ethnicity, and Language in an Islamic Nation* (Chapel Hill: University of North Carolina Press, 2006).

11. For the argument that Bangladesh is becoming the new center for militant Islamic activism in South Asia, see Hiranmay Karlekar, *Bangladesh: The Next Afghanistan?* (New Delhi: Sage Publications, 2006); for the counterargument, see Ali Riaz, *God Willing: The Politics of Islamism in Bangladesh* (Lanham, Md.: Rowman & Littlefield, 2004).

12. For background on the Chechnya conflict, see John B. Dunlop, *Russia Confronts Chechnya: Roots of a Separatist Conflict* (Cambridge: Cambridge

University Press, 1998); Andrew Meier, *Chechnya: To the Heart of a Conflict* (New York: W. W. Norton, 2004); Sebastian Smith, *Allah's Mountains: The Battle for Chechnya* (London: Tauris Parke, 2005); and Tony Wood, *Chechnya: The Case for Independence* (London: Verso, 2007).

13. For an excellent overview of Islamic political movements in Central Asia, see Ahmed Rashid, *Jihad: The Rise of Militant Islam in Central Asia* (New Haven: Yale University Press, 2002).

14. The English transcriptions of the names of these nations vary widely. I have chosen to use the forms that the current governments prefer, in some cases because the old spelling implies a Russified version of the names. Hence, I use Tajikistan rather than Tadzhikistan, and Kyrgyzstan rather than Kirghizia.

15. When the Republic of Tatar, surrounded entirely by Russia, declared itself a "sovereign state" in March 1992, President Boris Yeltsin was publicly nervous—not only because he feared the dissolution of the Russian Federation but also because he was concerned about forces within his own nation that might encourage the rising tide of Islamic nationalism on the southern boundaries.

16. Vladimir Klimenko, "Opposition Seizes Power in Tajikistan," *Los Angeles Times*, May 8, 1992, A45.

17. Abdulrahim Pulatov, leader of Birlik, quoted in Robin Wright, "Report from Turkestan," *New Yorker*, April 6, 1992, 60.

18. Mark Fineman, "Tide of Islam Stirs Forces in Soviet Asia," *Los Angeles Times*, November 5, 1991, A1.

19. Quoted in Ronald Wixman, "Ethnic Attitudes and Relations in Modern Uzbek Cities," in William Fierman, ed., *Soviet Central Asia: The Failed Transformation* (Boulder, Colo.: Westview Press, 1991), 174.

20. Quoted in Wixman, "Ethnic Attitudes," 172. Wixman reports that the Uzbek students were pleasantly surprised to hear that most American males were circumcised. He further reports that several Russians in the group who heard his description of American practices were shocked and explained that if this were the case, it was only because "the Jews control America." Quoted in Wixman, "Ethnic Attitudes," 174.

21. For the history and culture of Muslims in Central Asia, see Denis Sinor, *The Cambridge History of Inner Asia* (Cambridge: Cambridge University Press, 1990); Alexandre Bennigsen and S. Enders Wimbush, *Muslims of the Soviet Empire: A Guide* (London: C. Hurst, 1985); Shirin Akiner, *The Islamic Peoples of the Soviet Union* (London: Kegan Paul International, 1983); and R. Pierce, *Russian Central Asia, 1867–1917: A Study in Colonial Rule* (Berkeley: University of California Press, 1960).

22. See Hélène Carrère d'Encausse, *Islam and the Russian Empire: Reform and Revolution in Central Asia*, translated by Quintin Hoare (London: I. B. Tauris, 1988).

23. For the history of Soviet-Central Asian relations, see Alexandre Bennigsen and Marie Broxup, *The Islamic Threat to the Soviet State* (New York: St. Martin's Press, 1983); Edward Allworth, ed., *Central Asia: 120 Years of Russian Rule* (Durham, N.C.: Duke University Press, 1989); Yaacov Ro'i, ed., *The USSR and the Muslim World: Issues in Domestic and Foreign Policy* (London:

Allen & Unwin, 1984); and Geoffrey Wheeler, *The Modern History of Soviet Central Asia* (London: Weidenfeld & Nicolson, 1964).

24. Adeeb Khalid, *Islam after Communism: Religion and Politics in Central Asia* (Berkeley: University of California Press, 2007).

25. Cited in Wright, "Report from Turkestan," 56.

26. Francis X. Cline, "Defiance of Kremlin's Control Is Accelerating in Soviet Asia," *New York Times,* July 1, 1990, A1.

27. Wright, "Report from Turkestan," 56. See also "The Next Islamic Revolution," *Economist* September 21, 1991, 58–60.

28. Ahmed Rashid, "The Islamic Challenge," *Far Eastern Economic Review* 149 (July 12, 1990): 24. His fellow mullahs again attempted to oust the Tashkent mufti Muhammad Sady Muhammad Yusuf, in January 1992. Martha Brill Olcott, "Central Asia's Post-Empire Politics," *Orbis* 36, no. 2 (Spring 1992): 253–68.

29. Sahib Nazarov, pro-democracy member of the Communist-dominated parliament in Tajikistan, quoted in Fineman, "Tide of Islam," A1.

30. Moldokasymov in *Leninchil Zhash,* August 6, 1987, quoted in Azade-Ayse Rorlich, "Islam and Atheism: Dynamic Tension in Soviet Central Asia," in William Fierman, ed., *Soviet Central Asia: The Failed Transformation* (Boulder, Colo.: Westview Press, 1991), 192.

31. Regarding Uzbek political alignments, see James Critchlow, *Nationalism in Uzbekistan: A Soviet Republic's Road to Sovereignty* (Boulder, Colo.: Westview Press, 1991). For a more general background to Uzbek history and culture, see Edward A. Allworth, *The Modern Uzbeks: From the Fourteenth Century to the Present, a Cultural History* (Stanford, Calif.: Hoover Institution Press, 1990).

32. Tsumbai Lyusanov, quoted in Wright, "Report from Turkestan," 57.

33. Souad Mekhennet and Michael Moss, "Europeans Get Terror Training Inside Pakistan," *The New York Times* international edition, September 10, 2007, 1.

34. For background information on religion and politics in Tajikistan, see Muriel Atkin, *The Subtlest Battle: Islam in Soviet Tajikistan* (Philadelphia: Foreign Policy Research Institute, 1989); and Lena Jonson, *Tajikistan in the New Central Asia: Geopolitics, Great Power Rivalry, and Radical Islam* (London: I. B. Tauris, 2006).

35. Olcott, "Central Asia's Post-Empire Politics," 261.

36. Ibid., 262.

37. Wright, "Report from Turkestan," 74.

38. Vladimir Klimenko, "Wind of Islam Fans Politics in Emergent Tajikistan," *Los Angeles Times,* May 14, 1992, A4.

39. Ibid.

40. Quoted in Wright, "Report from Turkestan," 74.

41. For the historical background of present-day Kazakhstan, see Martha Brill Olcott, *The Kazakhs* (Stanford, Calif.: Hoover Institution Press, 1987); and George J. Demko, *The Russian Colonization of Kazakhstan, 1896–1916* (Bloomington: Indiana University, 1969); and Martha Brill Olcott, *Kazakhstan: Unfulfilled Promise* (Washington, D.C.: Carnegie Endowment for International Peace, 2002).

42. Wright, "Report from Turkestan," 68.

43. Olcott, "Central Asia's Post-Empire Politics," 260.

44. See Rorlich, "Islam and Atheism," 191.

45. Olcott, "Central Asia's Post-Empire Politics," 264.

46. See Francis X. Cline's essay, "Islamic Militance along Russia's Rim Is Less Than a Sure Bet," *New York Times,* February 9, 1992, E2.

47. See John Stratton Hawley, "Naming Hinduism," *Wilson Quarterly,* Summer 1991, 20–34.

48. Whether there actually was a Kautilya, a political adviser to the great ruler Candragupta Maurya, is a subject of scholarly dispute. The *Artha-sastra* came to light in the twelfth century C.E., and some scholars date the text some seven centuries later than the purported fourth century B.C.E. date.

49. The date the *panchayat* system developed in India is difficult to ascertain, but Basham reports a primitive form of it in ancient India. A. L. Basham, *The Wonder That Was India: A Survey of the Culture of the Indian Sub-continent before the Coming of the Muslims* (New York: Grove Press, 1954), 102–7.

50. Embree, "Brahmanical Ideology and Regional Identities," in *Imagining India,* 9–27. For the manner in which Brahmanical Hinduism encapsulates its competition, see Embree, "The Question of Hindu Tolerance," in *Utopias in Conflict,* 19–37. As early as the mid-1960s, van Leeuwen proclaimed that Hinduism was becoming the national ideology of India. Van Leeuwen, *Christianity in World History,* 365.

51. On the history of the RSS, see Walter K. Andersen and Shridhar D. Damle, *The Brotherhood in Saffron: The Rashtriya Swayamsevak Sangh and Hindu Revivalism* (Boulder, Colo.: Westview Press, 1987).

52. I discuss the Savarkar-Gandhi debate in my article, "Gandhi vs. Terrorism," *Daedalus,* Winter, 2007.

53. V. D. Savarkar, foreword to Savitri Devi, *A Warning to the Hindus* (Calcutta: Hindu Mission, 1939).

54. V. D. Savarkar, *Hindutva: Who Is a Hindu?* (Bombay: Veer Savarkar Prakashan, 1969).

55. Quoted in Ainslie T. Embree, "The Function of the Rashtriya Swayamsevak Sangh: To Define the Hindu Nation," in Martin E. Marty and R. Scott Appleby, eds., *Accounting for Fundamentalisms* (Chicago: University of Chicago Press, 1994).

56. Nehru, *Discovery of India,* 531.

57. For an analysis of the persistence of what the author calls Hindu fundamentalism in South Asia, see Robert Eric Frykenberg, "Revivalism and Fundamentalism: Some Critical Observations with Special Reference to Politics in South Asia," in James W. Bjorkman, ed., *Fundamentalism, Revivalists and Violence in South Asia* (Riverdale, Md.: Riverdale Company, 1986).

58. Another political issue that exercised Muslims was the Indian Supreme Court's 1986 decision in the *Shah Bano* case. At issue was the fairness of the Muslim laws regarding compensation for a divorced wife. A Muslim woman in Indore, Shah Bano, argued that she should receive compensation equal to what a divorced Hindu woman would receive, not the meager settlement allowed under Muslim law. The court agreed, and the chief justice added fuel to the fire

by calling for a unified legal code equally applicable to all religious communities in India. The outcry from Muslims in response was considerable; in Bombay a procession of 100,000 people denounced the court's verdict. At first Rajiv Gandhi's government defended the court, but after Muslim resistance mounted, it reversed itself, proposing legislation known as the Muslim Women's Bill. The bill would have partially overturned the Supreme Court's decision by exempting Muslims from the provisions of Section 125 of the Criminal Procedure Code, which prescribed alimony. The new bill attempted to be egalitarian, however, by allowing Muslim women to appeal to the Muslim *waqf,* the charitable fund, for compensation equal to what Hindu women in such circumstances would receive. The bill was attacked by Hindus, secularists, and feminists, but on May 6, 1986, it became law.

59. For background on the Bharatiya Janata Party and the rise of Hindu nationalism in India, see Peter van der Veer, *Religious Nationalism: Hindus and Muslims in India* (Berkeley: University of California Press, 1994); Thomas Blom Hansen, *The Saffron Wave* (Princeton: Princeton University Press, 1999); and Chetan Bhatt, *Hindu Nationalism: Origins, Ideologies, and Modern Myths* (Oxford: Berg Publishers, 2001).

60. Opinion poll conducted by *India Today* 16, no. 10 (May 31, 1991): 3.

61. See Peter van der Veer, "Hindu 'Nationalism' and the Discourse of 'Modernity': The Vishva Hindu Parishad," in Marty and Appleby, *Accounting for Fundamentalisms.*

62. The founding date was August 29, which in 1964 corresponded with the date of Lord Krishna's birth in the lunar calendar.

63. Swami Chinmayananda was a Shaivite Kshatriya from Kerala who had been active in the Indian independence movement before traveling to Rishikesh, where he sought out the reclusive Swami Topavana for spiritual edification. His Chinmaya Mission had centers in cities throughout India in addition to the main Sandeepany Sadhanalaya ashram near Bombay. He taught a reformed Hinduism emphasizing the value of self-esteem and the dangers of a secularized society. A number of young, Western spiritual seekers were attracted to his ashram in the 1970s, and a branch of the movement established a "Sandeepany West" in California in the 1980s. My thanks to Prof. Ann Berliner of California State University, Fresno, for information on Swami Chinmayananda and his mission.

64. Ayodhya was the third "most important issue" in the 1991 political campaign; "price increase" was first, and "political instability" was second. *India Today* 16, no. 10 (May 31, 1991): 4.

65. These figures were reported by *India Today.* The *Los Angeles Times* placed the number killed in Ayodhya-related incidents at more than a thousand. Mark Fineman, "India Arrests Hindu Party Chief, Sparks Crisis," *Los Angeles Times,* October 24, 1990, A12.

66. Quoted in Bernard Weinraub, "A Hindu Nationalist Stirs and Scares," *New York Times,* June 9, 1991, international edition, A10.

67. Rajiv Gandhi was killed during the campaign by a bomb blast on May 21, 1991, in the small southern Indian town of Sriperumbudur, where he had come to make a speech. Tamils involved in the Sri Lankan separatist movement were implicated in the conspiracy.

68. *India Today,* May 31, 1991, 59.

69. Quoted in Sanjoy Hazarika, "Hindu Fundamentalist Threatens India's Government over Temple," *New York Times,* October 18, 1990, international edition, A1.

70. Quoted in Mark Fineman, "Hindus Storm Mosque; 32 Die in India Strife," *Los Angeles Times,* October 31, 1990, A1.

71. Quoted in Fineman, "India Arrests Hindu Party Chief," A12.

72. Sarvepalli Gopal, introduction to Sarvepalli Gopal, ed., *Anatomy of a Confrontation: The Babri Masjid-Ramjanmabhumi Issue* (New Delhi: Penguin Books, 1991), 13.

73. Quoted in Bernard Weinraub, "A Hindu Nationalist Stirs and Scares," A10.

74. A. B. Vajpayee, BJP leader, quoted in V. Mahurkar, "Gandhian Humanism: BJP Agonizes over Striking New Posture," *India Today,* May 31, 1992, 16.

75. Dilip Awasthi and Shahnaz Anklesaria Aiyar, "RSS-BJP-VHP: Hindu Divided Family," *India Today,* November 30, 1991, 14–19.

76. In a cover story on Prime Minister Vajpayee, *India Today* compared him with U.S. President Ronald Reagan, calling him a "teflon president" who seemed immune to criticism (Saba Naqvi Bhaumik, "Man of the Moment," *India Today,* August 2, 1999).

77. Press Trust of India report published as "America Denies Visa to Narendra Modi," *ExpressIndia.Com,* March 19, 2005 (www.expressindia .com).

78. The page on the BJP website dedicated to its "philosophy" is located at www.bjp.org/philo.html.

79. See Michael Hunt, "Drafting the Nepal Constitution, 1990," *Asian Survey* 31, no. 11 (November, 11 1991): 1020–39.

80. See Jonathan Gregson, *Massacre at the Palace: The Doomed Royal Dynasty of Nepal* (New York: Hyperion, 2002).

81. The Unity March, led by BJP leader Murli Manohar Joshi, continued north to the Kashmir border, where Joshi and his marchers were denied access for security reasons. Joshi flew to the Kashmir capital, Srinagar, by airplane to complete the last leg of the march. In 1991, in the midst of the Ayodhya controversy, a similar incident occurred: a group of young Hindu students in Chandigarh, the capital of the Punjab, who were on a hunger strike to show their support for the BJP cause were shot dead by a passing cadre of militant Sikhs.

82. Some Sikhs, however, maintain that they have more in common with the BJP than with the secular Congress Party, and for that reason they supported the BJP in several national elections.

83. Interview with Jasvinder Singh, member of the Delhi Branch, All-India Sikh Students Federation (Mehta-Chawla group), at Rakabganj Gurdwara, New Delhi, January 13, 1991.

84. Interview with Darshan Singh Ragi, former jatedar, Akal Takhat, at Bhai Vir Singh Sadan, New Delhi, January 13, 1991.

85. Ibid.

86. Jarnail Singh Bhindranwale, "Address to the Sikh Congregation," transcript of a sermon given in the Golden Temple in November 1983, in *Struggle for Justice: Speeches and Conversations, Sant Jarnail Singh Bhindranwale*, translated by Ranbir Singh Sandhu (Columbus, Ohio: Sikh Religious and Educational Trust, 1999).

87. For a brief introduction to Guru Nanak and his relation to the other *bhakti* saints, see John Stratton Hawley and Mark Juergensmeyer, trans., *Songs of the Saints of India* (New York: Oxford University Press, 1988). The leading scholarly work on Guru Nanak's life and writings is W. H. McLeod, *Guru Nanak and the Sikh Religion* (Oxford: Clarendon Press, 1968). Whether Guru Nanak actually took an interest in the social issues of his day is a matter of some speculation.

88. See the title essay in W. H. McLeod, *The Evolution of the Sikh Community: Five Essays* (Oxford: Clarendon Press, 1976), 1–19.

89. See Embree, "A Sikh Challenge to the Indian State," in *Utopias in Conflict,* 113–32.

90. For a good account of the Punjab crisis and the events leading up to it, see Mark Tully and Satish Jacob, *Amritsar: Mrs. Gandhi's Last Battle* (London: Cape, 1985); also useful are Amarjit Kaur et al., *The Punjab Story* (New Delhi: Roli Books International, 1984); and Kuldip Nayar and Khushwant Singh, *Tragedy of Punjab: Operation Bluestar and After* (New Delhi: Vision Books, 1984).

91. Sandhu, *Struggle for Justice*. An analysis of some of Bhindranwale's speeches may be found in Mark Juergensmeyer, "The Logic of Religious Violence," *Journal of Strategic Studies* 10, no. 4 (December 1987), reprinted in David C. Rapoport, ed., *Inside Terrorist Organizations* (London: Frank Cass, 1988).

92. Fear of the absorption of Sikhism into Hinduism is the refrain of many modern Sikh writers, including the best known, Khushwant Singh. See, for instance, the final chapter of his *History of the Sikhs*, vol. 2 (Princeton: Princeton University Press, 1966). In Nayar and Singh, *Tragedy of Punjab*, 19–21, Khushwant Singh attributes many of the problems in the Punjab during the mid-1980s to the erosion of Sikh identity.

93. *Qaum* is a Persian word with a Muslim provenance that has traditionally been a part of the Sikh vocabulary, where it expresses a sense of religious nationhood. For a discussion of the political implications of the concept in the Punjab, see Mark Juergensmeyer, *Religion as Social Vision: The Movement against Untouchability in 20th Century Punjab* (Berkeley: University of California Press, 1982), 45.

94. Bhindranwale, "Address to the Sikh Congregation," in Sandhu, *Struggle for Justice*. The demand for Khalistan developed largely among Sikhs living abroad. The Indian government's account of Jagjit Singh Chauhan's campaign for a separate Sikh nation while he was in exile in London is detailed in a report prepared by the Indian Home Ministry, "Sikh Agitation for Khalistan," reprinted in Nayar and Singh, *Tragedy of Punjab,* 142–55.

95. On Bhindranwale's use of *miri-piri*, see Joyce Pettigrew, "In Search of a New Kingdom of Lahore," *Pacific Affairs* 60, no. 1 (Spring 1987).

96. Jarnail Singh Bhindranwale, "Two Lectures," given on July 19 and September 20, 1983, in Sandhu, *Struggle for Justice*.

97. Bhindranwale, "Address to the Sikh Congregation," in Sandhu, *Struggle for Justice.*

98. Indira Gandhi, "Don't Shed Blood, Shed Hatred," All India Radio, June 2, 1984, reprinted in V. D. Chopra, R. K. Mishra, and Nirmal Singh, *Agony of Punjab* (New Delhi: Patriot Publishers, 1984), 189.

99. See Ritu Sarin, *The Assassination of Indira Gandhi* (New Delhi: Penguin Books, 1990).

100. There is a good deal of evidence that many of the acts of the "mobs" were orchestrated, or at least facilitated, by anti-Sikh politicians. See *Who Are the Guilty? Report of a Joint Inquiry into the Causes and Impact of the Riots in Delhi from 31 October to 10 November* (Delhi: People's Union for Democratic Rights and People's Union for Civil Liberties, 1984); and Stanley Tambiah's interesting study of three riots in South Asia, including the Delhi riot of November 1984: *Leveling Crowds: Ethnic Violence in South Asia* (Berkeley: University of California Press, 1996).

101. The majority of those killed were themselves Sikhs. "Sikhs Worst Hit by Punjab Terrorism," *Times of India,* March 6, 1992, 1. One of the more notorious incidents in 1991 was the attack of Sikh extremists on the Indian ambassador to Romania in Bucharest. The Romanian government helped capture the Sikhs, who were killed; in October, in retaliation, militant Sikhs kidnapped a Romanian diplomat in Delhi.

102. Punjab police are often drawn from the so-called backward castes, such as blacksmiths and carpenters, as well as from the lowest, the scheduled castes, which include *chuhras* (sweepers). Urban sweepers, known as *balmikis*, have traditionally been Hindu and have allied with urban merchant-caste Hindus (such as *aroras* and *khatris*). Rural *chuhras* are often Sikh; known as *mazhabis* (believers), they have traditionally been allies of Jat Sikhs. In modern times, however, economic opportunities offered by government service have drawn large numbers into the army and the police. The assassin of Mrs. Gandhi, Beant Singh, was a *mazhabi* who had joined the police; he then reverted to his caste's traditional alliance with the Jats and became an instrument of their antipathy toward her. The other major group within the Punjab scheduled castes, the *chamars* (leatherworkers), who are both Sikh and Hindu, have become economically more successful and less dependent on Jat support than the *chuhras;* they tend increasingly to ally with *khatris.* Some, like their *mazhabi* counterparts, have entered government service. For background on Punjab untouchables, see Juergensmeyer, *Religion as Social Vision,* 11–21.

103. In Kashmir, where Muslims are in the majority, the rise of Hindu nationalism throughout India spurred a Muslim separatist movement. It erupted in 1986–87, led by the Muslim United Front, and in 1988 some elements of the opposition grew increasingly vocal, becoming a paramilitary operation: the Kashmir Liberation Front. Allegedly supported by Pakistan, the Front called for secession from India. Members organized demonstrations and responded to police attempts to suppress the operation by throwing bombs and shooting automatic weapons, incurring bloodshed on both sides. In May 1989 the separatists began calling themselves *mujahedin* (holy warriors) and characterized their conflict with the government as a holy war.

104. Sarin, *Assassination,* 149.

105. Ramesh Vinayak, "Striking Terror," *India Today,* September 30, 1995, 27.

106. Interview with Uduwawala Chandananda Thero, Kandy, Sri Lanka, February 2, 1988.

107. Ibid. For the role of Buddhist monks in contemporary Sri Lankan politics, see Stanley J. Tambiah, *Buddhism Betrayed? Religion, Politics and Violence in Sri Lanka* (Chicago: University of Chicago Press, 1992), and Donald Swearer, "Fundamentalist Movements in Theravada Buddhism," in Marty and Appleby, *Fundamentalisms Observed,* 628–90.

108. Interview with Uduwawala Chandananda Thero, Kandy, Sri Lanka, January 6, 1991.

109. The Pali Chronicles portray a grand Buddhist dynasty from the time of Mahinda up to the fall of the Buddhist capital at Anaradhapura. See Walpola Rahula, *History of Buddhism in Ceylon,* 2d ed. (Colombo: M. D. Gunasena, 1966); and Bardwell L. Smith, "The Ideal Social Order as Portrayed in the Chronicles of Ceylon," in Gananath Obeyesekere, Frank Reynolds, and Bardwell L. Smith, eds., *The Two Wheels of Dhamma: Essays on the Theravada Tradition in India and Ceylon* (Chambersburg, Pa.: American Academy of Religion, 1972), 31–57.

110. The origins of the Sri Lankan flag and the Tamil objections to it are described in Satchi Ponnambalam, *Sri Lanka: National Conflict and the Tamil Liberation Struggle* (London: Zed Books and Tamil Information Centre, 1983), 72–73.

111. Vejayavardhana, *The Revolt in the Temple.* The essay, "The Betrayal of Buddhism," is discussed in Tambiah, *Buddhism Betrayed?*

112. The Sinhalization of Sri Lankan politics is well documented in Gananath Obeyesekere, "Religious Symbolism and Political Change in Ceylon" in Obeyesekere, Reynolds, and Smith, *The Two Wheels of Dhamma,* 58–78; Donald Eugene Smith, "Ceylon: The Politics of Buddhist Resurgence," part 4 of Donald Eugene Smith, ed., *South Asian Politics and Religion* (Princeton: Princeton University Press, 1966), 453–546; "Religious Revival and Cultural Nationalism," chap. 6 of Wriggins, *Ceylon,* 169–270; and Urmila Phadnis, *Religion and Politics in Sri Lanka* (Columbia, Mo.: South Asia Books, 1976).

113. Ponnambalam, *Sri Lanka,* 2.

114. The government put the number of deaths at three hundred and fifty, but other estimates have gone as high as two thousand. Tambiah, *Sri Lanka,* 22. Useful collections of essays discussing the significance of the 1983 riots may be found in James Manor, *Sri Lanka in Change and Crisis* (London: Croom Helm, 1984); and Committee for Rational Development, *Sri Lanka, the Ethnic Conflict: Myths, Realities and Perspectives* (New Delhi: Navrang, 1984); see also the various monographs of the International Centre for Ethnic Studies, Kandy and Colombo, relating to the event, and Tambiah, *Leveling Crowds.*

115. Ponnambalam, *Sri Lanka,* 31.

116. Mark Fineman, "Rebels' Weapon: Cyanide," *Los Angeles Times,* January 20, 1992, A1.

117. I am grateful to Ainslie Embree for pointing out this bit of historical irony.

118. For a useful account of the rise and fall of the JVP in the 1980s, see Rohan Gunaratna, *Sri Lanka: A Lost Revolution? The Inside Story of the JVP* (Kandy, Sri Lanka: Institute of Fundamental Studies, 1990).

119. K. M. deSilva, *Managing Ethnic Tensions in Multi-ethnic Societies: Sri Lanka, 1880–1985* (Lanham, Md.: University Press of America, 1986), 204.

120. My information on the JVP comes from several interviews in Colombo, Matara, Tangalle, Humbantota, and Kandy, January 25 and February 6, 1988.

121. Interview with Mangala Moonesinghe, director, Political and Institutional Studies Division, Marga Institute, in Colombo, January 27, 1988.

122. Ibid.

123. Interview with W. G. Ganegama, coordinator, Sarvodaya Rural Technical Services, in Kandy, Sri Lanka, February 4, 1988.

124. Reuters report in *India West* 13, no. 15 (February 19, 1988): 1.

125. I saw the black flags myself in the city of Kandy and the surrounding countryside during the first week of February 1988.

126. This information came from my informal conversations with students at Peradeniya University in February 1988.

127. Interview with the Venerable Palipana Chandananda, mahana-yake, Asigiriya Chapter, Sinhalese Buddhist Sangha, in Kandy, Sri Lanka, February 3, 1988.

128. Interview with Uduwawala Chandananda Thero, Kandy, Sri Lanka, February 2, 1988.

129. Ibid.

130. Gunaratna, *Sri Lanka,* 306.

131. Ibid., 307.

132. Ibid., 296.

133. Interview with Merwyn Dominic, a taxi driver and a Roman Catholic Christian, in Colombo, January 3, 1991.

134. Interview with A. T. Ariyaratne, founder and president, Sarvodaya Shramadana Movement, in Moratuwa, Sri Lanka, January 2, 1991. The *Los Angeles Times* asserted that twenty thousand had been killed; no sources, however, were given for this figure. Mark Fineman, "Sri Lanka's Bizarre Leader Confounds His Foes," *Los Angeles Times,* January 26, 1992, A4.

135. Interview with Jamaluddin Farook and other students at the Peradeniya University canteen, January 4, 1991. They told me that soon after one of their friends, a Buddhist monk, publicly spoke out in support of the JVP and against the army's repression, he disappeared. They did not know whether he was hiding or had been killed.

136. These examples have been cited to me by Sri Lankans and others who visited the country in 1991 and 1992. See also Fineman, "Sri Lanka's Bizarre Leader," A4.

137. Premadasa also created ministries of Muslim and Hindu affairs (for which he did not serve as minister) and attempted to create a ministry of Christian

affairs. The Christians turned down the offer, preferring to stay free of government influence.

138. Interview with Palipana Chandananda, January 4, 1991.

139. Interview with Uduwawala Chandananda Thero, Kandy, Sri Lanka, January 5, 1991. For a summary of his earlier thoughts about the movement, see Juergensmeyer, "What the Bhikkhu Said."

140. Interview with Uduwawala Chandananda Thero, Kandy, Sri Lanka, January 5, 1991.

141. Ibid.

142. For efforts to broker a peace agreement in Sri Lanka, see Rohan Gunaratna, *Peace in Sri Lanka; Obstacles and Opportunities* (Colombo: Sansadaya, 2005); Chandrika Kumaratunga, "New Approach: The Democratic Path to Peace in Sri Lanka," *Harvard International Review* (June 1996); Saroj Pathak, *War or Peace in Sri Lanka* (New Delhi: Popular Prakashan, 2005); and Qadri Ismail, *Abiding by Sri Lanka: On Peace, Place, and Postcoloniality* (Minneapolis: University of Minnesota Press, 2005).

143. Interview with S. Bayantsagaan, president, Mogolyhn Siisegtnii Kholboo (Association of Mongolian Believers), and leader, Mongolian Buddhist Party, in Ulan Bator, April 12, 1992. Ordinarily Mongolians use only one name, the one given to them at birth. They have no family names. In order to help differentiate between one person's name and another, the first letter of the father's name often precedes a name in any formal identification, thereby providing a first initial.

144. For an overview of post-Soviet changes and political developments in Mongolia see Morris Rossabi, *Modern Mongolia: From Khans to Commissars to Capitalists* (Berkeley: University of California Press, 2005).

145. Interview with D. Oujun, scientific researcher for government archives and member of the Mongolian People's Revolutionary Party, in Ulan Bator, April 12, 1992.

146. B. Rinchen, ed., *Etnolingvisticheskiy atlas MNR* (Ethnolinguistic atlas of the MPR) (Ulan Bator: Academy of Sciences, 1979), 43–69, cited in Sanders, *Mongolia,* 124. The population of Mongolia at the end of the Cold War was roughly two million; fifteen years later it was almost three million.

147. Interviews with Y. Amgalan, deputy hamba lama (deputy head lama), Gandan Tegchinlen Monastery, in Ulan Bator, April 14, 1992, and Kushok Bakula, rinpoche and Indian ambassador, in Ulan Bator, April 12, 1992.

148. Interview with Y. Amgalan, Ulan Bator, April 14, 1992.

149. Interview with Kushok Bakula, Ulan Bator, April 12, 1992.

150. Interview with Y. Amgalan, Ulan Bator, April 13, 1992.

151. For a history of the Mongols and the conquests of the great khans, see Walther Heissig, *A Lost Civilisation: The Mongols Rediscovered* (London: Thames & Hudson, 1966), and *The Religions of Mongolia* (London: Routledge & Kegan Paul, 1980); J. J. Saunders, *The History of the Mongol Conquests* (London: Routledge & Kegan Paul, 1971); David Snellgrove and Hugh Richardson, *A Cultural History of Tibet* (London: Weidenfeld & Nicolson, 1968); Bertold Spüler, *History of the Mongols* (London: Routledge & Kegan Paul, 1968); and

Arthur Waley, *The Secret History of the Mongols* (London: Allen & Unwin, 1963).

152. See Morris Rossabi, *Khubilai Khan: His Life and Times* (Berkeley: University of California Press, 1988).

153. For the history of modern Mongolia, see Rossabi, *Modern Mongolia; C.R. Bawden, The Modern History of Mongolia* (New York: Praeger, 1968); Sanders, *Mongolia;* and Shirin Akiner, ed., *Mongolia Today* (London: Kegan Paul International, 1991). See also Michael Jerryson, *Mongolian Buddhism: The Rise and Fall of the Sangha* (Chiang Mai, Thailand: Silkworm Books, 2007).

154. Mongolians in present-day Inner Mongolia are in the minority because that region is inhabited largely by immigrants from China. However, there are areas with Mongolian majorities beyond Outer Mongolia, in Russian territory: Buryatia, north of present-day Mongolia, near the Russian city of Irkutsk; and Tuva, to the northwest.

155. Sanders, *Mongolia,* 125.

156. For a description of the Dalai Lama's visit, sponsored by the Asian Buddhist Conference for Peace, see Sanders, *Mongolia,* 126.

157. For a description of the problems faced in post-1989 Mongolia, see Fred Shapiro, "Starting from Scratch," *New Yorker,* January 20, 1992, 39–58; and Lincoln Kaye, "Faltering Steppes," *Far Eastern Economic Review,* April 9, 1992, 16–20.

158. See William R. Heaton, "Mongolia in 1990: Upheaval, Reform, but No Revolution Yet," *Asian Survey* 31 (January 1991): 50–56.

159. N. Zoljargal, quoted in Shapiro, "Starting from Scratch," 42.

160. Interview with A. Mekey, vice-rector, Mongolian State University, in Ulan Bator, April 11, 1992.

161. Quoted in Shapiro, "Starting from Scratch," 43.

162. See Paul C. Woy, "Rebirth of a Nation? Mongolia's Reincarnated Religious Leader," *Contemporary Review* 259 (November 1991): 234–41.

163. Interview with S. Bayantsagaan, Ulan Bator, April 12, 1992.

164. For the expansion of Buddhism after the 1990 reforms, see Alan J.K. Sanders, "Guardians of Culture," *Far Eastern Economic Review,* January 3, 1991, 20–23; David Holley, "In Mongolia, a Reincarnation of Buddhism," *Los Angeles Times,* October 8, 1991, H6; and John Noble Wilford, "Buddha and Genghis Khan Back in Mongolia," *New York Times,* July 22, 1991, A1.

165. Cited in Sanders, *Mongolia,* 127.

166. Interview with G. Lubsantseren, secretary general, Asian Buddhist Conference for Peace, in Ulan Bator, April 13, 1992.

167. Interview with C. Dambajav, Khambo Lama (head lama), Tashichoeling Monastery, in Ulan Bator, April 11, 1992.

168. Ibid.

169. Interview with S. Bayantsagaan, Ulan Bator, April 12, 1992.

170. The MPRP won 57 percent of the popular vote, with the rest divided among thirteen opposition parties. Out of the seventy-six seats at stake, the MPRP captured seventy, the Democratic Coalition (of three parties) garnered

four, the Social Democrats received one, and one seat was won by an independent allied with the MPRP. David Holley, "Ruling Party's Win Is Official in Mongolia," *Los Angeles Times,* July 3, 1992, A14.

171. Interview with S. Bayantsagaan, Ulan Bator, April 12, 1992.

172. Ibid.

173. For an overview of Tibet's relations with China, see Barry Sautman and June Teufel, *Contemporary Tibet: Politics, Development, and Society in a Disputed Region* (Armonk, N.Y.: M. E. Sharpe, 2005); John Heath, *Tibet and China in the Twenty-First Century: Non-Violence versus State Power* (London: Saqi Books, 2005); Gray Tuttle, *Tibetan Buddhists in the Making of Modern China* (New York: Columbia University Press, 2005); and Elliot Sperling, *The Tibet-China Conflict: History and Polemics* (Honolulu: East-West Center, 2005).

174. The Dalai Lama's "Five Point Peace Plan for Tibet" was presented to the U.S. Congress on September 21, 1987. A copy of the text may be found on www.tibet.com/proposal/5point.html.

175. See, for example, the Dalai Lama, *Ethics for the New Millennium* (New York: Riverhead Trade [Penguin Group], 2001).

176. Interview with Azyumardi Azra, Rector, Syarif Hidayatullah State Islamic University, in Jakarta, Indonesia, July 22, 2003.

177. Robert W. Hefner, "The Sword Against the Crescent: Religion and Violence in Muslim Southeast Asia," in Linell E. Cady and Sheldon W. Simon, eds., *Religion and Conflict in Southeast Asia* (London and New York: Routledge, 2007), 34.

178. See Christina Fink, *Living Silence: Burma Under Military Rule* (London: Zed Books, 2005).

179. See Joseph Chinyong Liow, *Muslim Resistance in Southern Thailand and Southern Philippines: Religion, Ideology, and Politics* (Honolulu: East-West Center, 2005); and the essays in Arabinda Acharya, Sabina Chua, and Rohan Gunaratna, eds., *Conflict and Terrorism in Southern Thailand* (Singapore: Marshall Cavendish Academic, 2006).

180. For an overview of the rise of the Jama'a Islamiyah and other radical Muslim groups in Indonesia, see Zachary Abuza, *Political Islam and Violence in Indonesia* (London: Routledge, 2006); and John Thayer Sidel, *Riot, Pogroms, Jihad: Religious Violence in Indonesia* (Ithaca, N.Y.: Cornell University Press, 2006). See also the essays in Robert Hefner and Patricia Horvatich, eds., *Islam in an Era of Nation-States: Politics and Religious Renewal in Muslim Southeast Asia* (Honolulu: University of Hawai'i Press, 1997). A narrative account, including first-person interviews with radical Muslim activists in Indonesia, may be found in Tracy Dahlby, *Allah's Torch: A Report from Behind the Scenes in Asia's War on Terror* (New York: William Morrow, 2005).

181. Sidney Jones, "New Developments within Jemaah Islamiya," paper presented at the Institute of Southeast Asian Studies, National University, Singapore; summary posted on the website of Indonesia Matters (www.indonesiamatters .com), January 5, 2006. The reports on the rise of radical Islam in Indonesia by Sidney Jones and other members of the Jakarta office of the International Crisis Group may be found at www.crisisgroup.org.

182. See Michael Vincent, "Concern over Bashir's Reduced Jail Sentence," transcript of "The World Today," *Australian Broadcasting Corporation*, March 10, 2004.

183. See "Hambali 'Planned Summit Attack'," report of the British Broadcasting Corporation, August 16, 2003, on the BBC News website (http://news .bbc.co.uk/1/hi/world).

184. The networks of operatives related to the Bali bombings are traced in Rohan Gunaratna, "Understanding Al Qaeda and its Network in Southeast Asia," and Zachary Abuza, "Al Qaeda in Southeast Asia: Exploring the Linkages," both in Kamar Ramakrishna and See Seng Tan, eds., *After Bali: The Threat of Terrorism in Southeast Asia* (Hong Kong: World Scientific Publishing Company, 2004).

185. See Thomas McKenna, *Muslim Rulers and Rebels: Everyday Politics and Armed Separatism in Southern Philippines* (Berkeley: University of California Press, 1998), and Liow, *Muslim Resistance in Southern Thailand and Southern Philippines.*

186. "Abu Sayyaf Group," backgrounder section of the website of the Council on Foreign Relations, January 23, 2007 (www.cfr.org/publication/9235).

187. Soon after Khadaffy Janjalani's death, in January 2007, Philippine troops supported by U.S. military advisors killed another Abu Sayyaf leader, Abu Sulaiman, who would likely have become Janjalini's successor. An older leader of the group, Radullan Sahiron, became titular leader of the group, though he probably did not play an active role since he was in his 70s and not in good health.

188. See Laurie Mylroie, "The World Trade Center Bomb: Who is Ramzi Yousef? And Why It Matters," *The National Interest*, Winter 1996.

CHAPTER 4: POST–COLD WAR REBELS: EUROPE, EAST ASIA, AND THE UNITED STATES

1. Sahib Nazarov, pro-democracy member of the communist-dominated parliament in Tajikistan, quoted in Mark Fineman, "Tide of Islam Stirs Forces in Soviet Asia," *Los Angeles Times*, November 5, 1991, A1. Fineman reported that attendance in mosques in the four southern republics of Central Asia had more than doubled and that the majority of the population appeared to favor "the re-establishment of the rule of Islam."

2. The *Great Soviet Encyclopedia* defines nationalism as "a bourgeois and petit bourgeois ideology." Quoted in Walker Connor, *The National Question in Marxist-Leninist Theory and Strategy* (Princeton: Princeton University Press, 1984), xiii.

3. Interestingly, both phrases occur in the same sentence, in a famous passage in Karl Marx, "Contribution to the Critique of Hegel's Philosophy of Right," reprinted widely, including in Reinhold Niebuhr, ed., *Karl Marx and Friedrich Engels on Religion* (New York: Schocken, 1964), 42.

4. See Connor, *National Question.*

5. Joseph Dzhugashvili, who adopted the name Stalin (man of steel) in 1913, had studied for the Russian Orthodox priesthood from 1884 to 1889 at a sem-

inary in Tiflis. He became a Marxist while he was in seminary and was expelled for insubordination.

6. For a history of the church's response to this repression, see Jane Ellis, *The Russian Orthodox Church: A Contemporary History* (Bloomington: Indiana University Press, 1986).

7. Richard N. Ostling, "Victory for a Dark Horse," *Time,* June 18, 1990, 71.

8. Ellis, *Russian Orthodox Church.* According to William Keller, former Moscow bureau chief for the *New York Times,* the Russian church's previous complicity with Communist leaders keeps it from playing an active political role (private conversation, Honolulu, January 16, 1992).

9. Regarding the revival of religion in Russia in the post–Cold War period, see the essays in Benjamin Forest, Juliet Johnson, Marietta T. Stephaniants, eds., *Religion and Identity in Modern Russia: The Revival of Orthodoxy and Islam* (Aldershot, Hampshire [U.K.] : Ashgate Publishing, 2005).

10. Nikolai Arzhannikov, a deputy in the Russian legislature, quoted in Russell Chandler, "A Russian Force Is Reborn," *Los Angeles Times,* September 28, 1991, A1.

11. Interview with Nikolai A. Kolesnik, chairman, Council on Questions of Religion, Ukrainian Soviet Socialist Republic Council of Ministers, at a meeting of the Working Group on Religion and Nationalism, United States Institute of Peace, Washington, D.C., June 20, 1990.

12. See Dan Ionescu, "Romania: Religious Denominations, Change and Resistance to Change at the Top," *Radio Free Europe Report on Eastern Europe* 1, no. 17 (April 17, 1990): 29–33; and Pedro Ramet, "Patterns of Religio-national Symbiosis in Eastern Europe: Poland, Czechoslovakia, Hungary," in *Eastern Europe: Religion and Nationalism,* Occasional Paper 3 (Washington, D.C.: East European Program, European Institute, Wilson Center, December 4, 1985), 48–51.

13. See Henry Kamm, "Rising Verbal Attacks Shake Romania's Jews," *New York Times,* June 19, 1991, international edition, A10.

14. In October 1991 Catholic churches in Serbia became a target of attack.

15. See Carol J. Williams, "Ethnic Mix Could Be Explosive in Yugoslav Republic," *Los Angeles Times,* June 10, 1991, A4.

16. Interview with Latvian prime minister Ivars Godmanis on CNN television news, August 27, 1991.

17. Quoted in Adam Brotnke, "A New Juncture in Poland," *Problems of Communism* 25, no. 5 (September–October 1976): 11, cited in Ramet, "Patterns of Religio-national Symbiosis in Eastern Europe."

18. Quoted in Bogdan Szajkowski, *Next to God . . . Poland: Politics and Religion in Contemporary Poland* (New York: St. Martin's Press, 1983), 17.

19. Carl Bernstein, "The Holy Alliance," *Time,* February 24, 1992, 28–35.

20. Quoted in Alain Touraine et al., *Solidarity: Poland, 1980–81,* translated by David Denby (Cambridge: Cambridge University Press, 1983), 46, cited in Ramet, "Patterns of Religio-national Symbiosis in Eastern Europe."

21. See "And unto Poland, What Is God's," *Economist,* May 25, 1991, 51.

22. Quoted in a news story from wire sources, "The Ukraine Declares Its Independence," *Honolulu Sunday Star-Bulletin and Advertiser,* August 25, 1991, A4.

23. The religious turmoil in independent Ukraine is described in David Little, *Ukraine: The Legacy of Intolerance* (Washington, D.C.: United States Institute of Peace Press, 1991).

24. Quoted in Jane Ellis, "The Russian Orthodox Church's Attitude to the Situation in Ukraine" (paper presented at the Working Group on Religion and Nationalism, United States Institute of Peace, Washington, D.C., June 21, 1990), 6.

25. Quoted in ibid.

26. Bohdan R. Bociurkiw, "Institutional Religion and Nationality in the Soviet Union," in S. Enders Wimbush, ed., *Soviet Nationalities in Strategic Perspective* (London: Groom Helm, 1985), 183, cited in Little, *Ukraine*, 53.

27. Interview with Ivan Hrechko, chairman, Commission on Religious Freedom of Rukh, Lviv Chapter, December 13, 1990, by David Little at the United States Institute of Peace. Quoted in Little, *Ukraine*, 74.

28. Denise Hamilton, "Independence Fever," *Los Angeles Times Magazine*, December 1, 1991, 54.

29. Father Frank Estocin, Summary of Remarks (presented at the Working Group on Religion and Nationalism, United States Institute of Peace, Washington, D.C., June 21, 1990), 3.

30. Ibid. He added that "*glasnost* and *perestroika* have opened the doors to this possibility."

31. Interview with Kolesnik, Washington, D.C., June 20, 1990.

32. For an overview of the relation of religion to the Chinese state in the post–Cold War era, see James Miller, *Chinese Religions in Contemporary Societies* (Santa Barbara, Calif: ABC-CLIO, 2006); Kim-Kwong Chan, *Religious Freedom in China: Policy, Administration, and Regulation; a Research Handbook* (Beijing: Institute for the Study of American Religion, 2005); and the essays in Daniel Overmyer, ed., *Religion in China Today* (Cambridge: Cambridge University Press, 2003). For religion-state issues in China in a historical context, see Anthony Yu, *State and Religion in China: Historical and Textual Perspectives* (Chicago: Open Court Publishing Co., 2005).

33. See Dru C. Gladney, *Dislocating China: Muslims, Minorities, and Other Subaltern Subjects* (Chicago: University of Chicago Press, 2004). Gladney discusses the problem that Islam and other religions pose for the Chinese government in seeking ways to accept them without allowing them to challenge the authority of the state and the identity of the nation.

34. See Maria Hsia Chang, *Falun Gong: The End of Days* (New Haven: Yale University Press, 2004), for a description of the movement and the challenge it presents for the Chinese authorities.

35. Richard Madsen, "Christian Communities in China," in Mark Juergensmeyer, ed., *The Oxford Handbook of Global Religion* (New York: Oxford University Press, 2006).

36. Ibid.

37. Some of the issues of controlling religion in postwar Vietnam are discussed in a study of popular religion in southern Vietnam, Philip Taylor, *Goddess on the Rise: Pilgrimage and Popular Religion in Vietnam* (Honolulu: University of Hawai'i Press, 2004).

38. These observations about the religious nature of *juche* thought came from my discussions with Korean officials in Pyongyang, North Korea, August 10–21, 1989.

39. Tambiah, *Buddism Betrayed?* 117–18.

40. Quoted in Chris Hedges, "Vatican II Reforms Gave Rise to Liberation Theology," *Dallas Morning News,* March 2, 1986, A29.

41. For a discussion of the importance of religion in the general context of the Nicaraguan revolution (and counterrevolution), see Luis Serra, "Ideology, Religion, and Class Struggle in the Nicaraguan Revolution," in Richard Harris and Carlos M. Vilas, eds., *Nicaragua: A Revolution under Siege* (London: Zed Books, 1985), 151–201; Roger N. Lancaster, *Thanks to God and the Revolution: Popular Religion and Class Consciousness in the New Nicaragua* (New York: Columbia University Press, 1988); and Michael Dodson and Laura Nuzzi O'Shaughnessy, *Nicaragua's Other Revolution: Religious Faith and Political Struggle* (Chapel Hill: University of North Carolina Press, 1990). I am grateful to Darrin McMahon for preparing a background paper on the Nicaraguan situation and its sources.

42. Services held in the streets were much better attended than those in the church building (interview with religious leaders in Managua, June 5, 1988).

43. Teofilo Cabestrero, *Revolutionaries for the Gospel: Testimonies of Fifteen Christians in the Nicaraguan Government,* translated by Phillip Berryman (Maryknoll, N.Y.: Orbis Books, 1986).

44. Ibid., 22.

45. I am grateful to Prof. Charles Hale for pointing out the nationalism of Nicaragua's Roman Catholic right wing as well as its left.

46. See Jocelyne Cesari, *Where Islam and Democracy Meet: Muslims in Europe and the United States* (New York: Palgrave Macmillan, 2006); Jytte Klausen, *The Islamic Challenge: Politics and Religion in Western Europe* (New York: Oxford University Press, 2005); and the essays in Barbara Daly Metcalf, ed., *Making Muslim Space in North America and Europe* (Berkeley: University of California Press, 1996).

47. Robert S. Leiken, "Europe's Angry Muslims" *Foreign Affairs,* July/August 2005; and Alkman Granitsas, "Europe's Next Immigration Crisis," *Yale-Global Online,* April 11, 2006 (www.yaleglobal.yale.edu).

48. See Gary Lease, "The Origins of National Socialism: Some Fruits of Religion and Nationalism," in Peter Merkl and Ninian Smart, eds., *Religion and Politics in the Modern World* (New York: New York University Press, 1983).

49. For a comparison of three European approaches to issues related to Muslim immigrants, see Joel S. Fetzer and J. Christopher Soper, *Muslims and the State in Britain, France, and Germany* (Cambridge: Cambridge University Press, 2004).

50. See John R. Bowen, *Why the French Don't Like Headscarves: Islam, the State, and Public Space* (Princeton: Princeton University Press, 2006); and Jonathan Laurence and Justin Vaisse, *Integrating Islam: Political and Religious Challenges in Contemporary France* (Washington, D.C.: Brookings Institution Press, 2006).

51. Sarkozy also said that the immigrant suburbs in France needed "indus-

trial cleaning" ("French Police Sent to Riot Towns," BBC News, November 3, 2005).

52. Sarkozy also appointed Senegalese-born Rama Yade as junior minister for human rights and feminist activist Fadela Amara to oversee public housing renovation (Associate Press news story by Jenny Barchfield, "Sarkozy Reaches Out to Minorities with Appointments," *Boston Globe*, June 20, 2007).

53. Tom Carter "Van Gogh's Killing Spurs Anger at Islam; Dutch Back Crackdown," *Washington Times,* November 10, 2004.

54. Knight Ridder report, "Wave of Anti-Muslim Legislation in Europe has Broad Support," posted on *Religion News Blog* (www.religionnewsblog.com), March 5, 2004.

55. Danish prime minister Andres Fogh Rasmussen, quoted in a report on Al Arabiya television and rebroadcast on Australian Broadcasting Corporation's *ABC News,* February 3, 2006.

56. I arranged for a class visit to the mosque while teaching a course on religion and violence at Lund University, Sweden, August 12, 2004.

57. For background on the tensions between Muslim religious parties and the secular state in Turkey, see Jenny B. White, *Islamist Mobilization in Turkey: A Study in Vernacular Politics* (Seattle: University of Washington Press, 2003); and M. Hakan Yavuz, *Islamic Political Identity in Turkey* (New York: Oxford University Press, 2005). See also the essays in Sibel Bozdogan, editor, *Rethinking Modernity and National Identity in Turkey* (Seattle: University of Washington Press, 1997); and M. Hakan Yavuz and John Esposito, eds., *Turkish Islam and the Secular State: The Gulen Movement* (Syracuse, N.Y.: Syracuse University Press, 2003).

58. *Turkish Daily News,* April 28, 2007; and Anthony Shadid, "A Journey to Defend Turkey's Secular Ideals," *Washington Post,* May 6, 2007.

59. A thoughtful analysis of global Islam that links the problems of assimilation into European society with the rise of jihadi ideology is Oliver Roy, *Globalized Islam: The Search for a New Ummah* (New York: Columbia University Press, 2006). See also Robert S. Leiken, "Europe's Mujahideen: Where Mass Immigration Meets Global Terrorism" *Center for Immigration Studies Backgrounder,* April 2005.

60. Charles M. Sennott, "Seeking Madrid Motives in a Cradle of Muslim Glory," *Boston Globe,* March 28, 2004.

61. Mohammad Sidique Khan, videotaped statement aired on Al-Jazeera television, September 1, 2005.

62. Shehzad Tanweer, videotaped statement aired on Al-Jazeera television, July 6, 2006.

63. Regarding the connection between immigrant experience and political Islam, see Roy, *Globalized Islam.*

64. See my essay on this topic, "The Ghadar Syndrome: Immigrant Sikhs and Nationalist Pride," in Mark Juergensmeyer and N. Gerald Barrier, eds., *Sikh Studies: Comparative Perspectives on a Changing Tradition* (Berkeley: Berkeley Religious Studies Series, 1979).

65. See David Chidester, *Shots in the Street: Violence and Religion in South Africa* (Boston: Beacon Press, 1991).

66. For a thoughtful discussion of the future of the Muslim community in Europe see Tariq Ramadan, *Western Muslims and the Future of Islam* (New York: Oxford University Press, 2005).

67. John Hickey, *Religion and the Northern Ireland Problem* (Totawa, N.J.: Barnes & Noble, 1984), 57–88; and W. Dennis D. Cooke, "The Religious Dimension in the Northern Ireland Problem," *Lexington Theological Quarterly* 16, no. 3 (July 1981): 85–93.

68. Interview with Tom Hartley, councillor and leader of the Sinn Féin party in the Belfast city council, Belfast, July 31, 1998.

69. I develop further the nonviolent aspects of the Northern Ireland case in my article "Gandhi vs. Terrorism," *Daedalus* 136, no. 1 (Winter 2007): 30–39; and in my book *Gandhi's Way: A Handbook of Conflict Resolution* (Berkeley: University of California Press, 2005).

70. Interview with "Takeshi Nakamura," Tokyo, January 12, 1996 (translation assistance provided by Amy Arakane and Prof. Susumu Shimazono). At the request of the interviewee I changed his name and omitted any personal information that might allow current members of the movement to identify him.

71. Shoko Asahara, *Disaster Approaches the Land of the Rising Sun: Shoko Asahara's Apocalyptic Predictions* (Tokyo: Aum Publishing Co., Shizuoka Japan, 1995), 190.

72. Ibid., 135–36.

73. Ibid., 136.

74. Interview with Nakamura, Tokyo, January 12, 1996.

75. Asahara, *Disaster Approaches*, 190.

76. Ibid., 190.

77. Ibid., 274.

78. Ibid., 275.

79. Ibid., 169.

80. Ian Reader, *A Poisonous Cocktail? Aum Shinrikyo's Path to Violence* (Copenhagen: Nordic Institute of Asian Studies, 1996), 35.

81. Interview with Susumu Shimazono, professor of religious studies, Tokyo, January 9, 1996. See also his articles "In the Wake of Aum," *Japanese Journal of Religious Studies* 22, nos. 3–4 (1995): 381–415 (which is a condensed version of Shimazono's book *Aum Shinrikyo no kiseki*, Robert Kisala trans.); and "New 'New Religions' and This World: Religious Movements in Japan after the 1970s and Their Beliefs about Salvation," *Social Compass* 42, no. 2 (1995): 193–202.

82. "Resurgence of Interest in Aum Shinrikyo," *New York Times*, October 28, 1998, A3. My interviews with members of the Aum movement are described more fully in my book *Terror in the Mind of God*.

83. See, for instance, Weston LaBarre, *The Ghost Dance: The Origins of Religion* (New York: Dell, 1970).

84. The first in the series is Tim F. LaHaye and Jerry Jenkins, *Left Behind: A Novel of the Earth's Last Days* (Carol Stream, Ill.: Tyndale Publishing House, 2000). For an analysis of the series as a publishing phenomenon, see Glenn Shuck, *Marks of the Beast: The* Left Behind *Novels and the Struggle for Evangelical Identity* (New York: New York University Press, 2004); Michael Standaert,

Skipping Towards Armageddon: The Politics and Propaganda of the Left Behind *Novels* (Brooklyn, N.Y.: Soft Skull Press, 2006); and the essays in Bruce David Forbes and Jeanne Halgren Kilde, eds., *Rapture, Revelation, and the End Times: Exploring the* Left Behind *Series* (New York: Palgrave Macmillan, 2004).

85. For a discussion of the rise of Christian religious political movements at the turn of the twenty-first century, see Michelle Goldberg, *Kingdom Coming: The Rise of Christian Nationalism* (New York: W. W. Norton, 2007); Chris Hedges, *American Fascists: The Christian Right and the War on America* (New York: Free Press, 2007); and Kevin Phillips, *American Theocracy: The Peril and Politics of Radical Religion, Oil, and Borrowed Money in the 21st Century* (New York: Penguin, 2007).

86. See, for instance, Stephen Bruce, "The Moral Majority: The Politics of Fundamentalism in Secular Society," in Lionel Caplan, ed., *Studies in Religious Fundamentalism* (Albany: State University of New York Press, 1987); and Capps, *The New Religious Right.*

87. Bruce Barron, *Heaven on Earth? The Social and Political Agendas of Dominion Theology* (Minneapolis: Zondervan, 1992).

88. "Manifesto for the Christian Church," *Crosswinds.* Quoted in Chip Berlet, John Salvi, *Abortion Clinic Violence, and Catholic Right Conspiracism* (Somerville, Mass.: Political Research Associates, 1996), 8.

89. The book that established Reconstruction Theology as a movement is Rousas John Rushdoony's two-volume *Institutes of Biblical Law* (Nutley, N.J.: Craig Press, 1973). Introductions to Cornelius Van Til's thought are found in R. J. Rushdoony, *By What Standard?* (Tyler, Tex.: Thoburn Press, 1978), and Richard Pratt, *Every Thought Captive* (Phillipsburg, N.J.: Presbyterian and Reformed Publishing Company, 1982). The journal of Reconstruction thought, *Chalcedon Report,* is published in Vallecito, California.

90. Gary North, *Backward, Christian Soldiers? An Action Manual for Christian Reconstruction* (Tyler, Tex.: Institute for Christian Economics, 1984), 267. According to North, the four main tenets of Christian Reconstruction are biblical law, optimistic eschatology, predestination, and "presuppositional apologetics," which North defines as a "philosophical defense of the faith" (*Backward, Christian Soldiers?* 267). North has authored or edited over twenty books, including *An Introduction to Christian Economics* (Tyler, Tex.: Institute for Christian Economics, 1973), *Unconditional Surrender: God's Program for Victory* (Tyler, Tex.: Institute for Christian Economics, 1988), *and Millennialism and Social Theory* (Tyler, Tex.: Institute for Christian Economics, 1990).

91. Gary North, *Lone Gunners for Jesus: Letters to Paul J. Hill* (Tyler, Tex.: Institute for Christian Economics, 1994), 2.

92. Interview with Michael Bray, Reformation Lutheran Church, Bowie, Maryland, March 20, 1998.

93. Michael Bray, *A Time to Kill: A Study Considering the Use of Force and Abortion* (Portland, Oregon: Advocates for Life, 1994).

94. Paul Hill explains the reasons for the shooting in his autobiographical statement "I Shot an Abortionist," on the Army of God website (www.armyofgod.com/PHill_ShortShot.html).

95. North, *Lone Gunners for Jesus,* 25.

96. Ibid.

97. Paul Hill, *Paul Hill Speaks* (pamphlet published by Reformation Press, Bowie, Maryland, June 1997), 1.

98. Ibid., 2.

99. Bray, *A Time to Kill*, 158.

100. Chester L. Quarles, *Christian Identity: The Aryan American Bloodline Religion* (Jefferson, N.C.: McFarland & Co., 2004). For a discussion of the significance of the radical Christian right on American politics and society, see Hedges, *American Fascists*; Goldberg, *Kingdom Coming*; Clyde Wilcox and Carin Larson, *Onward Christian Soldiers: The Religious Right in American Politics* (Boulder, Colo.: Westview Press, 2006); Robert Booth Fowler, Allen D. Hertzke, and Laura R. Olson, *Religion and Politics in America: Faith, Culture, and Strategic Choices* (Boulder, Colo.: Westview Press, 2004); and William Martin, *With God on Our Side: The Rise of the Religious Right in America* (New York: Broadway, 2005).

101. Morris Dees, *Gathering Storm: America's Militia Threat* (New York: HarperCollins, 1996), 165. Reports of McVeigh visiting Elohim City are made in David Hoffman, *The Oklahoma City Bombing and the Politics of Terror* (Venice, Calif.: Feral House, 1998), 83–84.

102. Andrew Macdonald [William Pierce], *The Turner Diaries* (New York: Barricade Books, 1996) (originally published by National Alliance Vanguard Books, Arlington, Va., in 1978).

103. Dees, *Gathering Storm*, 154.

104. Ibid., 158.

105. Although Pierce, the author of *The Turner Diaries*, denies knowing McVeigh or talking to him, two separate law enforcement sources claim to have telephone records proving that McVeigh placed a lengthy call to Pierce's unlisted number in West Virginia in the weeks before the bombing. This information was first reported by CNN and is mentioned in Dees, *Gathering Storm*, 165.

106. Amy C. Solnin, *William L. Pierce, Novelist of Hate: Research Report of the Anti-Defamation League* (New York: Anti-Defamation League, 1995), 8.

107. Macdonald [Pierce], *Turner Diaries*, 64.

108. Michael Barkun, *Religion and the Racist Right: The Origins of the Christian Identity Movement* (Chapel Hill: University of North Carolina Press, 1994).

109. Barkun, *Religion and the Racist Right*, 7.

110. Leonard Zeskind, *The "Christian Identity" Movement: Analyzing Its Theological Rationalization for Racist and Anti-Semitic Violence* (New York: Division of Church and Society of the National Council of Churches of Christ in the U.S.A., 1986), 12.

111. Zeskind, *"Christian Identity" Movement*, 14.

112. Jeffrey Kaplan, *Radical Religion in America: Millenarian Movements from the Far Right to the Children of Noah* (Syracuse, N.Y.: Syracuse University Press, 1997), 175.

113. Zeskind, *"Christian Identity" Movement*, 45.

114. Gerald Baumgarten, *Paranoia as Patriotism: Far-Right Influences on the Militia Movement* (New York: Anti-Defamation League, 1995), 17.

115. Gordon "Jack" Mohr (founder of the Christian Patriot Defense League), "Know Your Enemies," 1982 pamphlet, quoted in James Aho, *The Politics of Righteousness: Idaho Christian Patriotism* (Seattle: University of Washington Press, 1990), 96.

116. Aho, *Politics of Righteousness,* 91.

117. Kim Murphy, "Last Stand of an Aging Aryan," *Los Angeles Times,* January 10, 1999, A1.

118. Kim Murphy, "Hate's Affluent New Godfathers," *Los Angeles Times,* January 10, 1999, A14.

119. Michael Bray, "Running with Rudolph," *Capitol Area Christian News* 28 (Winter 1998–99): 2. Eric Rudolph's own explanation of why he exploded the bomb at Centennial Park emphasizes the attempt to punish and embarrass the United States government for its stand on abortion. See his autobiographical statement on the Army of God website (www.armyofgod.com/EricRudolph AtlantaCourtStatement.html).

120. Bray, "Running with Rudolph," 2.

121. Aho, *Politics of Righteousness,* 85.

122. I explore further this discussion of Christian activism in America in my book *Terror in the Mind of God,* where parts of this section were first published.

CHAPTER 5: TRANSNATIONAL NETWORKS: GLOBAL JIHAD

1. For an overview of the global expansion of the transnational jihadi movement, see Gilles Kepel, *Jihad: The Trail of Political Islam* (Cambridge, Mass.: Belknap Press of Harvard University Press, 2003); Marc Sageman, *Understanding Terror Networks* (Philadelphia: University of Pennsylvania Press, 2004); Fawaz A. Gerges, *The Far Enemy: Why Jihad Went Global* (Cambridge: Cambridge University Press, 2005); Rohan Gunaratna, *The Changing Face of Terrorism* (Singapore: Marshall Cavendish Corp, 2005); and Oliver Roy, *Globalized Islam: The Search for a New Ummah* (New York: Columbia University Press, 2006).

2. Sheik Omar Abdel-Rahman entered the United States on four occasions, beginning in 1986 at the invitation of a group of Muslim students in the United States. The first visa was alleged to have been arranged with the assistance of the Central Intelligence Agency (see Cooperative Research History Commons, July 1990, www.cooperativeresearch.org/context.jsp?item =a0790abdulrahman; MITP Terrorism Knowledge Base, http://www.tkb.org/ KeyLeader.jsp?memID=5651). In July 1990 he entered the United States to take up residency in New Jersey despite being on a terrorist watch list. The U.S. State Department launched an internal investigation in 1993 to find out how Abdel-Rahman had been able to enter the country and concluded that it was due to flaws in the computer system meant to identify undesirable immigrants (Douglas Jehl, "Flaws in Computer Check Helped Sheik Enter U.S." *New York Times,* July 3, 1993).

3. Sheik Omar Abdul-Rahman, quoted in the British newspaper *The Independent.* Cited in Kim Murphy, "Have the Islamic Militants Turned to a New Battlefront in the U.S.?" *Los Angeles Times,* May 5, 1993, 20.

4. The network surrounding Sheik Omar Abdel-Rahman that was involved in the 1993 World Trade Center bombing is detailed in Peter Caram, *The 1993 World Trade Center Bombing: Foresight and Warning* (London: Janus Publishing, 2001); and Jim Dwyer and Deidre Murphy, Peg Tyre, and David Kocieniewski, *Two Seconds under the World: Terror Comes to America—The Conspiracy Behind the World Trade Center Bombing* (New York: Crown, 1994).

5. Interview with Mahmoud Abouhalima, convicted co-conspirator in the 1993 bombing of the World Trade Center, at U.S. Federal Penitentiary, Lompoc, California, August 19, 1997.

6. Ibid.

7. Michael B. Mukasey, chief judge, United States District Court for the Southern District of New York, quoted in John J. Goldman, "Defendants Given 25 Years to Life in N.Y. Terror Plot," *Los Angeles Times*, January 18, 1996, A1.

8. For an excellent description of the radical ideology propounded by Egyptian jihadi thinkers, see Gilles Kepel, *Muslim Extremism in Egypt: The Prophet and Pharaoh* (rev. ed.: University of California Press, 2003).

9. Abd al-Salam Faraj, "The Neglected Duty," in Johannes J. G. Jansen, *The Neglected Duty: The Creed of Sadat's Assassins and Islamic Resurgence in the Middle East* (New York: Macmillan, 1986), 41.

10. It was published in *Al-Ahrar,* an Egyptian newspaper, on December 14, 1981. An English translation, accompanied by an extensive essay on the document, can be found in Johannes J. G. Jansen, *The Neglected Duty: The Creed of Sadat's Assassins and Islamic Resurgence in the Middle East* (New York: Macmillan, 1986). I have also found helpful the analysis of this document by David Rapoport in "Sacred Terror: A Case from Islam," unpublished paper delivered at the 1988 Annual Meeting of the American Political Science Association, Washington D.C., September 1–4, 1988. The political implications of the document are discussed in Mohammed Heikal, *Autumn of Fury: The Assassination of Sadat* (London: André Deutsch, 1983).

11. Faraj, *Neglected Duty*, in Jansen, 79.

12. Faraj, paras. 102 and 109, in Jansen, *Neglected Duty,* 210–11.

13. Faraj, para. 113, in Jansen, *Neglected Duty,* 212–13; see also paras. 109, 211.

14. For background on Osama bin Laden, see Peter Bergen, *Holy War, Inc.: Inside the Secret World of Osama bin Laden* (New York: Touchstone, 2001); Daniel Benjamin and Steven Simon, *The Age of Sacred Terror* (New York: Random House, 2002); Rohan Gunaratna, *Inside al Qaeda: Global Network of Terror* (New York: Columbia University Press, 2002); Bruce Lawrence, *Messages to the World: The Statements of Osama bin Laden* (London: Verso, 2005); and Peter Bergen, *The Osama bin Laden I Know* (New York: Random House, 2006).

15. Bin Laden was the only child that his mother produced while married to bin Laden's father (they were later divorced). She was said to be the least favored of his father's ten wives, and Jerrold Post speculates that this might have been a factor in bin Laden's psychological development. See Jerrold M. Post, introduction to Jerrold M. Post, ed., *Military Studies in the Jihad against the Tyrants: The Al-Qaeda Training Manual* (Maxwell Air Force Base, Alabama: USAF Counterproliferation Center, n.d. [ca. 2005]), 1.

16. Lawrence, *Messages to the World*, xii.

17. Interview with Afghanistan's former prime minister, Gulbuddin Hekmatyar, broadcast on Geo Television, Pakistan, January 10, 2007.

18. Robert I. Friedman, "The CIA and the Sheik" *The Village Voice*, March 30, 1993; Joseph Zulaika, "The Self-Fulfilling Prophecies of Counterterrorism," *Radical History Review* 85 (2003), 191–200.

19. Bergen, *Holy War, Inc.*, 80–82.

20. Lawrence, *Messages to the World*, 6.

21. Gunaratna, *Inside al-Qaeda*, 32–34.

22. An implicit connection between bin Laden and Ramzi Yousef in the 1980s is mentioned in the *Report of the National Commission on Terrorist Attacks upon the United States* ("*9/11 Commission Report*"), September 24, 2004 (www.9-11commission.gov/), 59.

23. Osama bin Laden, "The Betrayal of Palestine, December 29, 1994," in Lawrence, *Messages to the World*, 3–14.

24. *9/11 Commission Report*, 62. The report lists "intelligence reports" as its source for the al-Zawahiri connection to the attempted attempt to assassinate Mubarak.

25. Osama bin Laden, "Declaration of *Jihad*, August 23 1996," in Lawrence, *Messages to the World*, 23–30.

26. Osama bin Laden, "The World Islamic Front, February 23 1998," in Lawrence, *Messages to the World*, 61.

27. Michael Grunwald and Vernon Loeb, "Charges Filed Against bin Laden," *Washington Post*, November 5, 1998.

28. *9/11 Commisssion Report*, 145–52.

29. Reports on Khalid Sheik Mohammed's trail of terrorist activities are to be found in the *9/11 Commission Report*, chap. 5; Rohan Gunaratna, "Womanizer, Joker, Scuba Diver: The Other Face of al-Qaida's No. 3," *Guardian Limited*, March 3, 2003; Zakki Hakim, "Official Ties al-Qaida to Indonesia Terror," *Associated Press*, February 28, 2006.

30. Gunaratna, "Womanizer, Joker, Scuba Diver."

31. Khalid Sheik Mohammed, "Verbatim Transcript of Combatant Status Review Tribunal Hearing for ISN 10024," March 15, 2007, on www .globalsecurity.org.

32. J. M. Berger, "Mohammed Jamal Khalifa: Life and Death Secrets," Intelwire, January 31, 2007 (http://intelwire.egoplex.com).

33. Bin Laden, "The World Islamic Front," in Lawrence, *Messages to the World*, 61.

34. *9/11 Commission Report*, chap. 5.

35. Interview with Sheik Muhammad al-Kubaisi, deputy secretary general, Association of Muslim Clerics, at the Mother of All Battles Mosque, Baghdad, May 6, 2004.

36. A collection of these jihadi recruitment videos is located on www .jihadwatch.org.

37. *9/11 Commission Report*, chap 5, sec. 1.

38. See the discussion of the possible global jihadi links to terrorist incidents in Kashmir and Mumbai in chapter 3 of this book.

39. The Jordanian intelligence reports are cited in Lee Hudson Teslik, "Profile: Abu Musab al-Zarqawi," a background report on the website of the Council on Foreign Relations (www.cfr.org). See also Robert S. Leiken and Steven Brooke, "Who is Abu Zarqawi?" *Weekly Standard*, May 24, 2004.

40. Mary Ann Weaver, "Inventing al-Zarqawi," *Atlantic Monthly*, July/August 2006.

41. Ibid.

42. The possible global jihadi links of the Salafia Jihadia group in Morocco are discussed in chapter 2 of this book.

43. Statement of Mohammad Sidique Kahn broadcast on Al-Jazeera television, September 1, 2005.

44. Lawrence, *Messages to the World*, 100–275.

45. Al-Zawahiri, *Knights Under the Prophet's Banner*, serialized in *Al-Sharq al-Awsat*, a London-based Saudi-owned daily newspaper, in 2001.

46. "Letter from al-Zawahiri to al-Zarqawi," complete text of the letter from Ayman al-Zawahiri to Abu Musab al-Zarqawi, July 9, 2005, posted on GlobalSecurity.org (www.globalsecurity.org/security/library/report/2005).

47. Weaver, "Inventing al-Zarqawi."

CHAPTER 6: THE ENDURING PROBLEMS OF VIOLENCE,
DEMOCRACY, AND HUMAN RIGHTS

1. Excerpted from one of Bhindranwale's speeches, translated in Pettigrew, "In Search of a New Kingdom of Lahore."

2. Khomeini, *Collection of Speeches, Position Statements*, 7.

3. Interview with Lerner, Jerusalem, January 20, 1989.

4. Juergensmeyer, *Terror in the Mind of God*, chap. 8.

5. René Girard, *Violence and the Sacred*, translated by Patrick Gregory (Baltimore: Johns Hopkins University Press, 1977); and *The Scapegoat*, translated by Yvonne Freccero (Baltimore: Johns Hopkins University Press, 1986).

6. Osama bin Laden, "Among a Band of Knights—February 14, 2003," reprinted in Lawrence, ed., *Message to the World*, 188.

7. Bhindranwale, "Two Lectures," in Sandhu, *Struggle for Justice*.

8. Bhindranwale, "Address to the Sikh Congregation," in Sandhu, *Struggle for Justice*.

9. Bhindranwale, "Two Lectures," in Sandhu, *Struggle for Justice*.

10. Khomeini, *Collection of Speeches, Position Statements*, 6.

11. Bani-Sadr, *Fundamental Principles and Precepts of Islamic Government*, 28–35.

12. Khomeini, *Collection of Speeches, Position Statements*, 30.

13. Khomeini, *Islam and Revolution*, 27–28.

14. Khomeini, *Collection of Speeches, Position Statements*, 24.

15. Ibid., 3.

16. Ibid., 25.

17. Ernesto Cardenal, in Teofilo Cabastrero, *Ministers of God, Ministers of the People: Testimonies of Faith from Nicaragua*, translated by Robert R. Barr (Maryknoll, N.Y.: Orbis Books, 1983), 22–23.

18. My interviews with the bhikkhu Rev. Uduwawala Chandananda Thero were conducted in Sri Lanka on February 4–5, 1988, in English. For a fuller account, see Juergensmeyer, "What the Bhikkhu Said."

19. Meir Kahane, speech on the announcement of the creation of an independent state of Judea, Jerusalem, January 18, 1989 (from my notes taken on that occasion).

20. Ibid.

21. Interview with Lerner, Jerusalem, January 20, 1989.

22. "Guidelines for the Panth" and other excerpts from the speeches of Bhindranwale are included as an appendix in Surjeet Jalandhary, *Bhindranwale Sant* (Jalandhar, India: Punjab Pocket Books, n.d. [ca. 1985]), 164.

23. Bhindranwale, excerpt from a speech, in Pettigrew, "In Search of a New Kingdom of Lahore."

24. Bhindranwale, "Address to the Sikh Congregation," in Sandhu, *Struggle for Justice.* See also Jalandhary, *Bhindranwale Sant,* 165.

25. See Mohinder Singh, "Gandhi, Sikhs and Non-violence," *Khera* 9, no. 3 (July–September 1990): 72–87. For the ethic of nonviolence in Sikhism, see W. Owen Cole and Piara Singh Sambhi, *The Sikhs: Their Religious Beliefs and Practices* (London: Routledge & Kegan Paul, 1978), 138. For Sikh ethical attitudes in general, see Avtar Singh, *Ethics of the Sikhs* (Patiala, India: Punjabi University Press, 1970); and S. S. Kohli, *Sikh Ethics* (New Delhi: Munshiram Manoharlal, 1975).

26. Bhindranwale, "Two Lectures," 21, in Sandhu, *Struggle for Justice.*

27. On the development of the just-war doctrine in Christianity, with its secular parallels, see James Turner Johnson, *Ideology, Reason, and the Limitation of War: Religious and Secular Concepts, 1200–1740* (Princeton: Princeton University Press, 1975). For the idea of a "just revolution" in Christianity, see Robert McAfee Brown, *Religion and Violence,* 2d ed. (Philadelphia: Westminster Press, 1987), 56–61.

28. Interview with Kahane, Jerusalem, January 18, 1989.

29. Speech given by Kahane at the event proclaiming an independent state of Judea, Jerusalem, January 18, 1989. For a summary of the discussion in the Gush Emunim about the appropriateness of using violence, see Lustick, *For the Land and the Lord,* 93–100.

30. Kahane speech, Jerusalem, January 18, 1989.

31. Ibid.

32. Interview with Lerner, Jerusalem, January 20, 1989.

33. Interview with Kahane in Mergui and Simonnot, *Israel's Ayatollahs,* 52.

34. Ibid., 50.

35. Interview with Sheik Yassin, Gaza, January 14, 1989.

36. Ibid.

37. Interview with Rantisi, Khan Yunis, March 1, 1988. The Arabic word *izzat* can mean "pride" and "respect," as well as "honor."

38. Interview with 'Odeh in *Islam and Palestine,* Leaflet 5 (Limassol, Cyprus, June 1988).

39. Ibid.

40. Interview with Shitta, Cairo, January 11, 1989.

41. Interviews in Sri Lanka, January 1988.

42. Ibid.

43. Ibid.

44. Bandaranaike was gunned down by a bhikkhu, Talduwe Somarama Thero, when Somarama came to the prime minister's house with a group of petitioners on September 25, 1959. The court determined that the bhikkhu was part of a larger conspiracy masterminded by the most politically powerful monk of the day, Mapitigama Buddharakkhita Thero, whom Donald Smith has called the Rasputin of Sri Lankan politics. Donald Eugene Smith, "The Political Monks and Monastic Reform," in Donald Eugene Smith, ed., *South Asian Politics and Religion* (Princeton: Princeton University Press, 1966), 495.

45. For the social composition of the Iranian revolution, see Robin Wright, *Sacred Rage: The Wrath of Militant Islam* (New York: Linden Press, Simon & Schuster, 1985); Sick, *All Fall Down;* and Simpson, *Inside Iran.*

46. Kim Murphy, "Islamic Party Wins Power in Algeria," *Los Angeles Times,* December 28, 1991, A15.

47. Richard Gombrich and Gananath Obeyesekere, *Buddhism Transformed: Religious Change in Sri Lanka* (Princeton: Princeton University Press, 1988). See also Tambiah, *Buddhism Betrayed?*

48. This analysis is based on twenty obituaries printed in the *World Sikh News* during 1988. I appreciate the assistance of Gurinder Singh in compiling this information.

49. For a comparative study of this issue, see the essays in Hawley, *Fundamentalism and Gender.*

50. Quoted in Kim Murphy, "Algerian Election to Test Strength of Radical Islam," *Los Angeles Times,* December 26, 1991, 19.

51. Quoted in ibid.

52. The intense loyalties of male comrades in these militant groups suggest in some cases a homoerotic element. In India, some of the young men in militant Sikh cadres pair off and are bonded as blood brothers in a quasi-religious ceremony.

53. Frantz Fanon, *The Wretched of the Earth* (New York: Grove Press, 1963).

54. Gopal, *Anatomy of a Confrontation,* 13.

55. Quoted in Kim Murphy, "Algerian Election to Test Strength of Radical Islam," *Los Angeles Times,* December 26, 1991.

56. Dina Nath Mishra, *RSS: Myth and Reality* (New Delhi: Vikas, 1980), 73; see also Embree, "Function of the Rashtriya Swayamsevak Sangh," 9–17.

57. Interview with Sheik Yassin, Gaza, January 14, 1989.

58. Quoted in Mergui and Simonnot, *Israel's Ayatollahs,* 40–41.

59. Interview with Sheik Yassin, Gaza, January 14, 1989.

60. Interview with Uduwawala Chandananda Thero, Kandy, Sri Lanka, February 2, 1988.

61. Interview with el-Arian, Cairo, January 11, 1989.

62. Interview with Levinger, Jerusalem, January 16, 1989.

63. Abdulrahim Pulatov, quoted in Robin Wright, "Report from Turkestan," *New Yorker,* April 6, 1992, 60.

64. "The Great Divide: How Westerners and Muslims View Each Other," Pew Global Attitudes Project, released June 22, 2006 (www.pewglobal.org).

I am grateful to Roger Friedland for pointing out this correlation. His analysis of a 2003 Pew study showing a relationship between the appeal of democracy and Muslim politics may be found in Roger Friedland, "Constituting Violence," a paper presented at the 2006 European Amalfi Theory Meetings, cosponsored by the Italian Sociological Association.

65. Interview with Shitta, Cairo, January 10, 1989.

66. Interview with Sheik Yassin, Gaza, January 14, 1989.

67. Kahane, quoted in Mergui and Simonnot, *Israel's Ayatollahs,* 35.

68. "The goal of democracy is to let people do what they want," Kahane claimed. "Judaism wants to make them better." Quoted in ibid., 36.

69. Interview with Uduwawala Chandananda Thero, Kandy, Sri Lanka, February 2, 1988.

70. Plato, *The Republic,* translated by B. Jowett (New York: Modern Library, 1941), 312.

71. The separation of legislative and executive branches was a further attempt to balance these two functions of government, one representing particular districts and the other representing the whole. See Locke, "Of the Legislative, Executive, and Federative Power of the Commonwealth," chap. 12 *of The Second Treatise on Government,* 410.

72. See *The Federalist Papers* (New York: Mentor Books, 1961), 378.

73. Interview with el-Geyoushi, Cairo, May 30, 1990.

74. Speech by Yoel Lerner at the celebration to establish an independent state of Judea, Jerusalem, January 18, 1989. I appreciate the simultaneous translation of his speech at that occasion provided by Ehud Sprinzak and his students.

75. Interview with Lerner, Jerusalem, January 20, 1989.

76. For a discussion of the role of democracy in Islam, see John Esposito and John Voll, *Islam and Democracy* (New York: Oxford University Press, 1996). One Iranian theologian is quite adamant about the importance of democracy for Islam; see Abdolkarim Soroush, *Reason, Freedom, and Democracy in Islam: Essential Writings of Abdolkarim Soroush* (New York: Oxford University Press, 2002). An American author believes that democracy will solve many of the problems of the loss of legitimacy in Middle East regimes; see Noah Feldman, *After Jihad: America and the Struggle for Islamic Democracy* (New York: Farrar, Strauss, & Giroux, 2003).

77. Hamid Algar, trans., *Constitution of the Islamic Republic of Iran* (Berkeley: Mizan Press, 1980), 68.

78. The leader is leader for life, presumably, and when he dies, the constitution specifies that "experts elected by the people" will choose a new leader; if none is to be found, they will appoint three to five members of a leadership council, which will perform the leader's functions. Algar, *Constitution,* 66.

79. See H. E. Chehabi, "Religion and Politics in Iran: How Theocratic Is the Islamic Republic?" *Daedalus* (Summer 1991): 69–92. For the clergy's ambivalence toward politics in the period immediately prior to the revolution, see Shahrough Akhavi, *Religion and Politics in Contemporary Iran: Clergy-State Relations in the Pahlavi Period* (Albany: State University of New York Press, 1980).

80. Sick, *All Fall Down,* 193–94.

81. Ibid., 185.

82. Arjomand, "Victory for the Pragmatists," 57. See also Simpson, *Inside Iran,* 92–93.

83. Although Sikhism does not have a tradition of clergy, it does have groups of teachers in what amount to monastic orders; Bhindranwale was in one of these, the Damdami Taksal.

84. Interview with Sheik Yassin, Gaza, January 14, 1989.

85. Interview with Uduwawala Chandananda Thero, Kandy, Sri Lanka, February 2, 1988.

86. Interview with el-Arian, Cairo, January 11, 1989.

87. Interview with Uduwawala Chandananda Thero, Kandy, Sri Lanka, February 2, 1988.

88. Interview with Shitta, Cairo, January 10, 1989.

89. Interview with Kahane, Jerusalem, January 18, 1989. Michael ben Horin, a leader of the event for proclaiming a state of Judea, explained that all the delegates had been chosen from Judea and Samaria, two elected from each settlement. Leaders of the founding congress were elected by a secret ballot. The list of people nominated for the executive committee was read out (and other names could be added); each candidate gave a short nominating speech. Interview with Michael ben Horin, manager, Kach office, in Jerusalem, January 15, 1989.

90. See Louis Dumont, *From Mandeville to Marx: The Genesis and Triumph of Economic Ideology* (Chicago: University of Chicago Press, 1977).

91. Quoted in Mark Fineman, "Riding the Crest of India's Hindu Revival," *Los Angeles Times,* June 11, 1991, H1.

92. Interview with Kahane, Jerusalem, January 18, 1989.

93. Bani-Sadr, *Fundamental Principles and Precepts of Islamic Government,* 40.

94. The International Centre for Ethnic Studies in Colombo produced a series of television programs describing the "unity through diversity" in Sri Lankan society. The Hindu god Vishnu, for instance, was shown to be frequently worshiped at Buddhist temples, and the distinctly Sri Lankan god Kataragama was seen to be venerated equally by Buddhists and Hindus.

95. A solution frequently offered for India's problems with the Sikhs (and, perhaps more important, with the much larger Muslim minority) is the creation of an ethnic branch of government: either councils composed of representatives from each religious community to advise the government on social legislation or an upper house of parliament to provide representation on the basis of religious and ethnic affiliation.

96. Interviews with Shitta, Cairo, January 10, 1989; el-Arian, Cairo, January 11, 1989; el-Geyoushi, Cairo, May 30, 1990; and Sheik Yassin, Gaza, January 14, 1989. Their comments about a two-level *shari'a* were made without knowing that similar comments had been made by the others.

97. Interview with el-Geyoushi, Cairo, May 30, 1990.

98. Prabhu Chawla, "Ambitious Alliances," *India Today,* April 30, 1991, 44.

99. Interview with Kenneth Fernando, Colombo, Sri Lanka, January 28, 1988. Anthony Fernando, Kelaniya University, Colombo, has also written extensively on the importance of Buddhism for Christians.

100. Carl W. Ernst, "The Symbolism and Psychology of World Empire in the Delhi Sultanate" (paper given at a conference, *Religion and Nationalism*, at the University of California, Santa Barbara, April 20, 1989), 15. Ernst is quoting the chronicle of the fourteenth-century Muslim historian Ziyamal-Din Barani.

101. Algar, *Constitution*, 32, 36.

102. See Bakhash, *Reign of the Ayatollahs*, 24; and Simpson, *Inside Iran*, 213–19.

103. Interview with el-Arian, Cairo, January 11, 1989. El-Arian claimed that, like Muslims, Copts have their own concentric circles of identity, one of which is Egypt.

104. Interviews with Shitta, Cairo, January 10, 1989; and el-Geyoushi, Cairo, May 30, 1990.

105. Interview with Father Aramea Marcari, Coptic monk, in Abba Marcarios Monastery, Wadi Natrun, Egypt, May 28, 1990.

106. Interview with el-Hamamsy, Cairo, January 10, 1989.

107. Interview with Kahane, Jerusalem, January 18, 1989.

108. Ibid. See also Meir Kahane, *They Must Go* (Jerusalem: Institute of the Jewish Idea, 1981).

109. Interview with ben Horin, Jerusalem, January 15, 1989.

110. Interviews with Shitta, Cairo, January 10, 1989; el-Arian, Cairo, January 11, 1989; el-Geyoushi, Cairo, May 30, 1990; and Sheik Yassin, Gaza, January 14, 1989.

111. Interview with el-Geyoushi, Cairo, May 30, 1990.

112. For a discussion of human rights in comparative perspective, see David Little, John Kelsay, and Abdulaziz A. Sachedina, *Human Rights and the Conflict of Cultures: Western and Islamic Perspectives on Religious Liberty* (Columbia: University of South Carolina Press, 1988); Max L. Stackhouse, *Creeds, Society, and Human Rights: A Study in Three Cultures* (Grand Rapids, Mich.: W. B. Eerdmans, 1984); Arlene Swidler, ed., *Human Rights in Religious Traditions* (New York: Pilgrim Press, 1982); Leroy S. Rouner, ed., *Human Rights and the World's Religions* (Notre Dame, Ind.: University of Notre Dame Press, 1988); Kenneth W. Thompson, ed., *Moral Imperative of Human Rights* (Washington: University Press of America, 1980); and Irene Bloome, Paul Martin, and Wayne Proudfoot, eds., *Religious Diversity and Human Rights* (New York: Columbia University Press, 1996); and the essays in Liam Georon, ed., *Human Rights and Religion: A Reader* (Sussex, U.K.: Sussex Academic Press, 2003). For an exploration of the interesting thesis that human rights is itself a religious tradition, see Robert Traer, *Faith in Human Rights: Support in Religious Traditions for a Global Struggle* (Washington, D.C.: Georgetown University Press, 1991).

113. David Little, "The Development in the West of the Right to Freedom of Religion and Conscience: A Basis for Comparison with Islam," in Little, Kelsay, and Sachedina, *Human Rights and the Conflict of Cultures*, 30.

114. Several authors argue that Islam embraces human rights, albeit in its own way; see Abdullahi Ahmed An-Naim, *Toward an Islamic Reformation: Civil Liberties, Human Rights, and International Law* (Syracuse,

N.Y.: Syracuse University Press, 1996); and Ann Elizabeth Mayer, *Islam and Human Rights: Tradition and Politics* (Boulder, Colo.: Westview Press, 2006).

115. Speech given by Meir Kahane, Jerusalem, January 18, 1989 (the English translation was supplied to me on that occasion by Ehud Sprinzak and his students). See also the transcript of an interview with Kahane in Mergui and Simonnot, *Israel's Ayatollahs,* 33–34.

116. Robert Bellah et al., *Habits of the Heart: Individualism and Commitment in American Life* (Berkeley: University of California Press, 1985).

117. Alasdair MacIntyre, *After Virtue: A Study in Moral Theory* (Notre Dame: University of Notre Dame Press, 1981).

118. Interview with el-Arian, Cairo, January 11, 1989.

119. Algar, *Constitution,* 27.

120. Ibid., 38.

121. Ibid., 43.

122. Ibid., 91.

123. Interview with Sheik Yassin, Gaza, January 14, 1989.

124. A number of Muslims I interviewed maintained that Islam is especially tolerant of differences of opinion and open discourse because, as one of them put it, "aside from the Qur'an, everything in Islam is open to argument." Interview with Ashur, Cairo, May 27, 1990.

125. See Embree, "Function of the Rashtriya Swayamsevak Sangh," 5.

126. Zafar Agha, "BJP Government: What Will It Be Like?" *India Today,* May 15, 1991, 20–21.

127. Interview with Levinger, Jerusalem, January 16, 1989.

128. Madhu Jain, "BJP Supporters: Invasion of the Scuppies," *India Today,* May 15, 1991, 18–19.

129. Quoted in Murphy, "Algerian Election to Test Strength of Radical Islam," 19.

130. Lawrence, *Defenders of God,* 27.

131. Giddens, *Nation-State,* 215–16.

132. Craig Calhoun, *Nationalism* (Minneapolis: University of Minnesota Press, 1998), 67.

133. John Lie, *Modern Peoplehood* (Cambridge, Mass.: Harvard University Press, 2005).

134. Gerald Larson, "Fast Falls the Eventide: India's Anguish over Religion" (Presentation at a conference, *Religion and Nationalism,* at the University of California, Santa Barbara, April 21, 1989).

135. Wilfred Cantwell Smith, *Islam in Modern History* (Princeton: Princeton University Press, 1957), 47.

136. Sick, *All Fall Down,* 185.

CONCLUSION

1. Gary Sick, *All Fall Down,* 186.

2. Imam Abu Kheireiddine, quoted in Kim Murphy, "Islamic Party Wins Power in Algeria," *Los Angeles Times,* December 28, 1991.

3. Robert Pape, *Dying to Win: The Strategic Logic of Suicide Terrorism* (New York: Random House, 2005).

4. I explore the topic of male empowerment as a factor in violence in "Why Guys Throw Bombs" in my book *Terror in the Mind of God*, 198–209.

5. Interview with Abdul Aziz al-Rantisi, cofounder and political leader of Hamas, Khan Yunis, Gaza, March 1, 1998.

6. A "senior Administration official" quoted in Robin Wright, "U.S. Struggles to Deal with Global Islamic Resurgence," *Los Angeles Times*, January 26, 1992.

7. The appeals to religion come from both ends of the political spectrum. The conservative political theorist Eric Voegelin, for instance, called for greater influence of Christianity in American political thinking in order to counter what he regarded as a gnostic tendency toward utopianism that corrupts the "civil theology" of the modern West. Eric Voegelin, *The New Science of Politics: An Introduction*, 2d ed. (Chicago: University of Chicago Press, 1987), 162. Interestingly, Islamic activists have also encouraged the United States to take biblical religion more seriously. Alann Steen reports that while he was held hostage in Lebanon, his Islamic captors, loyal followers of the Ayatollah Khomeini, gave the hostages Bibles and encouraged them to read them. Interview with Alann Steen, in Honolulu, March 11, 1992.

8. Mohandas Gandhi, *Hind Swaraj, or Indian Home Rule* (Ahmedabad, India: Navajivan Press, 1938), 33–34.

9. Arthur Schlesinger, who served in the administrations of Franklin D. Roosevelt and John F. Kennedy, said that Niebuhr "cast an intellectual spell" on him and his generation of political thinkers (Arthur Schlesinger, Jr., "Reinhold Niebuhr's Long Shadow," *New York Times*, June 22, 1992, A13).

10. Reinhold Niebuhr, *Moral Man and Immoral Society* (New York: Scribner's, 1932), 255.

11. Embree, *Utopias in Conflict*, 45.

12. Niebuhr, *Moral Man and Immoral Society*, 277.

13. Ibid.

14. Ibid.

List of Interviews

Abdullah, Dr. Farooq (conversation). Chief minister, State of Jummu and Kashmir, India. In Jummu, India, January 20, 1998.

Abe, Yoshiya. Professor of religion, Kokugakuin University. In Tokyo, January 9, 1996.

Abouhalima, Mahmud. Political activist, convicted co-conspirator of World Trade Center bombing. At federal penitentiary, Lompoc, California, August 19, 1997; September 30, 1997.

———. Correspondence from Lompoc, September 25, 1996; October 21, 1996; January 3, 1997; June 15, 1997; July 20, 1997; August 28, 1997; January 7, 1998. From Leavenworth, Kansas, May 20, 1999.

Abu-Amr, Zaid. Professor of Philosophy and Cultural Studies, Bir Zeit University. In Jerusalem, August 15, 1995.

Ahmed, Showkat. Student, Aligarh Muslim University. In Pathankot, India, January 18, 1998.

Amgalan, Y. Deputy Hamba Lama (Deputy Head Lama), Gandan Tegchinlen Monastery. In Ulan Bator, April 14, 1992.

Amunagama, Dr. Sarath. Associate Secretary-General, Worldview International Foundation. In Colombo, January 2, 1991.

Arafat, Dr. Fathi. President, Palestine Red Crescent Society. In Cairo, May 30, 1990.

el-Arian, Essam. Medical doctor, member of the People's Assembly, and member of the Muslim Brotherhood. Cairo, January 11, 1989.

Ariyaratne, A. T. Founder and President, Sarvodaya Shramadana Movement. In Moratuwa, Sri Lanka, January 2, 1991.

Asafi, Dr. Muhammad, and other Palestinian refugee camp leaders. In Jabaliya camp, Gaza, January 14, 1989.

Asfour, Gaber. Professor of Arabic Literature, Cairo University. In Cairo, May 26, 1990.

Ashur, Prof. A. K. Dean of the Faculty of Education, Al-Azhar University. In Cairo, May 27, 1990.

Auda, Gehad. Research Scholar, Al Ahram Institute. In Cairo, May 31, 1990.

Azra, Azyumardi. Rector, Syarif Hidayatullah State Islamic University, Jakarta, Indonesia. In Jakarta, July 21, 2003.

Bakula, Kushok. Rinpoche and Indian Ambassador. In Ulan Bator, April 12, 1992.

bar Nathan, Arie. Settler in Mitzpeh Jericho. In Gush Emunim tent in front of Knesset, Jerusalem, January 16, 1989.

Batsukh, D. Official, Asian Buddhist Conference for Peace. In Ulan Bator, April 10, 11, and 13, 1992.

Bayantsagaan, S. President, Mongolyn Susegtnii Kholboo (Association of Mongolian Believers). In Ulin Bator, April 12, 1992.

Bayarsuren, Ts., Chairman, Mongolian Religious Party. In Ulan Bator, April 12, 1992.

Bayasakh, K. Director, School of Foreign Service, and Head, Department of Oriental Studies, Mongolia State University. In Seoul, April 10, 1992.

ben Horin, Michael. Manager, Kach Office. In Jerusalem, January 15, 1989.

Bishoy, Father Sedrack Anbas. Coptic monk. In Anbas Bishoy Monastery, Wadi Natrun, Egypt, May 28, 1990.

Bray, Rev. Michael. Pastor, Reformation Lutheran Church, and editor, *Capitol Area Christian News*. In Bowie, Maryland, April 25, 1996; March 20, 1998.

———. Correspondence from Bowie, Maryland, July 20, 1997; March 9, 1999.

Chandananda, Venerable Palipana. Mahanayake, Asgiri Chapter, Sinhalese Buddhist Sangha. In Kandy, Sri Lanka, February 3, 1988, and January 4, 1991.

Chandananda Thero, Rotapokune. Principal, Vidyasara Vidyayathana Pirvena. In Kalutara, Sri Lanka, January 3, 1991.

Chandananda Thero, Rev. Uduwawala. Member, Karaka Sabha, Asgiri Chapter, Sinhalese Buddhist Sangha. In Kandy, Sri Lanka, February 2, 1988, and January 5, 1991.

Chandra, Ram. Office-worker, Bharatiya Janata Party. In Delhi, January 10, 1991.

Charny, Israel W. Executive director, Institute of the International Conference on the Holocaust and Genocide. In Jerusalem, January 15, 1989.

Choijants, D. Lama, Gandan Monastery, and member, Great Hural (Upper House of Parliament). In Ulan Bator, April 12, 1992.

Coomaraswamy, Radhika. Research scholar, International Centre for Ethnic Studies. In Colombo, January 28, 1988.

Dambajav, C. Hamba Lama (Head Lama), Tashichoeling Monastery. In Ulan Bator, April 11 and 13, 1992.

Dandinsuren, B. Hamba Lama (Head Lama), Gandan Tegchinlen Monastery. In Ulan Bator, April 14, 1992.

deSilva, K. M. Chairman, International Centre for Ethnic Studies. In Kandy, Sri Lanka, January 4, 1991.

deSilva, Padmasiri. Professor of Philosophy, Peradeniya University. In Kandy, Sri Lanka, February 4, 1988.

Desouki, Ali. Member, Muslim Brotherhood. In Cairo, January 11, 1989.

Dewasumananayaka Thero, D. Buddhist Teacher, Dharmavijaya Pirivena. In Kalutara, Sri Lanka, January 3, 1991.

Dhaman, Kuldip Kumar. Student, Guru Nanak Dev University. In Amritsar, Punjab, January 11 and 12, 1991.

Dharmasiri, Gunapala. Professor of philosophy, Peradeniya University. In Kandy, Sri Lanka, February 5, 1988.

Dheerasekera, J. D. Professor, University of Colombo. In Colombo, February 2, 1988.

Dignan, Stuart. Office staff, Democratic Unionist Party. In Belfast, Northern Ireland, July 30, 1998.

Dominic, Merwyn. Member, Sri Lankan Catholic Church. In Colombo, January 3, 1991.

Dorji, D. Rector, Mongolian State University. In Seoul, April 10, 1992.

Eskin, Avigdor. Writer and political activist. In Jerusalem, March 3, 1998.

Faluji, Imad. Writer and political activist. In Gaza, August 19, 1995.

Falwell, Jerry (conversation). Pastor, Thomas Road Baptist Church. In Lynchburg, Virginia, February 23, 1997.

Farook, Jamaluddin. Student, Peradeniya University. In Kandy, Sri Lanka, January 4, 1991.

Fernando, Rev. Kenneth. Ecumenical Institute for Study and Dialogue. In Colombo, January 27, 1988.

Fruman, Manachem. Rabbi at Tuqua settlement. In West Bank, Israel, August 14, 1995.

Ganegama, W. G. Coordinator, Sarvodaya Rural Technical Services. In Kandy, Sri Lanka, February 4, 1988.

el-Geyoushi, Muhammad Ibraheem. Dean of the Faculty of *Dawah*, Al Azhar University. In Cairo, May 30, 1990.

Gibney, Jim (conversation). Sinn Féin Public Affairs Officer. In Belfast, Northern Ireland, July 30, 1998.

Gunatilake, Godfrey. Research Scholar, Marga Institute. In Colombo, January 28, 1988.

Gutierrez, Rev. Gustavo. Roman Catholic Priest. In Managua, Nicaragua, June 12, 1988.

el-Hamamsy, Leila. Director, Social Research Center, American University in Cairo. In Cairo, January 10, 1989.

Hanafi, Hasan. Student Leader, Muslim Brotherhood, Cairo University. In Cairo, May 30, 1990.

Haniu, Chieko. Public affairs officer, Tokyo office of Agonshu. In Tokyo, January 10, 1996.

Hartley, Tom. Councillor and leader of Sinn Féin in Belfast City Council. In Belfast, Northern Ireland, July 31, 1998.

Hassan, Ali. Student at Islamic University of Gaza and supporter of Hamas. In Gaza, March 1, 1998.

Hernandez, Norman J. Catholic student leader. In Managua, Nicaragua, June 14, 1988.

Hicham, Moulay (conversation). Prince of Morocco. In Isla Vista, California, February 5, 2007.

Hiramatsu, Yasuo. Public affairs officer, Tokyo office of Aum Shinrikyo. In Aoyama, Tokyo, January 13, 1996.

Ibrahim, Saad. Professor of sociology, American University in Cairo. In Cairo, January 10, 1989; in Santander, Spain, August 21, 2006.

Jawahir, A. L. Student, Peradeniya University. In Kandy, Sri Lanka, February 6, 1988.

Kahane, Rabbi Meir. Former member, Knesset, and Leader, Kach Party. In Jerusalem, January 18, 1989.

Kamal, Muhammad. Student at Islamic University of Gaza and supporter of Hamas. In Gaza, March 1, 1998.

Kamuro, Setsufumi. Secretary General of Tokyo office of Agonshu. In Tokyo, January 10, 1996.

Kaur, Surjit. President, Delhi Branch, Women's Akali Dal (Mann group). In Rakabganj Gurdwara, New Delhi, January 13, 1991.

Khalifa, Muhammad. Professor of comparative religion, Department of Oriental Languages, Cairo University. In Cairo, January 9, 1989.

Khisamutdinov, Amir. President, Far Eastern Studies Society, Vladivostok. In Honolulu, February 18, 1992.

Kolesnik, Nikolai A. Chairman, Council on Questions of Religion, Ukrainian Soviet Socialist Republic Council of Ministers. In a meeting of the Working Group on Religion and Nationalism, United States Institute of Peace, Washington, D.C., June 20, 1990.

al-Kubaisi, Sheik Muhammad. Deputy secretary general, Association of Muslim Clerics. At the Mother of All Battles Mosque, Baghdad, May 6, 2004.

Lamba, Navneet. Librarian, Bhai Vir Singh Sadan. In New Delhi, January 9, 1991.

Lerner, Yoel. Director, Sanhedrin Institute. In Jerusalem, January 20, 1989.

Levinger, Rabbi Moshe. Leader, Gush Emunim. In Gush Emunim tent in front of Knesset, Jerusalem, January 16, 1989.

Lubsantseren, G. Secretary general, Asian Buddhist Conference for Peace. In Ulan Bator, April 13, 1992.

al-Maliki, Jawad [also known as Nouri Kamel Mohammed Hassan al-Maliki]. Deputy director, Islamic Dawa Party, and later prime minister of Iraq. In Baghdad, Iraq, May 5, 2004.

Mann, Simranjit Singh. Former member of Parliament and leader of Akali Dal (Mann faction). In Chandigarh, Punjab, August 4, 1996.

Marcari, Father Aramea. Coptic monk. In Abba Marcarios Monastery, Wadi Natrun, Egypt, May 28, 1990.

Marzel, Baruch. Settler in Kalpat Arba, Hebron. In Jerusalem, January 17, 1989.

Mekey, A. Vice-rector, Mongolian State University. In Ulan Bator, April 11 and 14, 1992.

Miller, Davy (conversation). Sinn Féin supporter. In Belfast, Northern Ireland, July 30, 1998.

Moonesinghe, Mangala. Director, Political and Institutional Studies Division, Marga Institute. In Colombo, January 27, 1988.

Muraoka, Tatsuko. Secretary general of Tokyo office, Aum Shinrikyo. In Aoyama, Tokyo, January 13, 1996.

Mykmar, J. Assistant, Torgon Zam Co. In Ulan Bator, April 13, 1992.

Nakamura, Takeshi (pseudonym for a former member of Aum Shinrikyo). In Tokyo, January 12, 1996. (In English and Japanese; translation assistance provided by Prof. Susumu Shimazono and Amy Arakane.)

Nandy, Ashis. Research scholar, Center for Developing Societies. In Delhi, January 20, 1988.

Narang, Surjit Singh. Professor of political science, Guru Nanak Dev University. In Amritsar, Punjab, January 11, 1991.

Nasar, Mrs., and other Palestinian leaders. At Mama Hotel, Gaza, January 14, 1989.

Oujun, D. Scientific Researcher for government archives and member, Mongolian People's Revolutionary Party. In Ulan Bator, April 12, 1992.

Padmasiri, Rev. T. Sinhalese Monk. In Humbantota, Sri Lanka, February 3, 1988.

Palihawardene, Mahinda. Professor of English, University of Sri Jayawardena. In Colombo, January 27, 1988.

Pandher, Sarabjit. Principal correspondent, *The Hindu*. In Jummu, India, January 19, 1998.

Parajon, Gustavo. Leader, CEPAD. In Managua, Nicaragua, June 14, 1988.

Puri, Harish. Professor of political science, Guru Nanak Dev University. In Delhi, January 10, 1991; in Amritsar, Punjab, January 11, 1991.

Rabin, Leah (conversation). Widow of former prime minister Yitzhak Rabin. In Tel Aviv, March 2, 1998.

Ragi, Darshan Singh. Former Jatedar, Akal Takhat. In Bhai Vir Singh Sadan, New Delhi, January 13, 1991.

Rajagopal, Hari. Office-worker, BJP. In Delhi, January 9, 1991.

Rajapaksa, Mahinda. Lawyer and member, SLFP. In Tangalle, Sri Lanka, February 3, 1988.

Rantisi, Dr. Abdul Aziz, leader of the political wing of the Hamas movement. In Khan Yunis, Gaza, March 1, 1998.

al-Rawi, Isam, professor of geology at Baghdad University and member of the Association of Muslim Clerics, Iraq. In Cairo, March 12, 2005.

Rey, Roy (conversation). Staff member, Martyrs Memorial Free Presbyterian Church. In Belfast, Northern Ireland, July 30, 1998.

Salameh, Sheik. Spiritual teacher, al-Nur Mosque. In Cairo, May 28, 1990.

Salem, Mohamed Elmisilhi. Professor of educational psychology, Al-Azhar University. In Cairo, May 27, 1990.

Salomon, Gershom. Head, Faithful of Temple Mount. In Jerusalem, May 25, 1990.

Samarasinghe, S. W. R. deA. Director, International Centre for Ethnic Studies. In Kandy, Sri Lanka, January 4, 1991.

Saydhom, Arian. Member, Coptic Orthodox Church. In Cairo, May 28, 1990.

Schleiffer, Prof. Abdullah. Director, Communications Center, American University in Cairo. In Cairo, January 7, 1989.

Sekhon, Kuldip Singh. Lawyer for Sikh immigration cases. In Berkeley, June 1, 1996.
Shiha, Abdul Hamid. Professor of Dar el-Alum, Cairo University. In Cairo, May 27, 1990.
Shitta, Ibrahim Dasuqi. Professor of Persian literature, Cairo University. In Cairo, January 10 and 11, 1989.
Shohdy, Nancy A. Director of public and ecumenical relations, Coptic Orthodox Church. In Cairo, May 28, 1990.
Singh, Dr. Amrik. Member, All-India Sikh Students Federation (Mehta-Chawla group). In Rakabganj Gurdwara, New Delhi, January 13, 1991.
Singh, Bhagwan. Mulgranthi (chief worship leader), Golden Temple. In Amritsar, Punjab, January 11, 1991.
Singh, Gurmit. President, Delhi branch, All-India Sikh Students Federation (Mehta-Chawla group). In Rakabganj Gurdwara, New Delhi, January 13, 1991.
Singh, Gurnam. Professor of political science, Guru Nanak Dev University. In Amritsar, Punjab, January 11, 1991.
Singh, Harbinder. General secretary, Delhi branch, All-India Sikh Students Federation (Mehta-Chawla group). In Rakabganj Gurdwara, New Delhi, January 13, 1991.
Singh, Harcharand. Former Jatedar, Golden Temple. In Rakabganj Gurdwara, New Delhi, January 13, 1991.
Singh, Harjap. Council member of Amritsar Municipal Corporation and brother of Kanwarjit Singh, leader of Khalistan Commando Force, 1987–1989. In Sultanwind village, Amritsar, Punjab, January 20, 1998. (In English and Punjabi. Interview conducted with the assistance of Harish Puri, Harbhajan Singh, and Raminder Bir Singh.)
Singh, Jasvinder. Member, Delhi branch, All-India Sikh Students Federation (Mehta-Chawla group). In Rakabganj Gurdwara, New Delhi, January 13, 1991.
Singh, Mohinder. Director, National Institute for Punjab Studies. In Bhai Vir Singh Sadan, New Delhi, January 9, 1991.
Singh, Narinder. Retired major general, Indian army. In Chandigarh, Punjab, August 3, 1996.
Singh, Ramander Bir. Junior research fellow, Guru Nanak Dev University. In Amritsar, Punjab, January 20, 1998.
Singh, Sohan. Leader of Sohan Singh Panthic Committee. In Mohalli, Punjab, August 3, 1996.
Singh, Yashwant Pal. Manager, Delhi office, All-India Sikh Students Federation (Mehta-Chawla group). In Rakabganj Gurdwara, New Delhi, January 13, 1991.
Sodnom, Sh. Dean of the faculty, Mongolia State University. In Ulan Bator, April 11, 1992.
Steen, Alann. Former hostage held by Islamic militants in Lebanon. In Honolulu, March 11, 1992.
Sumanawansa Thero, N. Principal, Dharmavijaya Pirivena. In Kalutara, Sri Lanka, January 3, 1991.

Sutel, Seth. Correspondent for Associated Press. In Tokyo, January 9, 1996.

Thiruchelvam, Neelan. Director, International Centre for Ethnic Studies. In Colombo, January 27, 1988.

Tomoko (no last name given). Co-manager of Satian Bookstore, Aum Shinrikyo. Shibuya, Tokyo, January 11, 1996.

Wangchindorj, B. Editor-in-chief, *Buddhists for Peace*. In Ulan Bator, April 13, 1992.

Wangchuk, S. Assistant to Rinpoche Kushok Bakula. In Ulan Bator, April 12, 1992.

Wijesekera, Mahinda. Lawyer and member, SLFP. In Matara, Sri Lanka, February 2, 1988.

Wljeratne, Tissa. Manager, Sinhaputra Finance Co. In Kandy, Sri Lanka, February 6, 1988.

Yaghi, Ashraf. Hamas supporter. In Gaza City, August 19, 1995.

Yassin, Sheik Ahmed. Leader, Hamas. In Gaza, January 14, 1989.

Yokoyama, Minoru. Sociologist and professor of criminology, Kokugakuin University. In Tokyo, January 10, 1996.

Zamlot, Saleh. Student leader, Fateh, Palestine Liberation Organization. In Al-Azhar University, Cairo, May 27, 1990.

Zilberman, Dr. Ifrah. Research scholar, Hebrew University. In Jerusalem, January 18, 1989, and May 25, 1990.

Bibliography

GENERAL WORKS

Aho, James. *This Thing of Darkness: A Sociology of the Enemy.* Seattle: University of Washington Press, 1994.

Ali, Tariq. *The Clash of Fundamentalisms: Crusades, Jihads, and Modernity.* London: Verso, 2002.

Alpher, Joseph, ed. *Nationalism and Modernity: A Mediterranean Perspective.* New York: Praeger, 1986.

Anderson, Benedict. *Imagined Communities: Reflections on the Origin and Spread of Nationalism.* London: Verso, 1983.

Antoun, Richard T., and Mary Elaine Hegland, eds. *Religious Resurgence: Contemporary Cases in Islam, Christianity, and Judaism.* Syracuse, N.Y.: Syracuse University Press, 1987.

Appleby, R. Scott., ed. *Spokesmen for the Despised: Fundamentalist Leaders of the Middle East.* Chicago: University of Chicago Press, 1997.

Arendt, Hannah. *On Revolution.* New York: Viking Press, 1963.

Asad, Talal. *Formations of the Secular: Christianity, Islam, and Modernity.* Stanford: Stanford University Press, 2003.

Audi, Robert, and Nicholas Wolterstorff. *Religion in the Public Square: The Place of Religious Convictions in Political Debate.* New York: Rowman & Littlefield, 1997.

Baron, Salo Wittmayer. *Modern Nationalism and Religion.* New York: Harper & Bros., 1947.

Baumann, Red E., and Kenneth M. Jensen, eds. *Religion and Politics.* Charlottesville: University Press of Virginia, 1989.

Bellah, Robert, Richard Madsen, William Sullivan, Ann Swidler, and Steven Tipton, *Habits of the Heart: Individualism and Commitment in American Life.* Berkeley: University of California Press, 1985.

Benavides, Gustavo, and M. W. Daly, eds. *Religion and Political Power*. Albany: State University of New York Press, 1989.

Berger, Peter. *The Desecularization of the World*. Grand Rapids, Mich.: Eerdmans and the Ethics and Public Policy Center, 2000.

Beyer, Peter. *Religion and Globalization*. London: Sage Publications, 1994.

Breuilly, John. *Nationalism and the State*. Manchester: Manchester University Press, 1982.

Brinton, Crane. *The Anatomy of Revolution*. Rev. ed. New York: Random House, Vintage Books, 1957.

Burkert, Walter, René Girard, and Jonathan Z. Smith. *Violent Origins: Ritual Killing and Cultural Formation*. Edited by Robert G. Hamerton-Kelly. Stanford, Calif.: Stanford University Press, 1987.

Calhoun, Craig. *Nationalism*. Minneapolis: University of Minnesota Press, 1998.

Candland, Christopher, comp. *The Spirit of Violence: An Annotated Bibliography on Religious Violence*. New York: Harry Frank Guggenheim Foundation, 1993.

Caplan, Lionel, ed. *Studies in Religious Fundamentalism*. Albany: State University of New York Press, 1987.

Casanova, José. *Public Religions in the Modern World*. Chicago: University of Chicago Press, 1994.

———. "Rethinking Secularization: A Global Comparative Perspective." *The Hedgehog Review* 8 (2006): 7–22.

Cassirer, Ernst. *The Philosophy of the Enlightenment*. Boston: Beacon Press, 1955.

Connor, Walker. *The National Question in Marxist-Leninist Theory and Strategy*. Princeton: Princeton University Press, 1984.

Cox, Richard H. *Ideology, Politics, and Political Theory*. Belmont, Calif.: Wadsworth, 1969.

della Porta, Donatella, ed. *Social Movements and Violence: Participation in Underground Organizations*. Greenwich, Conn: JAI Press, 1992.

———. *Social Movements, Political Violence, and the State*. Cambridge: Cambridge University Press, 1995.

Detienne, Marcel, and Jean-Pierre Vernant. *The Cuisine of Sacrifice among the Greeks*. Translated by Paula Wissing. Chicago: University of Chicago Press, 1989.

Deutsch, Karl. *Nationalism and Social Communication*. Cambridge, Mass.: MIT Press, 1966.

Doob, L. *Patriotism and Nationalism*. New Haven: Yale University Press, 1964.

Douglas, Mary. "The Effects of Modernization on Religious Change." *Daedalus* 111, no. 1 (Winter 1982): 1–19.

Dumont, Louis. *From Mandeville to Marx: The Genesis and Triumph of Economic Ideology*. Chicago: University of Chicago Press, 1977.

Dumouchel, Paul, ed. *Violence and Truth: On the Work of René Girard*. Stanford, Calif.: Stanford University Press, 1988.

Dupré, Louis. *Transcendent Selfhood: The Loss and Rediscovery of the Inner Life*. New York: Seabury Press, 1976.

Dupuy, Jean-Pierre. *Ordres et désordres: Enquêtes sur un nouveau paradigme.* Paris: Éditions du Seuil, 1982.

Durkheim, Émile. *The Elementary Forms of the Religious Life.* 1915. Translated by Joseph Ward Swain. London: Allen & Unwin, 1976.

Emerson, Rupert. *From Empire to Nation: The Rise to Self-Assertion of Asian and African Peoples.* Boston: Beacon Press, 1960.

Falk, Richard. *Religion and Humane Global Governance.* New York: Palgrave Publishers, 2001.

Fanon, Frantz. *The Wretched of the Earth.* New York: Grove Press, 1963.

Foucault, Michel. *The Archaeology of Knowledge.* Translated by A. M. Sheridan Smith. New York: Pantheon Books, 1972.

———. *Power/Knowledge: Selected Interviews and Other Writings, 1972–1977.* New York: Pantheon Books, 1980.

Fox, Jonathan, and Shmuel Sandler, *Bringing Religion into International Relations.* New York: Palgrave Macmillan, 2004.

Fukuyama, Francis. *The End of History and the Last Man.* New York: Free Press, 1992.

———. "The End of History." *The National Interest* 16 (Summer 1989): 3–18.

Gauchet, Marcel. *The Disenchantment of the World: A Political History of Religion.* Translated by Oscar Burge. Princeton: Princeton University Press, 1997.

Geertz, Clifford. "Religion as a Cultural System." In William A. Lessa and Evon Z. Vogt, eds., *Reader in Comparative Religion: An Anthropological Approach,* 3d ed. New York: Harper & Row, 1972.

———. "Ideology as a Cultural System." In David Apter, ed., *Ideology and Discontent.* New York: Free Press, 1964.

———, ed. *Old Societies and New States: The Quest for Modernity in Asia and Africa.* New York: Free Press, 1963.

Gellner, Ernest. *Nations and Nationalism.* Oxford: Basil Blackwell, 1983.

Giddens, Anthony. *Central Problems in Social Theory: Action, Structure and Contradiction in Social Analysis.* Berkeley: University of California Press, 1979.

———. *The Nation-State and Violence.* Vol. 2 of *A Contemporary Critique of Historical Materialism.* Berkeley: University of California Press, 1985.

Girard, René. *The Scapegoat.* Translated by Yvonne Freccero. Baltimore: Johns Hopkins University Press, 1986. (Originally published as *Le bouc émissaire.* Paris: Éditions Grasset et Fasquelle, 1982.)

———. *Violence and the Sacred.* Translated by Patrick Gregory. Baltimore: Johns Hopkins University Press, 1977. (Originally published as *La violence et le sacré.* Paris: Éditions Bernard Grasset, 1972.)

Goldstone, Jack. *Revolution and Rebellion in the Early Modern World.* Berkeley: University of California Press, 1991.

Greenawalt, Kent. *Religious Convictions and Political Choice.* New York: Oxford University Press, 1988.

Gurr, Ted Robert. *Why Men Rebel.* Princeton: Princeton University Press, 1971.

Habermas, Jiirgen. *Legitimation Crisis.* Translated by Thomas McCarthy. Boston: Beacon Press, 1975.

Hadden, Jeffrey K., and Anson Shupe, eds. *Prophetic Religions and Politics.* Religion and the Political Order 1. New York: Paragon House, 1984.

Hanson, Eric, *Religion and Politics in the International System Today.* Cambridge: Cambridge University Press, 2006.

Hawley, John Stratton, ed. *Saints and Virtues.* Berkeley: University of California Press, 1987.

———. *Fundamentalism and Gender.* New York: Oxford University Press, 1994.

Hayes, Carleton J. H. *The Historical Evolution of Modern Nationalism.* New York: Richard R. Smith, 1931.

———. *Nationalism: A Religion.* New York: Macmillan, 1960.

———. *Essays on Nationalism.* New York: Russell and Russell, 1966.

Haynes, Jeff. *Religion in Third World Politics.* Boulder, Colo.: L. Rienner, 1994.

Hobsbawm, Eric J. *Revolutionaries.* New York: Pantheon Books, 1973.

———. *The Age of Empire, 1875–1914.* New York: Pantheon Books, 1987.

Huntington, Samuel P. *The Third Wave: Democratization in the Late Twentieth Century.* Norman: University of Oklahoma Press, 1991.

———. *The Clash of Civilizations and the Remaking of World Order.* New York: Simon and Schuster, 1998.

———. "How Countries Democratize." *Political Science Quarterly* 106, no. 4 (Winter 1991–92): 579–616.

Jelen, Ted G., ed. *Religion and Political Behavior in the United States.* New York: Praeger, 1989.

Johnson, Chalmers. *Revolutionary Change.* Boston: Little, Brown, 1966.

———. *Revolution and the Social System.* Stanford: Hoover Institution on War, Revolution, and Peace, 1964.

Johnson, James Turner. *Ideology, Reason, and the Limitation of War: Religious and Secular Concepts, 1200–1740.* Princeton: Princeton University Press, 1975.

Juergensmeyer, Mark. *The New Cold War? Religious Nationalism Confronts the Secular State.* Berkeley: University of California Press, 1993.

———. *Terror in the Mind of God: The Global Rise of Religious Violence.* 3d ed. Berkeley: University of California Press, 2003.

———. *Gandhi's Way: A Handbook of Conflict Resolution.* Berkeley: University of California Press, 2005.

———. "Nonviolence." In Mircea Eliade, ed., *The Encyclopedia of Religion,* vol. 10. New York: Macmillan, 1987.

———. "Sacrifice and Cosmic War." In Mark Juergensmeyer, ed., *Violence and the Sacred in the Modern World.* London: Frank Cass, 1992.

———. "Violence and Religion." In Jonathan Z. Smith, ed., *The Harper Dictionary of Religion.* New York: HarperCollins, 1995.

———. "Gandhi vs. Terrorism." *Daedalus* 136, no. 1 (Winter 2007): 30–39.

———, ed. *Violence and the Sacred in the Modern World.* London: Frank Cass, 1992.

Kedourie, Elie, ed. *Nationalism in Asia and Africa.* New York: New American Library, 1970.

Keyes, Charles F., ed. *Ethnic Change.* Seattle: University of Washington Press, 1981.

Kohn, Hans. *The Age of Nationalism.* New York: Harper, 1962.

———. *Nationalism: Its Meaning and History*. Princeton: D. Van Nostrand, 1955.

Kramer, Martin. "Sacrifice and Fratricide in Shi'ite Lebanon." In Mark Juergensmeyer, ed., *Violence and the Sacred in the Modern World*. London: Frank Cass, 1992.

Krejci, Jaroslav. "What Is a Nation?" In Peter Merkl and Ninian Smart, eds., *Religion and Politics in the Modern World*. New York: New York University Press, 1983.

Laqueur, Walter. *The Age of Terrorism*. Boston: Little, Brown, 1987.

———. "Postmodern Terrorism." *Foreign Affairs* 75 no. 5 (September 1996): 24–36.

Lawrence, Bruce B. *Defenders of God: The Fundamentalist Revolt against the Modern Age*. San Francisco: Harper & Row, 1989.

van Leeuwen, Arend Theodor. *Christianity in World History: The Meeting of the Faiths of East and West*. Translated by H. H. Hoskins. New York: Scribner's, 1964.

Lewy, Guenter. *Religion and Revolution*. New York: Oxford University Press, 1974.

Lincoln, Bruce. *Holy Terrors: Thinking about Religion after September 11*. Chicago: University of Chicago Press, 2002.

———, ed. *Religion, Rebellion, Revolution: An Interdisciplinary and Cross-cultural Collection of Essays*. New York: St. Martin's Press, 1985.

Little, David, John Kelsay, and Abdulaziz A. Sachedina. *Human Rights and the Conflict of Cultures: Western and Islamic Perspectives on Religious Liberty*. Columbia: University of South Carolina Press, 1988.

Livingston, Paisley, ed. *Disorder and Order: Proceedings of the Stanford International Symposium (Sept. 14–16, 1981)*. Stanford Literature Series 1. Saratoga, Calif.: Anma Libri, 1984.

London, Kurt. *New Nations in a Divided World: The International Relations of the Afro-Asian States*. New York: Praeger, 1983.

MacIntyre, Alasdair. *After Virtue: A Study in Moral Theory*. Notre Dame, Ind.: University of Notre Dame Press, 1981.

Madsen, Richard, William Sullivan, Ann Swidler, and Steven Tipton. *Meaning and Modernity: Religion, Polity, and Self*. Berkeley: University of California Press, 2001.

Mannheim, Karl. *Ideology and Utopia*. New York: Harcourt, Brace & World, 1936.

Martin, David. "Fundamentalism: An Observational and Definitional *Tour d'Horizon*." *Political Quarterly* 61, no. 2 (April–June 1990): 129–31.

Marty, Martin E., and R. Scott Appleby, eds. *Fundamentalisms Observed*. Chicago: University of Chicago Press, 1991.

———. *Accounting for Fundamentalisms: The Dynamic Character of Movements*. Chicago: University of Chicago Press, 1994.

McMahon, Darrin. *Enemies of the Enlightenment: The French Counter-Enlightenment and the Making of Modernity*. New York: Oxford University Press, 2002.

Merkl, Peter H., and Ninian Smart, eds. *Religion and Politics in the Modern World*. New York: New York University Press, 1983.

Mestrovic, Stjepan. *The Coming Fin de Siècle: An Application of Durkheim's Sociology to Modernity and Postmodernism.* London: Routledge, 1991.
———. *The Barbarian Temperament: Toward a Postmodern Critical Theory.* London: Routledge, 1993.
Mews, Stuart, ed. *Religion in Politics: A World Guide.* London: Longman, 1989.
Molnar, Thomas. "The Medieval Beginnings of Political Secularization." In George W. Carey and James V. Schall, eds., *Essays on Christianity and Political Philosophy.* Lanham, Md.: University Press of America, 1984.
Moore, Harrington, Jr. *The Social Origins of Dictatorship and Democracy: Lord and Peasant in the Making of the Modern World.* Boston: Beacon Press, 1966.
Nandy, Ashis. *The Savage Freud and Other Essays on Possible Retrievable Selves.* Princeton: Princeton University Press, 1995.
Niebuhr, Reinhold. *Moral Man and Immoral Society.* New York. Scribner's, 1932.
———. *The Nature and Destiny of Man,* vol. 2. New York: Scribner's, 1941.
———. *Man's Nature and His Communities.* New York: Scribner's, 1965.
———, ed. *Karl Marx and Friedrich Engels on Religion.* New York: Schocken, 1964.
Norris, Pippa, and Ronald Inglehart, *Sacred and Secular: Religion and Politics Worldwide.* Cambridge: Cambridge University Press, 2004.
Olcott, Martha Brill. *Kazakhstan: Unfulfilled Promise.* Washington, D.C.: Carnegie Endowment for International Peace, 2002.
Packard, Sidney R. *Twelfth-Century Europe: An Interpretive Essay.* Amherst: University of Massachusetts Press, 1973.
Pollard, Sidney. *Peaceful Conquest: The Industrialization of Europe, 1760–1970.* New York: Oxford University Press, 1981.
Rapoport, David C., "The Politics of Atrocity." In Y. Alexander and S. Finger, eds., *Terrorism: Interdisciplinary Perspectives.* New York: John Jay, 1977.
———, ed. *Inside Terrorist Organizations.* New York: Columbia University Press, 1988.
Rapoport, David C., and Yonah Alexander, eds. *The Morality of Terrorism: Religious and Secular Justifications.* New York: Pergamon Press, 1982.
Rawls, John, and Erin Kelly. *Justice as Fairness.* 2d rev. ed., edited by Erin Kelly. Cambridge, Mass: Harvard University Press, 2001.
Riesebrodt, Martin. *Pious Passion: The Emergence of Modern Fundamentalism in the United States and Iran.* Berkeley: University of California Press, 1990.
Rouner, Leroy S., ed. *Human Rights and the World's Religions.* Notre Dame, Ind.: University of Notre Dame Press, 1988.
Rubenstein, Richard L., ed. Spirit *Matters: The Worldwide Impact of Religion on Contemporary Politics.* New York: Paragon House, 1987.
Rudolph, Susanne Hoeber, and James Piscatori, eds. *Transnational Religion and Fading States.* Boulder, Colo.: Westview Press, 1997.
Sagan, Eli. *The Lust to Annihilate: A Psychoanalytic Study of Violence in Ancient Greek Culture.* New York: Psychohistory Press, 1972.

———. *Cannibalism: Human Aggression and Cultural Form*. New York: Psychohistory Press, 1974.

Sageman, Marc. *Understanding Terror Networks*. Philadelphia: University of Pennsylvania Press, 2004.

Sahliyeh, Emile, ed. *Religious Resurgence and Politics in the Contemporary World*. Albany: State University of New York Press, 1990.

Schafer, Boyd C. *Faces of Nationalism: New Realities and Old Myths*. New York: Harcourt Brace Jovanovich, 1972.

Schlesinger, Arthur, Jr. "Reinhold Niebuhr's Role in American Political Thought." In Charles W. Kegley, ed., *Reinhold Niebuhr: His Religious, Social and Political Thought*, rev. ed. New York: Pilgrim Press, 1984.

Schorske, Carl E. *Fin-de-Siècle Vienna: Politics and Culture*. New York: Knopf, 1980.

Sells, Michael A. *The Bridge Betrayed: Religion and Genocide in Bosnia*. Berkeley: University of California Press, 1996.

Seton-Watson, Hugh. *Nations and States: An Enquiry into the Origins of Nations and the Politics of Nationalism*. Boulder, Colo.: Westview Press, 1977.

Smart, Ninian. *Worldviews: Crosscultural Explorations of Human Beliefs*. New York: Scribner's, 1983.

———. "Religion, Myth, and Nationalism." In Peter H. Merkl and Ninian Smart, eds., *Religion and Politics in the Modern World*. New York: New York University Press, 1983.

Smith, Anthony D. *Theories of Nationalism*. London: Duckworth, 1971.

———. *Nationalism in the Twentieth Century*. Oxford: Martin Robertson, 1979.

———, ed. *Nationalist Movements*. New York: St. Martin's Press, 1977.

Smith, Donald Eugene, ed. *South Asian Politics and Religion*. Princeton.: Princeton University Press, 1966.

———. *Religion, Politics, and Social Change in the Third World: A Sourcebook*. New York: Free Press, 1971.

———. *Religion and Political Modernization*. New Haven: Yale University Press, 1974.

Smith, Wilfred Cantwell. *The Meaning and End of Religion: A New Approach to the Religious Traditions of Mankind*. New York: Macmillan, 1962.

Snyder, Louis L. *The Dynamics of Nationalism: Readings in Its Meaning and Development*. Princeton: D. Van Nostrand, 1964.

Soudan, François. "Jeune Afrique l'Intelligent." Paris, August 12–15, 2002. English translation in *World Press Review* 49, no. 11 (November 2002).

Sproxton, Judy. *Violence and Religion: Attitudes towards Militancy in the French Civil Wars and the English Revolution*. London: Routledge, 1995.

Stackhouse, Max L. *Creeds, Society, and Human Rights: A Study in Three Cultures*. Grand Rapids, Mich.: W. B. Eerdmans, 1984.

Strayer, Joseph. *Medieval Statecraft and the Perspectives of History*. Princeton: Princeton University Press, 1971.

Swatos, William H., Jr., ed. *Religious Politics in Global and Comparative Perspective*. New York: Greenwood Press, 1989.

Swidler, Arlene, ed. *Human Rights in Religious Traditions*. New York: Pilgrim Press, 1982.

Tambiah, Stanley. *Leveling Crowds: Ethnonationalist Conflicts and Collective Violence in South Asia*. Berkeley: University of California Press, 1996.

Taylor, Charles. *Sources of the Self: The Making of the Modern Identity*. Cambridge, Mass.: Harvard University Press, 1992.

———. *Modern Social Imaginaries (Public Planet)*. Durham, N.C.: Duke University Press, 2004.

———. *The Ethics of Authenticity*. Cambridge, Mass: Harvard University Press, 2007.

———. *A Secular Age*. Cambridge, Mass: Harvard University Press, 2007.

Thomas, Scott, *The Global Resurgence of Religion and the Transformation of International Relations*. New York: Palgrave Macmillan, 2005.

Tilly, Charles. *Coercion, Capital, and European States*. Cambridge, Mass.: Basil Blackwell, 1990.

de Tocqueville, Alexis. *The Old Régime and the French Revolution*. Translated by Stuart Gilbert. New York: Doubleday, Anchor Books, 1955.

Traer, Robert. *Faith in Human Rights: Support in Religious Traditions for a Global Struggle*. Washington, D.C.: Georgetown University Press, 1991.

van der Veer, Peter. *Transnational Religion*. Princeton: Princeton University Migration Working Papers, 2001.

Voegelin, Eric. *Science, Politics, and Gnosticism*. Washington, D.C.: Regnery Gateway, 1968.

———. *The New Science of Politics: An Introduction*, 2d ed. Chicago: University of Chicago Press, 1987.

de Vries, Hent, ed. *Religion: Beyond a Concept*. New York: Fordham University Press, 2007.

de Vries, Hent, and Lawrence Sullivan, eds., *Political Theologies: Public Religions in a Post Secular World*. New York: Fordham University Press, 2006.

Wallace, Anthony F. C. *The Death and Rebirth of the Seneca*. New York: Random House, 1969.

Wallerstein, Immanuel. *The Modern World-System*, 1: *Capitalist Agriculture and the Origins of the European World-Economy in the Sixteenth Century*. New York: Academic Press, 1974.

———. *The Modern World-System*, 2: *Mercantilism and the Consolidation of the European World-Economy, 1600–1750*. New York: Academic Press, 1980.

———. *Geopolitics and Geoculture: Essays on the Changing World-System*. New York: Cambridge University Press, 1991.

Walzer, Michael. *The Revolution of the Saints: A Study in the Origins of Radical Politics*. New York: Atheneum, 1974.

Waxman, Chaim I., ed. *The End of Ideology Debate*. New York: Simon & Schuster, 1964.

Weber, Max. "Politics as a Vocation." In Hans H. Gerth and C. Wright Mills, eds., *From Max Weber: Essays in Sociology*. New York: Oxford University Press, 1946.

Westerlund, David, ed. *Questioning the Secular State: The Worldwide Resurgence of Religion in Politics*. London: Hurst, 1996.

Whitehead, Alfred North. *Religion in the Making.* Reprinted in F. S. C. Northup and Mason W. Gross, eds., *Alfred North Whitehead: An Anthology.* New York: Macmillan, 1961.

Williams, James G. *The Bible, Violence, and the Sacred: Liberation from the Myth of Sanctioned Violence.* San Francisco: HarperSan Francisco, 1991.

Wolf, Eric R. *Europe and the People without History.* Berkeley: University of California Press, 1982.

Wright, Robin, and Doyle McManus. *Flashpoints: Promise and Peril in a New World.* New York: Knopf, 1992.

ISLAMIC ACTIVISM

Abdallah, Umar F. *The Islamic Struggle in Syria.* Berkeley: Mizan Press, 1983.

Abrahamian, Ervand. *Radical Islam: The Iranian Mojahedin.* London: I. B. Tauris, 1989.

Abu-Amr, Ziad. *Islamic Fundamentalism in the West Bank and Gaza: Muslim Brotherhood and Islamic Jihad.* Bloomington: Indiana University Press, 1994.

Abuza, Zachary. *Political Islam and Violence in Indonesia.* London: Routledge, 2006.

———. "Al Qaeda in Southeast Asia: Exploring the Linkages," in Kamar Ramakrishna and See Seng Tan, eds. *After Bali: The Threat of Terrorism in Southeast Asia.* Hong Kong: World Scientific Publishing Company, 2004.

Acharya, Arabinda, Sabina Chua, and Rohan Gunaratna, eds. *Conflict and Terrorism in Southern Thailand.* Singapore: Marshall Cavendish Academic, 2006.

Adams, Charles. "The Ideology of Mawlana Mawdudi." In Donald Eugene Smith, ed., *South Asian Politics and Religion.* Princeton: Princeton University Press, 1966.

Ahmad, Aziz. "The Ulama in Politics." In Nikki R. Keddie, ed., *Scholars, Saints, and Sufis.* Berkeley: University of California Press, 1972.

Ahmad, Jalal Al-e. *The School Principal.* Translated by John K. Newton. Minneapolis: Bibliotheca Islamica, 1974.

Ahmad, Mumtaz. "Islamic Fundamentalism in South Asia: The Jamaat-i-Islami and the Tablighi Jamaat." In Martin E. Marty and R. Scott Appleby, eds., *Fundamentalisms Observed.* Chicago: University of Chicago Press, 1991.

Akhavi, Shahrough. "The Impact of the Iranian Revolution on Egypt." In John L. Esposito, ed., *The Iranian Revolution: Its Global Impact.* Miami: Florida International University Press, 1990.

———. *Religion and Politics in Contemporary Iran: Clergy-State Relations in the Pahlavi Period.* Albany: State University of New York Press, 1980.

Akiner, Shirin. *The Islamic Peoples of the Soviet Union.* London: Kegan Paul International, 1983.

Algar, Hamid, trans. *Constitution of the Islamic Republic of Iran.* Berkeley, Calif.: Mizan Press, 1980.

Allworth, Edward, ed. *Central Asia: 120 Years of Russian Rule.* Durham, N.C.: Duke University Press, 1989.

———. *The Modern Uzbeks: From the Fourteenth Century to the Present. A Cultural History.* Stanford, Calif.: Hoover Institution Press, 1990.

Amjad, Mohammed. *Iran: From Royal Dictatorship to Theocracy.* Westport, Conn.: Greenwood Press, 1989.

Arjomand, Said Amir, *The Shadow of God and the Hidden Imam: Religion, Political Order, and Societal Change in Shi'ite Iran from the Beginning to 1890.* Chicago: University of Chicago Press, 1984.

———. *The Turban for the Crown: The Islamic Revolution in Iran.* New York: Oxford University Press, 1988.

———. "A Victory for the Pragmatists: The Islamic Fundamentalist Reaction in Iran." In James P. Piscatori, ed., *Islamic Fundamentalisms and the Gulf Crisis.* Chicago: Fundamentalism Project, American Academy of Arts and Sciences, 1991.

———, ed. *Authority and Political Culture in Shi'ism.* Albany: State University of New York Press, 1988.

Atkin, Muriel. *The Subtlest Battle: Islam in Soviet Tajikistan.* Philadelphia: Foreign Policy Research Institute, 1989.

Auda, Gehad. "An Uncertain Response: The Islamic Movement in Egypt." In James P. Piscatori, ed., *Islamic Fundamentalisms and the Gulf Crisis.* Chicago: Fundamentalism Project, American Academy of Arts and Sciences, 1991.

———. "The Normalization of the Islamic Movement in Egypt." In Martin E. Marty and R. Scott Appleby, eds., *Accounting for Fundamentalisms: The Dynamic Character of Movements.* Chicago: University of Chicago Press, 1994.

Azra, Azyurmardi. *Indonesia, Islam, and Democracy: Dynamics in a Global Context.* Jakarta, Indonesia: Solstice Publishing, 2006.

Baker, Raymond William. *Sadat and After: Struggles for Egypt's Political Soul.* Cambridge: Harvard University Press, 1990.

Bakhash, Shaul. *The Reign of the Ayatollahs: Iran and the Islamic Revolution.* New York: Basic Books, 1984.

Bani-Sadr, Abolhassan. *The Fundamental Principles and Precepts of Islamic Government.* Translated by Mohammed R. Ghanoonparvar. Lexington, Ky.: Mazda Publishers, 1981.

Baxter, Craig. *Bangladesh: From a Nation to a State.* Boulder, Colo.: Westview Press, 1997.

Benjamin, Daniel, and Steven Simon. *The Age of Sacred Terror.* New York: Random House, 2002.

Bennigsen, Alexandre, and Marie Broxup. *The Islamic Threat to the Soviet State.* New York: St. Martin's Press, 1983.

Bennigsen, Alexandre, and S. Enders Wimbush. *Muslims of the Soviet Empire: A Guide.* London: C. Hurst, 1985.

Bonner, Michael. *Jihad in Islamic History.* Princeton: Princeton University Press, 2006.

Bowen, John R. *Why the French Don't Like Headscarves: Islam, the State, and Public Space.* Princeton: Princeton University Press, 2006.

Bozdogan, Sibel, ed. *Rethinking Modernity and National Identity in Turkey.* Seattle: University of Washington Press, 1997.

Burke, Edmund, III, and Ira M. Lapidus, eds. *Islam, Politics, and Social Movements.* Berkeley: University of California Press, 1988.

Caram, Peter. *The 1993 World Trade Center Bombing: Foresight and Warning.* London: Janus Publishing, 2001.

Carrère d'Encausse, Hélène. *Islam and the Russian Empire: Reform and Revolution in Central Asia.* Translated by Quintin Hoare, London: I. B. Tauris, 1988. Originally published as *Réforme et révolution chez les Musulmans de l'empire russe.* Paris: Presses de la Fondation Nationale des Sciences Politiques, 1966.

Cesari, Jocelyne. *Where Islam and Democracy Meet: Muslims in Europe and the United States.* New York: Palgrave Macmillan, 2006.

Chehab, Zaki. *Inside Hamas.* New York: Nation Books, 2007.

Chehabi, H. E. "Religion and Politics in Iran: How Theocratic Is the Islamic Republic?" *Daedalus,* Summer 1991, 69–92.

Cole, Juan R. I., I. Routledge, and Nikki R. Keddie. *Shi'ism and Social Protest.* New Haven: Yale University Press, 1986.

Cook, David. *Understanding Jihad.* Berkeley: University of California Press, 2005.

Critchlow, James. *Nationalism in Uzbekistan: A Soviet Republic's Road to Sovereignty.* Boulder, Colo.: Westview Press, 1991.

Curtis, Michael, ed. *Religion and Politics in the Middle East.* Boulder, Colo.: Westview Press, 1981.

Dahlby, Tracy, *Allah's Torch: A Report from behind the Scenes in Asia's War on Terror,* New York: William Morrow, 2005.

Deeb, Marius. "Egypt." In Stuart Mews, ed., *Religion in Politics: A World Guide.* London: Longman, 1989.

Demko, George J. *The Russian Colonization of Kazakhstan, 1896–1916.* Bloomington: Indiana University, 1969.

Dessouki, Ali E. Hillal, ed. *Islamic Resurgence in the Arab World.* New York: Praeger, 1982.

Dunlop, John B. *Russia Confronts Chechnya: Roots of a Separatist Conflict.* Cambridge: Cambridge University Press, 1998.

Dwyer, James, David Kocieniewski, Deidre Murphy, and Peg Tyre. *Two Seconds under the World: Terror Comes to America—The Conspiracy behind the World Trade Center Bombing.* New York: Crown, 1994.

Emerson, Steven. *Jihad Incorporated: A Guide to Militant Islam in the U.S.* Amherst, N.Y.: Prometheus Books, 2006.

Enayat, Hamid. *Modern Islamic Political Thought: The Response of the Shi'i and Sunni Muslims to the Twentieth Century.* London: Macmillan, 1982.

Entelis, John P. *Algeria: The Revolution Institutionalized.* Boulder, Colo.: Westview Press, 1986.

Esposito, John L. *Islam and Politics.* Syracuse, N.Y.: Syracuse University Press, 1987.

———. *Unholy War: Terror in the Name of Islam.* New York: Oxford University Press, 2003.

———, ed. *Voices of Resurgent Islam.* New York: Oxford University Press, 1983.

———, ed. *The Iranian Revolution: Its Global Impact.* Miami: Florida International University Press, 1990.

Esposito, John, and John Voll. *Islam and Democracy.* New York: Oxford University Press, 1996.

Farazmand, Ali. *The State, Bureaucracy, and Revolution in Modern Iran: Agrarian Reforms and Regime Politics.* New York: Praeger, 1989.

Fetzer, Joel S., and J. Christopher Soper. *Muslims and the State in Britain, France, and Germany.* Cambridge: Cambridge University Press, 2004.

Fierman, William, ed. *Soviet Central Asia: The Failed Transformation.* Boulder, Colo.: Westview Press, 1991.

Forest, Benjamin, Juliet Johnson, and Marietta T. Stephaniants, eds. *Religion and Identity in Modern Russia: The Revival of Orthodoxy and Islam.* Aldershot, Hampshire [U.K.]: Ashgate Publishing, 2005.

Ganguly, Sumit. *The Crisis in Kashmir: Portents of War, Hopes of Peace.* Cambridge: Cambridge University Press, 1999.

Gerges, Fawaz. *The Far Enemy: Why Jihad Went Global.* Cambridge: Cambridge University Press, 2005.

———. *Journey of the Jihadist: Inside Muslim Militancy.* Orlando, Fla.: Harvest Books, 2007.

Ghayasuddin, M., ed. *The Impact of Nationalism on the Muslim World.* London: Open Press, Al-Hoda, 1986.

Gilsenan, Michael. *Recognizing Islam: Religion and Society in the Modern Arab World.* New York: Pantheon, 1982.

Gladney, Dru. *Muslim Chinese: Ethnic Nationalism in the People's Republic.* Cambridge, Mass.: Council on East Asian Studies, Harvard University, 1991.

———. *Dislocating China: Muslims, Minorities, and Other Subaltern Subjects.* Chicago: University of Chicago Press, 2004.

Gunaratna, Rohan. *The Changing Face of Terrorism.* Singapore: Marshall Cavendish Corp., 2005.

———. *Peace in Sri Lanka; Obstacles and Opportunities.* Colombo: Sansadaya, 2005.

———. "Understanding Al Qaeda and Its Network in Southeast Asia." In Kamar Ramakrishna and See Seng Tan, eds., *After Bali: The Threat of Terrorism in Southeast Asia.* Hong Kong: World Scientific Publishing Company, 2004.

Haddad, Yvonne V. "Sayyid Qutb: Ideologue of Islamic Revival." In John L. Esposito, ed., *Voices of Resurgent Islam.* New York: Oxford University Press, 1983.

Haynes, Jeff. *Religion and Politics in Africa.* London: Zed Books, 1996.

Hefner, Robert W. "The Sword Against the Crescent: Religion and Violence in Muslim Southeast Asia." In Linell E. Cady and Sheldon W. Simon, eds., *Religion and Conflict in Southeast Asia.* London: Routledge, 2007.

Hefner, Robert, and Patricia Horvatich, eds. *Islam in an Era of Nation-States: Politics and Religious Renewal in Muslim Southeast Asia.* Honolulu: University of Hawai'i Press, 1997.

Heikal, Mohammed. *Autumn of Fury: The Assassination of Sadat.* London: André Deutsch, 1983.

Hinnebusch, Raymond A. "The Islamic Movement in Syria: Sectarian Conflict and Urban Rebellion in an Authoritarian-Populist Regime." In Ali E. Hillal

Dessouki, ed., *Islamic Resurgence in the Arab World.* New York: Praeger, 1982.

Hopkins, Nicholas S., and Saad Eddin Ibrahim, eds. *Arab Society: Social Science Perspectives.* Cairo: American University in Cairo Press, 1985.

Humphreys, R. Stephen. *Between Memories and Desire: The Middle East in a Troubled Age.* Berkeley: University of California Press, 1999.

———. "The Contemporary Resurgence in the Context of Modern Islam." In Ali E. Hillal Dessouki, ed., *Islamic Resurgence in the Arab World.* New York: Praeger, 1982.

Hunter, Shireen T., ed. *The Politics of Islamic Revivalism: Diversity and Unity.* Bloomington: Indiana University Press, 1988.

Husain, Rizwan. *Pakistan and the Emergence of Islamic Militancy in Afghanistan.* Aldershot, Hampshire [U.K.]: Aldersgate Press, 2005.

Ibrahim, Raymond, ed. *The al Qaeda Reader.* New York: Broadway, 2007.

Ibrahim, Saad Eddin. "Islamic Militancy as a Social Movement: The Case of Two Groups in Egypt." In Ali E. Hillal Dessouki, ed., *Islamic Resurgence in the Arab World.* New York: Praeger, 1982.

Jansen, Johannes J. G. *The Neglected Duty: The Creed of Sadat's Assassins and Islamic Resurgence in the Middle East.* New York: Macmillan, 1986.

Jones, Owen Bennett. *Pakistan: Eye of the Storm.* New Haven: Yale University Press, 2003.

Jonson, Lena. *Tajikistan in the New Central Asia: Geopolitics, Great Power Rivalry, and Radical Islam.* London: I. B.Tauris, 2006.

Karlekar, Hiranmay. *Bangladesh: The Next Afghanistan?* New Delhi: Sage Publications, 2006.

Keddie, Nikki R., *Scholars, Saints, and Sufis.* Berkeley: University of California Press, 1972.

———. "Shi'ism and Revolution." In Bruce Lincoln, ed., *Religion, Rebellion, Revolution: An Interdisciplinary and Cross-Cultural Collection of Essays.* New York: St. Martin's Press, 1985.

———, ed. *Religion and Politics in Iran: Shi ism from Quietism to Revolution.* New Haven, Conn.: Yale University Press, 1983.

Keddie, Nikki R., and Eric Hooglund, eds. *The Iranian Revolution and the Islamic Republic.* Syracuse, N.Y.: Syracuse University Press, 1986.

Kelsay, John. *Islam and War: A Study in Comparative Ethics.* Louisville, Ky: Westminster/John Knox Press, 1993.

Kepel, Gilles. *Muslim Extremism in Egypt: The Prophet and Pharaoh.* Rev. ed. Berkeley: University of California Press, 2003.

Kepel, Gilles, and Anthony F. Roberts. *Jihad: The Trail of Political Islam.* Cambridge, Mass: Belknap Press of Harvard University Press, 2003.

Khalid, Adeeb. *Islam after Communism: Religion and Politics in Central Asia.* Berkeley: University of California Press, 2007.

Khomeini, Ayatollah Sayyed Ruhollah Mousavi. *Collection of Speeches, Position Statements.* Translated from *Najaf Min watha 'iq al-Imam al-Khomeyni did al-Quwa al Imbiriy-aliyah wa al-Sahyuniyah wa al-Raj'iyah* (From the Papers of Imam Khomeyni against Imperialist, Zionist and Reactionist Powers),

1977. Translations on Near East and North Africa 1902. Arlington, Va.: Joint Publications Research Service, 1979.

———. *Sayings of the Ayatollah Khomeini: Political, Philosophical, Social and Religious.* Extracts from *Valayate-Faghih* (The Kingdom of the Learned), *Kashfol-Asrar* (The Key to Mysteries), and *Towzihol-Masael* (The Explanation of Problems). Selected and translated into French by Jean-Marie Xavière and published as *Principes de l'Ayatollah Khomeiny: Philosophiques, sociaux et réligieux,* Paris: Éditions Libres-Hallier, 1979. Translated from the French by Harold J. Salemson and edited by Tony Hendra. New York: Bantam Books, 1980.

———. *A Clarification of Questions: An Unabridged Translation of* Resaleh Towzih al-Masael. Translated by J. Borujerdi. Boulder, Colo., and London: Westview Press, 1984.

———. *Islam and Revolution: Writings and Declarations.* Translated and annotated by Hamid Algar. Berkeley: Mizan Press, 1981; London: Routledge & Kegan Paul, 1985.

Klausen, Jytte. *The Islamic Challenge: Politics and Religion in Western Europe.* New York: Oxford University Press, 2005.

Kramer, Martin, ed. *Shi'ism, Resistance and Revolution.* Boulder, Colo.: Westview Press, 1987.

Lapidus, Ira M. *A History of Islamic Societies.* Cambridge: Cambridge University Press, 1988.

Laurence, Jonathan, and Justin Vaisse. *Integrating Islam: Political and Religious Challenges in Contemporary France.* Washington, D.C.: Brookings Institution Press, 2006.

Legrain, Jean-François. "Islamistes et lutte nationale palestinienne dans les territories occupés par Israel." *Revue française de science politique* 36, no. 2 (April 1986): 227–47.

———. "The Islamic Movement and the Intifada." In Jamal R. Nassar and Roger Heacock, eds., *Intifada: Palestine at the Crossroads.* New York: Praeger, 1990.

———. "A Defining Moment: Palestinian Islamic Fundamentalism." In James P. Piscatori, ed., *Islamic Fundamentalisms and the Gulf Crisis.* Chicago: Fundamentalism Project, American Academy of Arts and Sciences, 1991.

Leiken, Robert S. "Europe's Mujahideen: Where Mass Immigration Meets Global Terrorism." Center for Immigration Studies Backgrounder. April 2005.

———. "Europe's Angry Muslims." *Foreign Affairs,* July/August 2005.

Lewis, Bernard. *The Assassins: A Radical Sect in Islam.* New York: Oxford University Press, 1967.

———. *The Political Language of Islam.* Chicago: University of Chicago Press, 1988.

———. "The Return of Islam." In Michael Curtis, ed., *Religion and Politics in the Middle East.* Boulder: Westview Press, 1981.

———, ed. *Islam: From the Prophet Muhammad to the Capture of Constantinople.* 2 vols. New York: Oxford University Press, 1987.

Lewy, Guenter. "Nasserism and Islam: A Revolution in Search of Ideology." In Guenter Lewy, ed., *Religion and Revolution*. New York: Oxford University Press, 1974.

Liow, Joseph Chinyong. *Muslim Resistance in Southern Thailand and Southern Philippines: Religion, Ideology, and Politics*. Honolulu: East-West Center, 2005.

Lonsdale, John. *Religion and Politics in Kenya*. Henry Martyn Lectures. Cambridge: Henry Martyn Centre, 2005.

Martin, Richard C. "Religious Violence in Islam: Towards an Understanding of the Discourse *on Jihad* in Modern Egypt." In Paul Wilkinson and A. M. Stewart, eds., *Contemporary Research on Terrorism*. Aberdeen: Aberdeen University Press, 1987.

McKenna, Thomas. *Muslim Rulers and Rebels: Everyday Politics and Armed Separatism in Southern Philippines*. Berkeley: University of California Press, 1998.

Meier, Andrew. *Chechnya: To the Heart of a Conflict*. New York: W. W. Norton, 2004.

Metcalf, Barbara Daly, ed. *Making Muslim Space in North America and Europe*. Berkeley: University of California Press, 1996.

Mishal, Shaul, and Avraham Sela. *The Palestinian Hamas: Vision, Violence, and Coexistence*. New York: Columbia University Press, 2006.

Mitchell, Richard P. *The Society of the Muslim Brothers*. London: Oxford University Press, 1969.

Mortimer, Edward. *The Politics of Islam*. New York: Random House, Vintage Books, 1982.

Mottahedeh, Roy P. *The Mantle of the Prophet*. New York: Pantheon, 1986.

Munson, Henry, Jr. *Islam and Revolution in the Middle East*. New Haven, Conn.: Yale University Press, 1988.

Muslih, Muhammad. *The Origins of Palestinian Nationalism*. New York: Columbia University Press, 1988.

Mylroie, Laurie. "The World Trade Center Bomb: Who is Ramzi Yousef? And Why It Matters." *The National Interest*, Winter 1996.

An-Naim, Abdullahi Ahmed. *Toward an Islamic Reformation: Civil Liberties, Human Rights, and International Law*. Syracuse, N.Y.: Syracuse University Press, 1996.

Nassar, Jamal R., and Roger Heacock. *Intifada: Palestine at the Crossroads*. New York: Praeger, 1990.

Nettler, Ronald L. *Past Trials and Present Tribulations: A Muslim Fundamentalist's View of the Jews*. New York: Pergamon Press, 1987.

Olcott, Martha Brill. *The Kazakhs*. Stanford, Calif.: Hoover Institution Press, 1987.

———. "Central Asia's Post-Empire Politics." *Orbis* 36, no. 2 (Spring 1992): 253–68.

———. "Central Asia's Catapult to Independence." *Foreign Affairs* 71, no. 3 (Summer 1992): 131–45.

Oliver, Anne Marie, and Paul Steinberg. *The Road to Martyrs' Square: A Journey Into the World of the Suicide Bomber*. New York: Oxford University Press, 2006.

Peters, Rudolph. *Islam and Colonialism: The Doctrine of Jihad in Modern History*. The Hague: Mouton, 1979.

Pierce, R. *Russian Central Asia, 1867–1917: A Study in Colonial Rule*. Berkeley: University of California Press, 1960.

Piscatori, James P. *Islam in the Political Process*. Cambridge: Cambridge University Press, 1983.

―――, ed. *Islamic Fundamentalisms and the Gulf Crisis*. Chicago: Fundamentalism Project, American Academy of Arts and Sciences, 1991.

Post, Jerrold M. *Military Studies in the Jihad Against the Tyrants: The Al-Qaeda Training Manual*. Maxwell Air Force Base, Ala.: USAF Counterproliferation Center, n.d. (ca. 2005).

Qutb, Sayyid. *This Religion of Islam (Hadha'd-Din)*. Translated by Islamdust. Palo Alto, Calif.: Al-Manar Press, 1967.

Ramadan, Tariq. *Western Muslims and the Future of Islam*. New York: Oxford University Press, 2005.

Rashid, Ahmed. *Jihad: The Rise of Militant Islam in Central Asia*. New Haven: Yale University Press, 2002.

―――. *Taliban: Militant Islam, Oil, and Fundamentalism in Central Asia*. New Haven: Yale University Press, 2001.

―――. "The Islamic Challenge." *Far Eastern Economic Review* 149 (July 12, 1990): 24.

al-Razzaz, Munif. *The Evolution of the Meaning of Nationalism*. Translated by Ibrahim Abu-Lughod. Garden City, N.Y.: Doubleday, 1963.

Rekhess, Elie. "The Iranian Impact on the Islamic Jihad Movement in the Gaza Strip." In David Menashri, ed., *The Iranian Revolution and the Muslim World*. Boulder, Colo.: Westview Press, 1990.

Riaz, Ali. *God Willing: The Politics of Islamism in Bangladesh*. Lanham, Md.: Rowman & Littlefield, 2004.

Roberts, Hugh. *The Battlefield: Algeria 1988–2002. Studies in a Broken Polity*. London: Verso, 2003.

―――. "Radical Islamism and the Dilemma of Algerian Nationalism: The Embattled Arians of Algiers." *Third World Quarterly* 10, no. 2 (April 1988): 556–89.

Ro'i, Yaacov, ed. *The USSR and the Muslim World: Issues in Domestic and Foreign Policy*. London: George Allen & Unwin, 1984.

Rorlich, Azade-Ayse. "Islam and Atheism: Dynamic Tension in Soviet Central Asia." In William Fierman, ed., *Soviet Central Asia: The Failed Transformation*. Boulder, Colo.: Westview Press, 1991.

Rosen, Nir. *In the Belly of the Green Bird: The Triumph of the Martyrs in Iraq*. New York: Free Press, 2006.

Rowan, A.R. *On the Trail of a Lion: Ahmed Shah Massoud, Oil Politics and Terror*. Oakville, Ontario: Mosaic Press, 2005.

Roy, Olivier. *Islam and Resistance in Afghanistan*. Cambridge: Cambridge University Press, 1990. Originally published as *L 'Afghanistan: Islam et modernité politique*. Paris: Éditions du Seuil, 1985.

―――. *Globalized Islam: The Search for a New Ummah*. New York: Columbia University Press, 2006.

Sachedina, Abdulaziz Abdulhussein. *The Just Ruler* (al-sultan al-'adil) *in Shi'ite Islam: The Comprehensive Authority of the Jurist in Imamite Jurisprudence.* New York: Oxford University Press, 1988.

———. "Activist Shi'ism in Iran, Iraq, and Lebanon." In Martin E. Marty and R. Scott Appleby, eds., *Fundamentalisms Observed.* Chicago: University of Chicago Press, 1991.

Satha-Anand, Chaiwat. *Islam and Violence: A Case Study of Violent Events in the Four Southern Provinces, Thailand, 1976–1981.* Monographs in Religion and Public Policy. Tampa: Department of Religious Studies, University of South Florida, 1986.

Schofield, Victoria. *Kashmir in Conflict.* London: I. B. Tauris, 2000.

Sick, Gary. *All Fall Down: America's Tragic Encounter with Iran.* Rev. ed. New York: Penguin, 1986.

Sidel, John Thayer. *Riot, Pogroms, Jihad: Religious Violence in Indonesia.* Ithaca, N.Y.: Cornell University Press, 2006.

Siddiqui, Kalim. "Nation-States as Obstacles to the Total Transformation of the *Ummah.*" In M. Ghayasuddin, ed., *The Impact of Nationalism on the Muslim World.* London: Open Press, Al-Hoda, 1986.

Simpson, John. *Inside Iran: Life under Khomeini's Regime.* New York: St. Martin's Press, 1988.

Sinor, Denis. *The Cambridge History of Inner Asia.* Cambridge: Cambridge University Press, 1990.

Sivan, Emmanuel. *Radical Islam: Medieval Theology and Modern Politics.* New Haven, Conn.: Yale University Press, 1985.

———. "Sunni Radicalism in the Middle East and the Iranian Revolution." *International Journal for Middle East Studies* 21 (1989): 1–30.

———. "The Islamic Resurgence: Civil Society Strikes Back." *Journal of Contemporary History* [London] 25 (1990): 353–64.

Sivan, Emmanuel, and Menachem Friedman, eds. *Religious Radicalism and Politics in the Middle East.* Albany: State University of New York Press, 1990.

Smith, Sebastian. *Allah's Mountains: The Battle for Chechnya.* London: Tauris Parke, 2005.

Smith, Wilfred Cantwell. *Islam in Modern History.* Princeton, N.J.: Princeton University Press, 1957.

Soroush, Abdolkarim. *Reason, Freedom, and Democracy in Islam: Essential Writings of Abdolkarim Soroush.* New York: Oxford University Press, 2002.

Steinberg, Matti. "The PLO and Palestinian Islamic Fundamentalism." *Jewish Quarterly* 52 (Fall 1989): 37–54.

Syed, Anwar. *Pakistan: Islam, Politics, and National Solidarity.* New York: Praeger, 1982.

Tibi, Bassam. *The Challenge of Fundamentalism: Political Islam and the New World Disorder.* Berkeley: University of California Press, 1998.

Uddin, Sufia M. *Constructing Bangladesh: Religion, Ethnicity, and Language in an Islamic Nation.* Chapel Hill: University of North Carolina Press, 2006.

Wasserstein, Bernard. "Patterns of Communal Conflict in Palestine." In Ada Rapoport and Steven J. Zipperstein, eds., *Jewish History: Essays in Honour of Chimen Abramsky.* London: Peter Halban, 1988.

Watt, W. Montgomery. *Islamic Fundamentalism and Modernity*. London: Routledge, 1988.

Wendell, Charles, trans. *Five Tracts of Hasan al-Banna (1906–1949)*. Berkeley: University of California Press, 1978.

Wheeler, Geoffrey. *The Modern History of Soviet Central Asia*. London: Weidenfeld & Nicolson, 1964.

White, Jenny B. *Islamist Mobilization in Turkey: A Study in Vernacular Politics*. Seattle: University of Washington Press, 2003.

Wixman, Ronald. "Ethnic Attitudes and Relations in Modern Uzbek Cities." In William Fierman, ed., *Soviet Central Asia: The Failed Transformation*. Boulder, Colo.: Westview Press, 1991.

Wood, Tony. *Chechnya: The Case for Independence*. London: Verso, 2007.

Wright, Robin. *Sacred Rage: The Wrath of Militant Islam*. New York: Linden Press, Simon & Schuster, 1985.

———. *In the Name of God: The Khomeini Decade*. New York: Simon & Schuster, 1989.

———. *The Last Great Revolution: Turmoil and Transformation in Iran*. New York: Simon & Schuster, 2000.

———. "Report from Turkestan." *New Yorker*, April 6, 1992, 53–75.

———. "Islam, Democracy, and the West." *Foreign Affairs* 71, no. 3 (Summer 1992): 131–45.

Yavuz, M. Hakan. *Islamic Political Identity in Turkey*. New York: Oxford University Press, 2005.

Yavuz, M. Hakan, and John Esposito, eds. *Turkish Islam and the Secular State: The Gulen Movement*. Syracuse, N.Y.: Syracuse University Press, 2003.

JEWISH ACTIVISM

Agus, Jacob B. *Banner of Jerusalem: The Life, Times, and Thought of Rabbi Abraham Isaac Kuk*. New York: Bloch, 1946.

Aran, Gideon. "From Religious Zionism to Zionist Religion: The Roots of Gush Emunim." In Peter Medding, ed., *Studies in Contemporary Jewry*, vol. 2. New York: Oxford University Press, 1986.

———. "Jewish Zionist Fundamentalism: The Bloc of the Faithful in Israel (Gush Emunim)." In Martin E. Marty and R. Scott Appleby, eds., *Fundamentalisms Observed*. Chicago: University of Chicago Press, 1991.

Biale, David J. "Mysticism and Politics in Modern Israel: The Messianic Ideology of Abraham Isaac Ha-Cohen Kook." In Peter H. Merkl and Ninian Smart, eds., *Religion and Politics in the Modern World*. New York: New York University Press, 1983.

Buchanan, George W. *Revelation and Redemption: Jewish Documents of Deliverance from the Fall of Jerusalem to the Death of Nahmanides*. Dillsboro: Western North Carolina Press, 1978.

Cromer, Gerald. *The Debate about Kahanism in Israeli Society, 1984–1968*. Occasional Papers 3. New York: Harry Frank Guggenheim Foundation, 1988.

Frankel, Jonathan, ed. *Jews and Messianism in the Modern Era: Metaphor and Meaning.* Studies in Contemporary Jewry 7. New York: Oxford University Press, and Jerusalem: Institute of Contemporary Jewry, Hebrew University of Jerusalem, 1991.

Friedland, Roger, and Richard Hecht. *To Rule Jerusalem.* Cambridge: Cambridge University Press, 1996.

Friedman, Robert. *The False Prophet: Rabbi Meir Kahane—From FBI Informant to Knesset Member.* London: Faber & Faber, 1990.

Grossman, David. *The Fellow Wind.* Translated from the Hebrew by Haim Watzman. New York: Farrar, Straus & Giroux, 1988.

Kahane, Meir. *They Must Go.* Jerusalem: Institute of the Jewish Idea, 1981.

———. *Listen World, Listen Jew.* Jerusalem: Institute of the Jewish Idea, 1978.

Kotler, Yair. *Heil Kahane.* New York: Adama Books, 1986.

Lustick, Ian S. *For the Land and the Lord: Jewish Fundamentalism in Israel.* New York: Council on Foreign Relations, 1989.

Mergui, Raphael, and Philippe Simonnot. *Israel's Ayatollahs: Meir Kahane and the Far Right in Israel.* London: Saqi Books, 1987. Originally published as *Meir Kahane: Le rabbin qui fait peur aux juifs.* Lausanne: Éditions Pierre-Marcel Favre, 1985.

Metzger, Alter B. Z. *Rabbi Kook's Philosophy of Repentence: A Translation of "Orot Ha-Teshuvah."* Studies in Torah Judaism 11. New York: Yeshiva University Press, 1968.

Paz, Reuven. *Ha-'imna ha-islamit umichma'utah 'iyyon rechoni utargum* (The Covenant of the Islamicists and Its Significance—Analysis and Translation). Tel Aviv: Dayan Center, Tel Aviv University, 1988.

Reich, Walter. *A Stranger in My House: Jews and Arabs in the West Bank.* New York: Holt, Rinehart & Winston, 1984.

Sprinzak, Ehud. *Brother against Brother: Violence and Extremism in Israeli Politics from Altalena to the Rabin Assassination.* New York: Free Press, 1999.

———. *The Ascendance of Israel's Radical Right.* New York: Oxford University Press, 1991.

———. *Gush Emunim: The Politics of Zionist Fundamentalism in Israel.* New York: American Jewish Committee, 1986.

Weisburd, David. *Jewish Settler Violence: Deviance as Social Reaction.* University Park: Pennsylvania State University Press, 1989.

Zucker, Norman L. "Secularization Conflicts in Israel." In Donald Eugene Smith, ed., *Religion and Political Modernization.* New Haven, Conn.: Yale University Press, 1974.

BUDDHIST ACTIVISM

Abe, Yoshiya. "Violence and Cults: The Case of Aum Shinrikyo." Paper read at the meetings of the International Society for the Study of Religion, Quebec, Canada, June 1995.

Abeysekera, Charles, and Newton Gunasinghe, eds. *Facets of Ethnicity in Sri Lanka.* Colombo: Social Scientists Association, 1987.

Akiner, Shirin, ed. *Mongolia Today*. London: Kegan Paul International, 1991.

Asahara, Shoko. *Supreme Initiation: An Empirical Spiritual Science for the Supreme Truth*. New York: Aum USA, 1988.

———. *Beyond Life and Death*. Shizuoka, Japan: Aum, 1992.

———. *Declaring Myself the Christ: Disclosing the True Meanings of Jesus Christ's Gospel*. Shizuoka, Japan: Aum, 1992.

———. *Tathagata Abhidhamma: The Ever-Winning Law of the True Victors*. 2 vols. Shizuoka, Japan: Aum, 1992.

———. *The Bodhisattva Sutra: Salvation through Complete Reliance on the Power of the True Victor*. Shizuoka, Japan: Aum, 1994.

———. *Disaster Approaches the Land of the Rising Sun: Shoko Asahara's Apocalyptic Predictions*. Shizuoka, Japan: Aum, 1995.

Aung-Thwin, Michael. *Pagan: The Origins of Modern Burma*. Honolulu: University of Hawai'i Press, 1985.

Bawden, C. R. *The Modern History of Mongolia*. New York: Praeger, 1968.

Bechert, Heinz. "Buddhism and Mass Politics in Burma and Ceylon." In Donald Eugene Smith, ed., *Religion and Political Modernization*. New Haven: Yale University Press, 1974.

Bobilin, Robert. *Revolution from Below: Buddhist and Christian Movements for Justice in Asia: Four Case Studies from Thailand and Sri Lanka*. Lanham, Md.: University Press of America, 1988.

Brackett, D. W. *Holy Terror: Armageddon in Tokyo*. New York: Weatherhill, 1966.

Brown, William A., and Urgunge Onon, trans. *History of the Mongolian People's Republic*. Cambridge, Mass.: East Asian Research Center, Harvard University, 1976.

Bhikkhu Buddhadasa. *Dhammic Socialism*. Translated and edited by Donald K. Swearer. Bangkok: Thai Inter-religious Commission for Development, 1986.

Chan, Kim-Kwong. *Religious Freedom in China: Policy, Administration, and Regulation. A Research Handbook*. Beijing: Institute for the Study of American Religion, 2005.

Chang, Maria Hsia. *Falun Gong: The End of Days*. New Haven: Yale University Press, 2004.

Committee for Rational Development. *Sri Lanka, the Ethnic Conflict: Myths, Realities, and Perspectives*. New Delhi: Navrang, 1984.

Dalai Lama. *Ethics for the New Millennium*. New York: Riverhead Trade (Penguin Group), 2001.

Davis, Winston. "Fundamentalism in Japan: Religious and Political." In Martin E. Marty and R. Scott Appleby, eds. *Fundamentalisms Observed*. Chicago: University of Chicago Press, 1991.

———. "Dealing with Criminal Religions: The Case of Om Supreme Truth." *Christian Century* 112, no. 22 (1995), 708–12.

deSilva, K. M. *Managing Ethnic Tensions in Multi-ethnic Societies: Sri Lanka, 1880–1985*. Lanham, Md.: University Press of America, 1986.

Fink, Christina. *Living Silence: Burma Under Military Rule*. London: Zed Books, 2005.

Gombrich, Richard, and Gananath Obeyesekere. *Buddhism Transformed: Religious Change in Sri Lanka.* Princeton: Princeton University Press, 1988.

Goulet, Denis. *Survival with Integrity: Sarvodaya at the Crossroads.* Colombo: Marga Institute, 1981.

Gunaratna, Rohan. *Sri Lanka: A Lost Revolution? The Inside Story of the JVP.* Kandy, Sri Lanka: Institute of Fundamental Studies, 1990.

Hardacre, Helen. *Aum Shinrikyo and the Japanese Media: The Pied Piper Meets the Lamb of God.* New York: East Asian Institute Report, Columbia University, 1995.

Haselkorn, Avigdor. "Japan's Poison Gas Apocalyptics." *American Spectator* 28, no. 7 (July 1995), 22–26.

Heath, John. *Tibet and China in the Twenty-First Century: Non-Violence Versus State Power.* London: Saqi Books, 2005.

Heaton, William R. "Mongolia in 1990: Upheaval, Reform, but No Revolution Yet." *Asian Survey* 31 (January 1991): 50–56.

Heissig, Walther. *Lost Civilization: The Mongols Rediscovered.* London: Thames & Hudson, 1966.

———. *The Religions of Mongolia.* London: Routledge & Kegan Paul, 1980.

Ismail, Qadri. *Abiding by Sri Lanka: On Peace, Place, and Postcoloniality.* Minneapolis: University of Minnesota Press, 2005.

Jerryson, Michael. *Mongolian Buddhism: The Rise and Fall of the Sangha.* Chiang Mai, Thailand: Silkworm Books, 2007.

Kaye, Lincoln. "Faltering Steppes." *Far Eastern Economic Review,* April 9, 1992, 16–20.

Keyes, Charles F. *Thailand: Buddhist Kingdom as Modern Nation-State.* Boulder, Colo.: Westview Press, 1987.

Kitabatake, Kiyoyasu. "Aum Shinrikyo: Society Begets an Aberration." *Japan Quarterly* 42, no. 4 (1995): 376–83.

Kumaratunga, Chandrika. "New Approach: The Democratic Path to Peace in Sri Lanka," *Harvard International Review,* June 1996.

Lewy, Guenter. "Militant Buddhist Nationalism: The Case of Burma." In Guenter Lewy, *Religion and Revolution.* New York: Oxford University Press, 1974.

———. "The Sinhalese Buddhist Revolution of Ceylon." In Guenter Lewy, *Religion and Revolution.* New York: Oxford University Press, 1974.

Manogaran, Chelvadurai. *Ethnic Conflict and Reconciliation in Sri Lanka.* Honolulu: University of Hawai'i Press, 1987.

Manor, James. *Sri Lanka in Change and Crisis.* London: Groom Helm, 1984.

McGowan, William. *The Tragedy of Sri Lanka.* New York: Farrar, Straus & Giroux, 1992.

Miller, James. *Chinese Religions in Contemporary Societies.* Santa Barbara, Calif.: ABC-CLIO, 2006.

Moonesinghe, Mangala. *The Sri Lanka Ethnic Conflict: A Documentation of Literature 1983–1987.* Colombo: Marga Institute, 1987.

Mullins, Mark R., Shimazono Susumu, and Paul L. Swanson, eds. *Religion and Society in Modern Japan.* Berkeley: Asian Humanities Press, 1993.

Obeyesekere, Gananath, Frank Reynolds, and Bardwell L. Smith, eds. *The Two Wheels of Dhamma: Essays on the Theravada Tradition in India and Ceylon*. Chambersburg, Pa.: American Academy of Religion, 1972.

Okawa, Ryuho. *The Challenge of Religion*. Tokyo: Institute for Research into Human Happiness, 1993.

Overmyer, Daniel, ed. *Religion in China Today*. Cambridge: Cambridge University Press, 2003.

Pathak, Saroj. *War or Peace in Sri Lanka*. New Delhi: Popular Prakashan, 2005.

Phadnis, Urmila. *Religion and Politics in Sri Lanka*. Columbia, Mo.: South Asia Books, 1976.

Ponnambalam, Satchi. *Sri Lanka: National Conflict and the Tamil Liberation Struggle*. London: Zed Books and Tamil Information Centre, 1983.

Rahula, Walpola. *History of Buddhism in Ceylon*, 2d ed. Colombo: M. D. Gunasena, 1966.

Reader, Ian. *A Poisonous Cocktail? Aum Shinrikyo's Path to Violence*. Copenhagen: Nordic Institute of Asian Studies, 1996.

Rossabi, Morris. *China and Inner Asia: From 1368 to the Present Day*. New York: Pica Press, 1975.

———. *Khubilai Khan: His Life and Times*. Berkeley: University of California Press, 1988.

Rossabi, Morris. *Modern Mongolia: From Khans to Commissars to Capitalists*. Berkeley: University of California Press, 2005.

Sanders, Alan J. K. *Mongolia: Politics, Economics and Society*. London: Frances Pinter, 1987.

———. "Guardians of Culture." *Far Eastern Economic Review* 151 (January 3, 1991): 20–23.

Sarkisyanz, E. *Buddhist Backgrounds of the Burmese Revolution*. The Hague: Martinus Nijhoff, 1965.

Saunders, J. J. *The History of the Mongol Conquests*. London: Routledge & Kegan Paul, 1971.

Sautman, Barry, and June Teufel, *Contemporary Tibet: Politics, Development, and Society in a Disputed Region*. Armonk, N.Y.: M. E. Sharpe, 2005.

Sayle, Murray. "Nerve Gas and the Four Noble Truths." *New Yorker*, April 1, 1996, 56–71.

Shimazono, Susumu. *Aum Shinrikyo no kiseki*. Booklet no. 379. Tokyo: Iwanami, 1995.

———. "The Expansion of Japan's New Religions into Foreign Cultures." In M. Mullins, S. Shimazono, and P. Swanson, eds. *Religion and Society in Modern Japan*. Berkeley: Asian Humanities Press, 1993.

———. "In the Wake of Aum." *Japanese Journal of Religious Studies* 22, nos. 3–4 (1995): 381–415. (Condensed version of Shimazono's *Aum Shinrikyo no kiseki*, translated by Robert Kisala.)

———. "New New Religions and This World: Religious Movements in Japan after the 1970s and Their Beliefs about Salvation." *Social Compass* 42, no. 2 (1995): 193–202.

Smith, Bardwell L. "The Ideal Social Order as Portrayed in the Chronicles of Ceylon." In Gananath Obeyesekere, Frank Reynolds, and Bardwell L. Smith, eds., *The Two Wheels of Dhamma: Essays on the Theravada Tradition in India and Ceylon.* Chambersburg, Pa.: American Academy of Religion, 1972.

———, ed. *Religion and Legitimation of Power in Thailand, Laos, and Burma.* Chambersburg, Pa.: Anima Books, 1978.

Smith, Donald Eugene. "The Political Monks and Monastic Reform." In Donald Eugene Smith, ed., *South Asian Politics and Religion.* Princeton: Princeton University Press, 1966.

———, ed. *Religion and Politics in Burma.* Princeton: Princeton University Press, 1965.

Smith, Donald Eugene, Jeyaratnam Wilson, and D. S. Siriwardane. "Ceylon: The Politics of Buddhist Resurgence." Part 4 of Donald Eugene Smith, ed., *South Asian Politics and Religion.* Princeton: Princeton University Press, 1966.

Snellgrove, David, and Hugh Richardson. A *Cultural History of Tibet.* London: Weidenfeld & Nicolson, 1968.

Spencer, Jonathan. *Sri Lanka: History and the Roots of Conflict.* London: Routledge, 1990.

Sperling, Elliot. *The Tibet-China Conflict: History and Polemics.* Honolulu: East West Center, 2005.

Spüler, Bertold. *History of the Mongols.* London: Routledge & Kegan Paul, 1968.

Suksamran, Somboon. *Buddhism and Politics in Thailand: A Study of Sociopolitical Change and Political Activism of the Thai Sangha.* Singapore: Institute of Southeast Asian Studies, 1982.

Swearer, Donald K. *Buddhism and Society in Southeast Asia.* Chambersburg, Pa.: Anma Books, 1981.

———. "Fundamentalist Movements in Theravada Buddhism." In Martin E. Marty and R. Scott Appleby, eds., *Fundamentalisms Observed* (Chicago: University of Chicago Press, 1991).

Tambiah, Stanley J. *World Conqueror and World Renouncer: A Study of Buddhism and Polity in Thailand against a Historical Background.* Cambridge: Cambridge University Press, 1976.

———. *Sri Lanka: Ethnic Fratricide and the Dismantling of Democracy.* Chicago: University of Chicago Press, 1986.

———. *Buddhism Betrayed? Religion, Politics and Violence in Sri Lanka.* Chicago: University of Chicago Press, 1992.

———. *Leveling Crowds: Ethnic Violence in South Asia.* Berkeley: University of California Press, 1996.

Taylor, Philip. *Goddess on the Rise: Pilgrimage and Popular Religion in Vietnam.* Honolulu: University of Hawai'i Press, 2004.

Tuttle, Gray. *Tibetan Buddhists in the Making of Modern China.* New York: Columbia University Press, 2005.

Vejayavardhana, D. C. *The Revolt in the Temple: Composed to Commemorate 2,500 Years of the Land, the Race, and the Faith.* Colombo: Sinha Publications, 1953. Reprinted in Donald Eugene Smith, *Religion, Politics and Social Change in the Third World: A Sourcebook.* New York: Free Press, 1971.

von der Mehden, Fred R. *Religion and Nationalism in Southeast Asia: Burma, Indonesia, the Philippines.* Madison: University of Wisconsin Press, 1963.

――――. "Secularization of Buddhist Polities: Burma and Thailand." In Donald Eugene Smith, ed., *Religion and Political Modernization*. New Haven: Yale University Press, 1974.

Waley, Arthur. *The Secret History of the Mongols*. London: Allen & Unwin, 1963.

Woy, Paul C. "Rebirth of a Nation? Mongolia's Reincarnated Religious Leader." *Contemporary Review* 259 (November 1991): 234–41.

Wriggins, W. Howard. *Ceylon: Dilemmas of a New Nation*. Princeton: Princeton University Press, 1960.

Yoshino, Kosaku. *Cultural Nationalism in Contemporary Japan*. London: Routledge, 1992.

Yu, Anthony. *State and Religion in China: Historical and Textual Perspectives*. Open Court Publishing Company, 2005.

SIKH AND HINDU ACTIVISM

Andersen, Walter K., and Shridhar D. Damle. *The Brotherhood in Saffron: The Rashtriya Swayamsevak Sangh and Hindu Revivalism*. Boulder, Colo.: Westview Press, 1987.

Basham, A. L. *The Wonder That Was India: A Survey of the Culture of the Indian Sub-continent before the Coming of the Muslims*. New York: Grove Press, 1954.

Baxter, Craig. *The Jana Sangh: A Biography of an Indian Political Party*. Philadelphia: University of Pennsylvania Press, 1969.

Bhatt, Chetan. *Hindu Nationalism: Origins, Ideologies, and Modern Myths*. Oxford: Berg Publishers, 2001.

Bhindranwale, Jarnail Singh. "Two Lectures." Given on July 19 and September 20, 1983, translated from the videotaped originals by R. S. Sandhu, and distributed by the Sikh Religious and Educational Trust, Columbus, Ohio.

――――. "Address to the Sikh Congregation." Transcript of a sermon given in the Golden Temple in November 1983, translated by Ranbir Singh Sandhu, April 1985, and distributed by the Sikh Religious and Educational Trust, Columbus, Ohio.

Bjorkman, James W., ed. *Fundamentalism, Revivalists and Violence in South Asia*. Riverdale, Md.: Riverdale Company, 1986.

Bose, Sumantra. *Kashmir: Roots of Conflict, Paths to Peace*. Cambridge, Mass.: Harvard University Press, 2005.

Chaddah, Mehar Singh. *Are Sikhs a Nation?* Delhi: Delhi Sikh Gurdawara Management Committee, 1982.

Chatterjee, Margaret. *Gandhi's Religious Thought*. Notre Dame, Ind.: Notre Dame University Press, 1983.

Chopra, V. D., R. K. Mishra, and Nirmal Singh. *Agony of Punjab*. New Delhi: Patriot Publishers, 1984.

Citizens for Democracy. *Oppression in Punjab*. Columbus, Ohio: Sikh Religious and Educational Trust, 1985.

Cole, W. Owen, and Piara Singh Sambhi. *The Sikhs: Their Religious Beliefs and Practices*. London: Routledge & Kegan Paul, 1978.

Das, Veena, ed. *The Word and the World: Fantasy, Symbol and Record.* New Delhi: Sage Publications, 1986.

―――, ed. *Mirrors of Violence: Communities, Riots and Survivors in South Asia.* Delhi: Oxford University Press, 1990.

Devi, Savitri. A *Warning to the Hindus.* Calcutta: Hindu Mission, 1939.

Duara, Prasenjit. "The New Politics of Hinduism." *Wilson Quarterly,* Summer 1991, 35–42.

Editors of *Executive Review. Derivative Assassination: Who Killed Indira Gandhi?* New York: New Benjamin Franklin House, 1985.

Embree, Ainslie T. *Imagining India: Essays on Indian History.* Delhi and New York: Oxford University Press, 1989.

―――. *Utopias in Conflict: Religion and Nationalism in Modern India.* Berkeley: University of California Press, 1990.

―――. "The Function of the Rashtriya Swayamsevak Sangh: To Define the Hindu Nation." In Martin E. Marty and R. Scott Appleby, eds., *Accounting for Fundamentalisms.* Chicago: University of Chicago Press, 1994.

Fink, Christina. *Living Silence: Burma under Military Rule.* London: Zed Books, 2005.

Freitag, Sandria B. *Collective Action and Community: Public Arenas and the Emergence of Communalism in North India.* Berkeley: University of California Press, 1989.

French, Hal W., and Arvind Sharma. *Religious Ferment in Modern India.* New York: St. Martin's Press, 1981.

Frykenberg, Robert Eric. "Revivalism and Fundamentalism: Some Critical Observations with Special Reference to Politics in South Asia." In James W. Bjorkman, ed., *Fundamentalism, Revivalists and Violence in South Asia.* Riverdale, Md.: Riverdale Company, 1986.

Gandhi, Indira. "Don't Shed Blood, Shed Hatred." All India Radio, June 2, 1984. Reprinted in V. D. Chopra, R. K. Mishra, and Nirmal Singh, *Agony of Punjab.* New Delhi: Patriot Publishers, 1984.

Gandhi, Mohandas. *Hind Swaraj, or Indian Home Rule.* Ahmedabad: Navajivan Press, 1938.

Ganguly, Sumit. *The Crisis in Kashmir: Portraits of War, Hopes of Peace.* Cambridge: Cambridge University Press, 1997.

George, Alexandra. *Social Ferment in India.* New York: Athlone, 1986.

Gold, Daniel. "Organized Hinduisms: From Vedic Tradition to Hindu Nation." In Martin E. Marty and R. Scott Appleby, eds., *Fundamentalisms Observed.* Chicago: University of Chicago Press, 1991.

―――. "Rational Action and Uncontrolled Violence: Explaining Hindu Communalism." *Religion* 21 (1991): 357–70.

Gopal, Sarvepalli, ed. *Anatomy of a Confrontation: The Babri Masjid-Ramjanmabhumi Issue.* New Delhi: Penguin Books, 1991.

Graham, B. D. *Hindu Nationalism and Indian Politics: The Origins and Development of the Bharatiya Jana Sangh.* Cambridge: Cambridge University Press, 1990.

Gregson, Jonathan. *Massacre at the Palace: The Doomed Royal Dynasty of Nepal.* New York: Hyperion, 2002.

Gulati, Kailash Chander. *The Akalis Past and Present*. New Delhi: Ashajanak Publications, 1974.

Gupta, Lina. "Indian Secularism and the Problem of the Sikhs." In Gustavo Benavides and M. W. Daly, eds., *Religion and Political Power*. New York: State University of New York Press, 1989.

Hansen, Thomas Blom. *The Saffron Wave*. Princeton: Princeton University Press, 1999.

Hawley, John Stratton. "Naming Hinduism." *Wilson Quarterly*, Summer 1991, 20–34.

Hawley, John Stratton, and Mark Juergensmeyer, trans. *Songs of the Saints of India*. New York: Oxford University Press, 1988.

Hunt, Michael. "Drafting the Nepal Constitution, 1990." *Asian Survey* 31, no. 11 (November 1991): 1020–39.

Jaffrelot, Christophe. *Hindu Nationalism: A Reader*. Princeton: Princeton University Press, 2007.

Jalandhary, Surjeet. *Bhindranwale Sant*. Jalandhar, India: Punjab Pocket Books, n.d. (ca. 1985).

Jeffrey, Robin. *What's Happening to India? Punjab, Ethnic Conflict, Mrs. Gandhi's Death and the Test for Federalism*. New York: Holmes & Meier, 1986.

Juergensmeyer, Mark. *Religion as Social Vision: The Movement against Untouchability in 20th Century Punjab*. Berkeley: University of California Press, 1982. Revised edition: *Religious Rebels in the Punjab: The Social Vision of Untouchables*. Delhi: Ajanta Publications, 1988.

———. *Radhasoami Reality: The Logic of a Modern Faith*. Princeton: Princeton University Press, 1991.

———. "The Logic of Religious Violence." In David C. Rapoport, ed., *Inside Terrorist Organizations*. London: Frank Cass, 1988.

———. "India." In Stuart Mews, ed., *Religion in Politics: A World Guide*. London: Longman, 1989.

Juergensmeyer, Mark, and N. Gerald Barrier, eds. *Sikh Studies: Comparative Perspectives on Changing Tradition*. Berkeley Religious Studies Series 1. Berkeley, Calif.: Graduate Theological Union, 1979.

Kapur, Rajiv A. *Sikh Separatism: The Politics of Faith*. London: Allen & Unwin, 1986.

Kashmeri, Zuhair, and Brian McAndrew. *Soft Target: How the Indian Intelligence Service Penetrated Canada*. Toronto: J. Lorimer, 1989.

Kaur, Amarjit, Shourie Arun, J. S. Aurora, Khushwant Singh, M. V. Kamath, Shekhar Gupta, Subhash Kirpekar, Sunil Sethi, and Tavleen Singh. *The Punjab Story*. New Delhi: Roli Books International, 1984.

Kohli, S. S. *Sikh Ethics*. New Delhi: Munshiram Manoharlal, 1975.

Lal, Brij V. *Islands in Turmoil: Elections and Politics in Fiji*. Canberra: Asia Pacific Press, 2006.

Madan, T. N. "The Double-Edged Sword: Fundamentalism and the Sikh Religious Tradition." In Martin E. Marty and R. Scott Appleby, eds., *Fundamentalisms Observed*. Chicago: University of Chicago Press, 1991.

Mahmood, Cynthia Keppley. *Fighting for Faith and Nation: Dialogues with Sikh Militants*. Philadelphia: University of Pennsylvania Press, 1997.

———. "Sikh Rebellion and the Hindu Concept of Order." *Asian Survey* 29, no. 3, 1989: 326–40.

Majahid, Abdul Mali. *Conversion to Islam: Untouchables' Strategy for Protest in India.* Chambersburg, Pa.: Anima Press, 1989.

Malik, Yogendra, and Dhirendra Vajpeyi. "The Rise of Hindu Militancy: India's Secular Democracy at Risk." *Asian Survey* 29, no. 3 (1989): 308–25.

McLeod, W. H. *Guru Nanak and the Sikh Religion.* Oxford: Clarendon Press, 1968.

———. *The Evolution of the Sikh Community: Five Essays.* Oxford: Clarendon Press, 1976.

———. *Who Is a Sikh? The Problem of Sikh Identity.* Oxford: Clarendon Press, 1989.

Mishra, Dina Nath. *RSS: Myth and Reality.* New Delhi: Vikas, 1980.

Mulgrew, Ian. *Unholy Terror: The Sikhs and International Terrorism.* Toronto: Key Porter Books, 1988.

Nandy, Ashis. "An Anti-secularist Manifesto." In John Hick and Lament C. Hempel, eds., *Gandhi's Significance for Today: The Elusive Legacy.* London: Macmillan, 1989.

Nayar, Baldev Raj. *Minority Politics in the Punjab.* Princeton: Princeton University Press, 1966.

———. "Sikh Separatism in the Punjab." In Donald Eugene Smith, ed., *South Asian Politics and Religion.* Princeton: Princeton University Press, 1966.

Nayar, Kuldip, and Khushwant Singh. *Tragedy of Punjab: Operation Bluestar and After.* New Delhi: Vision Books, 1984.

Nehru, Jawaharlal. *The Discovery of India.* New York: John Day, 1946.

———. *A Bunch of Old Letters.* Bombay: Asia Publishing House, 1958.

O'Brien, Conor Cruise. "Holy War against India." *Atlantic Monthly* 262 (August 1988).

O'Connell, Joseph T., Milton Israel, and Willard G. Oxtoby, eds. *Sikh History and Religion in the Twentieth Century.* Toronto: Centre for South Asian Studies, University of Toronto, 1988.

Oddie, G. A., ed. *Religion in South Asia: Religious Conversion and Revival Movements in South Asia in Medieval and Modern Times.* Columbia, Mo.: South Asia Books, 1977.

Pettigrew, Joyce. "In Search of a New Kingdom of Lahore." *Pacific Affairs* 60, no. 1 (Spring 1987).

Premdas, Ralph R., S. W. R. de A. Samarasinghe, and Alan B. Anderson, eds. *Secessionist Movements in Comparative Perspective.* London: Pinter Publishers, 1990.

Sarin, Ritu. *The Assassination of Indira Gandhi.* New Delhi: Penguin Books, 1990.

Savarkar, V. D. *Hindutva: Who Is a Hindu?* Bombay: Veer Savarkar Prakashan, 1969.

Seshadri, H. V., ed. *RSS: A Vision in Action.* Bangalore, India: Jagarana Prakashana, 1988.

Singh, Amrik, ed. *Punjab in Indian Politics: Issues and Trends*. New Delhi: Ajanta Books, 1985.

Singh, Avtar. *Ethics of the Sikhs*. Patiala, India: Punjabi University Press, 1970.

Singh, Jagjit. *The Sikh Revolution*. New Delhi: Bahri Publications, 1981.

Singh, Khushwant. *History of the Sikhs*, vol. 2. Princeton: Princeton University Press, 1966.

Singh, Mohinder. "Gandhi, Sikhs and Non-violence." *Khera* 9, no. 3 (July–September 1990) 72–87.

Smith, Donald Eugene. *India as a Secular State*. Princeton: Princeton University Press, 1963.

Tambiah, Stanley J. *Leveling Crowds: Ethnic Violence in South Asia*. Berkeley: University of California Press, 1996.

Thapar, Romila. "Imagined Religious Communities? Ancient History and the Modern Search for a Hindu Identity." *Modern Asian Studies* 23, no. 2 (1989): 209–31.

Tully, Mark, and Satish Jacob. *Amritsar: Mrs. Gandhi's Last Battle*. London: Cape, 1985.

van der Veer, Peter. *Religious Nationalism: Hindus and Muslims in India*. Berkeley: University of California Press, 1994.

———. "God Must Be Liberated! A Hindu Liberation Movement in Ayodhya." *Modern Asian Studies* 21, no. 2 (1985): 283–301.

———. "Hindu 'Nationalism' and the Discourse of 'Modernity': The Vishva Hindu Parishad." In Martin E. Marty and R. Scott Appleby, eds., *Accounting for Fundamentalisms*. Chicago: University of Chicago Press, 1994.

Wallace, Paul, ed. *Region and Nation in India*. New Delhi: Oxford and IBH, 1985.

Wallace, Paul, and Surendra Chopra, eds. *Political Dynamics and Crisis in Punjab*. Amritsar: Guru Nanak Dev University Press, 1988.

Who Are the Guilty? Report of a Joint Inquiry into the Causes and Impact of the Riots in Delhi from 31 October to 10 November. Delhi: People's Union for Democratic Rights and People's Union for Civil Liberties, 1984.

CHRISTIAN ACTIVISM

Abanes, Richard. *American Militias: Rebellion, Racism and Religion*. Downers Grove, Ill.: InterVarsity Press, 1996.

Adams, Gerry. *Before the Dawn*. London: Mandarin Paperbacks, 1997.

Aho, James. *The Politics of Righteousness: Idaho Christian Patriotism*. Seattle: University of Washington Press, 1990.

Alexander, Yonah, and Dennis A. Pluehinsky, eds. *European Terrorism Today and Tomorrow*. Washington, D.C.: Brassey's, 1992.

Ammerman, Nancy T. "North American Protestant Fundamentalism." In Martin E. Marty and R. Scott Appleby, eds., *Fundamentalisms Observed*. Chicago: University of Chicago Press, 1991.

Balmer, Randall. *Mine Eyes Have Seen the Glory: A Journey into the Evangelical Subculture in America*. New York: Oxford University Press, 1989.

Barkun, Michael. *Religion and the Racist Right: The Origins of the Christian Identity Movement*. Chapel Hill: University of North Carolina Press, 1994.

————. *A Culture of Conspiracy: Apocalyptic Visions in Contemporary America*. Berkeley: University of California Press, 2003.

————, ed. *Millennialism and Violence*. London: Frank Cass, 1996.

Barron, Bruce. *Heaven on Earth? The Social and Political Agendas on Dominion Theology*. Grand Rapids, Mich.: Zondervan, 1992.

Batstone, David. *From Conquest to Struggle: Jesus of Nazareth in Latin America*. Albany: State University of New York Press, 1991.

Bellah, Robert N. "Transcendence in Contemporary Piety." In Donald R. Cutler, ed., *The Religious Situation: 1969*. Boston: Beacon Press, 1969.

————. "Civil Religion in America," *Daedalus* 96, no. 1 (Winter 1967): 1–21.

Bennett, David H. *The Party of Fear: The American Far Right from Nativism to the Militia Movement*. New York: Vintage Books, 1995.

Berlet, Chip. *The Increasing Popularity of Right Wing Conspiracy Theories*. Somerville, Mass.: Political Research Associates, 1996.

————, ed. *Eyes Right: Challenging the Right Wing Backlash*. Boston: South End Press, 1995.

Berlet, Chip, and Matthew N. Lyons. *Too Close for Comfort: Right-Wing Populism, Scapegoating, and Fascist Potentials in U.S. Political Traditions*. Boston: South End Press, 1996.

Berryman, Phillip. *Liberation Theology: The Essential Facts about the Revolutionary Movements in Latin America and Beyond*. Maryknoll, N.Y.: Orbis Books, 1984.

————. *The Religious Roots of Rebellion: Christians in Central American Revolutions*. Maryknoll, N.Y.: Orbis Books, 1984.

Blanchard, Dallas A., and Terry J. Prewitt. *Religious Violence and Abortion: The Gideon Project*. Gainesville: University Press of Florida, 1993.

Bociurkiw, Bohdan R. "Institutional Religion and Nationality in the Soviet Union." In S. Enders Wimbush, ed., *Soviet Nationalities in Strategic Perspective*. London: Groom Helm, 1985.

Borge, Tomas, Carlos Fonseca, Daniel Ortega, Humberto Ortega, and Jaime Wheelock. *Sandinistas Speak*. New York: Pathfinder Press, 1986.

Boyer, Paul. *When Time Shall Be No More: Prophetic Belief in Modern American Culture*. Cambridge, Mass.: Harvard University Press, 1992.

Bradstock, Andrew. *Saints and Sandinistas: The Catholic Church in Nicaragua and Its Response to the Revolution*. London: Epworth Press, 1987.

Bray, Michael. *A Time to Kill: A Study Concerning the Use of Force and Abortion*. Portland, Ore.: Advocates for Life, 1994.

Bruce, Stephen. "The Moral Majority: The Politics of Fundamentalism in Secular Society." In Lionel Caplan, ed., *Studies in Religious Fundamentalism*. Albany: State University of New York Press, 1987.

Bruce, Steve, Peter Kivisto, and William H. Swatos, Jr., eds. *The Rapture of Politics: The Christian Right as the United States Approaches the Year 2000*. New Brunswick, N.J.: Transaction, 1995.

Cabastrero, Teofilo. *Ministers of God, Ministers of the People: Testimonies of Faith from Nicaragua*. Translated by Robert R. Barr. Maryknoll, N.Y.: Orbis Books, 1986.

————. *Revolutionaries for the Gospel: Testimonies of Fifteen Christians in the Nicaraguan Government.* Translated by Phillip Berryman. Maryknoll, N.Y.: Orbis Books, 1986.

Capps, Walter H. *The New Religious Right: Piety, Patriotism, and Politics.* Columbia: University of South Carolina Press, 1990.

Carey, George W., and James V. Schall, eds. *Essays on Christianity and Political Philosophy.* Lanham, Md.: University Press of America, 1985.

Carey, Michael J. "Catholicism and Irish National Identity." In Peter H. Merkl and Ninian Smart, eds., *Religion and Politics in the Modern World.* New York: New York University Press, 1983.

Casaldaliga, Bishop Pedro. *Prophets in Combat: The Nicaraguan Journal of Bishop Pedro Casaldaliga.* Oak Park, Ill: Meyer-Stone Books, 1987.

Chidester, David. *Shots in the Streets: Violence and Religion in South Africa.* Boston: Beacon Press, 1991.

Chodak, Szymon. "People and the Church versus the State: The Case of the Roman Catholic Church in Poland." In Richard L. Rubenstein, ed. *Spirit Matters: The Worldwide Impact of Religion on Contemporary Politics.* New York: Paragon House, 1987.

Clarke, Sister Sarah. *No Faith in the System.* Cork, Ireland: Mercier Press, 1995.

Coates, James. *Armed and Dangerous: The Rise of the Survivalist Right.* New York: Hill & Wang, 1987.

Cooke, Dennis. *Persecuting Zeal: A Portrait of Ian Paisley.* Kerry, Ireland: Brandon, 1996.

————. "The Religious Dimension in the Northern Ireland Problem." *Lexington Theological Quarterly* 16, no. 3 (July 1981): 85–93.

Coppola, Vincent. *Dragons of God: A Journey Through Far-Right America.* Atlanta: Longstreet Press, 1996.

Corcoran, James. *Bitter Harvest: Gordan Kahl and the Posse Comitatus—Murder in the Heartland.* New York: Penguin Books, 1990.

Cox, Harvey. *Fire from Heaven: The Rise of Pentacostal Spirituality and the Reshaping of Religion in the Twenty-First Century.* Cambridge, Mass.: DaCapo Press, 2001.

Crabtree, Harriet. *The Christian Life: Traditional Metaphors and Contemporary Theologies.* Minneapolis: Fortress Press, 1991.

————. "Onward Christian Soldiers? The Fortunes of a Traditional Christian Symbol in the Modern Age." *Bulletin of the Center for the Study of World Religion* [Harvard University] 16, no. 2 (1989/90): 6–27.

Dees, Morris, with James Corcoran. *Gathering Storm: America's Militia Threat.* New York: HarperCollins, 1996.

Demko, George J. *The Russian Orthodox Church: A Contemporary History.* London and Sydney: Groom Helm Ltd., 1986.

Diamond, Sara. *Roads to Dominion: Right-Wing Movements and Political Power in the United States.* New York: Guilford, 1995.

————. *Spiritual Warfare: The Politics of the Christian Right.* Boston: South End Press, 1989.

Dillon, Martin. *God and the Gun: The Church and Irish Terrorism.* New York: Routledge, 1997.

Dodson, Michael, and Laura Nuzzi O'Shaughnessy. *Nicaragua's Other Revolution: Religious Faith and Political Struggle.* Chapel Hill: University of North Carolina Press, 1990.

Dunlop, John. *A Precarious Belonging: Presbyterians and the Conflict in Ireland.* Belfast: Blackstaff Press, 1995.

Ellis, Jane. *The Russian Orthodox Church: A Contemporary History.* Bloomington: Indiana University Press, 1986.

Flynn, Kevin, and Gary Gerhardt. *The Silent Brotherhood: Inside America's Racist Underground.* New York: Free Press, 1989.

Forbes, Bruce David, and Jeanne Halgren Kilde, eds. *Rapture, Revelation, and the End Times: Exploring the Left Behind Series.* New York: Palgrave Macmillan, 2004.

Fowler, Robert Booth, Allen D. Hertzke, and Laura R. Olson. *Religion and Politics in America: Faith, Culture, and Strategic Choices.* Boulder, Colo.: Westview Press, 2004.

Gibellini, Rosino, ed. *Frontiers of Theology in Latin America.* Translated by John Drury. Maryknoll, N.Y.: Orbis Books, 1983.

Girardi, Giulio. "Democracy and Ideological Struggle in Nicaragua Today." *Cross Currents* 39, no. 1 (Spring 1989).

Goldberg, Michelle. *Kingdom Coming: The Rise of Christian Nationalism.* New York: W. W. Norton, 2007.

Griffin, Leslie, ed. *Religion and Politics in the American Milieu.* Notre Dame, Ind.: Review of Politics and Office of Policy Studies, University of Notre Dame, 1989.

Gutierrez, Gustavo. *A Theology of Liberation: History, Politics, and Salvation.* Rev. ed. Maryknoll, N.Y.: Orbis Books, 1988.

Hammond, Phillip E. "Religion and Nationalism in the United States." In Gustavo Benavides and M. W. Daly, eds., *Religion and Political Power.* Albany: State University of New York Press, 1989.

Harris, Richard, and Carlos M. Vilas, eds. *Nicaragua: A Revolution under Siege.* London: Zed Books, 1985.

Haslam, David. *Faith in Struggle: The Protestant Churches and Their Response to the Revolution.* London: Epworth Press, 1987.

Haught, James A. *Holy Hatred: Religious Conflicts of the '90s.* Amherst, N.Y.: Prometheus Books, 1995.

Hedges, Chris. *American Fascists: The Christian Right and the War on America.* New York: Free Press, 2007.

Hickey, John. *Religion and the Northern Ireland Problem.* Totawa, N.J.: Barnes & Noble, 1984.

Hoffman, David S. *The Web of Hate: Extremists Exploit the Internet.* New York: Anti-Defamation League, 1996.

———. *The Oklahoma City Bombing and the Politics of Terror.* Venice, Calif.: Feral House, 1998.

Hoover, Arlie J. *The Gospel of Nationalism: German Patriotic Preaching from Napoleon to Versailles.* Stuttgart: Franz Steiner Verlag, 1986.

Hudson, Winthrop S., ed. *Nationalism and Religion in America: Concepts of American Identity and Mission.* New York: Harper & Row, 1970.

Ionescu, Dan. "Romania: Religious Denominations, Change and Resistance to Change at the Top." *Radio Free Europe Report on Eastern Europe* 1, no. 17 (April 17, 1990): 29–33.

Jarman, Neil. *Material Conflicts: Parades and Visual Displays in Northern Ireland*. Oxford and New York: Berg, 1997.

Kaplan, Jeffrey. "Right Wing Violence in North America." In Tore Bjørgo, ed. *Terror from the Extreme Right*. London: Frank Cass, 1995.

———. *Radical Religion in America: Millenarian Movements from the Far Right to the Children of Noah*. Syracuse, N.Y.: Syracuse University Press, 1997.

———. "The Context of American Millenarian Revolutionary Theology: The Case of the 'Identity Christian' Church of Israel." *Terrorism and Political Violence* 5, no. 1 (Spring 1993), 30–82.

Kennedy, Michael D., and Maurice D. Simon. "Church and Nation in Socialist Poland." In Peter H. Merkl and Ninian Smart, eds., *Religion and Politics in the Modern World*. New York: New York University Press, 1983.

LaBarre, Weston. *The Ghost Dance: The Origins of Religion*. New York: Dell, 1970.

LaHaye, Tim F., and Jerry Jenkins. *Left Behind: A Novel of the Earth's Last Days*. Carol Stream, Ill.: Tyndale Publishing House, 2000.

Lancaster, Roger N. *Thanks to God and the Revolution: Popular Religion and Class Consciousness in the New Nicaragua*. New York: Columbia University Press, 1988.

Lease, Gary. "The Origins of National Socialism: Some Fruits of Religion and Nationalism." In Peter Merkl and Ninian Smart, eds., *Religion and Politics in the Modern World*. New York: New York University Press, 1983.

Lewellen, Ted C. "Holy and Unholy Alliances: The Politics of Catholicism in Revolutionary Nicaragua." *Journal of Church and State* 31, no. 1 (Winter 1989): 15–31.

Lienesch, Michael. *Redeeming America: Piety and Politics in the New Christian Right*. Chapel Hill: University of North Carolina Press, 1993.

Little, David. *Ukraine: The Legacy of Intolerance*. Washington, D.C.: United States Institute of Peace Press, 1991.

Macdonald, Andrew. *The Turner Diaries*. Hillsboro, W. Va.: National Vanguard Books, 1978. Reprinted by the National Alliance, Arlington, Va., in 1985, and by Barricade Books, New York, 1996.

Madsen, Richard. "Christian Communities in China." In Mark Juergensmeyer, ed., *The Oxford Handbook of Global Religion*. New York: Oxford University Press, 2006.

Marrin, Albert, ed. *War and the Christian Conscience: From Augustine to Martin Luther King, Jr.* Chicago: Regnery, 1971.

Marsden, George M. *Fundamentalism and American Culture: The Shaping of Twentieth-Century Evangelicalism, 1870–1925*. New York: Oxford University Press, 1980.

Martin, William. *With God on Our Side: The Rise of the Religious Right in America*. New York: Broadway, 2005.

McManners, John. *The French Revolution and the Church*. Westport, Conn.: Greenwood Press, 1969.

McVeigh, Joseph. *A Wounded Church: Religion, Politics and Justice in Ireland*. Dublin: Mercier Press, 1989.

Motyl, Alexander J. *Sovietology, Rationality, Nationality: Coming to Grips with Nationalism in the USSR*. New York: Columbia University Press, 1990.

———, ed. *Thinking Theoretically about Soviet Nationalities: History and Comparison in the Study of the USSR*. New York: Columbia University Press, 1992.

Noble, Kerry. *Tabernacle of Hate: Why They Bombed Oklahoma City*. Prescott, Ontario: Voyageur, 1998.

North, Gary. *Backward Christian Soldiers? An Action Manual for Christian Reconstruction*. Tyler, Tex: Institute for Christian Economics, 1984.

———. *Conspiracy: A Biblical View*. Fort Worth, Tex: Dominion Press, 1986.

———. *The Dominion Covenant: An Economic Commentary on the Bible*. Tyler, Tex: Institute for Christian Economics, 1987.

———. *The Judeo-Christian Tradition: A Guide for the Perplexed*. Tyler, Tex: Institute for Christian Economics, 1990.

———. *Millennialism and Social Theory*. Tyler, Tex: Institute for Christian Economics, 1990.

———. *Lone Gunners for Jesus: Letters to Paul J. Hill*. Tyler, Tex: Institute for Christian Economics, 1994.

———. *Is the World Running Down? Crisis in the Christian Worldview*. Tyler, Tex: Institute for Christian Economics, 1998.

North, Gary, and Gary DeMar. *Christian Reconstruction: What It Is, What It Isn't*. Tyler, Tex: Institute for Christian Economics, 1991.

O'Brien, Conor Cruise. "God and Man in Nicaragua." *Atlantic Monthly* 258, no. 2 (1986).

Paisley, Ian R. K. *Sermons on Special Occasions*. Belfast: Ambassador Productions, 1996.

Paneth, Donald. *The Literature of the Apocalypse: Far-Right Voices of Violence*. New York: Anti-Defamation League, 1996.

Phillips, Kevin. *American Theocracy: The Peril and Politics of Radical Religion, Oil, and Borrowed Money in the Twenty-First Century*. New York: Penguin, 2007.

Quarles, Chester L. *Christian Identity: The Aryan American Bloodline Religion*. Jefferson, N.C.: McFarland & Co., 2004.

Ramet, Pedro, ed. *Eastern Christianity and Politics in the Twentieth Century*. Durham, N.C.: Duke University Press, 1988.

———. "Patterns of Religio-national Symbiosis in Eastern Europe: Poland, Czechoslovakia, Hungary." In *Eastern Europe: Religion and Nationalism*. Occasional Paper 3. Washington, D.C.: East European Program, European Institute, Wilson Center, December 4, 1985.

———, ed. *Religion and Nationalism in Soviet and East European Politics*. Durham, N.C.: Duke University Press, 1989.

Randall, Margaret. *Christians in the Nicaraguan Revolution*. Translated by Mariana Valverde. Vancouver: New Star Books, 1983.

Risen, Jim, and Judy L. Thomas. *Wrath of Angels: The American Abortion War*. New York: Basic Books, 1998.

Robinson, Peter. *The Union Under Fire: United Ireland Framework Revealed.* Belfast: Ambassador, 1995.

Rose, Dorothy. *The Jubilee: New Voice of the Far Right.* New York: Anti-Defamation League, 1996.

Roy, Joseph T., ed. *False Patriots: The Threat of Antigovernment Extremists.* Montgomery, Ala: Southern Poverty Law Center, Klanwatch Project, 1996.

Rushdoony, Rousas John. *The Institutes of Biblical Law.* Nutley, N.J.: Craig Press, 1973.

———. *Christianity and the State.* Vallecito, Calif: Ross House Books, 1986.

Sanders, Thomas G. "The New Latin American Catholicism." In Donald Eugene Smith, ed., *Religion and Political Modernization.* New Haven: Yale University Press, 1974.

Serra, Luis. "Ideology, Religion, and Class Struggle in the Nicaraguan Revolution." In Richard Harris and Carlos M. Vilas, eds., *Nicaragua: A Revolution under Siege.* London: Zed Books, 1985.

Shaeffer, Francis. *A Christian Manifesto.* Westchester, Ill.: Crossway Books in association with Nims Communication, 1982.

Shuck, Glenn. *Marks of the Beast: The Left Behind Novels and the Struggle for Evangelical Identity.* New York: New York University Press, 2004.

Sigmund, Paul. *Liberation Theology at the Crossroads: Democracy or Revolution?* New York: Oxford University Press, 1990.

Sizer, Sandra. *Gospel Hymns and Social Religion: The Rhetoric of Nineteenth-Century Revivalism.* Philadelphia: Temple University Press, 1978.

Smith, Brent L. *Terrorism in America: Pipe Bombs and Pipe Dreams.* Albany: State University of New York Press, 1994.

Solnin, Amy C. *William L. Pierce: Novelist of Hate.* New York: Anti-Defamation League, 1995.

Standaert, Michael. *Skipping toward Armageddon: The Politics and Propaganda of the Left Behind Novels.* Brooklyn, N.Y.: Soft Skull Press, 2006.

Stern, Kenneth S. *A Force Upon the Plain: The American Militia Movement and the Politics of Hate.* New York: Simon & Schuster, 1996.

Strozier, Charles B. *Apocalypse: On the Psychology of Fundamentalism in America.* Boston: Beacon Press, 1995.

Strozier, Charles B., and Michael Flynn. *Two Thousand: Essays on the End.* New York: New York University Press, 1997.

Suall, Irwin. *The Skinhead International: A Worldwide Survey of Neo-Nazi Skinheads.* New York: Anti-Defamation League, 1995.

Szajkowski, Bogdan, *Next to God . . . Poland: Politics and Religion in Contemporary Poland.* New York: St. Martin's Press, 1983.

Tabor, James D., and Eugene V. Gallagher. *Why Waco: Cults and the Battle for Religious Freedom in America.* Berkeley: University of California Press, 1995.

Vasquez, Manuel, Anna Lisa Peterson, and Philip J. Williams, eds., *Christianity, Social Change, and Globalization in the Americas.* New Brunswick, N.J.: Rutgers University Press, 2001.

Walker, Thomas. *Nicaragua: The Land of Sandino.* Boulder, Colo.: Westview Press, 1981.

Walter, Jess. *Every Knee Shall Bow: The Truth and Tragedy of Ruby Ridge and the Randy Weaver Family.* New York: HarperCollins, 1995.

Whitsel, Brad. "The Turner Diaries and Cosmotheism: William Pierce's Theology of Revolution." *Nova Religio: The Journal of Alternative and Emergent Religions* 1, no. 2 (April 1998): 183–97.

Wilcox, Clyde, and Carin Larson. *Onward Christian Soldiers: The Religious Right in American Politics.* Boulder, Colo.: Westview Press, 2006.

Wills, Garry. *Under God: Religion and American Politics.* New York: Simon & Schuster, 1990.

Wlasowsky, Ivan. *Outline History of the Ukrainian [Autocephalous] Orthodox Church.* New York: Ukrainian Orthodox Church, 1974.

Wright, Stuart A., ed. *Armageddon in Waco: Critical Perspectives on the Branch Davidian Conflict.* Chicago: University of Chicago Press, 1995.

Vinz, Warren L. *Pulpit Politics: Faces of American Protestant Nationalism in the Twentieth Century.* Albany: State University of New York Press, 1996.

Zeskind, Leonard. *The "Christian Identity" Movement: Analyzing Its Theological Rationalization for Racist and Anti-Semitic Violence.* New York: Division of Church and Society of the National Council of the Churches of Christ in the U.S.A., 1986.

Index

Abbas, Mahmoud, 72
ABCP. *See* Asian Buddhist Conference for Peace (ABCP)
Abdullah Azzam Brigade (Egypt), 209
Abdul-Rahman, Sheik Omar: entries into U.S., 303n2; *fatweh* of 1981 by, 42; global jihad and, 193–94, 196; World Trade Center bombing (1993), 42, 193–94, 195, 199–200, 205
Abouhalima, Mahmud, 194–95, 199
absolutism of conflict, 255–57
Abu Sayyaf movement (Philippines), 148–50, 204
accommodation of religion: in Egypt, 27–28; in India, 107–8; in Iran, 50–51, 54; in Israel, 54–63; minority rights and, 233, 234–36, 237; in Morocco, 81–82; in newer nations, 27–29; possibilities for, 17; in Soviet Union, 153–55; in Sri Lanka, 133; in the West, 26–27
Adams, Gerry, 177, 178
Adelet ve Kalkinma Partisi (AKP, Justice and Development Party), 172–73
al-Adl wal-Ihsan (Justice and Welfare Group), 82
Advani, Lal Krishna, 103–4, 110–11, 112, 113, 232–33, 234
Afghanistan: anti-Americanism and, 247; bin Laden and, 201, 205, 210; *mujahadin* movement and, 85–86, 197–200, 207; Muslim political networks and, 85–88, 246; reign of Taliban in, 85–88, 224, 225; Shi-a Hazara

tribal group in, 54; Soviet Union and, 85, 247; U.S. attack on, 87–88, 208, 250
Africa: attacks on U.S. embassy in, 205; religious nationalism in, 79–83
Agudat Israel Party (Israel), 56
ahimsa (the force of truth), 105, 220
Ahmadinejad, Mahmoud, 53, 224
Ahmed, Sharif Sheik, 81
Ajaj, Ahmad Muhammad, 195
Akali Dal (Band of the Immortal One, Sikh movement), 118, 119, 121, 122–23, 124
Akayev, Askar A. (Kyrgyzstan president), 102
Akbar (Mogul emperor), 234–35
AKP. *See* Adeler ve Kalkinma Partisi (AKP, Justice and Development Party)
Alash Party (Kazakhstan), 102, 103
Albanian nationalism, 157
Aleksy, Metropolitan, of Leningrad, 155
Aleph movement, 181, 258
Algeria, 10, 281n134; France and, 246; modernity in, 241–42; religious rebellion in, 80–81, 221, 222–23
Ali, Ayaan Hirsi, 170
Ali, Siddig, 194
Ali family, 48–49
Alliance for the Future of America, 169
Ambrose, Saint, 218
"American pattern" of society, 27
American Revolution, 15
Amir, Yigal, 61–62
Anderson, Benedict, 19, 24

Text and Display:	Sabon
Compositor:	Binghamton Valley Composition, LLC
Indexer:	Marcia Carlson
Printer and Binder:	Maple-Vail Manufacturing Group